SEEKING THE CENTER

Politics and

Policymaking at

the New Century

Martin A. Levin, Marc K. Landy,
and Martin Shapiro
Editors

Georgetown University Press
Washington, D.C

Georgetown University Press, Washington, D.C.
© 2001 by Georgetown University Press. All rights reserved.
Printed in the United States of America

10 9 8 7 6 5 4 3 2 1   2001

This volume is printed on acid-free offset book paper.

Library of Congress Cataloging-in-Publication Data

Seeking the center: politics and policymaking at the new century / Martin A.
Levin, Marc K. Landy, Martin Shapiro, editors.
　　p.　cm.
　　Includes index.
　　ISBN 0-87840-866-5 (cloth : alk. paper)—ISBN 0-87840-867-3 (pbk. : alk. paper)
　　1. United States—Politics and government—1993–2001. 2. United
States—Politics and government—1993–2001—Decision making. 3. United
States—Politics and government—2001– 4. United States—Politics and
government—2001——Decision making. 5. United States—Economic
policy—1993– 6. United States—Economic policy—1993——Decision
making. 7. United States—Social policy—1993– 8. United States—Social
policy—1993——Decision making. I. Levin, Martin A. II. Landy, Marc
Karnis. III. Shapiro, Martin M.

JK271 .S415 2001   2001023264
320'.6'0973—dc21

Contents

List of Figures   vi

Preface   vii

PART I ▪ Introduction   1

1 Durability and Change   3
Martin A. Levin, *Brandeis University* and
Marc K. Landy, *Boston College*

PART II ▪ Taxing and Spending   33

2 Budgeting More, Deciding Less   35
Eric M. Patashnik, *University of California, Los Angeles*

3 From Expansion to Austerity: The New Politics of Taxing
and Spending   **54**
Paul Pierson, *Harvard University*

4 Four Pathways of Power: Probing the Political Dynamics of
Federal Tax Policy in the Turbulent 1980s and 1990s   **81**
David R. Beam, *Illinois Institute of Technology* and
Timothy J. Conlan, *George Mason University*

PART III ▪ Rights Policies 111

5 **Immigration Reform Redux** 113
Peter H. Schuck, *Yale University*

6 **Republican Efforts to End Affirmative Action:**
Walking a Fine Line 132
John David Skrentny, *University of California, San Diego*

7 **On the Resilience of Rights** 172
Thomas F. Burke, *Wellesley College*

PART IV ▪ Social Welfare Policy 191

8 **The Evolving Old Politics of Social Security** 193
Martha Derthick, *University of Virginia*

9 **The Politics of Rights Retraction:** Welfare Reform from
Entitlement to Block Grant 215
Steven M. Teles, *Brandeis University* and
Timothy S. Prinz, *United Hospital Fund of New York City*

10 **The New Politics of the Working Poor** 239
Christopher Howard, *College of William and Mary*

11 **Dead on Arrival?** New Politics, Old Politics, and the Case of
National Health Reform 264
Cathie Jo Martin, *Boston University*

12 **The New Politics of the Census** 292
Peter Skerry, *Claremont McKenna College* and
The Brookings Institution

PART V ▪ Foreign Trade 311

13 **The Postwar Liberal Trade Regime:**
Resilience under Pressure 313
David Vogel, *University of California, Berkeley*

PART VI ▪ **Durability and Change** **337**

14 Much Huffing and Puffing, Little Change **339**
David R. Mayhew, *Yale University*

15 Bill Clinton and the Politics of Divided Democracy **350**
Sidney M. Milkis, *University of Virginia*

16 Two-Tier Politics Revisited **381**
Wilson Carey McWilliams, *Rutgers University*

17 Exit "Equality," Enter "Fairness" **401**
Eugene Bardach, *University of California, Berkeley*

18 The Politics and Policy of the Regulated Market, Efficiency-Constrained Welfare State **425**
Martin Shapiro, *University of California, Berkeley*

Contributors **439**

Index **443**

List of Figures

FIGURE 3.1 Outlays by Budget Enforcement Act Category as a Percentage of GDP   **62**

FIGURE 3.2 Outlays by BEA Category Excluding Health Care   **71**

FIGURE 4.1 The Four Pathways of Power   **84**

Preface

We are passing through a period in which Democrats and Republicans each get about 50 percent of the votes and 50 percent of the government. But this kind of politics does not necessarily mean a policy deadlock.

Seeking the Center: Politics and Policymaking at the New Century analyzes the politics of policymaking since the writing of *The New Politics of Public Policy* in the early 1990s. It is a book about the determinants of public policy. Our analyses describe what happened in national policymaking and explain why it happened by examining the political dynamics of what government does. This is the realm of that crucial, though rarely considered, connection between politics and policymaking.

Tracking the political dynamics of governmental activity is indeed what most people think political science is all about. But this is not the case. Increasingly, the discipline of political science has become devoted to abstract theorizing and formalisms of various sorts. The public policy schools bring the study of government closer to earth. But their goal is problem solving and efficiency, not political analysis. For the most part, they try to fix the leaks in the plumbing rather than understand the political roots of policy developments. Similarly, the think tanks devote themselves to the technicalities of policy analysis, partisan policy advocacy, or a complex mixture of both. This book restores the politics of policymaking to the forefront of the political science agenda.

Indeed, separating politics and policy has obscured one of *Seeking the Center*'s fundamental findings: An intensely competitive, evenly balanced two-party system operating within a broad public consensus has produced highly partisan political posturing and moderate, incremental, but substantial policy innovations.

The 1990s saw policy persistence as well as policy changes. But these disparate pieces of policy add up to a surprisingly coherent whole—a policy regime dominated by moderation. While politics and the policymaking process have been marked by episodes of extreme partisan discourse, policy outcomes were largely moderate.

The myth of the lone scholar is just that—a myth. As Plato knew, "The older I grew, the more I realized how difficult it is to manage a city's affairs rightly. For I saw that it was impossible to do anything without friends." Research and writing, like most pursuits, are done best in community.

We have been fortunate to be members of many fine research communities. This book began in the nurturing intellectual environment of the Gordon Public Policy Center. But it came to full flower in the newly assembled community of "The New Politics of Public Policy" project. The authors of the first volume in this series, and the new ones attracted by the promise of the second volume, generously created an interactive conversation from which we all have learned much. Their creative feedback and suggestions through the long process of preliminary seminars, first drafts, conference papers, and then draft chapters produced a rich dialogue. It transformed a series of initially individual works by many authors into a book with coherent themes, arguments, and conclusions. We are grateful to them and this process for this rich product and the stimulating ride.

We had the fine administrative assistance of the Gordon Center's energetic staff: Liz Miller, Emily Silver, Shellie Gutman, Alexis D'Arcy, Allison Charney, Linda Boothroyd, and Rosanne Colocouris. Laura Lawson was an excellent copy editor. In recent years the Gordon Center's luminosity has been heightened by the intellectual and personal contributions of Steve Teles. He has had a major impact on this work in many ways.

We appreciate the intelligent and well-managed editorial process provided by Georgetown University Press. John Samples, the Press's former director, gave us important initial advice and encouragement, and Gail Grella, Deborah Weiner, and Sally Barrows not only improved the final product but significantly smoothed the procedure.

We have benefited from much help and support from Boston College. Its Thomas P. O'Neill Jr. Endowment funded a national conference that provided a stimulating forum for presenting drafts of this book's chapters. We also wish to thank William Neenan, S.J., the former academic vice president, for his support. We appreciate the tireless efforts on behalf of this project of Sandra MacDonald, the administrator of the political science department.

The trustees of the Gordon Foundation of Chicago—John Adelsdorf, Sandy Bank, Burton Feldman, Robert Green, and David Silberberg—deserve special thanks. Their faith in this project, as well as the other endeavors of the Gordon Center, has been gracious and strong.

PART I

Introduction

1

Durability and Change

Martin A. Levin, *Brandeis University*
Marc K. Landy, *Boston College*

Since the writing of *The New Politics of Public Policy* in the early 1990s, there have been several major policy innovations. Most of them were moderate in ways we will explain shortly.[1] These included welfare reform (Temporary Assistance for Needy Families [TANF]); continual and ultimately successful deficit reduction and the consequent fiscalizaton of policymaking; the North American Free Trade Agreement (NAFTA) and the China Permanent Normal Trade Relations (PNTR)–World Trade Organization legislation; telecommunications, banking, and agricultural deregulation; budgeting procedures reforms; and the Earned Income Tax Credit (EITC). Accompanying these policy changes was a unique pattern of political party interaction: frequent alternation in power among evenly divided parties. We analyze the significant connections between these party dynamics and policy outcomes.

As Sherlock Holmes would have understood, those dogs may bark loudest that don't bark at all. The lack of change in important and hitherto controversial public policies like affirmative action is at least as noteworthy as their vitiation or demise would have been. Hence this chapter's title, "Durability and Change," indicating that both barking and nonbarking dogs are part of the mysteries to be investigated. As our authors show, the continuities include the resiliency of Social Security and Medicare (Derthick), immigration reforms (Schuck), budget procedures on which new changes were layered (Patashnik), and many rights-based polices (Burke) including the much maligned federal affirmative action programs (Skrentny). In an era of sometimes divided government, powerful appeals to rights, and parity among competitive parties, there has been both policy persistence and policy change.

A Policy Regime Dominated by Moderation

But more is at stake than the explanation of particular anomalies. These disparate pieces of policy do add up to a surprisingly coherent whole—a policy regime dominated by moderation. Although ambitious health care reform was proposed and fought for, it did not pass (Martin). Welfare reform, which may be the "signature" policy development of the 1990s, was an exception to this pattern. But even this major entitlement reform only constrained welfare state policy. It left, as Teles and Prinz explain, the basic outline of the entitlement state intact. It maintained cash payments to eligible welfare recipients, but they were tied to time limits and those hallmarks of the market—work and training. Thus, even with this major reform of welfare, the predominant pattern was policies that uphold this moderate status quo, along with political leaders pursuing what we will describe as "positive small government."

In explaining these moderate policy results in the 1990s, we distinguish between policy and process. Policy is the product of the policymaking process. Intimately interwoven into that process may be the type of politicking or positioning and competing for power that happens in campaigns and in partisan legislative rhetoric and posturing. Thus, a policymaking process marked by episodes of extreme partisan discourse, nevertheless, has produced largely moderate policy outcomes in the period under study here.

As Mayhew concludes, it was "quite a decade for markets." Three major deregulatory initiatives were enacted: telecommunications reform, the Freedom to Farm Act, and banking reform. But these deregulatory policies were moderate in that they were intermediate: They did not fully end government involvement, and they created neither a complete free market nor government ownership. The Freedom to Farm Act, for example, is more market-oriented than previous post–New Deal farm programs, but it still retains government subsidies. And, the support for these measures crossed both party and ideological lines.

NAFTA, the World Trade Organization (WTO), and the China PNTR-WTO were also both substantial and incremental. WTO followed in the direction charted by the previous Uruguay round. Its trade barrier cuts were modest. NAFTA increased the openness of trade with two nations that were already major American trading partners. It adopted a regional trade zone model that has become common around the world. The legislation granting China permanent most favored nation-trading status in the last months of the Clinton administration was hotly debated. But, as Vogel shows, this was an incremental policy: It simply made permanent what Congress had in fact been doing on an annual basis for the previous twenty years.

As the congressional Republicans demonstrated after taking over the House in 1994, political behavior in this period has not been consistently moderate. But their more extreme initiatives were blunted. Immoderate moments surfaced during the 1990s. These included the effort by the House Republicans to shut down the government and the Clinton health care initiative. But they were almost always pursued on pain of eventual electoral defeat by a public opting for more moderate positions. Ironically, increased polarization in Congress did not, on the whole, lead to more extreme policymaking. Divided and even highly partisan government can act.

The policies of the 1990s were more the product of presidential initiative and action than congressional initiative. There was increased polarization in the congressional process, but it coexisted with a good deal of moderation among the electorate and at the presidential level. Thus, the most important policy development of the 1990s was the triumph of moderation. This is the key dependent variable to be explained.

In addition to essential centrist driving dynamics of American politics, we explain these 1990s outcomes in terms of several economic, intellectual, and political forces as the key independent variables. The overarching economic influence has been the economic boom, which dates back at least to 1992 and, arguably, to 1982. The chief intellectual development is the rise of a consensus, at least at the broad level of public opinion, regarding the virtues of both the *regulated* free market and the *constrained* entitlement state. The key political developments are, first, the advent of a new party dynamic of pragmatism and opportunism born of close competition between evenly divided parties that frequently alternated power and, second, the political implications of what McWilliams terms the "two-tier polity." What Pierson terms "the fiscalization of policymaking"—a phenomenon resulting from the persistent impact of budgetary deficit—is the third development: When the budget was in deficit, as it was for most of the 1980s and 1990s, a more moderate sort of policymaking resulted—deficit reduction, retrenchment, moderate entitlement cuts, and budget procedure reforms.

The Meaning of Moderation

To substantiate our claim about the dominance of moderation, we must clarify what we mean by the term. *Moderation* is not a synonym for *inconsequential*. The moderate policies discussed in this book are substantial, significant, and sometimes even innovative. Yet they were moderate because they were modest in size and effect and represented incremental changes in policy direction. Typically, they were intermediate in the sense of being between the two policy poles of left and right. Welfare reform is a case of this type of intermediate innovation and moderate change. It was a substantial and significant change, but it was moderate in the sense of being halfway between a pure cash grant entitlement and a pure employment and training program. The very name of its original form—workfare—emphasized its intermediate character. EITC is an intermediate program in which people receive cash grants but only to supplement what is earned by working. Similarly, the national park system was expanded in the 1990s. But, as environmentalists complained, the expansion was only moderate.

The moderate style of programs of this period is captured in the political slogans of this period. No new domestic "wars" were declared. Instead, programs were proposed that combined these poles: Bill Clinton vowed to combine entitlement with responsibility to "end welfare as we know it" and announced the end of "the era of big government is over," while George W. Bush promised a "compassionate conservatism." In a striking reversal of political style, the former liberal "new age" California governor Jerry Brown advocated a military-style (complete with uniforms) college preparatory charter school program.

The 1990s has indeed witnessed a profound political development. The center has been relocated somewhere to the right of its previous location. Reagan's rightward shift was confirmed and fully legitimized by Clinton and the New Democrats. The moderate, incremental policy product of this period is consonant with this shift in political geography.

Welfare Reform and Deficit Reduction

The two seeming exceptions to the principle of moderation in policy change during the 1990s were welfare reform and deficit reduction. Both reflected marked breaks with previous conditions and encompassed sweeping change. But neither vitiates the broader point about the dominance of moderation. Welfare reform was Clinton's "trip to China." It was the price of victory for his broader agenda of entitlement defense and moderate governmental expansion. As far back as the 1992 campaign, he had pledged to "end welfare as we know it." He was convinced that the Democrats were suffering electorally because of their defense of welfare as an entitlement. He set in motion a political dynamic that made retrenchment of welfare a political inevitability. Although he considered the Republican initiative too sweeping, he knew that to veto it would guarantee his defeat in 1996. He also sensed that a veto would make impossible what turned out to be a very successful defense of the other, larger entitlements such as Medicare and Social Security and incremental expansions of other programs. The proclaimed boldness of welfare reform was in the service of moderation. Although it imposed time limits and compulsory work and training, it also maintained the preexisting program of cash grants to eligible recipients. The true test of its reforms will come when the country moves from full employment to some degree of unemployment.

The virtual elimination of the federal deficit in the late 1990s ranks as one of the most significant policy developments of the last twenty-five years. But it was not the product of any radical policy initiative. Nor was it even driven by direct policy changes. Instead, it derived from the extraordinary economic growth and the absence of any major change in tax policy—taxes were not radically reduced during the Clinton administration. The result was massive increases in tax revenues. No major budget cutting took place. (The budget cuts made generally were modest. In some cases—such as defense—there were no cuts but rather reductions in the rate of increases in government spending.) In the face of such bounteous revenue expansion, balancing the budget resulted from the maintenance of budgetary status quo.

The sequel to deficit reduction—decisions on how to spend the new apparent surplus—has also been moderate. The Democrats have not proposed large new social programs or efforts to cure poverty. Rather, they want to shore up existing entitlements—Social Security and Medicare—fund small increases in some existing programs, and, in the vein of "positive small government," create modest new ones, such as HMO reform and a patients' bill of rights. Republicans have focused on shoring up Social Security and Medicare and using whatever surplus is left over for modest tax cuts. The Republican version of "positive small government" involves such programs as Ed/Flex (allowing the states flexible spending of already granted federal education funds).

The Changing Nature of Parties, Partisanship, and Party Competition

The regime of moderation owes much to political change that occurred during the 1990s. Perhaps the most significant was the transformed nature of party competition. Our national government has always been characterized by separate institutions sharing power. But in the 1990s this sharing came to include a high degree of alternation in power and parity between the parties: no one party dominated either the presidency or Congress for the entire decade.

During the 1980s, the Republican party reversed almost fifty years of history to become, in Samuel Lubell's words, the "sun" party. In his view, the normal party dynamic is for one party to establish the agenda for policymaking, as the sun generates the light for the solar system. The other party must react and adapt to the sun and live in its reflected glow, much as the moon depends on the sun for its illumination. In contradistinction to the New Deal and the Great Society epochs, the policy agenda for the 1980s was set by the Republicans. The Democrats were relegated to the unaccustomed position of the "moon."

Despite the election and reelection of a Democratic president, this pattern did not reverse in the 1990s. The Republicans continued as the agenda-setting party. But, as Republican leaders bitterly acknowledge, Clinton hunted by moonlight, stealing their agenda—deficit reduction, welfare reform, and crime control. His success was reflected not only in his own reelection but in the Democrats' success by the end of the decade in reducing Republican control of Congress to the narrowest of margins.

Indeed, the common view prior to the 1990s (argued in detailed theories such as in Ginsberg and Shefter's *Politics by Other Means*) turned out to be quite wrong. It held that because of a putative "electoral college lock," the Republicans would continue to monopolize control of the presidency, and the Democrats would continue to exercise a similar degree of control over the Congress. But the 1992 and 1996 Democratic presidential successes exploded the idea of a Republican presidential monopoly. The 1994 Republican congressional success shows that the House of Representatives is not permanently under the control of the Democrats. The Democrats' rebound near victory in the House in 1998 and the 2000 elections suggest a good deal of parity with neither party having a lock on any of our federal policymaking institutions.

The political implications of this close competition are complex, but the policy implications have been simple. In policy formulation, moderation almost always prevails. This may seem ironic given the polarizing tone of the 1994 Republican congressional campaign. But the Republican Revolution was short lived. Thermidor set in even before the Democratic presidential resurrection a mere two years later. Indeed, the political pattern of the 1990s was that any concerted effort to depart from the regime of moderation was punished by the electorate. The Republican victory in 1994 was caused by voter repugnance at what was perceived to be an excessively radical and intrusive Democratic health care initiative. Clinton's reelection victory in 1996 was due to his ability to depict the congressional Republicans as extremists. The heroic race of both parties to seize the middle ground yielded the virtual dead heat of the 2000 elections.

This close competition explains the seeming anomaly of polarized parties producing centrist results. Indeed, in one sense the two parties are more polarized than ever. There are almost no liberal Republicans in Congress and many fewer conservative Democrats than there were twenty years ago. But the lack of strong Republican majorities in the two houses has given inordinate political power to the more moderate members of both parties who continually find themselves in a position to provide the margin of victory. Although most Democrats opposed NAFTA and PNTR for China, both bills passed because President Clinton was able to convince a sufficiently large minority of Democrats to support those measures.

In his concluding chapter, Mayhew describes this ironic anomaly of polarized parties producing centrist results in terms of the process and policy distinction noted earlier. "[M]otored by aggressive ideological activists on both sides [who tried to] 'enact their medians,'. . . the congressional parties drew farther apart on major issues even as each grew more cohesive. . . . [But] the 1990s brought largely a history of disappointing or failed crusades that have not left major traces in policy. . . .That is, anyone focusing on the decade's election results, flashy party programs, and ideological crusades might have missed the actual policy results" (pp. 6–7).*

Thus, in the 1990s this parity in party power seemed to have pushed each party toward more pragmatic and moderating policy positions. Indeed, rather than creating stasis, this divided government—in ways that Mayhew's classic *Divided We Govern* would predict—has actually served to increase the competition for policy innovation and enhance the power of strategically placed policy entrepreneurs. More generally, the parties seem to be changing from initiators and organizers of coherent patterns of ideas to strategic and opportunistic choosers of particular ideas that attract voters and sustain interest group support.

As Shapiro suggests, "a series of themes recur in story after story. . . . Low-visibility interest group, old-style policymaking persists. There is, however, a significant high-visibility overlay characterized by electoral competition between the parties and a politics of credit claiming and blame avoidance. Neither party wishes to appear unfair or mean-spirited. Both push their claims to posses new ideas and/or higher competence to govern."

---

*Mayhew concludes that "in the American system it is not easy to carry off-median projects to completion." He details this with his description of "three especially aggressive [and unsuccessful] efforts by one party or the other to 'enact its median.'. . . The Republican impeachment drive of 1998–1999 . . . ran up against a hostile public opinion median. So did the Gingrich-Dole budget drive of 1995–1996, which culminated and came apart through 'shutting down' the government. No less off-median were the Clinton-led Democrats in 1993–1994 as they advanced their policies on gays in the military, the expensive 'investments' woven in the early version of the 1993 budget package, and their prodigious plan for health care reform" (p. 343).

Policymaking as a Political Chess Match

Since they each continually sensed the possibility of either gaining or losing control of Congress, both parties deviated from partisan doctrine and became increasingly opportunistic. Because the prize, control of Congress, was so great, the value of appealing to the median voter rose concomitantly. Policymaking thus came to resemble a political chess match. The Democrats moved to adopt this chess playing strategy in the early 1990s—supporting deficit reduction and welfare reform. The Republicans adopted it somewhat later—supporting raises in the minimum wage, dropping efforts to weaken environmental regulation, and pursuing such positive small government policies as Ed/Flex.

Not all members of Congress adopted this strategic posture. But in the cases mentioned earlier, and others as well, enough members departed from previous party doctrine to enable the party as a whole to claim that it was in support of these popular initiatives. And, as we noted, electoral results supported the value of party pragmatism. At almost every juncture, when the public perceived immoderation in a candidate or a party, it was defeated.

Moderate Policymaking at the Presidential Level

Moderation has consistently characterized presidential aspirants, both winning and losing. The two losing Republican candidates of the 1990s, Dole and Bush, represented the moderate wing of the party. The 2000 victor, George W. Bush, called himself a "compassionate conservative" and made no secret of his willingness to adopt policy initiatives from the "New Democrat" think tank, the Progressive Policy Institute. Thus, he took more moderate campaign positions than most Republicans in Congress. Bush acted as if he had stolen a page from Clinton's moderate playbook and moved toward something of what the conservative publisher William Kristol called a "Clintonizing" of the Republican party. This is much like Reagan's even more significant moderatizing of the Democrats that brought about their presidential transformation. During the 1992 campaign and again in the wake of the 1994 debacle, Clinton sought to transform the image of the Democratic party in the minds of the voters from one of uncritical defender of big government to a "third-way" party dedicated to pragmatic problem solving. He declared in his 1996 State of the Union Address that "the era of big government is over." He signed the welfare reform legislation despite the profound animosity which most party activists felt toward it. After an early Ralph Nader–inspired rhetorical move toward some populist positions, Democratic presidential candidate Al Gore carefully avoided any claim to the banner of liberalism.

Perhaps most important, President Clinton accepted the primacy of deficit reduction. Shortly after taking power in the spring of 1993, he flirted with the idea of increasing spending via a so-called capital budget. By distinguishing between expenditures geared toward consumption, which he pledged to reduce, and expenditures geared toward improving physical and human capital stock, he hoped to create a politically acceptable rationale for expanding the latter. But his desire to win over the deficit-obsessed voters who had voted for Reform party candidate Ross Perot caused him to abandon this effort and wholeheartedly adopt the cause of deficit reduction that dominated his whole first term in office. By joining both the Republicans and the Perotistas in trumpeting the deficit reduction cause, Clinton ensured the primacy of what Pierson calls the "fiscalization of policy"—the domination of policymaking by the exigencies of budget balancing. He chose instead to compete for the Perot voters by committing himself wholeheartedly to reducing the budget.

These actions, leading to his "comeback" victory in 1996, demonstrated that this shift in the Democratic party toward a "third way," and the tacit acceptance of the Republican "sun" that it implied, was serious and sustained. Further evidence of this shift was the 2000 primary contest in which Clinton's anointed successor, Gore, hewed to the "New Democratic" agenda, including what had come to be its most controversial intraparty aspect, trade liberalization. It may be that future Democratic aspirants will hew more closely to the "old-time religion," but as of 2000 Clinton's "third way" is the dominant party orthodoxy.

Indeed, this pattern of voters punishing perceived *non*moderation could be seen as early as the mid-1980s: In 1984 Walter Mondale was hurt by his liberal image, especially because of his proposal to raise taxes. In 1988 Michael Dukakis allowed himself to be portrayed as being nonmoderate—as a "liberal"—and he, too, was defeated. By contrast, in 1992 Clinton worked hard to avoid these Mondale and Dukakis images. He declared himself a "New Democrat" and proposed a middle-class tax cut and, unlike Dukakis, supported the death penalty.

The notion of a marked difference between congressional and presidential party politics is not new. It was true of the 1950s as well. But in that earlier era both congressional parties were more conservative than their presidential counterparts. In the 1990s, by contrast, the Democratic congressional delegation was more liberal than its presidential leader and the Republican delegation more conservative than its presidential candidates. This usually represents a rational strategy on the part of congressional candidates. Their districts typically tend either to be more liberal or more conservative than the national median. Thus, they must move to more extreme positions than the national party norm to capture their districts median voter.

Precisely because the close partisan balance forces policy moderation, the two congressional parties have sought to differentiate themselves electorally in other ways. These include a high degree of partisan rhetoric, especially when one party sensed a tactical advantage against a supposedly vulnerable opponent. The Republicans, for example, took this tack in the Clinton impeachment process. The Democrats took it in attacking the Republicans over Medicare and Social Security.

Competing for the Middle in Policy

Despite partisan bombast, in policymaking, the parties have tended to compete for the middle. As noted, a key political variable is the party dynamic defined by partisan competition for the middle: their district's middle (or median voter) for Congress members; the national middle (or median voter) for presidential politicians which tends to be more moderate than the median in most congressional districts.[†]

---

† This analysis follows the Downs-Hotelling model of the rational competition for the median voter using the analogy of where to locate the hot dog stand on a long beach full of scattered people—the middle. Indeed, this is where American elections have traditionally been won. The model is particularly persuasive in the context of the entrenched American two-party system. U.S. constitutional arrangements, however, create two different kinds of beaches. The presidential election beach involves competition for the national median voter. That median voter is more moderate than the median voter in most congressional districts. We should also note that the Downs model makes the not-always realistic assumption that the voters are evenly spread out on the beach. Thus, our argument is further strengthened by the fact that in this period, in fact, the voters tend to be bunched in the middle of the beach rather than spread evenly. We described this earlier in the section on moderate policymaking at the presidential level with the cases of Clinton being more moderate than the congressional Democrats and, in 2000, George W. Bush being more moderate than the congressional Republicans.

This dynamic will sometimes be modified when members of Congress vote or speak closer to the national median because they are concerned about the success of their national ticket. This concern is most likely to arise in presidential election years, as seen in the many congressional Republicans softening their conservatism as the 2000 race came upon them. Similarly, during the 2000 campaign, when President Clinton vetoed the repeal of the estate tax, of the sixty-five congressional Democrats who initially had voted for repeal, twelve switched their votes to help the national ticket. This was almost precisely the necessary margin of votes—fourteen were needed—to sustain the veto.[2]

Two Political Tiers

McWilliams describes the mass electorate outside the centers of government as being "weakly articulated, mostly baffled." He calls this the second tier of our polity and contrasts it with its first tier—"the world in and around the centers of government that, in contrast to the thinness of the first tier, is thick and dense with organized interest and policy advocates and highly articulated" (p. 382). In the 1990s, the second tier of our polity found new importance in policy-making. Sometimes this influence was felt in a radical direction at odds with the durability of federal policy. While federal policy about affirmative action did not change substantially in this period, both California and Washington passed referenda repealing affirmative action and bilingual education as well. Also, as Patashnik shows, folk wisdom triumphed over professional expertise in the second tier's acceptance of balanced budget notions rather than Keynesian deficit-spending policies. On the other hand, the most extraordinary impact of the second tier was to maintain the status quo, blocking the effort of congressional Republicans to force Clinton from office. Early in the Lewinsky scandal, it appeared that even the Democratic first tier was prepared to desert the president. It was the decidedly underwhelming response of public opinion at large that emboldened prominent Democrats to come to his defense and stave off a vote against him in the Senate.

Moderation normally implies a degree of security and satisfaction with the status quo that does not quite fit with the surliness and disengagement that seems to characterize much of the populace. Its resistance to political change seems more borne of fear than of fidelity. Clinton's very high approval ratings coupled with the very low esteem in which he is held suggests that support for him may have been totemic in character, as if his removal from office in 1999 might, in some magical way, have caused a stock market crash or a new crime wave.

As McWilliams shows, as the ties binding the broader polity to the political system grow increasingly thin, the ability of ordinary people to make sense of public affairs, or even to try, weakens. The vote serves less as an instrument for realizing positive goals and more as a club to bludgeon those who seem to threaten the public's tenuous grip on sanity and stability. How else to explain one of the true political innovations of the 1990s, the moderate demagogue. In 1992 Ross Perot created a new American political type: a man who exploited political alienation in the style of a demagogue but whose own political program was slavishly middle of the road—social liberalism combined with fiscal austerity. One can hardly imagine Huey Long or George Wallace trying to charm the voters away from their traditional political loyalties with the pie charts and bar graphs and quasi-religious appeals to the sanctity of a balanced budget. And Perot was no flash in the pan. In 1998 his Minnesota acolyte, a former professional wrestler named Jesse Ventura, was elected governor of Minnesota. Ventura defeated respectable Democratic and Republican candidates with a Perotian combination of contempt for "politics as usual" and a middle-of-the-road policy platform.

But these developments do not gainsay the continued power and importance of the first tier. The thick politics of Washington makes policy innovation, even in an era of divided government, the coin of the realm for politicians, their staffs, and the policy intellectuals who people the think tanks and advocacy organizations. To an unprecedented extent, policy change is their raison d'être. The conventional view of politics as a game played to divide the spoils "who gets what when and where" endures, but the political and institutional context of that game has changed markedly. The number of people whose job it is to analyze, formulate, and market policy innovation has grown astronomically. This growth has been registered in the increased size of congressional staff, but that is only the tip of the iceberg. The number and diversity of nongovernmental organizations with this mission have grown even more rapidly.

And, even though the executive branch has not grown apace, a great change has occurred in the outlook of departmental and Executive Office of the President employees who see themselves less as either technicians or servants of the president and more as policy entrepreneurs. The political deadlock of the 1990s clearly put a damper on these efforts, but only a damper, not a lid. One might compare this situation to the human reproductive process. New policy ideas have become so plentiful they come to resemble the hordes of male sperm searching out the scarce female egg. So many try that some few are bound to succeed.

Because the second tier is frequently averse to the changes sought by members of the first tier, a plausible way for policy specialists to make significant policy changes is through stealth approaches. Neither the public nor partisan enemies can oppose change that they do not know about. Therefore, the aim of change proponents might be to make their changes as invisible as possible. They may well avoid mobilizing their supporters for fear of alerting their opponents. Rather than confront unpalatable proposals directly, they may content themselves with using the "fine print" of laws, regulations, and executive orders to recover in fact what they appear to have conceded in principle. They could try to embed time bombs in seemingly innocuous or consensual laws. These explosive devices could take many guises—they might be camouflaged in funding formulas, waivers, or legal definitions, as Teles and Prinz's analyses of welfare reform suggest. Well hidden, they would remain invisible to the "enemy" and be timed to explode when no one is likely to be paying attention.

A similar and related way of pushing policy is the tendency for innovative policymaking to occur more readily in the shadows—the making of policy at a low level of visibility when the issue is of relatively low salience to the public. In an era of less institutional cover and risk-averse policymakers driven as much by blame avoidance as credit claiming, politicians manage the scope of conflict by lowering the visibility of policymaking.

And policy change seems to be more likely to spring from these shadows than from the stage of heightened public glare and high drama. Skrentny and Howard show this as they describe the initial development of affirmative action and EITC, respectively. Skrentny also emphasizes blame avoidance as a driving force. By contrast, we find high-visibility blocking innovation in Martin's description of the 1993 failure of the health care reform initiative and contributing to the retraction (via high-visibility referenda) to the rollback of affirmative action and bilingual education in California in the late 1990s. More generally, as Shapiro suggests, along with a low-visibility politics of experts in which technical consensus on relatively narrow, programmatic policy ideas dominates, there is also a pattern of "entrenched vested interests, discensus among experts or more or less political manipulation reinforced by the media that may move particular policy issues from low to high visibility. Skerry tells one such story [about census policy]. Beam and Conlan make this dynamic the central theme of their analysis of tax policy."

Explaining Moderate Policy Results: Fiscalization and New Party Dynamics

We explain moderate policy results by reference to several key political, economic, and intellectual forces. Because each of these independent variables appears to influence the others, we cannot offer a precise causal chain specifying the relationship.

The Fiscalization of Policymaking

One of the chief engines of policymaking since the early 1980s has been the size and direction of the budget deficit. When the budget was in deficit—as it was for most of this period—a more moderate policymaking resulted: deficit reduction, retrenchment, moderate entitlement cuts, and budget procedure reforms. It also encouraged policymaking that would not have an impact on the budget. Such policy could take either the regulatory route (environmental regulations, affirmative action, and expansion of handicap rights) or the deregulatory route (economic deregulation of various kinds, immigration reform).

When the budget was in surplus, beginning in the late 1990s, a very different and more expansionist policymaking tended to result. There was more generous and somewhat expansionary entitlement reform (Social Security and Medicare), modestly expansionary environmental and education policies, and modest increments to support welfare reform.

Prosperity and Consensus: Accepting Both the Free Market and the Entitlement State

The 1990s have been a time of unusually sustained and strong domestic and international prosperity. During the 1960s, prosperity served as an engine for policy innovation. A huge budget surplus enabled Lyndon Johnson to initiate expansive new policies without placing new demands on taxpayers. The 1990s were radically different. First, they were accompanied for most of the time by budget deficit, not surplus, which, as Ronald Reagan had so fervently hoped, served to brake enthusiasm for expensive new policies. Indeed, no ambitious funding initiative was undertaken throughout this whole period. Ambitious programs, such as the Americans with Disabilities Act (ADA), were indeed launched, but they were pursued via regulation and therefore had minimal budgetary import.

But the dearth of new initiatives should not be laid solely at the door of the budget deficit. Unlike that of the 1960s, this boom occurred at a time of very low public trust in government and an equally low level of belief in the efficacy of government programs. Furthermore, this negative view of government was combined with an extraordinarily high respect for the free market and a strong public desire not to see it excessively shackled.

The negative view of government does not imply, however, a desire to reduce the entitlements that are the core of federal domestic policy. As Shapiro argues, neither the left nor right, nor the public at large, was willing to challenge essential aspects of either the free market or the entitlement state. Instead, a consensus has formed around a *regulated* free market and a *constrained* entitlement state. Even the much-touted welfare reform left the basic outline of the entitlement state intact. And even as deregulation moved ahead on many fronts, new regulations were added to temper market imperfections. Therefore, arguments about political economy and service delivery occurred at the margin, as both parties sought to maintain a satisfactory balance between efficiency and equity by pursuing moderate policymaking.

How did this moderating dualism develop, and what are its components? Since the early 1990s—and in many respects since the early 1980s—politicians on both the left and right have faced three major political economy patterns that seem to have contributed to this moderation producing dualism: (1) sustained and very strong domestic and international economic prosperity; (2) the apparent success of deregulation; and, as Pierson shows, (3) a growing concern about welfare costs.

Politicians on both the left and right have come to support both the free market and the entitlement state. They favor the market over economic planning and a high degree of regulation. They also favor the welfare state over an unfettered free market that threatens to unfairly harm some individuals. As Shapiro points out in his concluding chapter, from both the European and American perspective, "there is almost total agreement . . . in persons of every political persuasion and economic circumstance that the rigors of free markets must be tempered by the welfare state. Of course, work is best, but no one is going to be allowed to starve to death in the street. . . . Democrats and Republicans fully accept the welfare state, but both are concerned about its cost." Both right and left seek to resolve the overarching tension between market efficiency and individual equity by pursuing policymaking in the center.

Toward Positive Small Government

This support of both the free market and the entitlement state also has led to a shift from an era of big new ideas being played out in big government programs to one of modest policy ideas played out in modest programs—"positive small government." The Democrats started to pursue positive small government in 1995; the Republicans followed suit in the late 1990s. Following his denunciation of big government, in his second term, President Clinton pressed for fewer and cheaper policies that often had greater symbolic than substantive import. This approach was epitomized by his school uniform proposal and the Kennedy-Kassenbaum incremental approach to health care reform. These very small steps were deemed to be evocative of bigger goals. The school uniforms proposal was a neat device for announcing Democratic concern for creating more order in the schools. Kennedy-Kassenbaum was not so much about mandating portability for individuals' health insurance as it was a symbol that something positive albeit small could be achieved short of comprehensive health care reform.

Following their setback in the 1998 congressional election, the Republicans struggled to find positive small government alternatives such as Ed/Flex (allowing the states flexible spending of already granted federal education funds), HMO reform and a patients' bill of rights (but with more limitations and covering fewer people than the

Democrats' version), and a very limited gun control bill. The 2000 Republican presidential nominee adopted the slogan "compassionate conservatism," borrowed from and echoing Clinton's small symbolic endeavors. The two candidates argued about which would provide better, but thrifty and incremental, benefits for the elderly and how much and what kinds of tax cuts would be equitable and contribute to economic efficiency.

Clinton called for "positive small government" to rid himself of the "big government" label often pinned on Democrats without giving up the Democratic faith in positive government. Similarly, at the outset of the George W. Bush administration, we see a call for "communitarianism" emphasizing local and private institutions. This is a way of simultaneously expressing traditional Republican suspicions of "big government," avoiding accusations that Republicans are indifferent to the plight of the poor, and acknowledging Republican sympathy for religious endeavors. Both presidents proclaim that they want enough government—somewhere between big government and laissez-faire.

The Strong Economy as an Alternative Explanation

An alternative and more parsimonious explanation of the phenomena we are trying to analyze would focus exclusively on the impact of prosperity. Whether this unprecedented economic strength was the result of the noninterventionist policies of their Republican predecessors, the appeal of "if it's not broken, don't fix it" must have necessarily been strong to the Clinton administration. In policy terms this approach meant moderate polices. If the Democrats in 1992 stressed that it was "the economy, stupid," then in the 1996 election they stressed that it was "the *strong* economy, stupid." They repeated that in the 1998 election as a counter to Republican impeachment efforts. Indeed, the strong economy in part generated and certainly supported the intellectual consensus on markets and the welfare state. The strong economy seems to be key in both the market being held in high regard and the welfare state being accepted once and for all.

But a closer examination reveals more complexity than this more parsimonious explanation allows. The strong economy of the 1990s did not start until 1993 and 1994. But positioning toward moderation by the Democrats started in 1992, prior to which they typically had not been moderate in their national ticket. In 1992 the New Democrats took control of the national ticket. They stressed the economy, but they campaigned just as much on moderate policy positions such as ending welfare "as we know it" and crime control. Clinton was the first Democratic presidential candidate in a very long time who supported the death penalty.

Once in office, these New Democrats initiated moderate policymaking in 1993 even while the economy was still weak. This moderate policy positioning was at least as much a response to Perot's 1992 electoral strength as it was an effort not to rock the boat in good economic times.

By the 1995–1996 run-up to the presidential campaign, the economy had become much stronger. But to whatever extent the Democrats' moderate policymaking then was an effort to avoid "rocking the boat," it also was, as we have shown, in large part a strategic backtracking to counter the failure of their nonmoderate 1993–1994 health care reforms followed by the strong 1994 Republican victory.

The Republican's move toward moderation in the late 1990s seems to be another instance of factors other than the strong economy pushing policymaking toward the center. Republican moderation was at first halting and then proceeded by very small steps in Newt Gingrich's last two years, as we have described. After their setbacks in the impeachment process and in the 1998 election, Republicans made additional but modest moves toward moderation, as we will describe shortly. But both of these shifts seem to have at least as much to do with the party's strategic competitive concerns we have discussed as with the strong economy. Although we cannot provide weights to the various independent variables we have described, it is clear that all of them push in the same direction—toward the center.

In this, as in most efforts at political analysis, economic understanding proves crucial but insufficient. Prosperity was indeed a key factor, but prosperity alone would have permitted a variety of different policy outcomes. To understand more fully what actually transpired in terms of policy definition and design requires the "thicker" and more nuanced political analyses we endeavor to provide.

Producing Particular Moderate Policies and Maintaining Others: The Role of Rights and Ideas

So far we have sought to explain the overall moderate tone of policymaking in the 1990s. We have shown how political party dynamics (especially party parity, frequent alternation, and a new sun and moon party dynamic), the fiscalization of policymaking, the two-tier division of the polity, and the dualistic consensus on maintaining both the free market and the entitlement state have created a "regime of moderation." But this regime has not adopted every moderate policy proposal. What distinguished those that passed from those that did not and what caused some policies to be more durable than others has been appeals to rights and to other ideas that the polity holds dear. These ideas include "fairness," "work," "market efficiency," and the notion of a balanced budget. Policy proposals wrapped in these notions were more likely to pass (deficit reduction, deregulation, EITC). Existing policies already wrapped in them were more likely to endure (Social Security, affirmative action, *Miranda*). Existing policies that are not associated with them are less likely to endure (Aid to Families with Dependent Children [AFDC]).

The Force of Rights: Promoting New Policies and Maintaining Old Ones

Some durable policies do not have either widespread public support or expert consensus behind them, yet they endure because they appeal to rights, especially those that are what Burke calls "morally entrenched" rights. Without this rights attachment, other policies either fail of enactment or prove impermanent. Skrentny, Burke, Derthick, and Schuck show this to be true with regard to affirmative action, the ADA, Social Security, and immigration reform. Affirmative action's durability is especially noteworthy because, as Skrentny shows, support for it was lukewarm from the outset, while opposition was always strong and vocal. In addition, the expert consensus in support of it, which may have existed at one time, has now broken down.

Social Security's durability also seems to fit this pattern. Experts have always supported it. But, as Derthick shows, a significant number of them now favor significant changes in its policy architecture. Nevertheless, Social Security endures unchanged, because of the widespread perception of it as a fundamental economic right. Burke points out one highly explicit acknowledgment of this power of rights from a source not notably rights oriented. In *Dickerson v. United States,* Justice Rehnquist's majority held that "*Miranda* has become so embedded in routine police practice to the point where warnings have become part of our national culture" and so was no longer open to policy change "whether or not we would agree with . . . [its] . . . reasoning" (*Dickerson v. United States,* 2000 U.S. Lexis 5911 [2000]). The *Dickerson* decision is reminiscent of the 1992 *Planned Parenthood v. Casey* (505 U.S. 833 [1992]) decision reaffirming the constitutional right to abortion. It was joined by justices who acknowledged that they might well have not have voted for *Roe v. Wade* in 1973.

Conversely, when the attachment of a policy to rights is weak, that policy is far more vulnerable to change. As Burke, Teles, and Prinz explain, AFDC was never morally entrenched as a right and therefore it was susceptible to retrenchment.

The Force of Ideas

The Notion of a Balanced Budget

We learn from both Pierson and Patashnik that policymaking in this period has been greatly affected by the fiscalization of public policy. This is, in large part because, as McWilliams and Patashnik show, whatever the demurs of the experts, the public maintains a powerful commitment to the idea of a balanced budget. This attachment played a major role in the policy dynamics that led to the deficit reductions and the various changes in policymaking that flowed from this fiscalization of policymaking.

Patashnik explains that this strong attachment to the balanced budget notion percolated up from the polity's second tier rather than down from the first tier. Indeed, he describes the growth in this attachment in the 1980s and 1990s as an instance of the reassertion of folk wisdom over professional economics. The latter held to the Keynesian view that an unbalanced budget was necessary when there was a weak economy and even tolerable at almost all other times. This particular reassertion of folk wisdom seems to be an example of the first and second tier dialectics that McWilliams describes. He observes that one of the times that ordinary people can successfully oppose policy experts is when their "common experience" doesn't square with expertise. Ordinary people know they cannot long sustain an unbalanced family budget, and, rightly or wrongly, they firmly believe that their private experience should guide public budget policy as well.

This balanced budget predilection had important and widespread policymaking implications. As Howard and Skrentny show, policies like EITC and affirmative action that appeared to contribute little to the budget deficit were more likely to pass and more likely to endure than those that would have strained the budget. EITC also seems to have been helped by the era of fiscalization in another way. It was introduced through an omnibus budget package, an instrument often used in deficit reduction policymaking. As our prior discussion of "stealth" indicated, this mode of introduction may have been the only way that EITC could have survived given its innovative content. By contrast, as Teles and Prinz and Schuck indicate, policies that were thought to contribute much to the deficit like AFDC and benefits for immigrants were not resilient. In reality, AFDC and immigrant benefits do not have a large budgetary impact, but they are perceived to be expensive, and that perception made them vulnerable.

Fairness

The notion of fairness resonates strongly with both the polity's first and second tier, as Bardach's chapter on "exit equality, enter fairness" shows. As the 1986 Tax Reform Act and the 1990s deficit reduction illustrate, posing an issue in terms of "fairness" helps its passage. In particular, proponents were able to portray them as being fairer policies for future generations.

Conversely, when a policy can be successfully portrayed as being "unfair," it becomes vulnerable to repeal. Skrentny shows this with regard to affirmative action repeal in the California referendum and the court decision against race-based quotas in the Boston Latin affirmative action court case (*McLaughlin v. Boston School Committee* [938 F.Supp. 1001 [1996]]). He observes that in the 1990s the public came to view color-blind policies as fair to the same profound degree that it had come to accept desegregation as fair during the late 1950s through the mid-1960s (at least in the North). Then as now, the effect of the notion of fairness on policymaking took some time to percolate through agencies and courts, and so actual policy change lagged behind change in public opinion.

The Notion of Work

The notion of work always has had a strong place in American social and political culture. Those who work tend to be considered "deserving" and those who do not—for whatever reason—tend to be considered "undeserving." Work is highly praised by elite experts and ordinary officeholders. But its major force in shaping policymaking seems to come from the strong commitment to it in the polity's second tier. Indeed, this powerful attachment to the notion of work has been the necessary condition for passage of both EITC and TANF (i.e., welfare reform). The work emphasis also resonates with the evolving consensus on both the regulated free market and the constrained entitlement state.

This attachment to the notion of work seems to have the same positive impact on policy durability as does the notion of rights. Indeed, they are sometimes closely allied. AFDC was not a right because you didn't work to get it. Social Security is a right because you do.

Market Efficiency

The idea of market efficiency animated politicians during the 1990s. NAFTA (1993), telecommunications reform (1996), the deregulation of agriculture in the Freedom to Farm Act (1996), and banking reform (1999) were major innovations that dramatically affected people's lives. But with the exception of NAFTA, these innovations did not seem to arouse the degree of controversy commensurate with their innovativeness. None of them sparked much ideological or partisan discord because the idea of market efficiency transcended partisanship. Where market principles could not be successfully appealed to, such as in the budget debates of the mid-1990s and the health care reform proposals of 1993–1994, discord and deadlock prevailed. Under any pure interest-based theory of politics, NAFTA was doomed. Its greatest benefits were thinly spread over the general public and non-immediate. Its costs were tangibly concentrated in specific geographically defined sets of voters. The interest group push of the exporting industries cannot account for the political success of NAFTA. Surely it was the intellectual power of the market idea that provided the margin of victory in the interest group struggle.

This seems to be a further sign of a gradual erosion of party differences in comparison to party cleavages during the New Deal. Indeed, the New Deal was animated by the notion of market inefficiency. Policymaking aimed to create a welfare state and other regulations to compensate for market inadequacies such as those in farming and banking. Indeed, initially the New Deal resorted to deliberately anticompetitive devices such as the National Industrial Recovery Act (NIRA) and restrictive licensing in the trucking industry. The political cleavages around this policymaking were what came to be the classic liberal Democratic and conservative Republican positions for almost the next half-century. Even as recently as the New Frontier and the Great Society, an "affluent society" tried to have the government deal directly with poverty rather than addressing the problem through increasing market efficiency. The political cleavages of the 1960s still fit the traditional New Deal pattern.

But in the mid-1970s stagflation was the problem at hand. Economic experts' ideas about efficiency through a deregulated market gained policy entrepreneurs' attention. As several chapters of *The New Politics of Policymaking* showed, the resulting deregulation of the transportation, telephone, and banking industries in the 1970s and 1980s was pathbreaking. But none of the legislation elicited traditional partisan conflict as these polices passed with bipartisan support in both Democratic and Republican administrations. By the 1990s market efficacy had an even stronger hold on both Democrats and Republicans. NAFTA and, even more, the innovative telecommunications, farming, and banking reforms passed with bipartisan support even while there was a good deal of noise in the background from other partisan rhetoric. The nonmarket strategy of dealing with poverty—AFDC—was abandoned. With bipartisan support, it was replaced by a policy that tied the amelioration of poverty to the market-friendly mechanisms of employment and training.

Evolving Patterns

The period from the late 1980s through the 1990s was one in which patterns evolving over the previous twenty-five years reached culmination. Analysts have underrated these phenomena because they have become accustomed to conceptualizing distinctive policy eras based on their unique policy contributions. Thus, the Great Society is linked to its innovative efforts to fight poverty, and the 1970s are thought of as the era of deregulation and the 1980s as the era of budget cuts. With the exception of welfare reform, the 1990s had no "signature" programs. Instead, it witnessed more the fruition of trends that preceded it.

The first pattern was the budget and deficit reduction policy resulting in the fiscalization of policymaking. During the Reagan-Bush administrations, a major peak was reached with the

Gramm-Rudman budget procedure reforms in 1987. A further and perhaps decisive peak was reached in 1992, after the elder Bush's first term and with Perot's presidential candidacy. That candidacy was based largely of the issue of deficit reduction and received 19 percent of the vote—the second largest third-party vote in the twentieth century. Then, under Clinton in the mid-1990s, the Democratic "moon party" opportunistically shifted and adopted more of a deficit-reducing policy as it sought—successfully—to win over more of these Perot voters. In 1998 and 1999 the deficit became a surplus, and policymaking took a new turn toward somewhat more generous and expansionary policymaking.

The second pattern was the Republican party's full ascendancy as the agenda-setting "sun party." This was followed by the equally significant Democratic party response of becoming a quite adaptively opportunistic "moon party." This stimulus and response in turn culminated in the unique party dynamic of frequent alternation in power between evenly divided parties. The 2000 election continued this pattern. The presidential and Senate elections were virtual dead heats and resulted in changed party control of the White House. The House Republican margin in 1999 had been thirteen seats and became only nine in 2001.

This close party competition combined with frequent alternation in power has led to a third pattern of the parties becoming opportunistic choosers of particular ideas that attract voters and sustain interest group support. The 1990s competitiveness meant that in each election each party, though the Democrats more so, acted opportunistically. The following chapters show a similar though less pronounced pattern of strategic opportunism among the Republicans. As Shapiro's chapter argues, under Reagan the Republicans moved to cut the entitlement state. They succeed in reducing it. But ultimately Reagan could do no better than strategically accepting a constrained welfare state. And by 1996 this trend toward Republican acceptance of the entitlement state continued again after Gingrich's short-lived "Republican revolution." (Indeed, Gingrich in part led this acceptance, which brought him to blows with his most conservative peers.) Skrentny's chapter on affirmative action comes to a similar conclusion. Despite their dislike of it, the Republicans abjured repealing it to avoid punishment at the polls for what would have been perceived as an extreme "antirights" and antiminority position.

Again, we must stress critical qualifications and exceptions to this pattern: we are focusing on policymaking and policy outcomes. These were primarily the product of presidential initiative and action. However, during the 1990s there was more polarizing and partisan political behavior in Congress. Much of this was confined to campaigning and symbolic congressional rhetoric. But at critical times, a good deal of this ideological activity manifested itself in policymaking attempts: the 1994–1995 budget stand-off between the parties is the clearest case. But the ideological steadfastness of the Republicans was met with rejection at the polls in 1996. After 1996, these same Republicans, under a chastened Gingrich, became more opportunistic in policymaking as they sought to avoid further punishment at the polls. Gingrich studiously sought budget compromise with the Democratic White House in 1997 and 1998—so much so, according to his most conservative colleagues, that they ousted him.

But then again in 1998, the Clinton impeachment hearings raised the incentive for ideological political behavior and rhetoric. In this context, Democrats matched Republicans with regard to party purity and cohesion. In the House of Representatives, the votes on the Articles of Impeachment were cast virtually along party lines. And, again, in the 1998 congressional elections, the Republicans, who were perceived as the more vociferous of the two parties, suffered losses in the House. Once more, this failed ideological foray was followed by opportunistic backtracking: the House Republicans abandoned their effort to abolish the Department of Education and supported positive small government proposals like Ed/Flex. In the run-up to the 2000 presidential nominating process, such staunch conservatives as Tom DeLay and Dick Armey supported the newly "moderated" George W. Bush. Likewise, congressional Democrats chose not to go "too far" on such volatile issues as gun control and free trade.

Despite this opportunistic backpedaling in actual policymaking situations, both parties maintained ideological distance in terms of their general rhetoric and party positioning. The Democrats, for example, sought to maintain a distinctively "liberal" position on race and rights policies. The Republicans staked out the clearly "conservative" position on antiregulatory policies and the primacy of free enterprise.

The fourth pattern is "the end of big ideas and big programs." This is the climax of a trend away from expensive new government programs that began in the 1970s. The 1990s were a time of unusually sustained and strong domestic and international economic prosperity. With this has come what Shapiro in his conclusion calls the movement of almost all political leaders on the left and right toward supporting a dualism of efficiency and equity—supporting both the free market and the welfare state. An agreement has been reached that free markets are the best way to allocate goods and services but that the rigors of free markets must be tempered by the welfare state. Consequently, Clinton declared the end of the era of big government, and both parties moved toward making it a time of positive small government.

Even a large government surplus led to few calls of major expansion of the sphere of national government. Instead, the debate was about fiscal fine-tuning, incremental regulatory change, small adjustments in the balance between national and local authority, and minor redirections of the flow of government benefits.

A final pattern is broached by Mayhew. He argues that the 1990s witnessed greater concurrence between public opinion and policymaking. Welfare reform, reducing the budget deficits, and affirmative action rollbacks at the state level, for instance, were all in line with mass opinion. There also was the triumph of folk wisdom over professional economics with the elite acceptance of the notion of a balanced budget. The durable policies of the 1990s also seem to reflect mass preferences. Many experts and professional politicians sought to change Social Security radically and dismantle big entitlements. But both endured pretty much in the 1990s without major changes.

By contrast, the 1970s and 1980s were a time of incongruity between public opinion and policymaking. As *The New Politics of Public Policy* showed—especially James Q. Wilson's concluding chapter—signature policies of that earlier period such as entitlements' expansion, deficit spending, and immigration reform were not popular. They were all the products of elite opinion.

What seems to explain this shift? Perhaps it is merely a lag effect. It may simply take public opinion a period of years to find means for mobilizing itself to countervail elite imposed policies. Or, perhaps the degree of congruity between elite and mass opinion is influenced by budgetary considerations. During a period of severe budgetary pressure, such as the early and middle 1990s, more issues tend to rise to higher levels of visibility and salience. Thus, it is harder to accomplish policy change through stealth. Elite politicians find it more difficult to foist unpopular policies on the public. Those policies that do pass despite a lack of popular support are those that have the least budgetary impact. This is because they either are not very costly (EITC) or do not appear as public budget items at all (NAFTA).

By contrast, in a expansionary fiscal period—the 1960s and 1970s—or one in which there are fewer budgetary pressures—the middle and late 1970s—many elite issues tend not to rise to higher levels of visibility and saliency. Thus, these policy realms are more likely to remain dominated by elites. Hence the panoply of Great Society social programs in the former period. In the latter period, policies that were not yet demanded by the public such as deregulation and environmental and consumer reforms were nevertheless produced.

In considering these hypotheses, how much difference do these budgetary pressures or their absence make? How much difference have they made in recent years? We can get some idea of their relative impact in the 1990s by examining the criticisms and prescriptions of a thoughtful analyst on the absence of concerns about budgetary constraints in the 1980s. James Q. Wilson, writing in his concluding chapter for *The New Politics of Public Policy,* argued that the absence of sufficient concern about the budget in the 1980s allowed Congress and the presidents to avoid making hard policy choices. It permitted them to run irresponsibly against Washington at the same time they were voting for popular spending measure and against unpopular taxes. Thus, they had not come to grips with the problem of collective action—the problem of combining individual preferences into a policy that will command general assent over the long term.

Wilson felt so strongly that this insufficient budgetary concern was creating serious policymaking irresponsibility that he then went so far as to advocate a balanced budget amendment as a way of institutionalizing such budgetary pressures: "to create further barriers—not only to elite actions, but also to the short-sighted pursuit of our own preferences. . . . [A] balanced budget amendment is the one proposal that is easiest to envision and most consistent with the key problem of collective choice. . . . It would require the president and Congress to make harder choices than they are now disposed to make."

The results Wilson hoped for transpired without a balanced budget amendment. He had thought that the budgetary pressures were not sufficient to prevent irresponsible dealing with the problem of collective choice. But an indication of how salient and powerful these pressures had become in this age of the fiscaliziation of policymaking is that the deficits were reduced without a balanced budget amendment. Put differently, these pressures had become so visible and salient that they became a de facto balanced budget amendment. As Pierson shows, these pressures came to subject almost all policies to a "fiscalization test"—what was their fiscal impact on the deficit. Another mark of their power and significance is that at the end of the 1990s hardly anyone was calling for a de jure balanced budget amendment.

Some Final Thoughts

The student of policymaking is inevitably attracted to the bold. Yet the sources of policymaking are just as important to dissect when the results are moderate. From some future vantage point, these innovative changes and continuities may well prove of greater significance and durability than the flashier programs and policies emblematic of other political times. The policies discussed in this book are moderate, yet in no way are they of minor significance. Moreover, the 1990s were a time at which many important streams of political and policy development merged and reached their flood tide. The following essays provide a sense of the richness, the importance, and the subtlety of these developments.

Whether these patterns that reached a kind of culmination during the 1990s will endure remains to be seen. The Kosovo and Middle East crises bridging the new millennium may indicate that one of the most anomalous aspects of that decade—the lack of a serious foreign policy crisis—may not continue. Also, the late 1990s witnessed two significant challenges to the consensus about the virtues of free markets. There was a growth in power of, in Vogel's terms, a "left-right populist coalition" that included conservative Republicans with a populist shading à la Pat Buchanan and liberal environmentalists, trade unionists, and consumer groups. This coalition successfully opposed fast-track reauthorization on the grounds that further trade liberalization would play havoc with domestic businesses, workers, and the environment and also contribute to the loss of "sovereignty." In addition, concern about global economic volatility was not confined to the second tier. In the wake of the Asian financial crisis of the late 1990s, even some segments of the elite have begun to advocate reregulating international capital flows.

Neither of these developments is yet powerful enough to undermine the broad political consensus behind market expansion. Yet they do show that considerable differences exist regarding the proper extent of market domination and the best means for bringing market excesses within bounds. Indeed much of the current political and policy consensus, with its odd mix of surliness and resistance to change, may only be an economic recession or a foreign policy disaster away from dissolving. The careful reader will therefore want to tease out from the following essays those aspects of the deeply textured narratives that most strongly represent enduring sources of policy durability and change from those that are merely artifacts of a post–Cold War/Impeachment Follies political interregnum.

Notes

1. This chapter has benefited mightily from the comments and suggestions of David Beam, Tom Burke, Nia Lane Chester, John Coleman, Tim Conlan, Chris Howard, David Mayhew, Eric Patashnik, Peter Schuck, John Skrentny, Steve Teles, and Jeane Whitehouse.
2. See "Veto of Estate Tax Repeal Survives Vote in the House," *New York Times*, September 8, 2000, p.14.

PART II

Taxing and Spending

2

Budgeting More, Deciding Less

Eric M. Patashnik, *University of California, Los Angeles*

"Budgeting is governing," declares Pete V. Domenici, chair of the Senate Budget Committee, on the back cover of the leading annual guide to the federal budget process.[1] Few would challenge this statement. Budgeting has always been at the heart of policymaking. Since the early 1980s, however, the budget has been the major issue of American politics. As Norman Ornstein observes, elected officials, businessmen, and journalists alike became "obsessed with the budget process, endlessly analyzing and arguing over it."[2] Though people might disagree about how well (or poorly) the budget process is working, few doubt that the budget matters more than it once did.

But while budget issues undeniably acquired a new prominence in the 1980s and 1990s because of the struggle to control the budget deficit, the budget-making process has in fact declined in importance as a framework for governing the economy and setting national priorities. I certainly do not want to be understood as saying that the budget process is unimportant. The national budget mobilizes resources and maintains the bureaucracy. Politicians continue to make budget decisions that materially affect the lives and prospects of real citizens. And while the federal pork barrel is smaller than it once was, plenty of benefits remain for legislators to ladle out.[3]

Still, I contend that budgeting has become a less important setting for deciding public policy—even as it has become a more significant arena for political debate. This seemingly paradoxical state of affairs is the product of dramatic changes in economic ideas, political institutions, and the composition of the federal budget itself. The budget has moved to the center of political life in the United States because budget politics is a major battleground for partisan and ideological struggles over the future of activist government. Yet while the budget involves high political stakes, the policy importance of budget-making has declined over time. In the 1950s and 1960s, the Keynesian revolution elevated the importance of the national budget because effective fiscal policy was viewed as the key to economic prosperity. But now most policymakers place their economic faith in monetary policy and the Federal Reserve. Meanwhile, the budget has become a less powerful instrument for directing spending priorities because more and more of the budget goes for entrenched long-term programs like Social Security. Politicians may be fighting over budget issues more—but they are deciding less. And as I explain in this chapter, while the unanticipated emergence of budget surpluses in the last few years could fundamentally change these dynamics, there are good reasons to expect it won't. The budget story is a case study of the contradictions of the modern American polity.

The Fiscalization of the Policy Debate

Since the early 1980s, the budget has been the dominant issue of American national politics, overshadowing all other policy concerns. The policy debate has become "fiscalized." A good indicator is media coverage. According to David W. Brady and Craig Volden, the attention paid to the budget by the media has increased dramatically. During the 1970s, the *New York Times* ran an average of about 200 stories per year on the budget; during the 1980s, it averaged 1,800 stories a year. This trend continued into the 1990s. When reporters cover Congress, their stories are frequently budget related.[4]

The reason journalists focus heavily on budget issues today is not because they are deeply interested in the substance of public policy (though some reporters no doubt are) but because reporters instinctively love a good political fight—and the budget process is where some of the biggest recent clashes have been. Think of the Clinton-Gingrich budget battle of 1995. Or the squabble between House Republicans and President George H. W. Bush over Bush's abandonment of his "no new taxes" pledge at the 1990 budget summit at Andrews Air Force Base. The arcane federal budget process is now the stuff of high politics.

This is a relatively new development in American government. Traditionally budgeting attracted little political attention. Standard accounts of federal budgeting during the 1950s and 1960s—such as the late Aaron Wildavsky's classic 1964 book *The Politics of the Budgetary Process*—described budgeting as a vital, but sedate, process of incremental bargaining between Congress and bureau chiefs. Budgeting was considered so technical and dull when the book was first published that Wildavsky felt compelled to reassure his readers on the book's first page that the topic was actually of some political interest.[5]

Budgeting in the 1950s and 1960s lacked obvious drama for three main reasons. First, budget deficits were generally small as a percentage of gross domestic product (GDP). While programs were growing, spending was considered under control. Second, a rough ideological consensus existed among politicians over many taxing and spending issues. To be sure, liberals and conservatives during this era had their budget fights. But the scope of conflict over the budget was muted by the backdrop of the Cold War, the distributive nature of many spending programs—the pork barrel was still growing—and the existence of large numbers of political moderates in Congress. Finally, congressional budgeting created an artificial, yet meaningful, distinction between money decisions and policy decisions—and thus between high politics and mundane public administration. Under the pre-1974 rules, Congress did not consider the budget as a whole. When people spoke of the "budget," they meant the president's budget, which was then (as now) submitted to Congress each year, right after the president's State of the Union address. But the president's budget is only a set of executive proposals. Significantly, Congress did not debate these proposals as a package in the 1950s and 1960s. Rather, the president's budget proposals were taken up piecemeal by the thirteen appropriations subcommittees in each chamber. The effect was to cordon off funding skirmishes from broader political battles.

By the 1980s, all this had changed. First, the economic and budgetary situation had worsened. Budget deficits began rising after the mid-1970s and exploded after 1981. The main causes included an economic slowdown, rising entitlement spending, and the Reagan tax cut.

Second, as Sarah Binder of the Brookings Institution has documented, the number of political moderates on Capitol Hill declined.[6] The Democratic congressional caucus become more liberal; the Republican conference, more conservative. When congressional scholar Steven E. Schier conducted extensive interviews on Capitol Hill in the mid-1980s, he found that virtually all members of the House and Senate approached budget issues from an ideology encompassing fundamental concepts about the appropriate size and role of government. Unsurprisingly, conservatives displayed concern about the overall level of public spending. They also believed that defense spending was a high priority and worried about the effect of redistribution on economic incentives. By contrast, liberals focused less on the total size of government, viewed social spending as more important than defense, and were concerned about the achievement of a fair distribution of income.[7]

Finally, the rules of federal budgeting were transformed. Provoked by President Nixon's blatant abuse of his impoundment authority and by concern about increasing budget deficits, Congress adopted a landmark reform, the Budget Act of 1974. The measure curbed impoundments, created the Congressional Budget Office (CBO), and established new budget committees in each chamber. The House and Senate budget committees were given the job of formulating overall budget packages ("budget resolutions") for lawmakers to debate and decide on. The major aims of the new process were to restore the balance of power between the branches and help Congress coordinate its budget work. Although budget deficits continued to grow after 1974, they may well have been even larger had the process not been reformed. Quantitative analysis indicates that federal spending levels entered a period of sharply restrained growth just as the new budget process was being implemented.[8] Budget reform thus probably contributed to the "regime of austerity" that Pierson analyzes in chapter 3.

These three factors—rising budget deficits, the disappearance of the political center, and congressional budget reform—combined to create a wholly new and different budget regime. Because the deficit was large, lawmakers faced tough budget choices. Because Republicans and Democrats were more ideologically distant from one another, partisan conflict over budget matters increased. And because Congress now had to vote on total spending, taxing, and deficit levels—that is, on the total direction of national public policy—the conflicts between the parties took on heightened meaning, especially because top party leaders like the Speaker came to play an active role in appointing members of the key budget committees and crafting omnibus budget legislation.

The budget deficit was not just another policy issue during the 1980s and the 1990s. It was the master issue, subsuming all the others. Policy experts began speaking of "the fiscalization of the policy debate." By this phrase, they meant a new tendency for programs to be debated not according to their particular merits but according to their impact on the government's overall fiscal condition. "The measure of all arguments became dollars," observes former CBO director Robert D. Reischauer.[9] The key question became "What would the policy do to the deficit?" The obsession with the budget deficit transformed the political debate. As Pierson has elsewhere argued, the preoccupation with budget constraints displaced pragmatic disagreements over operational details with "broader, more abstract arguments about the appropriate role of government."[10]

Nothing inherent in budget deficits must produce ideological and partisan conflict. Given the context of American national politics in the 1980s and the 1990s, however, fundamental disagreement over the budget was virtually guaranteed. The underlying policy differences between the two congressional parties were large. Moreover, the new budget process forced these differences out into the open. Some 40 percent of congressional roll calls votes on budget resolutions between 1976 and 1990 found 75 percent or more of Republicans opposing 75 percent or more of Democrats. On 10 percent of the roll calls, 90 percent or more of one party opposed 90 percent or more of the other.[11] Even though the gap between Democrats and Republicans was hard to bridge, party leaders pushed their agendas in the context of the budget process because budget measures enjoyed special procedural advantages not available to other legislation. The budget became a leading example of the increasing resort to "omnibus" lawmaking.[12] Thus, Republicans in 1995 tried to use the budget process not only to lower deficits but to cut taxes, kill programs, reform welfare, restructure Medicare and Medicaid, and send power back to the states. Of course, many of these proposals failed. The important point is that the budget process became the leading legislative game in town.

Under the rules of the game, every measure must confirm to budget enforcement provisions. The leading keeper of the rules is the CBO. Because the CBO's scorekeeping decisions can have a decisive impact on policy outcomes, politicians complain vigorously when rulings don't go their way—as in House Republicans' ongoing complaint that the CBO fails to recognize the "dynamic" impact of tax cuts in its statistical models. As political sociologist Theda Skocpol notes, back in the Progressive era and the time of the New Deal, drafters of legislation spent a lot of time trying to guess what the Supreme Court would accept as constitutional. Today, lawmakers live in fear that the CBO will "reject their proposals as not 'costed out.'"[13]

With the establishment of a new budget process in 1974, Congress began a twenty-year experimentation with budget reform. The 1974 Act was in turn followed by the Gramm-Rudman Act in 1985 (which set declining deficit targets until balance was reached after six years) and the Budget Enforcement Act (BEA) in 1990 (which established caps on discretionary spending and pay-as-you-go rules for entitlements and revenues). In general, the reforms worked best as fiscal control devices when they discouraged Congress from creating major new budgeting commitments (the BEA) and were least successful when they sought to engineer massive cuts in existing programs (Gramm-Rudman).[14]

Each new budget reform typically did not replace what came before. Instead, the new rules and procedures were simply grafted onto the old ones.[15] For example, the traditional piecemeal appropriations process was not eliminated. Rather, appropriations committees and budget committees became organizational rivals, and discretionary spending was capped. Such "institutional layering" created all sorts of organizational frictions within Congress.[16] At the same time, it made the overall taxing and spending process more complex. The federal budget became like a foreign language. Newly elected members of Congress could hardly understand it.[17] This increased the power of those few policy elites who did understand (and could manipulate) the arcane rules of the budget game.

Macrobudgeting versus Microbudgeting

In sum, everything is now a budget issue, and the congressional budget process has become more centralized, complex, and politically adversarial. Meanwhile, the power of professional budget forecasters has greatly increased. What makes these developments all the more interesting is that they occurred during an era when the annual budget process has been of declining importance. The budget can be used to steer the economy (macrobudgeting) and to direct government priorities (microbudgeting).[18] The federal budget performs both of these functions to a much lesser extent than it once did.

Keynesianism's Rise and Fall

With the triumph of Keynesian economics—or at least the applied version of it—in the 1950s and the 1960s, the budget became the supposed key to governing the American economy. Before World War II, policymakers' lack of scientific knowledge about how the economy works inhibited them from using the budget as a tool to promote economic growth with low inflation. Politicians were also constrained by the belief that the budget must be balanced every year. As James Savage of the University of Virginia has shown, since the nation's founding a balanced federal budget has carried a symbolic importance far beyond its objective economic meaning, signaling democratic control, social harmony, and the preservation of republican government. By contrast, budget deficits have stood for inefficiency and corruption.[19] Even Franklin D. Roosevelt, whose New Deal programs resulted in a string of massive peacetime deficits, never really abandoned the view that government ordinarily had a moral obligation to balance its books.

By the late 1950s, however, leading economists increasingly saw the balanced budget dogma as the main obstacle to rational economic policymaking. With the triumph of Keynesian doctrine in the early 1960s, that obstacle was temporarily removed. President Kennedy's economic advisers believed in fiscal activism—that is, in deliberately pursuing the precise level of aggregate taxing and spending most appropriate given the current state of the economy. If economic conditions were disappointing, fiscal policies should try to improve them. Budget deficits were no longer evil in themselves; what mattered was their impact on aggregate output and consumer demand. "The federal budget can help achieve the overall economic goals of a high level of employment and reasonable price stability," confidently asserted two Brookings economists in 1971. "To serve this purpose, the amount of stimulus or restraint coming from the budget must be responsive to the needs of the economy at any particular time."[20] Although monetary policy was not entirely discounted, most Keynesians during this era believed that fiscal policy would be more effective.

The national budget thus came to be seen as the key to economic prosperity. Keynesianism's greatest triumph came with the large tax cut enacted by Congress in 1964. Whether the Kennedy-Johnson tax cut actually achieved its stated goal of spurring economic growth remains a matter of dispute among professional economists. But clearly elected officials believed it had worked. To deny the essential correctness of Keynesian prescriptions was to declare oneself a know-nothing.

The Keynesian intellectual revolution did not convert everyone, however. Public opinion surveys indicate that ordinary Americans never really abandoned the traditional belief that budget deficits are intrinsically decadent and immoral. "Keynesian arguments for simulative deficits—and attacks on the family budget analogy as misleading—seem to have made little headway with the public, except perhaps for short periods during major recessions," write leading scholars of American public opinion.[21] What James Q. Wilson calls the "elite abandonment" of fiscal orthodoxy in the 1960s thus opened a normative gap between leaders and ordinary citizens on deficit spending.[22]

But in the United States the values of ordinary citizens are not easily brushed aside. Many Keynesian experts took the position that budget balancing was no more than an accounting fetish. Yet few politicians were willing to tell the public it was foolish. Keynesian presidential advisers therefore developed a hybrid concept, the "full-employment" budget. Instead of strict balance, the idea was that the government would adopt fiscal policies that would cause the budget to be in balance at full employment. The Kennedy-Johnson tax cut was explicitly sold to the public on these grounds. According to the late Herbert Stein, "Keynesian economists were willing to make use of the vulgar prejudice in favor of a balanced budget, even if they did not share it."[23]

Within the stratum of policy elites, Keynesian ideas found somewhat greater acceptance in the executive than in Congress. This difference was rooted in the electoral incentives created by the two political institutions. More so than executives, members of Congress have an incentive to adopt popular understandings of policy issues.

As David Mayhew elsewhere points out, Keynesianism received a "chillier reception on the Hill than in the White House" during the 1960s "not because Congress [was] more 'conservative' but because it is in a sense more 'democratic'; the image of a balanced family budget is a powerful one."[24]

The power of Keynesian thought was substantially tied to its standing among professional economists. But economic theories can be discredited if the world doesn't work as predicted. When the economy experienced "stagflation" in the mid-1970s, Keynesians were bewildered and lost confidence. "Belief in the government's ability to manage the economy so as to yield high employment, stable prices, and stable growth, generally heralded in the early and mid 1960s, has been shattered by the simultaneous appearance of the worst recession and the worst inflation of the past thirty years," observed two Brookings scholars in 1976.[25] The dominant economic goal shifted from stimulating consumer demand to controlling inflation and boosting productivity. Economists continued to accept the idea of protecting family income through the use of "automatic stabilizers" such as food stamps and unemployment insurance. But they increasingly argued that politicians were incapable of "fine-tuning" fiscal policy to the business cycle. Primary responsibility for the nation's economic performance, they said, was better left to unelected experts at the Federal Reserve.

As the 1970s came to a close, the idea of a full-employment budget was heard less and less. In the 1984 presidential campaign, every major Democratic candidate condemned deficit spending. Over the remainder of the decade, the balanced budget idea became increasingly powerful as politicians increasingly embodied the traditional fiscal orthodoxy of average citizens.[26] As columnist Robert Samuelson observes, the recovery of the balanced budget concept can be seen as a "reassertion of folk wisdom over professional economics."[27]

By the mid-1980s, very few politicians or mainstream economists believed anymore in using the budget to manage the economy. We were all monetarists now. This was enormously frustrating to those few remaining activist liberals in the executive, who believed the government should use spending increases to boost economic performance. "In case you hadn't noticed, America's domestic policy is now being run by Alan Greenspan and the Federal Reserve Board," lamented former Labor Secretary Robert Reich. "Their decisions about interest rates are determining how many of us have jobs and how many of us get a raise. . . . Congress is out of this loop.[28] President Clinton did emphasize the need for government "investment" early in his first term. But the administration proposed only a very modest economic stimulus plan, which Congress ultimately scaled back under deficit pressures and the new elite consensus.

The Expansion of Long-Term Commitments

As the Fed was acting with dispatch to control inflation in the 1980s and 1990s, the congressional budget process was coming apart at the seams. Politicians talked endlessly about the urgency of getting the nation's fiscal house in order. Yet appropriations bills were constantly late. Between 1981 and 1985, the federal government shut down six times. Three more government shutdowns occurred between 1986 and 1990, and two more during the historic budget battles of 1995–1996. These funding interruptions were not inconsequential. "Nonessential" federal workers were furloughed. Tourists hoping to see the pandas found the National Zoo closed.[29] But the most sensitive parts of the budget—the massive income transfer programs—were only modestly affected. For most Americans the functioning of the budget process— the topic of endless news coverage—simply wasn't that important.

Of course, even as fiscal policy became less central to economic management, budgeting could still have remained a vital process for setting national spending priorities. Certainly it is difficult to imagine a time when budgeting will not matter for resource allocation. Policymakers will always confront questions about how to divvy up scarce tax dollars. Nonetheless, the scope for priority setting in the U.S. budget is much narrower than many believe. As Wildavsky explained in 1964, the budget is *never* actively reviewed as a whole every year. The calculative burden is simply too overwhelming. To save energy and time, politicians generally accept the prior year's budget as a starting point for the current one, confining their attention to changes at the margins. But—and this point is crucial—there is even less room for shaping government priorities through the budget today than there was in the 1950s and 1960s. There are two main reasons for this. First, the federal government's era of massive program building is all but over. Second, a greater share of spending goes for long-term commitments such as Social Security.

It is easy to forget just how much program building took place over the postwar period. Reischauer provides a useful reminder: "In the mid-1950s, numerous government agencies did not exist. A partial list includes the Departments of Transportation, Education, Energy, and Housing and Urban Development and agencies such as NASA, EPA, the Nuclear Regulatory Commission, the National Endowments for the Arts and Humanities, the Federal Emergency Management Agency, and the Legal Services Corporation."[30] Last year's budget may have been the most important determinant of current outcomes during the "classical period" of federal budgeting between 1945 and 1974—that was Wildavsky's point—but government growth and policy innovation still left space for Congress to make important funding decisions.

By the 1980s, however, the federal government was involved in numerous policy sectors, programs were mature, and most spending items were deeply entrenched. The very permanence of big government narrowed the scope for active decision making and increased the overall stability of budget results. According to an important recent study in the *American Journal of Political Science,* year-to-year changes in domestic spending priorities were actually more volatile during the postwar decades than during the 1980s and early 1990s, even though the modern budget process is so much more rancorous and conflictual.[31]

The increased stability of budget outcomes is not merely the product of the maturation of big government. It reflects as well an erosion of budgetary flexibility. Since the 1950s, annual appropriations paid out of general tax revenues—the accounts over which politicians possess the most discretion—have declined from more than two-thirds to less than one-third of the budget. This development reflects the growth of entitlement spending (mainly for Social Security and Medicare), the expansion of earmarked taxes dedicated to specific trust fund programs, and the adoption of automatic cost-of-living adjustments for social benefits and the tax code.[32] These precommitment devices do not eliminate the possibility of policy change. Indeed, at times, they may even *encourage* significant reforms. The prospect of the Social Security Trust Fund's "bankruptcy" in 1983, for example, led to some tax hikes and benefit reductions. Net, however, the three mechanisms make the budget more rigid, less responsive than ordinary appropriations to the preferences of current officeholders.

Because so much of future budgets is already spoken for, the CBO is further encouraged to make long-term budget forecasts. Yet, because future budgets are so sensitive to changes in economic conditions, these forecasts often turn out to be quite wrong. For example, no one foresaw the disappearance of the budget deficit in 1998. One effect of long-term public commitments has thus been simultaneously to reduce uncertainty for program beneficiaries and increase uncertainty for budget projections.

Entitlements, in particular, have stabilized budget outcomes and destabilized the budget process. Standard incrementalist theory, which assumes that programs are subject to discretionary control at the margins, has difficulty accounting for entitlements.[33] To be sure, spending for programs like Social Security has tended to grow gradually over time. The typical pattern during the 1960s was for Congress to increase benefits marginally every two years. Yet the pure incremental model, by focusing on serial choice, obscures the fact that such expansions are piled on top of commitments inherited from past Congresses. Moreover, incrementalism focuses on a short period of time, normally one or two budget cycles. But entitlement commitments stretch over generations. The growth of entitlements during the 1960s and 1970s reflects not incrementalism but rather "inheritance through political inertia."[34]

While entitlements made spending results more stable, they transformed budgetary relationships. In the 1950s and early 1960s—before the big increase in entitlement spending—the budget process was relatively insulated. Budget officials had relatively cordial relations and seemingly bargained in good faith. Interest groups could testify at appropriations hearings and seek to influence key legislators and bureaucrats. They could form coalitions. But clientele groups—and the media—were generally shut out from the committee meetings where the crucial deals were made. As Wildavsky wrote of budgeting during this era, "outsiders are barred . . . secrecy is maintained."[35]

The implicit rationale for this closed-door policy was that the U.S. budget was fundamentally the *government's* business—not the public's. Most federal spending during this era financed goods and services, especially defense. In short, clientele demands were mediated by the institutional structure of the administrative state. But most entitlements are income transfers. The expansion of entitlements thus made ordinary Americans increasingly dependent on the government for their personal well-being. Whereas during the 1950s the budgetary process looked inward to federal agencies and their staff, now it increasingly faces outward to the citizenry.[36] As Allen Schick observes, entitlements gave a host of clientele groups—the elderly, coal miners, and others—a direct, "open-ended draw on the Treasury." These budget claimants "brought demands, rights, and intense conflict to what once had been a sedate process."[37] In the new era of entitlements, a closed, secretive budget process could no longer be sustained.

Entitlements conflict with classical bargaining norms. Traditionally, claimants had to petition for their fair share increase; they had no right to more spending. But entitlement costs automatically rise absent an explicit—and often politically difficult—decision to cut programs. Entitlements thus shift attention away from the maintenance of a fair bargaining process toward the achievement of specific results.[38] Of course, democratic politics offers no policy guarantees. The AFDC (Aid to Families with Dependent Children) entitlement, for example, was abolished. But AFDC is the exception rather than the rule. Most means-tested entitlements have in fact been quite resilient.

The Struggle over the Budget Deficit

The budget deficit grew between the mid-1970s and mid-1990s chiefly because spending on inherited entitlement commitments, especially those for health care, outpaced economic growth. To be sure, the Reagan administration in 1981 won the enactment of a major budget package featuring a significant tax cut, reduction in domestic discretionary spending, and defense buildup. Between the mid 1980s and mid 1990s, however, the impact of current political decisions on budget outcomes was relatively modest.[39]

Virtually every influential politician, Democrats and Republicans alike, agreed on the need for courageous action on the budget. Yet for all the political emphasis on deficit reduction, the actual level of legislative progress made in easing the deficit was comparatively modest. When the Gramm-Rudman spending reduction targets started to bite in 1987, they were postponed. A number of beneficiaries (especially Medicare providers, upper-income taxpayers, and the defense sector) suffered genuine losses, and deficit reduction bills during the 1980s and 1990s definitely caused some pain.[40] Yet strong political support for the federal government's long-term promises severely circumscribed the range of feasible domestic spending cutbacks.

Efforts to make deep reductions in the deficit were also thwarted by ideological dissensus in Congress. Both liberals and conservatives developed coherent deficit reduction plans. But neither had the votes to go it alone, making compromise necessary. Despite the resort to bipartisan summits over the 1980s and 1990s, conflict, stalemate, and delay were the rule. During the intense, highly partisan battle over the 1996 budget, thirteen separate stopgap measures had to be enacted.[41]

In sum, the deficit wars did not make budget outcomes nearly as volatile as one might expect. While budget reforms like Gramm-Rudman and the BEA probably did help restrain spending on existing programs to some extent, their most important effect was to prevent Congress from creating expensive new budget promises.[42] This implied that deficits would eventually recede as economic growth caught up with the rate of entitlement growth. And that is basically what occurred. The legislative changes made in the Balanced Budget Act of 1997 were not expected to bring about a balanced budget until 2002. Congress achieved a balanced budget in 1998, four years ahead of schedule, primarily because medical inflation slowed, the savings from Medicare cutbacks were larger than planned, tax revenues surged, and (most important) the economy performed exceptionally well.

Future Prospects

During the 1980s and 1990s, the budget became a major issue of American politics. At the same time, the use of the budget as a framework for governing the economy declined and spending priorities became increasingly entrenched. This is ironic, to say the least. Before 1974, Congress had little organizational capacity for fiscal activism even though Keynesianism was the dominant economic theory. After the establishment of a top-down congressional budget process in 1974, legislators had the budgetary tools for discretionary economic management. By then, however, the idea of using the budget to drive the economy had lost legitimacy. An even deeper irony is the gap between the tremendous attention paid to current budget battles and the narrow maneuvering room of the contestants. The most important decisions affecting today's budget were made by politicians no longer in office. When inherited commitments crowd out the freedom to choose, the budget comes to reflect policy priorities more than set them.[43]

The projection of large federal budget surpluses—which of course is based on assumptions about future economic growth and political behavior that may not come true—definitely creates some new policy options. What remains to be seen is whether the political economy of the budget will fundamentally change. This could occur in at least three ways.

First, politicians could again embrace Keynesian "fine-tuning"—the idea of using discretionary changes in taxes and spending to boost economic performance on a routine basis. But, given the current state of macroeconomic theory and the political and economic constraints on elected officials in an era of capital market integration, this outcome seems unlikely. To be sure, President George W. Bush in 2001 did use the softening economy as political ammunition in selling his tax cut proposals, arguing that rate reductions were an "insurance policy" against a prolonged slowdown. But this hardly signified a revival of Keynesian fine-tuning. Bush never seriously challenged the idea that monetary policy is the nation's primary tool for guiding the economy. He was also at pains to emphasize that his tax plan was "affordable," noting that federal taxes were at their highest level as a percentage of GDP in thirty years.

Second, political support for the government's long-term spending commitments could crumble. But this possibility also seems remote. Even advocates of Social Security privatization recognize that any large-scale reforms will have to be phased in gradually. If fundamental changes are made to current benefit structures, they are unlikely to be implemented overnight.

Finally, the political economy of the budget would change if strong demands emerged for major new programs. Whether this will occur will depend in part, of course, on future electoral outcomes. It is highly unlikely, though, that politicians will allow discretionary domestic spending to decline in real terms due to inflation (as some budget projections unrealistically assume). New pork barrel projects will be adopted.

Given the large unified budget surpluses projected for the coming decade, however, what is most remarkable is the degree of spending restraint politicians have thus far displayed—a product of partisan maneuvering for electoral advantage, the continuing power of the balanced budget symbol, and a recognition among policy elites that deficits may well return when the baby boomers begin to retire. A strong bipartisan consensus emerged in late 1999 that the Social Security surpluses should be saved. If this commitment is kept, the amount of surplus revenue available to finance new expenditures will greatly decrease.

The availability of surplus revenue will further decrease, of course, if Congress adopts tax cuts in the years ahead. This point was not lost on liberal Democrats, who recognized correctly that Bush's tax cut proposals were intended to make it harder for them to propose new expenditures without identifying offsetting reductions elsewhere in the budget. Given the scope of federal entitlement commitments and an apparent unwillingness to accept a permanent increase in federal tax levels, it seems that fiscal slack—the key to preserving budgetary flexibility—will remain a thing of the past.

In sum, while new programs and tax cuts will almost certainly be adopted, yesterday's promises will continue to dominate today's budget outcomes. Of course, it remains possible that unexpected developments will serve to increase politicians' budgetary power and discretion. Until that happens, however, Washington policymakers will continue to budget more and decide less.

Notes

1. Stanley E. Collender, *The Guide to the Federal Budget: Fiscal 1997* (Lanham, Md.: Rowman & Littlefield, 1996).

2. Norman Ornstein, "The Deficit: A Look at the Bright Side" [book review of Joseph White and Aaron Wildavsky, *The Deficit and the Public Interest*], *New York Times Book Review*, June 30, 1990, section 7, p. 14.

3. Erika Niedowski, "Republican Hypocrites: GOP Budget Cutters are Hawks—Until It Comes to Trimming Their Own Pork," *Washington Monthly* (July–August 1997): 24–27. On the decline of pork barrel spending and the importance of particularistic benefits for legislative coalition building, see John W. Ellwood and Eric M. Patashnik, "In Praise of Pork," *The Public Interest* (Winter 1993): 19–33; for a fundamental defense of the pork barrel, see James Q. Wilson, "Democracy Needs Pork to Survive," *Wall Street Journal*, August 14, 1997, p. A12.

4. David W. Brady and Craig Volden, *Revolving Gridlock* (Boulder, Colo.: Westview, 1998), 56.

5. Aaron Wildavsky, *The Politics of the Budgetary Process* (Boston: Little, Brown, 1964).

6. See Sarah A. Binder, "The Disappearing 'Political Center,'" *Brookings Review* (Fall 1996): 36–39.

7. Steven Schier, *A Decade of Deficits: Congressional Thought and Fiscal Action* (Abany: State University of New York Press, 1992).

8. Bryan D. Jones, James L. True, and Frank R. Baumgartner, "Does Incrementalism Stem from Political Consensus or from Institutional Gridlock?" *American Journal of Political Science* 41 (October 1997): 1319–1339.

9. Robert D. Reischauer, "The Congressional Budget Process," in *Federal Budget Policy in the 1980s,* ed. Gregory B. Mills and John L. Palmer (Washington, D.C.: Urban Institute, 1984), 406.

10. Paul Pierson, "The Deficit and the Politics of Domestic Reform," in *The Social Divide: Political Parties and the Future of Activist Government,* ed. Margaret Weir (Washington, D.C.: Brookings Institution, 1998).

11. The data are taken from John J. Coleman, *Party Decline in America* (Princeton, N.J.: Princeton University Press, 1996), table 3.1, 75.

12. See Barbara Sinclair, *Unorthodox Lawmaking: New Legislative Processes in the U.S. Congress* (Washington, D.C.: Congressional Quarterly Press, 1997).

13. Theda Skocpol, *Boomerang* (New York: Norton, 1996), 67.

14. On the incompatibility of Gramm-Rudman with congressional incentives, see John W. Ellwood, "The Politics of the Enactment and Implementation of Gramm-Rudman-Hollings: Why Congress Cannot Address the Deficit Dilemma," *Harvard Journal on Legislation* 25, no. 2 (Summer 1988): 553–575; on the success of the Budget Enforcement Act in controlling discretionary spending, see Matthew Miller, "Cap Gains," *The New Republic,* May 27, 1996, pp. 19–21; on the effectiveness of the Congressional Budget Act as a device for empowering congressional majorities, see Allen Schick, "The Majority Rules," *Brookings Review* (Winter 1996): 42–45.

15. Aaron Wildavsky, *The New Politics of the Budgetary Process* (New York: HarperCollins, 1992), 35.

16. For a provocative theoretical discussion of how new and old institutional arrangements grate against one another, see Karen Orren and Stephen Skowronek, "Beyond the Iconography of Order: Notes for a 'New Institutionalism'" in *The Dynamics of American Politics,* ed. Lawrence C. Dodd and Calvin Jillson (Boulder, Colo.: Westview, 1994).

17. Phil Joyce, "Congressional Budget Reform: The Unanticipated Implications for Federal Policymaking," *Public Administration Review* (July/August 1996): 317–325.

18. The distinction between macrobudgeting and microbudgeting has been made by Allen Schick. See his informative essay, "Why Study Microbudgeting?" in *The Budget Puzzle,* ed. John F. Cogan, Timothy J. Muris, and Allen Schick (Palo Alto, Calif.: Stanford University Press, 1994).

19. James Savage, *Balanced Budgets and American Politics* (Ithaca, N.Y.: Cornell University Press, 1988).

20. Charles L. Schultze, Edward R. Fried, Alice M. Rivlin, and Nancy H. Teeter, *Setting National Priorities: The 1972 Budget* (Washington, D.C.: Brookings Institution, 1971), 2–3.

21. Benjamin Page and Robert Shapiro, *The Rational Public* (Chicago: University of Chicago Press, 1992), 148.

22. James Q. Wilson, "New Politics, New Elites, Old Publics," in *The New Politics of Public Policy,* ed. Marc K. Landy and Martin A. Levin (Baltimore, Md.: Johns Hopkins University Press, 1995), 257.

23. Herbert Stein, *The Fiscal Revolution in America* (Chicago: University of Chicago Press, 1969), 455.

24. David R. Mayhew, *Congress: The Electoral Connection* (New Haven, Conn.: Yale University Press, 1974), 139. See also David Mayhew, "Legislation," in *Law and the Social Sciences,* ed. Leon Lipson and Stanton Wheeler (New York: Russell Sage Foundation, 1986).

25. Henry Owen and Charles L. Schultze, "Introduction," in *Setting National Policies: The Next Ten Years* (Washington, D.C.: Brookings Institution, 1976), 7.

26. The fact that it was elites, rather than ordinary citizens, that changed their minds about the wisdom of peacetime deficits supports Wilson's argument that "elite ideas are always more volatile than popular ones." Wilson, "New Politics, New Elites, Old Publics," in Landy and Levin, *The New Politics of Public Policy,* 256.

27. Samuelson piece was published in the *Washington Post,* May 7, 1997. To be sure, Reagan's supply side advisers—very much like the Keynesians before them—renewed the familiar argument that budget balance is of little intrinsic economic importance. But the brief supply-side episode hardly revised fiscal activism. Supply siders were not interested in using the budget to govern the economy; they wanted to get the government out of the way. What really mattered, they argued, was the incentives for individuals and corporations to save, produce, and invest. Private entrepreneurship, not public budgeting, was their watchword.

28. Robert Reich, "Trial Ties Up Senate? Don't Worry, Congress Is Irrelevant," *USA Today,* January 7, 1999, p. 15A.

29. Donald F. Kettl, *Deficit Politics* (New York: Macmillan, 1992), 8.

30. Robert D. Reischauer, "The Unfulfillable Promise: Cutting Nondefense Discretionary Spending," in *Setting National Priorities: Budget Choices for the Next Century,* ed. Robert D. Reischauer (Washington, D.C.: Brookings Institution, 1997), 144.

31. Jones et al., "Does Incrementalism Stem from Political Consensus or from Institutional Gridlock?"

32. See Joseph J. Cordes, "How Yesterday's Decisions Affect Today's Budget and Fiscal Options," in *The New World Fiscal Order,* ed. Eugene C. Steurele and Mashairo Kawai (Washington, D.C.: Urban Institute, 1996); see also R. Kent

Weaver, *Automatic Government: The Politics of Indexation* (Washington, D.C.: Brookings Institution, 1988), and Eric M. Patashnik, *Putting Trust in the U.S. Budget: Federal Trust Funds and the Politics of Commitment* (Cambridge: Cambridge University Press, 2000).

33. Lance LeLoup, "From Microbudgeting to Macrobudgeting: Evolution in Theory and Practice" in *New Directions in Budget Theory,* ed. Irene S. Rubin (Albany: State University of New York Press); but see Joseph White, "Entitlement versus Bureau Budgeting," *Public Administration Review* (1998).

34. Richard Rose and Philip L. Davies, *Inheritance in Public Policy: Change without Choice in Britain* (New Haven, Conn.: Yale University Press, 1994).

35. Wildavsky, *The Politics of the Budgetary Process*, 190.

36. Ibid., 274.

37. Schick, "From the Old Politics of Budgeting to the New," *Public Budgeting and Finance* (Spring 1994): 137.

38. See Hugh Heclo, "The Sixties' False Dawn: Awakenings, Movements, and Postmodern Policy-making," *Journal of Policy History* 8, no. 1 (1996): 35–63.

39. Measured in constant 1989 dollars, budget authority for domestic discretionary programs decreased by 16 percent between 1981 and 1982. In the next seven years, however, inflation-adjusted budget authority for these activities grew by nearly 13 percent. See John F. Cogan and Timothy J. Muris, "Changes in Discretionary Domestic Spending in the Reagan Years," in Cogan et al., *The Budget Puzzle.*

40. When omnibus deficit reduction bills *were* passed, the savings they contained were often less than met the eye. Budget norms were subtly reworked to make it easier for politicians to claim credit for deficit reduction while avoiding blame for major funding reductions. Key to this ploy was the evolution of the concept of budget "baselines." The traditional budget process centered around fair share departures from the base, approximated by the actual level appropriated for the previous year. With the passage of the CBA, however, *assumed* measures of the base became crucial. This enabled policymakers to label actual spending increases relative to last year's level as spending "cuts" relative to the baseline. See Timothy J. Muris, "The Uses and Abuses of Budget Baselines," in Cogan et al., *The Budget Puzzle.*

41. James A. Thurber, "Centralization, Devolution, and Turf Protection in the Congressional Budget Process," in *Congress Reconsidered,* 6th ed., ed. Lawrence C. Dodd and Bruce I. Oppenheimer (Washington, D.C.: Congressional Quarterly Press, 1997).

42. Medicaid expansions for pregnant women and low-income children are an important exception. These expansions often served as sweeteners in budget reconciliation bills.

43. The distinction between setting and recording budget priorities is made in Joseph White, "What Budgeting Cannot Do: Lessons of Reagan's and Other Years," in Rubin, *New Directions in Budget Theory.*

3

From Expansion to Austerity

The New Politics of Taxing and Spending

Paul Pierson, *Harvard University*

The scope and time horizons of scholarly discussions of American politics have become increasingly circumscribed in recent years. On the one hand, "scientific" aspirations have fostered a concentration on discrete and "tractable" (i.e., quantifiable) questions, particularly related to the study of voters and of Congress. The search for deductive and potentially generalizable "laws" of politics has prompted analysts to narrow their focus. Parsimonious treatment of highly formalized and insulated relationships has largely replaced efforts to make sense of the broad contours of any particular political system taken as a whole, including the contemporary American one. On the other hand, "policy studies" have remained more inductive and more willing to eschew the goal of theoretical generalization in search of persuasive characterizations of a particular time and place. Yet these analyses also tend to be of modest scope, driven by a heavy orientation toward single case studies. Furthermore, such cases are often selected because they are dramatic or surprising in some respect—features that make them a questionable foundation for efforts to characterize the political system as a whole. In addition, such analyses tend to restrict their investigations to very short stretches of time.[1]

Working on such a restricted empirical canvas has come at a price. The price is a lack of attention to both the ways in which various parts of the American political system are connected, and to slow-moving but fundamental shifts in that system. In her admirable

Policymaking for Social Security, Martha Derthick highlights both dangers. Concerning the latter, she notes:

> Much of the scholarly literature that analyzes policymaking focuses on "leading" or controversial cases—moments of crisis that are intrinsically interesting and undoubtedly important, but not in themselves typical. Policymaking is a compound of exciting, innovative events, in which political actors mobilize and contest with one another, and not-so-exciting routines that are performed without widespread mobilization, intense conflict, or much awareness of what is going on except among the involved few. . . . The absence of conflict, I suggest, does not signify the absence of change, and what is routine, though it may not be interesting to analysts at a given moment, is cumulatively very important.[2]

This chapter follows Derthick's advice. The goal is to characterize the fiscal regime that has emerged in the United States over the past two decades. Highlighting broad trends, it makes only a limited effort to specify the causal processes that have generated this new fiscal environment. Indeed, since it is highly probable that the explanation for these shifts involves complex interactions, with various components operating as both causes and effects, any attempt to extract a short list of explanatory factors would be problematic. Rather, the purposes here are to bring these prominent trends into the foreground, to highlight likely interconnections within the resulting configuration of organized interests, institutions, and policies, and to suggest some major implications for the new politics of public policy.

A principal benefit of examining the broad configuration of fiscal arrangements is to place the contemporary budgetary climate in Washington in perspective. In the past few years, the long era of deficits, stretching from the early 1980s through the mid-1990s, has given way to modest surpluses, with projections of larger surpluses on the way. It will be tempting to suggest that the end of the deficit will produce a major shift in domestic policymaking. The argument of this essay is that one needs to distinguish the particular political dynamics associated with the deficit from the broader constraints imposed by the longer-term shift to what I will term a fiscal regime of austerity. The deficit era may be over, but the regime of austerity remains. It is therefore crucial to sort out the consequences of each. The end of the deficit will have real implications for the politics of public policy, but postdeficit politics will remain austerity politics.

From Policy Analysis to Fiscal Sociology

To frame a discussion of public policy around the structure of taxing and spending is to engage in what Joseph Schumpeter once termed "fiscal sociology": "The public finances are one of the best starting points for an investigation of society, especially though not exclusively of its political life. The full fruitfulness of this approach is seen particularly at those turning points . . . during which existing forms begin to die off and to change into something new, and which always involve a crisis of the old fiscal methods."[3] Schumpeter's perspective is echoed in Theda Skocpol's claim that "a state's means of raising and deploying financial resources tell us more than could any other single factor about its existing (and immediately potential) capacities to create or strengthen state organizations, to employ personnel, to co-opt political support, to subsidize economic enterprises, and to fund social programs."[4] A similar analysis, placing taxing and spending at the center of our understanding of public power, has been offered by Daniel Bell, who identifies "the public household" as the third realm of economic activity in modern societies, along with the domestic household and the market economy:

> I prefer the term "public household," with its sociological connotations of family problems and common living, to the more neutral terms such as "public finance" or "public sector." The public household, as expressed in the government budget, is the management of state revenues and expenditures. More broadly, it is the agency for the satisfaction of public needs and public wants, as against private wants. It is the arena for the register of political forces in the society. As Rudolf Goldscheid, a socialist economist, wrote almost 60 years ago, "the budget is the skeleton of the state stripped of all misleading ideologies."[5]

If the budget offers a good lens on the polity at a particular moment, then one can hope to track important shifts in the polity by following changes in the fiscal climate over time.[6] That is the approach adopted here. At the center of my analysis is the concept of a *fiscal regime,* by which I mean the configuration of political interests, institutions, and policy arrangements that structure conflicts over taxes and spending. This analysis both builds on and contrasts with the important contributions to W. Elliot Brownlee's recent *Funding the Modern American State,* with which the current analysis has obvious affinities.[7] I seek to extend their framework in two critical respects. First, one cannot treat finances as somehow detached from spending. The odd but essentially universal tendency in policy studies to separate the analysis of financing from the analysis of public expenditure draws attention away from the crucial connections between the two. Especially in political terms, taxing and spending are not two distinct realms but opposite sides of the same coin. The treatment of taxation as somehow occupying a separate political universe from spending is perhaps in part why Brownlee, Martin, and others can speak of *the* postwar tax regime, whereas I wish to argue that there have in fact been two quite distinct postwar fiscal regimes.

Second, and as a related point, I wish to focus to a greater degree on the concept of a regime—a term that Brownlee and Martin employ but do not systematically discuss.[8] In utilizing the concept of a fiscal regime, I want to stress the connectedness of different aspects of the policymaking environment in a particular historical configuration.[9] As Gosta Esping-Andersen has noted in a different but related context, "to talk of 'a regime' is to denote the fact that in the relation between state and economy a complex of legal and organizational features are systematically interwoven."[10]

The dynamics of taxing and spending are shaped and reinforced by a particular political context of institutions, powerful organizations, public policies, and dominant ideas. Because sustainable policy requires supportive politics, the explanation of policy trends requires attention to key features of the political setting within which policy is made. At the height of a particular fiscal regime, the critical components—policies, politics, and institutions—will be mutually reinforcing. Economists speak of organizational and institutional complementarities—in which the benefits of each element are increased when it operates in the context of the others.[11] A consolidated regime exhibits political complementarities. The whole is in a real sense greater than the sum of its parts.

Over the past half-century, the United States has had two quite different fiscal regimes. From roughly 1950 to the early 1970s, the fiscal regime was *expansionist.* A variety of factors—crucially but not exclusively unprecedented rates of economic growth—combined to make the introduction of new spending initiatives and the expansion of already existing ones an attractive option for policymakers. Beginning in the mid-1970s, this regime rapidly gave way to another, harsher one—a regime of austerity. In this new regime, politicians scrambled to keep existing programs in check, and significant spending initiatives were effectively precluded. That second regime is still in place; the emergent budget surplus is one of its consequences, rather than an indication that the regime is exhausted. In the next three sections of this chapter, I first outline the distinct features of the expansionist fiscal regime. I then review the process of its erosion and consider the key characteristics of the new regime of austerity. Finally, I briefly consider the (limited) implications of the emerging budget surplus.

The Expansionist Fiscal Regime

Steuerle has aptly termed the period from 1950 to the early 1970s the "era of easy finance."[12] He emphasizes four factors that combined to make this a period in which government spending could be expanded without imposing significant political pain—an era of winners rather than losers. First and most important, the "peace dividend" allowed a gradual but pronounced shift in fiscal resources from defense to domestic spending. The tax state was built on the need to wage war, but as that need waned, money could be used for public purposes without raising new taxes. Second, the government was able to raise payroll "contributions"—a low-visibility and popular tax base—greatly enhancing federal fiscal capacity in the process. Steuerle's third and fourth factors both relate to the relatively high inflation of the period. High inflation devalued existing government debt, reducing interest payments stemming from wartime borrowing. At the same time, it generated "bracket creep"—pushing taxpayers into higher brackets and once again filling the treasury without requiring open action to raise revenues.

These are indeed key features of the postwar fiscal environment, and Steuerle correctly identifies the commonality among them: each generated potential resources for domestic spending at low political cost. Several points need to be added, however, to characterize the expansionist fiscal regime more fully.

First, a fundamental background condition was the high rate of economic growth during this period. The recent upsurge in economic growth has served as a strong reminder of the fiscal consequences of prosperity. Rapidly rising real incomes from 1950 to 1973 created a positive-sum environment. Revenues grew rapidly, and taxpayers experiencing unprecedented growth in take-home pay were likely to be less vigilant in monitoring the government's share of revenues.[13]

Second, the exceptionally favorable political dynamics of the crucial motor of government expansion—a pay-as-you-go system of payroll tax–financed social insurance—needs to be underscored. This pay-as-you-go framework offered extraordinary political advantages during its early stages of development. As Robert Brown has put it:

> Politically, it can be argued that a PAYGO system creates two dollars of benefits for every dollar of contributions. Actuaries know that in a PAYGO scheme, every dollar of contribution that comes in the morning becomes a dollar of benefits that are paid out in the afternoon. So the contributions to the scheme have that dollar of value. At the same time, however, the worker who makes the dollar contribution has created the expectation that there is now a one dollar commitment that (s)he will get a dollar's worth of benefits (plus interest) when it is his (her) turn to retire.[14]

Nor are the immediate political benefits of introducing pay-as-you-go schemes limited to the fact that two dollars of benefits can be offered for one dollar of taxes. In their early years, pay-as-you-go systems generate a highly favorable demographic profile. Usually only small numbers of citizens will have paid sufficient contributions to qualify for benefits, while the entire working population is available to pay taxes. Thus, taxes can be kept far lower—and benefits higher—than the levels required to keep the system running at a steady state. Most of this long transition period took place during the postwar expansionist regime. During this phase, the federal government could simultaneously maintain payroll taxes at a rate far lower than what would eventually be needed to fund the benefits promised to current workers. At the same time, it could offer benefits to new retirees (and to those who benefited from other Social Security programs) far in excess of what would have been possible in a funded, actuarial system.

High benefits, low perceived costs—Social Security was a politician's dream come true. The extraordinary possibilities of this transitional period help to explain why the Social Security system—the political cornerstone of the expansionary fiscal regime—became enormously popular. For its first fifty years, Social Security offered an exceptional deal to those contributing to the program. It is small wonder that workers did not object to intermittent increases in payroll tax rates. In this instance an anecdote is telling. The "first" Social Security recipient, Ida May Fuller, received twenty-five years of pension benefits after her retirement in 1940. She had paid a grand total of $24.50 in payroll taxes.

The final point to be made about the expansionist regime concerns the role of supporting political interests. For several decades, the expansionist political regime was buttressed by a strengthening array of organized political actors. Politicians' votes for popular programs enhanced their electoral standing, allowing them to consolidate the advantages of incumbency and push for further expansions. As Jack Walker's research demonstrated, policy created interest groups at least as much as interest groups created policy.[15] In a process of policy feedback, government programs provided resource bases for organized interests, such as the American Association of Retired Persons (AARP), which then became formidable lobbyists for further programmatic extensions. Thus, at its height, the expansionist fiscal regime was characterized by virtuous circles, in which interests, policies, and institutions aligned to reinforce the dominant political dynamic.

The Regime of Austerity

In hindsight, one can see that this expansionist regime collapsed in a relatively short period. Domestic spending grew more rapidly under Richard Nixon than under any other president. Gerald Ford and Jimmy Carter were already managing austerity. With the election of Ronald Reagan the contours of the new fiscal regime began to take more coherent shape. The crucial background condition, of course, was the sharp fall in economic growth in the mid-1970s as the long postwar boom came to an abrupt end. One sign that these economic underpinnings were indeed crucial is the fact that the change in fiscal climate was evident throughout the advanced industrialized world, although the shift to a new fiscal regime occurred sooner in the United States than in most other countries.

Poor economic performance generated fiscal strain both by dampening revenue growth and by pushing up public expenditure in some programs. More fundamentally, it led to stagnant real incomes for most of the population. With incomes flat, concern about taxation increased. So did skepticism about the public household.

Three Adverse Policy Trends

This sharp deterioration of economic conditions had rapid effects, in part, because it was reinforced by broad policy shifts that were adverse to the regime of expansion. Three policy trends helped fuel the shift to a climate of austerity: the decline of sources of "easy finance," the maturation of existing governmental commitments that crowd out potential new spending initiatives, and the expanding role of tax expenditures in the federal budget. Each of these trends has been slow-moving, the result of distinct social developments as well as policy choices. Some shifts were generated by conscious interventions, while others were the unanticipated or at least largely unnoticed longer-term consequences of decisions taken in the fairly distant past. What links all of these trends is that they combined to intensify pressure for expenditure constraint on the federal budget.

Steuerle describes the late 1970s and early 1980s as the beginning of "the fiscal straightjacket era." He stresses four distinct shifts in the government's opportunity structure for raising revenues that occurred beginning after 1975. First was the virtual exhaustion of the "peace dividend," through which declining relative allocations for defense had created fiscal slack for domestic programs.[16] Second, with the decline of inflation beginning in 1982, a long period of cheap borrowing, in which debt incurred at times of low interest rates was paid off in inflated dollars, was also coming to an end. Third, beginning in the late 1970s there was a growing aversion to higher payroll taxes—a traditional source of low-visibility finance for Social Security and Medicare. Perhaps most important of all, the indexation of tax brackets introduced in 1981 made it far more difficult to raise revenues without voters noticing. Prior to 1981, politicians had been able to rely on inflation to push taxpayers slowly into higher tax brackets. In the context of "bracket creep," tax policy had taken the enviable form of returning some of this cash to voters in the form of "tax cuts," while retaining some of it for new or expanded government programs. After 1981, by contrast, governments seeking higher revenues would face the politically precarious task of voting openly for new revenues.[17]

Although the federal government has faced new and serious pressures on the revenue side, it is crucial to recognize that federal receipts as a percentage of gross domestic product (GDP) have fluctuated within a narrow band since 1980. Payroll taxes have risen further, and some tax expenditures have been cut to offset losses of revenue elsewhere. What ended was the era of *easy* finance. In recent years, attempts to increase federal receipts have required more visible allocations of pain than was true in the past. Not surprisingly, politicians have become more skittish about the actions required to do so.

If life has gotten harder for politicians on the revenue side, the story is much the same on the spending side. The second crucial policy trend shaping the new fiscal regime has been the maturation of governmental commitments in domestic programs.[18] As Figure 3.1 indicates, growth in public expenditure after the early 1970s occurred largely among the mandatory spending or "entitlement"

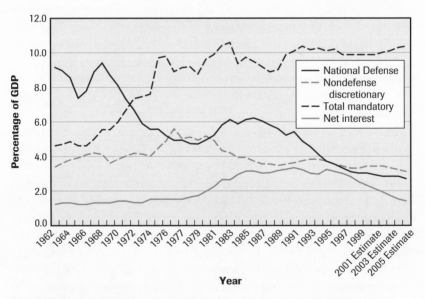

FIGURE 3.1.   Outlays by Budget Enforcement Act Category as a Percentage of GDP

programs, along with rising interest payments. Higher interest payments reflected the deficits of the 1980s, themselves a result of a failure to adequately finance these maturing commitments.

Almost all of this entitlement spending takes place in programs adopted before 1975. New government activities, or recent legislation funding old activities more generously, have not played a significant role. Except for modest expansions of Medicaid, increased spending on entitlement programs largely reflects the interaction of preexisting statutory requirements with societal changes (including shifts in demographics and the distribution of income, and especially rampant health care inflation). In fact, the overwhelming source of expenditure strain has been the increase in health care outlays. Federal expenditures on health programs, mostly for Medicare and Medicaid, rose from 2.5 percent of GDP in 1980 to 4.4 percent of GDP in 1995.[19] These increases have mostly reflected rising costs in the health care sector as a whole.

Thus, where costs have trended upward, the heavy hand of the past looms large, both in the form of legal rules requiring the provision of benefits to those meeting specified criteria and in the form of interest payments which reflect the lagged effects of previous policy decisions. Indeed, legislated changes (i.e., explicit policy choices) in entitlements over the past twenty years have almost always been in the direction of retrenchment rather than expansion. This new context of maturing commitments can be seen, in both fiscal and political terms, as the flip side of the favorable policy dynamic during the start-up phase of the big social insurance programs. Then, politicians could make attractive policy promises while deferring most of the costs. Now, the bill has come due, and politicians must finance the costs without getting much in the way of credit for the programs enacted by their predecessors.

The maturation of governmental commitments has added significantly to the general atmosphere of fiscal austerity. Major entitlement programs have significant political advantages, including their broad constituencies, the sense that benefits have been "earned" through contributions, and the fact that cuts in mandatory spending programs, unlike discretionary ones, require new legislation. In a Darwinian budgetary struggle, the political strength of entitlement programs has intensified pressure on other components of federal spending. Between 1963 and 1993, discretionary outlays fell from 70.4 percent of the budget to 37.2 percent. In turn, as mandatory spending has crowded out discretionary spending, outlays are determined more and more by broad social trends and prior policy commitments, and less and less by year-to-year adjustments of policymakers.[20]

A third major policy trend, the growth of tax expenditures, has had roughly similar effects. The federal government operates a vast, largely hidden array of policies that subsidize private activities through the tax code.[21] Most economists agree that these subsidies are analytically equivalent to budgetary outlays. The only difference is that the government, rather than writing a check to a particular group, simply indicates to the favored party that it can write a smaller check to the government.

Tax expenditure politics is low-visibility politics—which is to say that it favors the well organized. Most of the largest of these subsides were enacted decades ago, often with little debate, at a time when their budget implications were small because overall tax rates were low. On the whole, these programs have grown without any significant scrutiny. There is very little discussion of the effectiveness of particular tax expenditures as policy instruments. They are subject to very infrequent review because once enacted such programs face no systematic fiscal constraints.[22] Like entitlement programs, costs are determined by program rules, and if eligible applications rise, costs will rise even without new legislation.

In the past two decades, tax expenditures have grown very rapidly as the favored activities (e.g., private retirement savings, mortgage interest) have expanded (no doubt in part because of favorable tax treatment). An analysis by Christopher Howard showed that while social spending had grown twice as fast as tax expenditures between 1967 and 1975, this pattern reversed at that point. From 1975 to 1995, the real rate of growth of social policy–related tax expenditures was 4.3 percent, compared to a growth rate for on-budget social spending of 3.2 percent (the gap would be larger if inflation-induced increases in health care expenditures were excluded from these calculations). These tax expenditures are very expensive, and their expansion leaves gaping holes in the federal government's fiscal position. Howard estimated the total revenue loss from this "hidden welfare state" to be almost $350 billion in 1995.[23] By 2001, the estimated revenue loss from tax expenditures will be $92.4 billion for corporate retirement pensions, $80.6 billion for corporate health insurance, and $99.5 billion from the mortgage interest deduction and other tax breaks for home ownership.[24]

The growth of tax expenditures represents a third major source of pressure on the public household. The parallel between tax expenditures and on-budget spending is most apparent when one considers their implications for the federal budget. Like "regular" spending, tax expenditure growth can be financed in only three ways: through higher taxes on less favored groups and activities, cuts in public spending, or increases in the deficit. The option of large deficits can be employed only temporarily, at the cost of worsening already hard trade-offs later on. Thus, along with the end of the era of easy finance and the maturation of governmental commitments, the rise in tax expenditures has helped fuel a dramatically new budgetary climate marked by fierce, zero-sum conflict among competing expenditure priorities.

Four Adverse Political Trends

One of the main themes of the discussion so far is the extent to which the contemporary policymaking environment is the result of long-term, slow-moving trends—many of which cannot be described as the intended results of strategic political action. Political actors are often relatively unconcerned with the long term. Even if they are concerned about it, there is ample room for unintended consequences. When one considers the slow accretion of government spending commitments over long periods of time, or the contemporary implications of a system of tax expenditures that was introduced haphazardly and with no expectation of the eventual fiscal magnitude of such provisions, one needs to acknowledge that policy often "happens" rather than being "made." Adam Ferguson long ago put the same point more broadly: society "is the result of human action, but not of human design."[25]

Yet the new climate of austerity is not simply something that has happened "behind the backs" of political actors. Four important political shifts complemented the policy changes just discussed in transforming the fiscal regime. The first and most important has been the increasing strength of the Republican party in national politics and of antispending sentiment within that party. This increasing strength has both reflected and for the most part reinforced a second major change: growing popular ambivalence about the public sector. The third political trend has been the weakening of organized interests supportive of public spending. The fourth—less fundamental but still consequential—is a shift in the institutional rules governing budgetary decision making.

The first of these trends has, of course, been the most evident major change in American politics over the past three decades.[26] Republican strength has grown at every level. Most critically for budgetary politics, since 1978 there has been a fairly steady transformation in the composition of Congress. The year 1994 marked the culmination of this trend, with Republicans capturing the House for the first time in forty years. Yet the Reagan administration had shown as early as 1981 that in practice even Democratic Congresses could command a working majority only by being attentive to the concerns of fiscally conservative members.

As significant as this shifting partisan balance has been the growth of antigovernment sentiment among Republican politicians. The end of the Cold War, the emergence of the South as the new center of electoral and organizational strength within the party (reflected in the geographic makeup of the party leadership), and the routing of moderate Republican forces through ideological combat and generational replacement all fueled a much harsher stance toward "Washington" in general and public spending in particular.

Of course, the increasingly tough antispending posture of Republicans in national politics would not have been possible had it not resonated to some degree with the electorate. The second major political transition has been a hardening of popular views of the public sector. Public attitudes toward federal spending remain ambivalent if not contradictory—as the Republicans learned to their dismay following their balanced budget debacle of 1995–1996. Voters remain attached to most elements of public spending. Open attempts to cut programs generally provoke a strong reaction.[27] Yet over the past two decades, an economic climate in which most Americans were struggling hard just to sustain their standard of living, declining public confidence in government, and the protracted specter of the budget deficit along with the associated rhetoric of government profligacy have made voters more receptive to calls for a tough fiscal stance.

The trends in policy discussed earlier have helped fuel these sentiments. The "end of the era of easy finance" has made issues of taxation far more visible. Any rise in revenues now requires legislative action. Payroll taxes were raised in 1983 as part of a plan to shore up Social Security, but except under those peculiar circumstances, broad-based tax increases have proven impossible. Former presidents Clinton and Bush were each able to raise taxes on the wealthiest 1 percent of taxpayers as part of deficit reduction initiatives. Clinton's effort to introduce a "BTU tax" to provide a new revenue base, however, was defeated. The increasing visibility of taxes, of course, has made the costs of government spending more salient.

At the same time, the maturation of governmental commitments has required the imposition of "new" burdens to sustain "old" promises. The deferred cost of deficits, in the form of debt interest payments, has worsened the problem. Not only is there no money for new initiatives, but a significant share of current taxes must be diverted to cover the costs of past spending. In fiscal terms, the federal government must run harder and harder just to stand still. Voters could reasonably ask why they have had to pay more (e.g., in payroll taxes) for what look like the same, or even diminished, benefits.

Finally, the growth of tax expenditures, which, like entitlements, have become increasingly costly even in the absence of new initiatives, has had a similar effect. Furthermore, these tax subsidies for private activity lead many upper-middle-class voters to see the private sector (e.g., home ownership, mutual funds) rather than government (e.g., Social Security) as the guarantor of protection against life's economic hazards. For Republicans seeking to curb and rechannel the role of the public sector, tax expenditures possess multiple virtues. They direct fiscal resources to upper-income Republican constituencies, they diminish the revenue stream available to government for other initiatives, and they do both these things in the form of tax "cuts" or breaks that are rarely perceived as instances of government largesse. Tax expenditures are the antigovernment form of government spending.

Thus, in multiple ways, the new fiscal regime of austerity generates reinforcing political tendencies, strengthening the position of those seeking to enforce curbs on the public household. As the strength of antitax, antispending forces has waxed, that of their opponents has waned. This third consequential political shift is most evident in the position of organized labor—along with the Democratic party the strongest and most encompassing advocate of extensive public social provision. Intermittent pronouncements of a rejuvenated labor movement fly in the face of four decades of uninterrupted decline. Continuing changes in the structure of economic activity (especially from manufacturing to services) remain highly unfavorable to union organizing in the context of America's highly fragmented system of industrial relations.

Organized interests that cluster around individual sectors of public activity have largely supplanted labor's role in protecting public expenditure. The most dramatic example (because of both its scale and the scope of the programs that it "defends") is the AARP. Such organized interests remain a crucial bulwark supporting public spending, but their issue-specific focus prevents them from advancing a coherent case for the public household. The increasingly zero-sum competition among such interests for scarce federal dollars, which reinforces a narrow stance of mobilizing in support of each constituency's particular program, makes the task even more difficult. In short, there is a fundamental asymmetry between the organized advocates of public spending, who favor *particular* governmental initiatives, and their opponents, who (at least rhetorically) criticize government spending in general and on principle. The posture of organized supporters of public spending is increasingly fragmented, reactive, and ad hoc.

These trends among political elites, voters, and organized interests in turn have given rise to a final political shift: institutional reforms that reinforce the same dynamic. Many of these institutional reforms are discussed in Eric Patashnik's chapter 2 for this volume. The trend toward more centralized budgeting has highlighted trade-offs among programs and between tax cuts and spending. Even under Clinton, this has clearly operated as a constraint on public expenditure.[28] The Budget Enforcement Act (BEA) of 1990 imposed tough new budget rules. "Pay-as-you-go" requirements, which held that new initiatives must be adequately financed (either by taxes or cuts in other programs) over the medium run, imposed further discipline.[29] Tight overall caps on discretionary spending, requiring substantial real cuts over time, have pushed in the same direction and have reinforced the already considerable advantages of existing entitlements ("old spending") over new initiatives.

Thus, the new fiscal regime of austerity is based on not only adverse policy trends but a political configuration in which elites with a strong antispending stance hold powerful political positions, are reasonably credible to voters, confront weakened opponents, and operate in an institutional setting conducive to austerity. Given voter ambivalence, contesting elites, and the political advantages that American political structures confer on the status quo, such a regime by no mean insures significant cuts in public spending. It does, however, virtually foreclose any possibility of advancing new governmental initiatives that carry significant budgetary implications— as the Clinton administration rapidly discovered.[30] The consolidation of "no new taxes" as a virtual trump-card argument in American politics was strikingly confirmed in the recent collapse of tobacco legislation. The powerful tobacco lobby seemed acutely vulnerable following an aggressive and effective public relations campaign launched by public health advocates and the Clinton administration. Yet cigarette manufacturers and their Republican allies discovered that they could generate adequate political cover by framing the dispute as a tax matter rather than a public health issue.

In this new political configuration, efforts to further diminish the fiscal capacity of the federal government have become a persistent feature of American politics. Like most attempts at reform in a Madisonian system, these initiatives usually fail—but some of them (e.g., the indexation of tax brackets) succeed. Far-sighted and entrepreneurial Democrats used to sprinkle budgets with small spending programs that might eventually grow into more formidable sites of public activity. Now, far-sighted and entrepreneurial Republicans sprinkle the budget with small tax expenditures, designed to increase dramatically over the long term and open additional large holes below the water line of the federal budget.

To take a recent and telling example, the IRS Restructuring and Reform Act of 1998 included two substantial tax expenditures, each overwhelmingly targeted at the well-to-do. The first, a cut in the capital gains tax, was a revenue loser over the first ten years. Current law required that this initiative be financed by spending cuts or tax increases elsewhere. The "funding" that Congress selected revised the treatment of Individual Retirement Accounts (IRAs) for wealthy individuals, encouraging them to roll over traditional IRAs into Roth IRAs. This plan was cleverly designed to bring in cash during the immediate period relevant for budgetary requirements. It did so, however, by providing the affluent with incentives to make small tax payments now in return for even larger tax subsidies down the road. Although permitted under current budget rules, *both* these provisions benefiting the wealthy will cost the federal government revenues over the long run—an estimated $30 billion over the second decade stretching from 2008 to 2017.[31]

A similar dynamic played out on a larger scale in the budget agreement of 1997, contained in twin bills, the Balanced Budget Act and Taxpayer Relief Act. The agreement, made in the shadow of the acrimonious budget battles of the prior two years and in the aftermath of Clinton's reelection, involved a carefully negotiated compromise. The Clinton administration and its congressional allies were allowed modest initiatives on health care and immigrant aid along with education tax credits for the middle class. For the Republicans, there were tight caps on discretionary spending and a variety of tax cuts, including lower capital gains and estate taxes and an expansion of individual retirement accounts.

Yet in sharp contrast to earlier deficit reduction packages, this one included net tax reductions rather than increases. These tax reductions were not only heavily weighted toward the well-to-do but were designed to grow considerably over time. Indeed, while both the modest spending initiatives and the tax benefits for middle-income families (the education and child credits) declined in real terms over time (because they were not indexed), benefits for the affluent were carefully designed to start small (often producing net revenue increases in the first few years) but grow rapidly in later years. Funding for five of the six modest social program initiatives either terminates or declines after the first few years. Combined spending on these initiatives is lower in the second five years (fiscal years 2003–2007) than in the first five years (1998–2002) of the budget plan. By contrast, the revenue loss from tax cuts for high-income households is over *four times* as great in the second five-year period as it is in the first period.[32] In short, the details of this bipartisan agreement clearly signal the workings of a well-entrenched fiscal regime of austerity.

Over the past quarter-century, the evolution of policy on both the tax and spending sides has produced much greater pressure on the federal budget, forcing more visible and more painful trade-offs. Political shifts which have favored those eager to enforce expenditure constraint have worked in the same direction. In short, American politics has moved from an expansionary fiscal regime to one of essentially permanent austerity. It is this fiscal regime of austerity that has come to define the new politics of public policy.

The clearest indication that this combination of policy shifts and political changes has produced a new fiscal regime lies in the spending numbers themselves. Figure 3.2 is a somewhat modified version of the data presented in Figure 3.1. Because the goal is to measure the

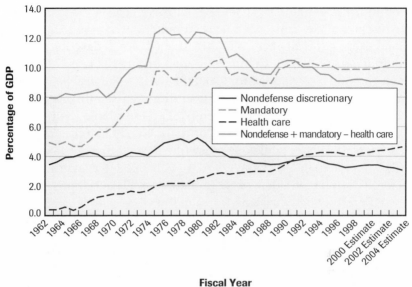

Fiscal Year

FIGURE 3.2.   Outlays by BEA Category Excluding Health Care

fiscal space available for contemporary policymakers, interest on the debt is excluded. Health care expenditure (which has grown significantly) is excluded because it largely reflects the overall rise in the costs of American health care rather than the expansion of government policy. What is left is everything else in the domestic budget—from food stamps to national parks to Social Security. The downward trend is striking. Between 1975 and 1984, spending ranged from 12.5 to 13.5 percent of GDP. By 1998 it was 10.3 percent, and current projections are that by 2002 it will be 9.9 percent.

For the past twenty-five years there has been a slow, steady, undramatic process of retrenchment for most elements of federal domestic expenditure. Modest vagaries of the business and electoral cycles aside, the shift in budgetary climate is clear and continuous. There have been no dramatic breaks—not Reagan's initiatives of 1981, or Clinton's attempt to introduce new public "investments" in 1993. Some programs—especially discretionary spending—have proven more vulnerable than others, but almost all have faced the harsh winds of austerity.

The result of these long-term trends has been a peculiar but systematic and revealing combination of continuity and change.

Continuity is evident at the level of *programs*. The effort to dismantle public policies fully, with its requirement of visible and radical change, has generally been a failure. If one were to describe the key components of American domestic spending in the late 1970s, and then compile a second list for 2000, the two lists would be remarkably similar. Of the major public spending items, only one (Aid to Families with Dependent Children [AFDC]—replaced by the block grant system of Temporary Assistance for Needy Families [TANF]) has been abolished, while one other (the Earned Income Tax Credit [EITC]) has expanded from very marginal status to a significant social role.[33] In the broadest programmatic terms, everything else has stayed pretty much the same.

Yet this striking continuity conceals a gradual, quiet erosion of the public household. Year after year of modest savings at the margin has taken its cumulative toll. Most domestic programs have been partly hollowed out—their mandates essentially unchanged but their capacities declining in proportion to an expanding economy and population. As Figure 3.2 indicates, the shift has been particularly evident for the nontransfer areas of the federal budget. Programs requiring new authorizations (and thus subject to the BEA's spending caps) have been most exposed to the cold climate of the new fiscal regime.

In addition to its immediate impact on public expenditure, this persistent era of austerity has had important consequences for policymaking more generally. Some of these have already been discussed. Existing programs (including tax expenditures) that do not require new budgetary authorizations have obtained a tremendous advantage over potential competitors. This highlights the analytical advantages of viewing policymaking processes over an extended period of time. *When* programs were enacted turns out to be a critical predictor of political success. Programs that failed to get through the fiscal door before it closed in the late 1970s were far less likely to make significant progress later on. Again, the EITC (adopted in 1974 but trivial until 1986) is exceptional rather than typical in this respect.

At the same time, the persistent atmosphere of retrenchment, permitting few significant new initiatives, fuels voters' skepticism about the possible contribution of government to their quality of life. Politicians are likely to reinforce public disappointment. Increasingly, they turn to "boutique" initiatives, which are high on rhetoric but, given budget constraints, inevitably low on content. Furthermore, the zero-sum budgetary climate weakens and fragments coalitions supportive of a more expansive public household.

Additional consequences of the new fiscal regime are worth highlighting. Of tremendous importance is the shift in government activism toward regulatory policy. It is no accident that this collection of essays focuses heavily on the politics of rule making rather than spending. Governments short on money but desiring to have an impact are likely to be drawn to regulatory mechanisms. This approach represents an important change in the character of the public sector. As the room for fiscal maneuver has declined, regulatory activity has been sustained and, in many cases, expanded. Furthermore, many of the main policy conflicts of the past few years—over federal "mandates" on state and local governments, the Clinton health care reforms, a patients' bill of rights, and tobacco legislation—have been at the interface of the regulatory and fiscal states. In the first three cases, the government attempted to use rule making to achieve public purposes that in an earlier era (and in other countries) were pursued primarily through taxing and spending. In the last case, politicians operating in the traditional regulatory arenas of public health and consumer protection tried to use public hostility to the tobacco industry and the specter of massive litigation as a justification for introducing sharp hikes in (thinly disguised) cigarette taxes. It was evident that one of the chief attractions of tobacco legislation for its supporters was the prospect of generating significant new revenues for government initiatives. Thus, much of the contemporary politics of regulation must be understood as itself in part a consequence of the new fiscal regime.

Finally, in a tight budgetary context, a wide range of governmental activity has come to be seen largely through a fiscal lens. Budgetary impact crowds out other criteria for evaluating public programs. Even activities with relatively modest fiscal implications and addressed to matters of national importance—for instance, in foreign policy domains such as the funding of international organizations or foreign aid—came to be scrutinized largely in terms of their budgetary ramifications. "Welfare reform" in 1995 was radically restructured from earlier Republican proposals in order to make the Republican leadership's target of a balanced budget compatible with promised tax cuts.[34] This tendency to "fiscalize" almost all policy issues was reinforced by institutional arrangements that encourage the fashioning of huge budget packages. Policy advocates seeking a fast track for reforms, especially ones that they knew would not survive an open vote, tried to get their agenda incorporated into these broad budget deals.

A durable fiscal regime emerged in the past two decades, grounded in mutually reinforcing political and policy trends. It has been marked by tough new constraints on taxing and spending. These constraints both limit and channel new governmental initiatives and help define the contemporary politics of public policy.

After the Deficit?

Perhaps, however, this is all behind us. The big news on the budgetary front over the past few years has been the rapid movement from a deficit—widely regarded by politicians as public enemy number one as late as 1997, when Congress and the president agreed on a plan to balance the budget—to significant surpluses. As of June 2000, the administration was projecting that the cumulative non–Social Security surplus, given no policy changes, would be on the order of $1.9 trillion over ten years. That certainly seems like a lot of money. Many observers argue that this represents a fundamental shift in the political climate, with major implications for public policy.

There are good reasons for skepticism. Most obviously, any projections about future budgets must be viewed with caution. The track record of government forecasting, even for periods as short as twelve months, has been unimpressive. The 1990 budget agreement was supposed to have brought the deficit under control, but by early 1993 analysts were projecting a deficit of $350 billion. Projections for five years hence should be viewed as educated guesses at best. Any significant downturn will render them unreliable.

These guesses are the best we have, however, and for analytical purposes it is useful to take them as a baseline. A more fundamental caveat is that the estimates greatly exaggerate the amount of fiscal slack available for new spending or tax cuts. They include surpluses in the Medicare trust funds, which are unlikely to be used for such purposes. They assume the expiration of a number of tax credits and other time-limited programs that have been routinely renewed even during periods of deficit. They assume that the government sustain very stringent budgetary caps on discretionary spending over an extended period of time—again, something that did not happen completely even in the shadow of the deficit. And they make no provision for an infusion of funds to address long-term financing needs of Social Security and Medicare—something both major parties have committed themselves to. Once plausible corrections for these unrealistic assumptions are made, the projected surplus falls to $400 billion over the next decade.[35]

How much of an impact on policymaking would this produce? In the language of this essay, does the end of the deficit mean that we are in a new "postausterity" fiscal regime? In a word, no. Two points need to be emphasized. First, all of the longer-term policy trends that generated acute fiscal pressure and narrowed the maneuvering room of public spending advocates remain in place. The "era of easy finance" is a distant memory. Any potential tax increases remain highly visible and salient. There could be no clearer indication of this than the conspicuous absence of payroll tax hikes from the range of options being considered to shore up the finances of Social Security, the flagship of public expenditure programs. Tax expenditures continue to occupy expanding fiscal space, crowding out other options. Maturing governmental commitments, especially associated with Medicare, will be well placed to compete for any fiscal slack that might otherwise allow new spending.

The second reason for skepticism is that "postdeficit" politics are not the same as "predeficit" politics. There is no return to the status quo ante. As Patashnik puts it in his chapter, "new politics" gets layered on top of "old politics." In this case, postdeficit politics gets layered on top of a range of political trends and institutional innovations discussed earlier in this essay, which have greatly enhanced the bargaining position of those hostile to expanded public expenditure. There are now more resources to be distributed, but they will be distributed in the context of long-term shifts in institutional settings, public policies, popular attitudes, and the balance of political power—both between the parties and among organized interests—which have given public expenditure skeptics the upper hand.

That discussions of taxing and spending in this new postdeficit climate remain firmly anchored in a regime of austerity can be seen in the evolving discussion of the budget surplus. The Clinton administration again demonstrated its improved skill at budgetary tactics when Clinton paired the surpluses with Social Security, arguing that any actions with major budget implications should be tabled until the finances of the popular pension system had been shored up. The Republican leadership, eager for large tax cuts, was placed on the defensive by this gambit. It remains, however, a limited and revealing stance for a president who began with activist aspirations but essentially acquiesced to his role as the manager of austerity. Ironically, the emerging debate on Social Security suggests that even "reserving" the surpluses for Social Security has opened up the possibility of using them to facilitate another project long dear to opponents of big government: the introduction of a more individualized, "funded" component to public retirement provision. Although such a project remains a political long shot, the fact that prominent Republicans can now aggressively advance it suggests a great deal about the contemporary environment.[36]

What is notably missing from current discussions of the surplus is the idea that they might be employed for significant new public spending initiatives—or even to relax seriously the current tough spending constraints on domestic expenditure that call for further real cuts in public provision over time. Debate over new initiatives instead takes the form of competing tax cuts. Of course, many of these tax cuts—targeted on particular activities of particular groups (e.g., saving for retirement or for education)—represent a disguised form of government activism. Yet the terrain of tax expenditures is systematically skewed toward Republican constituencies and the conservative agenda. Just as traditional public expenditure generated positive feedback by strengthening attachments between organized interests and the federal government, tax expenditures reinforce an atomized system of social provision in which the "private welfare state," the market, and individual initiative are seen as the sources of economic security and the federal government is perceived as either irrelevant or intrusive.

That there is no return to predeficit politics can be seen in the fiscal posture adopted by Al Gore's campaign for president in 2000. Paying down the debt was presented as the fiscal cornerstone of progressive politics. Tax expenditures, rather than new spending, were proposed to advance traditional Democratic priorities in education, health care, and child care. Even the one major new spending initiative, which called for adding a prescription drug benefit to Medicare, is revealing. It reflects the declining Democratic hold on a key constituency, the elderly. Republican gains have been particularly evident among the "young old," who are more likely to rely extensively on the private welfare state than the "old old" and have also received significantly lower rates of return from Social Security. Thus, even in the absence of the deficit, the Democrats' political agenda reflects the continuing erosion of the remnants of the old expansionist fiscal regime and the evident need to accommodate the ascendant regime of austerity.

None of this suggests that the vanishing of the deficit will not have important consequences. For almost two decades the deficit served as a powerful symbol of government failure and gave a kind of moral force to arguments for retrenchment. It also created pressure for large budget "packages," which generated distinct political dynamics. Finally, it fueled a negative-sum version of politics focused on and facilitating the imposition of losses. In short, in the absence of the deficit new possibilities will emerge in budgeting and in policymaking more generally. It is far more doubtful, however, that this development marks an end to the broader fiscal regime of austerity.

One central uncertainty concerns the future rate of economic growth. Although policy changes contributed significantly to the deficit's recent demise, a sudden and sharp increase in economic growth has mattered more. Should the recent improvement in productivity growth prove to be long lasting, this will remove one very important constraint on public expenditure. Whether it would also serve to undermine the overall regime of austerity is much less clear. Most of the key features of that regime—maturing governmental commitments, expanding tax expenditures, a powerful antitax party, public skepticism about government, weakening constituencies for public expenditure, and restrictive budgetary institutions— remain in place. Postdeficit politics is not predeficit politics. There is no reason to believe that a balanced budget is inconsistent with continuing austerity.

This is, of course, the justification for talking about a fiscal *regime:* a configuration of interlocking, complementary institutions, interests, and policies. During particular periods the distinct pieces of a regime fit together in a reasonably coherent way, each reinforced by the others. Such a regime continues to operate in the United States. It acts as a very effective block on new federal initiatives that require significant fiscal resources.

Notes

1. The major exception to these generalizations appears in the work of students of American political development, exemplified in the journal *Studies in American Political Development*. Yet while these scholars work on a broader empirical canvas and investigate longer stretches of time, they have largely retreated from efforts to investigate the contemporary American political system, focusing instead on earlier phases of political development.

2. Martha Derthick, *Policymaking for Social Security* (Washington, D.C.: Brookings Institution, 1979), 9.

3. Joseph Schumpeter, "The Crisis of the Tax State," in *International Economic Papers*, no. 4, ed. Richard A. Musgrave (New York: Macmillan, 1954 [1918]), 7.

4. Theda Skocpol, "Bringing the State Back In: Strategies of Analysis in Current Research," in *Bringing the State Back In*, ed. Peter B. Evans, Dietrich Rueschemeyer, and Theda Skocpol (Cambridge: Cambridge University Press, 1985), 17.

5. Daniel Bell, *The Cultural Contradictions of Capitalism* (New York: Basic Books, 1976), 221.

6. A major flaw of such a framework is that it shortchanges the second major venue of government activism—namely, regulatory policy. I briefly note some of the interconnections between changes in the American fiscal regime and regulatory politics in the final section of this chapter, but the topic deserves much more sustained attention than I can offer here.

7. W. Elliot Brownlee, ed., *Funding the Modern American State, 1941–1995: The Rise and Fall of the Era of Easy Finance* (Cambridge: Cambridge University Press, 1996).

8. Steurle, who like me sees the dynamics of the 1960s and early 1970s as quite different from those of the more recent period, speaks of "eras" rather than "regimes," which is revealing. His important analysis is oriented toward tracking trends (especially on the revenue side) rather than investigating the political context which supports or challenges those trends.

9. Ira Katznelson, "Structure and Configuration in Comparative Politics," in *Comparative Politics: Rationality, Culture, and Structure*, ed. Mark Irving Lichbach and Alan S. Zuckerman (Cambridge: Cambridge University Press, 1997), 81–112.

10. Gosta Esping-Andersen, *Three Worlds of Welfare Capitalism* (Princeton, N.J.: Princeton University Press, 1990), 3.

11. Paul Milgrom and John Roberts, "Complementarities and Systems: Understanding Japanese Economic Organization," 1994, unpublished manuscript.

12. C. Eugene Steuerle, "Financing the American State at the Turn of the Century," in Brownlee, *Funding the Modern American State*, 409–444.

13. High wage growth also meant buoyant payrolls. With the gradual expansion of a pay-as-you-go, payroll tax–financed system of social insurance (discussed later), this was extremely helpful for keeping payroll tax rates down.

14. Robert L. Brown, "The Future of Canada/Quebec Pension Plans," Research Report 93-10 (Waterloo (Ontario, Canada): Institute of Insurance and Pension Research, 1993).

15. Jack L. Walker Jr., *Mobilizing Interest Groups in America* (Ann Arbor: University of Michigan Press, 1991).

16. Following the Reagan defense buildup of the early 1980s, a second peace dividend kicked in after 1985. Reliance on reductions in defense has eased pressure on the rest of the budget, but the magnitude of these effects was far more modest than the peace dividend available during the expansionist fiscal regime.

17. For a discussion of the political implications of bracket indexation, see R. Kent Weaver, *Automatic Government* (Washington, D.C.: Brookings Institution, 1988).

18. Richard Rose, "Inheritance Before Choice in Public Policy," *Journal of Theoretical Politics* 2, no. 3 (1991): 263–291; Joseph Cordes, "The Yoke of Prior Commitments: How Yesterday's Decisions Affect Today's Budget and Fiscal Options," in *The New World Fiscal Order,* ed. C. Eugene Steurle and Masahiro Kawai (Washington, D.C. Urban Institute Press, 1996); Paul Pierson, "Irresistible Forces, Immovable Objects: Post-Industrial Welfare States Confront Permanent Austerity," *Journal of European Public Policy* 5, no. 4 (1998). See also Erik Patashnik's chapter 2 in this volume.

19. Office of Management and Budget, *Historical Statistics* (Washington, D.C.: U.S. Government Printing Office, 1996), table 16.1.

20. See the comments of Norman Ornstein in "Symposium: President Clinton's Budget and Fiscal Policy: An Evaluation Two Budgets Later," *Public Budgeting and Finance* (Fall 1994): 7–10.

21. For an excellent political analysis of tax expenditures see Christopher Howard, *The Hidden Welfare State: Tax Expenditures and Social Policy* (Princeton, N.J.: Princeton University Press, 1997).

22. Most tax expenditures are highly regressive because affluent households are generally able to spend more on the activities that are subsidized, and because the value of the deduction is greatly affected by one's tax bracket. For example, 97.7 percent of the value of the mortgage interest deduction went to households earning more than $30,000 a year, with 59.1 percent going to households earning at least $75,000. Joint Committee on Taxation, *Estimates of Federal Tax Expenditures for Fiscal Years 1994–1998* (Washington, D.C.: Government Printing Office, 1993).

23. Howard, *The Hidden Welfare State,* table 1.2, 26.

24. Office of Management and Budget, *Budget of the United States Government. Analytical Perspectives, Fiscal Year 2001* (Washington, D.C.: Government Printing Office, 2000), table 5.3.

25. Quoted in Jon Elster, *Nuts and Bolts for the Social Sciences* (Cambridge: Cambridge University Press, 1989), 91.

26. Dan Balz and Ronald Brownstein, *Storming the Gates: Protest Politics and the Republican Revival* (Boston: Little, Brown, 1996). On party realignment, see David W. Rohde, *Parties and Leadership in the Postreform House* (Chicago:

University of Chicago Press, 1991), and James M. Glaser, *Race, Campaign Politics, and the Realignment in the South* (New Haven, Conn.: Yale University Press, 1996).

27. Paul Pierson, *Dismantling the Welfare State? Reagan, Thatcher and the Politics of Retrenchment* (Cambridge: Cambridge University Press, 1994).

28. Paul Pierson, "The Deficit and the Politics of Domestic Reform," in *The Social Divide*, ed. Margaret Weir (Washington, D.C.: Brookings Institution, 1998), 126–178.

29. For the first time, they also put tax expenditures and on-budget spending on a level playing field, since tax subsides are also subject to pay-as-you-go rules. This arrangement only applies to *new* initiatives, however. As indicated below, Congress has also found ways to work around it in some cases.

30. Pierson, "The Deficit and the Politics of Domestic Reform."

31. "IRS Reform Bill Includes New Salvo of Tax Cuts for Wealthy," Center on Budget and Policy Priorities, Washington, D.C., June 26, 1998.

32. Robert Greenstein, "Looking at the Details of the New Budget Legislation," Center on Budget and Policy Priorities, Washington, D.C., August 12, 1997.

33. It is worth noting that this volume on "the new politics of public policy" contains chapters on both AFDC and the EITC. In 1996, combined federal outlays for the EITC and family support (which included AFDC) totaled $36.7 billion—less than 2.4 percent of total federal spending. This reinforces Derthick's claim that the most dramatic stories frequently are not the most typical ones or necessarily the most revealing about the character of a particular system of policymaking. House Ways and Means Committee, *1998 Greenbook* (Washington, D.C.: U.S. Government Printing Office), WMCP 105-7, appendix tables I-2 and I-4.

34. Although the press hardly noticed, most of the large savings in the "welfare reform" bill came from restrictions on the eligibility of legal immigrants for social safety net programs other than AFDC.

35. James Horney and Robert Greenstein, "How Much of the Enlarged Surplus Is Available for Tax and Program Initiatives?," Center on Budget and Policy Priorities, Washington, D.C., July 7, 2000.

36. Steven Teles, "The Dialectics of Trust: Ideas, Finance and Pensions Privatization in the U.S. and U.K.," paper presented to Max Planck Institute Conference on Varieties of Welfare Capitalism, Cologne, June 1999.

4

Four Pathways of Power

Probing the Political Dynamics of Federal
Tax Policy in the Turbulent 1980s and 1990s

David R. Beam, *Illinois Institute of Technology*
Timothy J. Conlan, *George Mason University*

Long confined to the esoteric world of tax lawyers and accountants, tax policy has emerged during the past two decades as one of the most prominent and important arenas of national policymaking. Over these years, proposed and enacted tax law changes have regularly made headlines. In the words of one close observer and key participant, "taxes came to dominate the public agenda" beginning in the 1980s.[1]

As tax policy became more visible, it also became less stable. Between 1978 and 1997, an astonishing number of major revenue enactments were adopted, including most prominently the Economic Recovery Tax Act of 1981 (ERTA), the Tax Equity and Fiscal Responsibility Act of 1982 (TEFRA), the Deficit Reduction Act of 1984 (DEFRA), the Tax Reform Act of 1986 (TRA86), the Omnibus Budget Reconciliation Acts (OBRA) of 1990 and 1993, and the Taxpayer Relief Act of 1997 (TRA97). During the period 1981–1990 alone, this amounted to some eight thousand pages of statutory fine print.[2]

Accentuating this activity, the goals of tax policy shifted abruptly from one piece of legislation to the next. ERTA comprised the biggest package of tax cuts in American history, offering breaks for individuals, corporations, and a welter of special interests. The very next year TEFRA sharply reversed course, significantly augmenting revenues by raising taxes and closing loopholes. The omnibus budget acts of 1990 and 1993 each raised tax rates for the wealthy. In contrast, the Taxpayer Relief Act of 1997 cut taxes for high-income payers and introduced a parade of new special tax breaks and incentives for a variety of purposes and constituencies.

The Tax Reform Act of 1986 (TRA86)—in many respects the most prominent and certainly the most unusual bill in this string—charted a unique and quite different course, which we examined in detail elsewhere.[3] Designed to be "revenue-neutral"—neither increasing nor decreasing federal receipts—TRA86 simultaneously reduced the number of tax brackets and lowered tax rates while broadening the base of taxable income by eliminating a host of "special interest" provisions. Intended to simplify the system, making it both more comprehensible and "fairer," TRA86 followed the general path long favored by tax experts, working uphill against substantial political obstacles that made its passage seem implausible from start to finish.[4]

This tax reform measure was important, both substantively and politically. But it, like a number of other key domestic policy changes, turned out not to be very durable. Instead, by 1993, a close observer could say that the newest tax legislation "marked a distinct retreat from the principles of tax reform that had shaped TRA, reversing the movement for lower tax rates and broadening of the tax base that had distinguished the 1986 act. The politics of tax reform was nowhere to be found."[5] Another commentator stated similarly, but more strongly:

> The nature of the changes [produced by the 1993 Clinton Tax Act] represent a dramatic departure from the Tax Reform Act of 1986 philosophy of simplification, lower rates, and the goal of removing tax considerations from investment planning. . . . The death knell has been sounded for the principles underlying [TRA86]. Taxes will again assume their common historic role of stimulating investment; tax rate disparities will encourage tax-oriented investment strategies; and the progressive tax rates have been enhanced so the more you make, the more you pay. Any thought of a flat tax or tax simplification is gone.[6]

That final forecast proved quite incorrect, however, as by 1996 political candidates and other advocates were again pressing for a new or greatly modified national tax system. But, despite this renewed interest, many new, complicated, and dubious provisions were introduced into the tax code with the TRA97. Proposals to eliminate the current income tax code by the year 2002 passed the House of Representatives in mid-July 1998 and a major IRS "reform" bill with a new oversight board and an expanded set of "taxpayer rights" was signed into law later the same month.

The Task of Explanation and Analysis

This outpouring of tax legislation activity further challenges the presumption that, in the absence of war or crisis, America's Madisonian system of checks and balances will produce only stalemate or modest, incremental policy outcomes. Even in an era characterized by divided government, Congress's output of tax legislation has been impressive in scope and volume, if not consistency.

But explaining why these numerous and varied bills have passed in the forms that they did is a complex task, and one that we can only begin here. In our prior works, however, we suggested the applicability of three different models of the policy process, which were termed the pluralist-incrementalist, presidential-majoritarian, and the entrepreneurial-ideational or "the new politics of reform."[7] This approach has, we believe, considerable merit, as each of these models offers insight into processes through which many key tax (and other) statutes were enacted, linking the nature of legislative outcomes with the patterns or styles of political leadership and activity that produced them.

At the same time, further reflection and more recent tax policy developments suggest the utility of certain modifications to this framework. Because of these changes, we now see the need for adding to our typology a fourth style or category, which we term "symbolic."

Some might describe the slide away from a more comprehensive, "flatter" system established in 1986 as simply a return to "business as usual"—in our scheme, the pluralist-incrementalist model. But in important respects that characterization is inadequate. Although the modest tangible outcomes are consistent with the "triumph of moderation" described in chapter 1—particularly the renewed proliferation of tax breaks and preferences—traditional pluralism is a poor description of the underlying political process. The pluralist-incrementalist model emphasized low-visibility agreements struck with interest groups, rather than the high-profile, popularly mobilized campaigns and extensive controversy that have characterized recent tax policies. Furthermore, both political parties and policy ideas have figured too importantly in the recent debates.

Instead, we believe that the many changes in tax policy and politics during the past two decades suggest a need for considering policymaking more strategically, looking at the methods by which policy initiators or advocates build support for their proposals—whether to help move them down the often difficult road toward enactment or simply to gain public attention and score political points. To this end, we offer a modified typology.

This typology, summarized in Figure 4.1, distinguishes four "pathways to power" differentiated by the *scope or scale of mobilization* (whether specialized or mass) and the *method of mobilization* (principally utilizing organizations or ideas). Not only does this alternative framework provide for a more comprehensive interpretation of the movement toward passage of the 1986 TRA; it also offers a useful foundation for discussing the numerous other, often-competing policy changes that have swept through the tax arena during the 1980s and 1990s.[8]

In addition, we would now like to emphasize, more strongly than in our previous writings, that these four models do not represent independent and discrete policy types. Rather, they are distinc-

	Scope of Mobilization	
	Specialized	**Mass**
Ideational Form of Mobilization	**Analytic** (Treasury I–1986; TRA86)	**Symbolic** (supply-side economics; most flat-tax proposals; proposals to eliminate IRS Code)
Organizational	**Pluralist** (normal "incremental" tax politics)	**Partisan** (Clinton 1993 Tax Act; ERTA 1981)

- Actors can mobilize support through either political organizations or political ideas.
- The scope or scale of mobilization can be either limited or broad (the "inside" or "outside" game).
- The four pathways of power or methods of political coalition building each typify a style of tax (and other) policymaking.
- Legislation often moves through multiple sectors on its way toward defeat or passage.

FIGURE 4.1.   The Four Pathways of Power (with prototypical examples listed)

tive "pathways of power"—dynamic and changeable strategies by which political actors can seek to build support for their proposals. While it often is accurate to characterize a particular bill as "mostly" presidential-majoritarian or "chiefly" incremental-pluralist, others resist being pigeonholed so neatly. The four can represent phases of activity, separate stages in the process by which a bill becomes law— or more than one may be in play simultaneously. Indeed, even TRA86, which is in our interpretation "mostly" ideational-entrepreneurial or "expert" legislation, had aspects or stages in which each of the other three models played important contributory roles.

This chapter outlines our revised fourfold policy framework and briefly demonstrates its applicability to other significant items of tax legislation. Finally, it considers the potential insights this framework may offer into additional arenas of public policy. We believe that the model is helpful for understanding the dynamics of other recent policy initiatives, from health care and welfare reform to various examples of education and environmental policy.

Two Traditional Methods of Mobilization: The "Politics of Organization"

Policymakers and advocates all face the need to build support for their proposals if they hope to see them move toward enactment. Traditionally, they have done so by relying on two types of specifically political organizations: so-called interest or lobby groups and the two major political parties.

Interest groups were, for many years, regarded as the principal source and chief beneficiaries of governmental action. Furthermore, they—along with specialists in the executive branch and within Congress itself—were essentially alone in possessing the scarce resources of time, attention, and information that would let them participate effectively in developing or modifying programs.

Political parties, of course, were designed more for electoral purpose than for advancing particular legislative objectives. The selection (or "ratification") of candidates, and not the drafting of a platform of principles, is the principal business at the quadrennial national party conventions. But, nonetheless, parties—and especially the party headed by the incumbent president—do devise and help advance a legislative program.

The Pluralist Pathway

In Washington, D.C., interpretations of "politics as usual" typically employ a "pluralist" perspective, which views policymaking chiefly as a process of adjustment among contending organized interests. Politicians assume the role of brokers, while legislatures essentially "referee the group struggle" by ratifying interest group victories and defeats in statutory terms.

The theory of budgetary and legislative incrementalism, to which pluralism is often wedded, emphasizes outcomes as well as processes. It recognizes that new policies usually involve only small departures from their predecessors, in part because of cognitive limitations: no individual decision maker can rationally evaluate all the alternative means to multitudinous ends they might favor. Small, simple changes, various marginal adjustments, are more readily understood. But incrementalism also has a strong political rationale, because incremental change is normally the path of least resistance where there is a pluralistic distribution of political power. Since the existing allocation of benefits should conform to the allocation of political influence—and typically have been spread widely in a "distributive" pattern—any attempt to revise policies dramatically could be expected to spark heated opposition.

At least prior to the 1980s, the usual pattern of U.S. tax politics closely fit this pluralist-incrementalist model. The federal income tax grew enormously in fiscal importance and complexity after 1913, with the most significant revisions associated with periods of crisis: wartime emergencies and the Great Depression. But, setting aside these important but relatively brief and infrequent moments, the tax system did not change in basic structure and proposals to alter it fundamentally seldom advanced very far. John Witte correctly described the standard pattern as beginning with

> marginal adjustments to the existing structure. . . . Applicable rates, bracket changes, exemption levels, standard deductions, depreciation percentages, investment credits, depletion allowances—the list of changes that can be accomplished by simply altering a number is very long. . . . Tax laws can also be easily and marginally altered by expanding or contracting eligible groups, actions, industries, commodities, or financial circumstances.[9]

Furthermore, the creation and expansion of tax preferences, which is among the more obvious "incremental" additions and changes, has

traditionally been attributed to the influence of organized beneficiary groups.[10]

But, however generally useful, this pluralist model does not
describe TRA86, the most important of the numerous tax law
changes of the past twenty years. First and foremost, that act was
remarkable because it was adopted in the face of significant opposition from most organized groups, many of which lost significant tangible, financial benefits. Major losers included real estate, heavy
industry, large defense contractors, and a host of others. On the other
hand, perhaps the clearest economic "winners" from tax reform—the
millions of low income former ratepayers who were entirely
removed from the rolls—were neither well organized nor so professionally represented. Of course, TRA86 also was too far-reaching in
scope to be described as merely incremental. Instead, it provided for
a substantial rewrite of both the individual and corporate tax code.

Certainly in other recent cases the usual sorts of interest group
influence played an important role. Sheldon Pollack notes that much
of "the Taxpayer Relief Act of 1997 reads like a Christmas-list of special tax provisions targeted at the constituents of the Republican
Party," including, for example, the reduction in the maximum capital gains tax rate and increased exemptions for the federal gift and
estate taxes.[11] But exceptions to the pluralist-incrementalist model
certainly abound in the tax initiatives of the 1980s and 1990s. Indeed,
as Pollack also says, during this period

> the normal distributive politics of the federal income tax
> [seemed] to come unglued . . . . Both the strong partisan tax
> policies advanced by the Republican Party in 1981 and 1995 and
> the politics of tax reform that prevailed in 1986 were outside the
> realm of the "normal" nonpartisan distributive policymaking
> typically associated with a pluralist political structure. . . . [T]he
> politics of the income tax in the 1980s departed from a pure dis-
> tributive politics that would otherwise have been predicted by
> a incrementalist/pluralist model.[12]

The Partisan Pathway

Traditionally, the American system has overcome the obstacles and
political inertia that block nonincremental policy changes only on
those rare occasions when it resembles the ideal of responsible
party government. Typically, a strong president—as was Franklin
Roosevelt in 1932 or Lyndon Johnson in 1964—sweeps into office

with large party majorities in both chambers of Congress. He mobilizes the resources of his office to construct a coherent legislative program, rallying the public and his party followers behind it. Because presidents have typically provided the essential leadership for such partisan action, we previously termed this the "presidential-majoritarian" model.

The Republican party's midterm electoral landslide in 1994, however, illustrated an alternative variant, with leadership coming from the legislative branch, rather than the White House. Under the direction of House Speaker Newt Gingrich of Georgia, Republican members succeeded in moving many of the initiatives contained in its far-reaching "Contract with America"—in effect, a binding party platform—through the House of Representatives in what was termed the "Republican Revolution." Some bills survived the somewhat more temperate Republican Senate as well, though many met with presidential vetoes from the incumbent Democrat, Bill Clinton. The interparty deadlock that resulted, as dramatized by shutdowns of the federal government beginning in November 1995, meant that the overall level of legislative activity for the 104th Congress was not particularly impressive. But the episode did show the ability of members of Congress to formulate, initiate, and advance a far-reaching legislative program without the participation of the White House.[13]

Such partisan politics illuminated elements, but by no means fully explained, the adoption of TRA86, as we emphasized in our prior account. Although Ronald Reagan placed the topic of tax reform squarely on the national agenda following his landslide victory in November 1984, it was congressional Republicans who were least enthralled with the idea. Their mass defection in the House nearly killed the legislation in 1985. In the Senate, too, Finance Committee Chair Bob Packwood and most of his party colleagues initially viewed tax reform as a direct attack on their most supportive constituencies and their preferred style of government which favored tax incentives over government-provided services. At the same time, certain Democrats—such as Senators Bill Bradley and Richard Gephardt—played an important role in initiating the concept, while it was Ways and Means Chair Dan Rostenkowski who essentially forced the Republican Senate to act by working reform legislation through his committee and the House.

Partisan leadership did play a notable role in some other prominent tax legislation of the 1980s and 1990s, including the

Republican-led ERTA 1981 tax cuts and the related Omnibus Budget Reconciliation Act (OBRA), with its sizeable spending reductions, as well as the proposals that became the 1997 Taxpayer Relief Act. As C. Eugene Steuerle comments on the former, "Eventually, it became apparent that a new, popularly elected president was going to get his way."[14] And as Conlan emphasizes, "For the single critical year of 1981 the narrow interest group subsystem politics and congressional fragmentation that characterized the Nixon and Carter years gave way to a highly visible, majoritarian style of presidential policy leadership."[15]

Indeed, the final vote on ERTA in the House divided the parties more sharply than any other tax vote since 1921. But, even so, this was not a purely partisan case, as Democrats joined Republicans in a "bidding war," matching their tax cut proposals nearly one for one, instead of steadfastly maintaining opposition.[16]

Adopted during a short two-year period when Democrats held control of both the presidency and Congress, Bill Clinton's 1993 deficit reduction package was nearly purely "partisan" in form. Assembled by his administration as a result of a campaign pledge to reduce the mounting deficit, the proposal resulted in bitter fights in Congress and never attracted the support of even a single Republican on any of eight critical votes.[17]

Yet these are unusual cases. While there is a bit of truth to caricaturing Republicans as stridently "antitax" and anti-IRS—particularly desiring rate reductions benefiting the wealthy, including capital gains cuts—and the Democrats as more accepting, concerned especially for the well-being of the lower and middle classes, this division holds up far better in the media and on the campaign trail than in reality. In truth, neither party developed or stuck to a consistent platform on tax issues, and no other bills were enacted strictly by mobilizing the party faithful. It was a Democrat, Jimmy Carter, who called the income tax a "disgrace to the human race" during the 1976 campaign, promising and preparing—but not getting enacted—a major overhaul along the same lines as TRA86.[18] In a move that launched the modern era of party competition discussed in chapter 1, many Democrats joined into the tax-cutting fever the latter president started in 1981, escalating ERTA to new heights of fiscal irresponsibility.

But it was the Republican Senate that took the lead in scaling back ERTA's excesses, with a vote strictly on party lines—with

Republicans voting for tax increases that repudiated their administration's initiative of the previous year.[19] Reagan himself reversed course, presiding over a significant series of "revenue enhancing" measures: in two terms as president, he signed eighteen separate tax bills, fourteen of which raised taxes.[20]

Reagan's successor and former vice president, George Bush, made a famous pledge—"Read my lips: no new taxes"—on the occasion of his August 1988 nomination acceptance speech. But, under threats from escalating deficits, a faltering economy, and the prospect of a mandatory budget sequester, he, too, reversed himself and accepted, following a lengthy bipartisan "budget summit," a 1990 budget act based more on tax increases than expenditure cuts.[21] In 1995 and 1996, both president Clinton and the Republican majority in Congress—as well as candidate Bob Dole—promised tax cuts as part of their proposals to balance the budget.[22] Such were in fact delivered with TRA97, which included provisions developed out of the Republicans' Contract with America and others—including a number of education benefits—that Clinton himself specifically favored.

Of key bills, then, only Clinton's 1993 Budget Act and, to a lesser degree, ERTA of 1981, closely fit the form suggested by the traditional partisan mobilization model. An explanation for the frequent, dramatic, contradictory and in many ways "unprincipled"[23] changes in tax law during the 1980s and 1990s must be sought in other quarters.

New Methods of Mobilization:
Two Variants on the "Politics of Ideas"

Traditional models emphasizing interest group pressure and partisan politics may well help explain the great majority of legislative enactments, but an increasing number of key statutes are difficult to account for in these ways. To interpret them, different or at least supplementary models are necessary.

These alternative approaches are informed by, and take into account, important changes in the American political environment during the past three decades. One of the many important developments is that the "foot soldiers" traditionally provided by political parties to work out in the precincts have become far less important then formerly. In contrast, money—needed for the hiring of campaign consultants, direct mail blitzes, and particularly the purchase of costly television advertising time—matters more. Especially with the rise of more numerous and highly publicized primaries, the battle for election to the presidency is fought out more "in the air" than, as in days past, "on the ground."

Congressional organization and procedures have been altered as well. To single out again one of the most important changes, in the early 1970s power was decentralized to a considerable degree, giving first-term freshmen a degree of visibility and opportunities for influence that would have been impossible to imagine in prior decades. At the same time, the legislative branch acquired staff capabilities (as well as access to other sources of information) that put it on a more equal position with the executive in terms of the capacity to identify problems and formulate or evaluate legislation.

Concurrently, the media have become evermore central to both electoral and policy politics. A great deal of governmental activity is under its close scrutiny—or has the possibility of becoming so— but, typically, in a manner emphasizing entertainment values: contests for power, the drama of debate and conflict, and of course financial scandals and moral improprieties. Consequently, politicians—young ones bred on them and their seniors bowing to the new realities—have discarded traditions of deference and courtesy that once were commonplace in legislative operations and become more aggressively offensive and warily defensive in campaigning and policy positioning.

The Expert Pathway

The best-recognized new approach to interpreting politics and policymaking begins by emphasizing the significance of *ideas*. Because it lacks the strong ideological passions and commitments found in Europe, American politics has commonly been viewed as quite pragmatic and interest based. But, especially during the 1980s, more and more political scientists came to emphasize the role of ideas, beliefs, and values as an important and independent influence. James Q. Wilson, for one, concluded after studying a number of regulatory statutes that "a complete theory of politics . . . requires that attention be paid to beliefs as well as interests. Only by the most extraordinary theoretical contortions can one explain [these laws] by reference to the economic stakes involved."[24] John Kingdon ended his influential study of agenda setting by pointing out that "if we try understand public policy solely in terms of [such concepts as power, influence, pressure and strategy] we miss a great deal. The content of . . . ideas themselves, far from being mere smokescreens or rationalizations, are integral parts of decision making in and around government."[25]

The increasing importance and influence of ideas in the public arena has vaulted intellectuals and experts—the natural generators and propagators of ideas—into positions of greater prominence. And when such experts and professionals are employed in and around government—in both staff agencies and think tanks, as has been increasingly the case since the 1960s and 1970s—they can sometimes influence policy quickly and directly. Daniel Patrick Moynihan traced much of Lyndon Johnson's War on Poverty to what he termed "the professionalization of reform."[26] Similarly, Samuel H. Beer noted that, throughout these two decades, "people in government service, or closely associated with it, acting on the basis of their specialized knowledge . . . first perceived the problem, conceived the program, initially urged it on the president and Congress, went on to help lobby it through to enactment, and then saw to its administration."[27] Another leading case in point was the deregulation of the airline, trucking, and telecommunications industries in the late 1970s and early 1980s, which also depended heavily on the views of experts and the "politics of ideas."[28] A more general factor has been the growing size and importance since the mid-1960s and early 1970s of both official staff research units and independent think tanks.[29]

Compared to other policy areas, the tax domain is unusual in that it includes such an extensive, well-informed, and highly committed professional community of experts in positions of considerable influence. Its members may be found especially in the Treasury Department's Office of Tax Policy and on the staff of the unique Joint Committee on Taxation (JCT), as well as at the Congressional Budget Office (CBO) and the Congressional Research Service, the Brookings Institution and Urban Institute, and elsewhere. Most of these participants share a commitment to a specific view of what would constitute "good" or "sound" policy—an agreement on a set of normative "principles" that, in their view, should guide legislative action.

Although no statute is ever a pure type, the 1986 Tax Reform Act is an outstanding example of the operation and influence of "expert" politics, which was especially important in its formative stages. The movement for tax reform rested above all else on the shared conviction of knowledgeable experts in and outside government that the federal income tax system had grown indefensible from the standpoint of professionally salient values. Furthermore, by the mid-1980s there was widespread agreement among these tax specialists on the basic features of an ideal income tax system: it should be horizontally equitable, investment neutral, and administratively efficient. All three goals could be attained by broadening the tax base and lowering rates, as Joseph A. Pechman had demonstrated in the 1950s and as had been more recently emphasized by the "flat-tax," Bradley-Gephardt, and Kemp-Kasten proposals.[30]

This professional consensus was especially important in shaping the first draft reform bill, dubbed "Treasury I." "Political considerations were irrelevant," Secretary Donald Regan had told his staff. Consequently, the initial Treasury Department plan was an astonishingly pure expression of expert views. Although never formally proposed as legislation, it—rather than current tax law—became the standard against which subsequent proposals were measured, and the basic contours of the final TRA—base broadening, reduced rates, revenue and distributional neutrality—all were fixed at this early stage. Expert consensus also accounted for the removal of a large number of the poor from the tax rolls, a particularly costly feature, and for the sharp hike in the corporate tax rate, which helped pay for lower individual rates.

As one would expect, professional ideas were less dominant throughout the remainder of the legislative process, but they were still influential. For example, the vast scope of the reform initiative overwhelmed members, leaving an enormous number of issues to be decided by the JCT staff. JCT staff also exercised life-or-death power over countless alternatives considered by decision makers by controlling the all-critical revenue estimates.

TRA86 represented the high-water mark of expert influence on tax policy. But elements of some similar impact can of course be found in other legislation, including the large 1982 TEFRA tax hike, which was forced by CBO's estimates of dangerously escalating deficits. As Steuerle describes it:

> In particular, Robert Dole, then chairman of the Senate Finance Committee, began the arduous task of grafting together a package of proposals he could get through the Senate. He was supported with technical assistance by the increasingly important congressional staff of the Senate Finance Committee and the

Joint Committee on Taxation and, within the administration, by the Office of Management and Budget and the Office of Tax Policy within the Treasury Department. Thus was born the Tax Equity and Fiscal Responsibility Act of 1982.[31]

Most legislation since 1986 has lacked the TRA's degree of relatively principled coherence. OBRA 1990, for example, "reflected no clear principles or ideology, nor did it suggest any new, emerging trends in tax policy. . . . With the 1990 act, a decade of intense tax legislating came to an end with policy adrift and no clear direction evident."[32]

Even more clearly, the 1997 Taxpayer Relief Act (and its associated budget act) departed sharply by adding a host of special tax breaks and new provisions that greatly increased the complexity of the tax system. Bemused and troubled tax experts engaged in debates about which were the worst features in a bill that had, in their mind, few good ones. Complaints and publicity immediately following its enactment quickly led to renewed calls for replacing the current income tax with a greatly simplified flat tax, in some cases by the same legislators who had supported the newly complicated provisions just adopted.

Similarly, the 1998 IRS reform bill was, particularly as initially proposed, strongly opposed by both tax experts and many professionals in public administration. Urged forward to address some highly publicized but often exaggerated abuses of authority by IRS agents, important aspects of the plan were deemed simply unworkable and others quite unwarranted or unwise by those familiar with IRS operations.

In short, if TRA86 can best be characterized as legislation in which the "experts won," to at least a significant degree, the principal developments since have found the same tax experts and the ideas that they support mostly on the losing side. Part of this can be explained by the influence of interest group and partisan politics, but it also is necessary to take into account the highly charged atmosphere that has surrounded tax questions and shaped the manner in which they have been formulated and debated as a result.

The Symbolic Pathway

Policy experts are concerned, in most cases above all else, with the actual substance of policy. For most, the key question is "will it work"—will it "do good" by accomplishing its objectives.

But proposals are very frequently advanced for other reasons as well. Programs may be designed around a popular prejudice or to fit a widespread preconception or even clearly recognized misconception. Sloganeering (e.g., "three strikes and you're out" for certain crimes or "two years and you're off" and "end welfare as we know it" concerning public assistance) can sometimes dictate substance.

Furthermore, candidates frequently promise actions or results that they (or their advisers) know have little chance of being realized. Advocates may urge initiatives to gain attention to themselves or to a cause, even if the positions advanced are unlikely to be adopted or implemented successfully. Issues also may be raised simply to embarrass opponents or to force a legislative vote that can be used as a campaign weapon during the next electoral cycle. For example, a Republican spokeswoman said that they never expected the recent House bill abolishing the Internal Revenue Code in 2002 to become law but hoped that it would "make some [Democrats'] lives miserable for defending the current tax code."[33]

We would term these "symbolic" policy proposals, as they draw the bulk of their appeal simply by appearing to respond to a problem in a manner that is easily comprehensible to the public.[34] Such initiatives are associated more with their abstract goal than evaluated according to the technical concerns such as program structure. Established or anticipated effectiveness is a secondary (or sometimes even nonexistent) concern.

The symbolic pathway contrasts with more traditional means of fashioning support for legislation, such as compromising over the provisions of an act, logrolling many different benefits into one program, or deferring to the expertise of individual legislative specialists. Compared with these methods, it is a faster and less expensive means to win support. Although to be successful, symbolic proposals must strike a rich preexisting vein of sympathy, their advocates need not possess a reservoir of power or resources for bargaining with a broad array of interests. So long as Congress's attention can be focused on some widely shared (or possibly greatly feared) legislative aim—rather than on more complex questions about which program approach is most appropriate to address the goal—coalition building can be greatly simplified. Such proposals may ultimately reach the floor in a form that essentially compels approval, in a way that no one can afford to oppose. "Position taking" and "blame avoidance" loom large.

The symbolic pathway, then, has both familiar and distinctive characteristics:

- It differs most sharply from the normal "pluralist" arena, in which deals are commonly struck among organized interests and compromising, logrolling legislators that rarely receive and might not withstand public scrutiny. Traditional pluralist politics is the politics of the back room, rather than the front page.

- It shares with the partisan pathway the possibility of making large, nonincremental, and unexpected changes in public policy. But it differs from it in that, when symbolic concerns are dominant, divisions of views along party lines are typically muted or absent. So commanding are the objectives thought to be that opposition by members of either party may seem unsavory and dangerous. Instead of taking conflicting positions, both Republicans and Democrats may climb on board to gain credit for advancing or avoid blame for blocking popular legislation.

- Symbolic politics shares with expert policymaking a focus on ideas of a sort. But these ideas need not be based on a broad consensus or agreement among these best-informed and most attentive specialists or be well grounded in research. Instead, the ideas at its focus often come from out of left (or right) field, backed by little in the way of evidence, drawing their sustenance more from their ties to widely shared values than from any carefully developed and thoughtfully deliberated principles.

In the case of tax policy in particular, the entire arena has been greatly shaped by popular resentment of taxation and, especially in recent years, an exaggerated distrust or fear of the IRS itself. The federal income tax, which had long been considered the "best" and "fairest" of all taxes by both experts and the public, has come to be widely condemned and reviled.

It is not difficult to find and draw upon a current of antitax sentiment in the United States. Such views are deeply rooted in our nation's history. But tax issues first moved to a high level of prominence in the modern era following the proposition 13 property tax freeze initiative adopted by California's voters in 1978. President Ronald Reagan took the Californians' complaints to Washington, claiming that high taxes and other aspects of "big government" were the principal cause of the economic problems in which the nation was then deeply mired.

It is often said that if something sounds too good to be true, it probably is. The supply-side policies championed by Reagan in 1981 to move the nation out of its economic doldrums were a noteworthy example, holding out the prospect of reducing taxes to increase economic performance and thus also reducing the deficit—all gain, no pain.

This notion is a curious example of the politics of ideas, as it shows the influence of "bad" ideas, not ones rooted in carefully certified expert opinion. While its proponents claim a hoary lineage, the theory's key propositions were not and are not now widely accepted among economists and, unlike the movement for economic deregulation that also was influential at the time, had not worked their way over the decades from academic journals, winning supporters with each slow step. Rather, the concept was what journalist William Greider describes as the work of a handful of "intellectual guerrillas" who never found much favor outside of the editorial page of the *Wall Street Journal*—and, of course, in the Oval Office itself.[35]

But oversimplification—which experts fear and disdain—is often a virtue in the symbolic arena, and proposals designed to travel this pathway are frequently shaped accordingly. For example, key components of Reagan's initial 1981 tax proposals—the "10-10-10" rate reduction over three years and the "10-5-3" plan for depreciation of buildings and various types of equipment—"had a certain flair to them," Steuerle writes, "and gave the illusion that the complexities of the tax law could be described in simple terms."[36]

In 1981, the combination of the announced aim of a popular new president, a understandable wish that taxes could be cut without also reducing services, and a patchwork of ideas that gave this improbable scheme a thin veneer of intellectual respectability led to huge tax cuts that were joined in by members of both parties. Furthermore, in the voting on OBRA, in particular, "The battle was over perception as much as reality. The Reagan Administration cast it this way: You were either for the President and economic recovery, or you were against it. Cool deliberation took a back seat. . . . Congress simply didn't have time to do a good job. Substance gave way to symbolism."[37]

In contrast to ERTA, the Tax Reform Act of 1986 moved forward on a firm foundation of "expert" politics, as well as receiving a significant impetus from party leaders. But, to obtain support beyond the narrow circle of experts, even the best technical proposals usually have to be trimmed and tapered according to the less-informed public's fashion. Such factors were not unimportant in shaping the content of the TRA or in moving it toward adoption. As we wrote previously, the shift from Treasury I—the original staff draft—to Treasury II, which was presented to the public, "signified the passage of tax reform into a very different arena from the one dominated by civil servants and academic experts. It was a domain in which politicians, not professionals, had the upper hand, a place where appearances and symbols often outweighed evidence and substance in decision making."[38]

Even earlier, symbolic rather than substantive considerations led to the development of a 15-25-35 rate structure for Treasury I, rather than the more awkward sounding 16-28-37 initially devised by staffers. Later, maintaining at least the appearance of a simple, two-rate structure became the focus of attention, particularly in the Senate. And, ultimately, "the power of the ideas that actually propelled the adoption of tax reform seemed to lie more in the realm of symbolism than of intellectual rigor. They appealed to greed and fear, as well as to logic and reason. . . . [V]ague but powerful symbols, plus a concern for appearances—sometimes cynically manipulated—lent dynamic force to the reform campaign."[39]

Just two years later, President George H. W. Bush employed the Hollywood symbolism of Dirty Harry with his "read-my-lips" pledge to oppose new taxes. But, like Republican legislators in 1982, he was forced by the escalating deficit to reverse himself: a sound move economically but a disastrous one politically.

The most recent tax debates and actions also seem to be marked more by the excessive enthusiasm, oversimplification, and obfuscation that are common to symbolic politics than hard-headed discussions of either "How well will it work?" (the expert's concern) or "What's in it for me?" (the pluralist's touchstone). This is the case whether the issue is such lesser reforms as elimination of the so-called marriage penalty or far-reaching calls to replace the income tax altogether.

For example, the various flat tax proposals, which gained renewed prominence during the 1996 presidential campaigns, look far better at a distance than when examined close up. While it is true that the theoretical idea of taxing consumption rather than income—which lies behind some (though not all) of these plans—has a lengthy intellectual pedigree, its main attraction is the promise of simplicity: a tax return form so short that it could fit on a postcard, according to the initial popularizers, Robert E. Hall and Alvin Rabushka.

But this superficial simplicity is overstated, to condense severely a lengthy set of complex criticisms. Indeed, two writers for the *Wall Street Journal,* the same publication where the Hall-Rabushka plan first made its appearance in a March 1981 article, have cautioned that the debate is surrounded with exaggerations and myths:

> First, none of the most highly publicized flat-tax plans being peddled by politicians today really are flat. . . . Second, contrary to what you may be hearing from politicians and economists, it is virtually impossible for anyone to predict with precision how the flat tax will affect you or the nation. . . . [Furthermore], some smart people think that the flat-tax proposals are flawed ideas that sound great in theory but just won't work. . . . What is on the surface a highly appealing idea is really a very complex proposal to scrap a system that has served us well—perhaps not as well as we would like—and replace it with an entirely new and untested system whose impact is largely unpredictable.[40]

Adding to these and other objections, the political obstacles facing change, the economic and financial uncertainty that would result from a wholly new tax system, and the enormous technical difficulties in "transitioning" from our present income tax to a consumption or "flat" tax, it is hard not to view the flat tax question as principally a soapbox for a strange coalition of (a few serious) intellectual theorists and (many more) political opportunists, rather than a significant effort at practical reform. As Sease and Herman add:

> We all know rationally that taxes are absolutely necessary to the functioning of our government. Yet we resent the levels at which we are taxed, we feel inadequate in the face of the complexity of the tax system, and we fear the agency that administers that system. Politicians play on those resentments and fears to win or keep office and they are playing especially loudly these days. As a consequence, Americans can expect tax policy to be at the forefront of the political process for many years [and that the] debate will often be rancorous, confusing, and emotional.[41]

That statement, and other similar ones, seems a good summary of our present situation. Indeed, in general, the growing importance of the "symbolic pathway" has had a deleterious effect on political deliberations. The effort by a wide range of political actors—included among them many otherwise "pragmatic" politicians, interest groups, and both political parties—to devise ideas that have a significant political cachet has simultaneously reduced the near-monopoly of traditional expert elites, led to the development of contending groups of "counterexperts," and promoted the "dumbing down" of policy proposals and its related political discussion. Oversimplifications, distortions, and the drama of discord have become increasingly important. As one journalist recently commented in a quite different context, "Although we do not like to admit it, America seems addicted to scraping the bottom of the barrel. We're getting cruder, more self-involved, and more over-the-top by the minute. . . . The merger of entertainment and politics that began with John Kennedy and Ronald Reagan reached a sour note with Bill Clinton . . . [who] campaigned and governed using low-brow forums of popular entertainment."[42]

Conclusion

Over the past twenty years, the direction of federal tax policy has wavered and wobbled from one enactment to the next, and the politics of these laws have varied as dramatically as their content. How should we account for this volatility in the policy process in an established field long and quite accurately characterized as "highly incremental"?[43]

There are many ways to go about answering this question. Here, we have suggested that it is helpful to look at the policy-making system strategically, from the standpoint of actors trying to build a coalition of support for their policy proposals. Such a perspective contrasts with the most common textbook image, which depicts policymaking as a singular process in which legislation marches through a predictable series of stages on route to passage, from initiation to adoption and implementation. This approach has its merits, but it also obscures important variations in the policymaking process that occur from one issue to the next, as seen throughout this discussion. The policy process can vary widely—not only according to the type of issue involved, as Lowi, Wilson, and others have observed[44]—but from program to program within individual policy domains, such as taxation, welfare, health care, or the environment.

Consequently, we suggest thinking of the policymaking system as a network of distinct but interconnected pathways of power, which constrain actors in the system but also provide strategic avenues by which to advance their aims. Each of these pathways tends to function best in a certain environment, favors particular tools of decision making, employs a unique style of coalition building, and is associated with a characteristic type of policy outcome. Each also tends to appeal to particular actors in the policy system, who seek to steer issues onto a path most familiar to them and conducive to their success. Strategically minded actors may attempt to borrow a successful decision making technique from another pathway or to switch tracks altogether, but they are likely to change the overall style of policymaking in the process.

Because each pathway has distinctive attributes, policies that are advanced along one avenue tend to differ in predictable ways from those developed in another. It makes a difference, for example, whether tax policies are devised and advanced along carefully engineered and professionally policed routes through the expert community or whether they are fashioned by entrepreneurs who are interested in moving public opinion along a symbolic superhighway.

Partly because different tax policy enactments over the past twenty years have followed different routes to passage, both the processes responsible for these laws and their substantive content have tended to vary one from the next. For example, the 1978 Revenue Act saw Congress seize the tax writing initiative from the Carter administration and construct a modestly sized but loophole-laden bill that epitomized the workings of interest group pluralism.[45] Three years later, ERTA, a much larger and far more comprehensive tax cut package, was passed by Congress, reflecting the power of a popular president to seize an issue, expand the scope of conflict, and mobilize his party and the media to help advance it. The characteristics of expert-driven reform were highlighted in the Tax Reform Act of 1986, while the politics of symbolism took center stage in the congressional actions of 1997 and 1998, which culminated in measures for "taxpayer relief" and "IRS reforms" that were anathema to most tax professionals in or close to government.

Looking beyond Tax Policy

We have found this framework to be helpful in understanding and interpreting the substance and volatility of recent tax policy, but it is just as applicable to other policy fields as well. For example, many traditional agricultural policies were shaped and advanced within the protective confines of a specialized policy subsystem.[46] Thus, in describing the politics of the nation's basic pesticide law—the Federal Insecticide, Fungicide, and Rodenticide Act (FIFRA) of 1947—Christopher Bosso wrote that "The 1947 act . . . was essentially the product of close cooperation among members of the House committee on Agriculture, mid-level personnel within the U.S. Department of Agriculture, and those representing the major agricultural pesticides makers—a classic 'iron triangle.'"[47] Until the 1970s, the resulting pesticides policy bore all the marks of pluralist-incremental policymaking, including a remarkable stability and resistance to change. When change did come, it was because policy formation was forced onto a "symbolic" track, driven initially by the entrepreneurial activities of environmentalists like Rachel Carson and the explosion of media interest that followed.

Education policy also offers examples of different policy paths at work. The landmark act of federal involvement in education, the Elementary and Secondary Education Act of 1965 (ESEA) was a classic example of the partisan model. Its enactment, according to one study, was a story in which "the Executive initiates," "the House acts," and the "Senate assents," all in the wake of the Democrats' landslide election victory in 1964.[48] Republicans, who were disgruntled by the Democrats' success in ramming the bill through Congress, even employed the metaphor of a policy pathway when they dubbed it "the railroad act of 1965."[49] The politics of the ESEA stood in stark contrast to those of the Family Educational Rights and Privacy Act of 1974 (FERPA), the so-called Buckley amendment. That provision, designed to guarantee the privacy of student records, had all the hallmarks of symbolic policymaking. It emerged suddenly—seemingly out of nowhere insofar as most higher education experts were concerned—having been initiated by an entrepreneurial senator who read about the problem in *Parade* magazine, a Sunday newspaper supplement. It swiftly passed the Congress—with no hearings, little debate, and serious technical problems—by virtue of its appeal to symbols of personal privacy.[50]

While many pieces of legislation closely fit one of the models described here, this framework does not imply that all—or even most—legislation is advanced along a single policy pathway. Many tax bills examined in this paper switched tracks at different stages of enactment. In fact, it may be the norm for enactments to move along different pathways as different functions in the political system (representation, interest aggregation, legitimation) are performed.

Moreover, certain actors in the policy process have incentives to switch tracks as they seek to move issues onto more friendly or familiar terrain. Others fight to retain control over issues by working to keep them within their own domain. Thus, while interest groups and specialists may prefer to address issues within the comfortable confines of their established policy networks, presidents and congressional leaders are interested in seizing issues around which they can rally their entire party, while policy entrepreneurs are generally interested in crafting hot issues that they can market to institutionally powerful actors and the mass media. Sophisticated practitioners of the policy process understand their own strengths and weaknesses and are likely to follow the path that maximizes their resources.

Both the character of the policy process and a proposal's substantive content are likely to change—sometimes unexpectedly—when issues switch or are moved onto different tracks. Experts who spent years conducting studies to investigate work disincentives in welfare programs suddenly found that "values trump analysis" once issues were moved to a broader public arena where "two years and you're off" was all it took to capture the public imagination.[51] Similarly, professional specialists who sought to craft a program guaranteeing affordable health insurance for all found their concerns were quickly shunted aside when opposing interests mounted a costly and effective media campaign playing on fears of "big government" and the loss of an individual's ability to select his or her personal physician. In other instances, a broad party mandate may be captured by specific interest groups once issues move from the realm of electoral pronouncements to the backrooms of congressional committee, as occurred when the broad value statements in the Contract with America were translated into hundred-page bills by congressional committees and their interest group allies.

The Ascendance of Symbolic Politics

The growing importance of symbolic politics over time is evidence of the new role played by "second-tier" politics, discussed elsewhere in this volume (see chapter 16). It also is a source of unpredictability and volatility in tax and other policies. Whereas pluralist politics tend to be highly stable, changing only as the alignment and interests of dominant groups shift slowly over time, symbolic politics tend to be impulsive and unpredictable, subject to the breathless lifecycle of media attention and the changing eddies and currents of public opinion.

We have witnessed a relative shift away from the interest group and partisan arenas, as the local foundations of parties have become less important and as groups have splintered and multiplied, while the two ideational forms of politics have become more prevalent. The expanding volume and complexity of knowledge, increased levels of education, and the growing demands on government have all fostered the politics of expertise. But, in an often conflicting current, changes in the nature of electoral campaigns and the growing influence of the mass media have tended to elevate symbolic politics. [52] So has the precipitous decline in legitimacy of established policymaking institutions, particularly Congress. This has encouraged policymakers to "go public" with issues, in the hopes of establishing a kind of populist legitimacy, much as reformers sought to embrace forms of direct democracy during the crisis of institutional legitimacy at the close of the nineteenth and early twentieth centuries. Whereas policy textbooks once called congressional enactment the "legitimation stage," Congress has lost so much public confidence in recent years that alternative forms of legitimation have become more attractive. Thus, the increased volatility of policy in recent years may be evidence in itself of the shift from pluralist and party politics towards the expert and symbolic forms.

At the same time, old policy dogs have proven adept at learning new tricks. In attempting to maintain control over issues that are important to them, interest groups have been going beyond traditional methods of interest representation and adopting techniques borrowed from political parties, expert, and symbolic politics.[53] Thus, the big growth areas of interest group activity in recent years have been grass-roots organizing, coalition formation, and media marketing.[54] Although many groups have a long history of participation in party politics, they have become increasingly sophisticated actors in the electoral arena. They contribute soft money for "party-building" efforts, run ads during election campaigns, and inform and mobilize voters. On the ideational tracks, groups hire their own experts, create their own think tanks or mobilize counterelites, and seek to play in the realm of symbolic politics by mounting independent media campaigns and issue advocacy drives. Thus, tobacco companies successfully fought off recent antismoking legislation with a major ad campaign that focused on the negative symbols of government interference and excessive new taxes, quickly killing a bill that had previously seemed certain of adoption. Political parties have also gone the ideational route, building links to their own think tanks and using the techniques of symbolic manipulation, as exemplified by the Contract with America.

In sum, looking back over tax policy developments over a period of a dozen years, we still believe that the 1986 Tax Reform Act should be viewed as exemplifying a style of political mobilization in which deference was paid to experts and their ideas, aided by ardent policy entrepreneurs and close media attention, as well as more traditional forms of political leadership. TRA86 may be joined with other legislation, perhaps most particularly airline deregulation, as demonstrating the viability of a "new politics of reform."

But the same changing political environment that permitted such "expert" politics has also facilitated the development of another political style, which we term "symbolic"—and which may, indeed, eclipse it. Such symbolic politics also relies on "ideas," but they often are not ideas to which a broad spectrum of experts would be willing to lend support and many often oppose. Rather, they are ideas tailored for their popular acceptance, devised more for public relations value than for technical effectiveness and efficiency. As Eric Patashnik observes in his analysis of the evolving politics of budget policy in chapter 2 of this volume, "it is not only the ideas of policy elites . . . that shape policy; popular symbols and beliefs matter also." He cites columnist Robert Samuelson's apt phrase that we have seen a "reassertion of folk wisdom over professional economics."[55]

The growing prevalence of idea based politics in general and symbolic politics in particular has implications for the "regime of moderation" outlined in chapter 1 of this volume. As we argue in *Taxing Choices,* idea based politics of both the symbolic and expert varieties provide an important avenue for nonincremental—and presumably nonmoderate—policy changes. Regarding TRA, we said that its astonishing adoption showed that "our governmental system has acquired new potential for surmounting the political obstacles of organized interests and bridging the seemingly unbridgeable gaps between separated institutions and divided parties."[56] Similarly, the deregulatory drive of the late 1970s, which had been built upon decades of work by serious researchers, was "within a very short time . . . transformed from a lonely cause with poor political prospects into a buzzword and a bandwagon. . . . Just as everyone in 1956 was in favor of defense, everyone in 1980 was in favor of deregulation."[57] This was ultimately a virtue, to Derthick and Quirk as to us, because it showed the American political system "working well," to be "capable of innovation," and "able to overcome particularism."[58]

The symbolic pathway holds the potential for making large policy changes as well—changes that in some cases might well be called immoderate. Political symbolism can be used to advance ill-considered ideas as well as thoroughly grounded ones; it can crucially determine the content of legislation, not just tuck and tailor its nomenclature or lesser features, and it can be used to oppose as well as to support far-reaching change. The forces of symbolism can be mobilized by the relatively ignorant as well as the seemingly enlightened, and by the privileged as well as the dispossessed. Its consequences are often surprising, leading to unexpected or rapid changes in the fate of initiatives that come under its influence—and subject to rapid decay, when the spotlight of attention turns away. Thus, symbolic politics is inherently unpredictable, which raises the possibility that a regime of moderation could be quickly and unexpectedly upended, as nearly occurred on more than one occasion during the 1990s.

Though it originated with the civil rights, consumer protection, and environmental movements of the 1960s and early 1970s, this pattern of symbolic politics has become increasingly important and more widely utilized. Some twenty-five years ago, James Q. Wilson—perhaps our keenest observer of political trends—commented that the growth of these "purposive" organizations might mean that

> leaders capable of producing concerted action on the basis of
> ideas [will become] more important. But only a few such lead-
> ers will succeed in institutionalizing their influence. . . . Their

importance in politics will thus be *episodic* and *limited* to those few policy areas that can be made the target of aroused passion. Meanwhile, other associations with their allied government agencies, immune for the moment from passion or purpose, will continue to maintain control over [their] policy domains . . . . One who wishes to describe "the policy making process" will be free to choose either the language of stasis or turmoil, interest or ideology, depending upon where he allows his gaze to fall.[59]

In this, as in so much else, Wilson was right. But the proportions have changed drastically over the intervening decades. The influence of what we have called "symbols" is now less episodic, less limited than formerly, and "aroused passions" are more commonplace. Indeed, they—as much as particularistic economic or social interests, partisan organizations and loyalties, and the ideas of experts—are a key component of the contemporary American political system.

Some observers might conclude otherwise, but we would hold with Mary Ann Glendon, who views what she terms the impoverishment of political discourse with alarm: "When political actors resort to slogans and images rather than information and explanations, they hinder the exercise of citizenship."[60] Linked with a distrust of government and an animosity toward taxation and perceived or real tax inequities, the multiplicity of pathways to power and especially the growing importance of symbolic politics has helped give tax issues a degree of prominence, volatility, and inconsistency that they typically lacked prior to the late 1970s. To a considerable degree, all traditional actors and forms—lobbyists, party politicians, bureaucrats, and tax experts—have suffered diminished influence as a result. So, too, in many ways, have the coherence of tax policy itself and the well-being of the public at large.

Notes

1. C. Eugene Steuerle, *The Tax Decade: How Taxes Came to Dominate the Public Agenda* (Washington, D.C.: Urban Institute Press, 1992).

2. In contrast, during the 1950s, 1960s, and 1970s, there were typically only two or three major tax bills each decade. See Michael J. Graetz, *The Decline (and Fall?) of the Income Tax* (New York: Norton, 1997), 86, 87.

3. The most detailed account is Timothy J. Conlan, Margaret T. Wrightson, and David R. Beam, *Taxing Choices: The Politics of Tax Reform* (Washington, D.C.: CQ

Press, 1990). See also Timothy J. Conlan, Margaret T. Wrightson, and David R. Beam, "Policy Models and Political Change: Insights from the Passage of Tax Reform," in *The New Politics of Public Policy*, ed. Marc K. Landy and Martin A. Levin (Baltimore: Johns Hopkins University Press, 1995), 121–142.

4. Ibid., chap. 1.

5. Sheldon D. Pollack, *The Failure of U.S. Tax Policy: Revenue and Politics* (University Park: Pennsylvania State University Press, 1996), 132–133.

6. Martin M. Shenkman, *Investment Strategies after the New Tax Act* (New York: Wiley, 1994).

7. Conlan et al., *Taxing Choices*, chapter 9.

8. The paths listed in Figure 4.1 cover the types we have observed in contemporary tax policymaking, but they are not meant to be an exhaustive listing. As other chapters make clear, another policy path is centered around the courts, whose lead actors are lawyers and judges and whose method of coalition building is equally unique. Still, a great deal of high-profile litigation involves legislation where the "symbolic" content is unusually high.

9. John F. Witte, *The Politics and Development of the Federal Income Tax* (Madison: University of Wisconsin Press, 1985), 244–245. For a recent analysis of the politics of tax expenditures, see Christopher Howard, *The Hidden Welfare State: Tax Expenditures and Social Policy in the United States* (Princeton, N.J.: Princeton University Press, 1997).

10. Stanley S. Surrey, "The Congress and the Tax Lobbyist: How Special Tax Provisions Get Enacted," *Harvard Law Review* 70 (May 1957): 1145–1182.

11. Sheldon D. Pollack, "The Politics of Taxation: Who Pays What, When, How," paper prepared for delivery at the 1998 Annual Meeting of the American Political Science Association, Boston, September 3–6, 1998, 13.

12. Pollack, *The Failure of U.S. Tax Policy*, 264.

13. John B. Bader argues that legislative party leaders often have played a more important role than generally recognized. See his *Taking the Initiative: Leadership Agendas in Congress and the "Contract with America"* (Washington, D.C.: Georgetown University Press, 1996).

14. Steuerle, *The Tax Decade*, 41.

15. Timothy J. Conlan, *New Federalism: Intergovernmental Reform from Nixon to Reagan* (Washington, D.C.: Brookings Institution, 1998), 114.

16. Ibid., 137. See also Graetz, *The Decline*, 124–126.

17. George Hager and Eric Pianin, *Mirage: Why Neither Democrats Nor Republicans Can Balance the Budget, End the Deficit, and Satisfy the Public* (New York: Random House, 1997), 223.

18. Graetz, *The Decline*, 120.

19. Pollack, *The Failure of U.S. Tax Policy*, 95.

20. Hager and Pianin, *Mirage*, 127.

21. Pollack, *The Failure of U.S. Tax Policy*, 118–120; Graetz, *The Decline*, 162–170.

22. Graetz, *The Decline*, 174.

23. This lack of principle in many specific bills and among legislative enactments is a major observation and concern of Pollack.

24. James Q. Wilson, ed., *The Politics of Regulation* (New York: Basic Books, 1980), 372.

25. John W. Kingdon, *Agendas, Alternatives, and Public Policies* (Boston: Little, Brown, 1984), 131. See also Deborah A. Stone, *Policy Paradox and Political Reason* (Glenview, Ill.: Scott Foresman, 1988), 25.

26. Daniel P. Moynihan, "The Professionalization of Reform," *The Public Interest* 1 (Fall 1965): 6–16.

27. Samuel H. Beer, "Federalism, Nationalism, and Democracy in America," *American Political Science Review* 72 (March 1978): 17.

28. See the masterful study by Martha Derthick and Paul J. Quirk, *The Politics of Deregulation* (Washington, D.C.: Brookings Institution, 1985).

29. On the latter see David M. Ricci, *The Transformation of American Politics: The New Washington and the Rise of Think Tanks* (New Haven, Conn.: Yale University Press, 1993), and James A. Smith, *The Idea Brokers: Think Tanks and the Rise of the New Policy Elite* (New York: Free Press, 1993).

30. See Joseph A. Pechman, "Erosion of the Individual Income Tax," *National Tax Journal* 10 (March 1957). Summaries of key reform proposals appear in Joseph A. Pechman, ed., *A Citizen's Guide to the New Tax Reforms: Fair Tax, Simple Tax, Flat Tax* (Totowa, N.J.: Rowman & Allanheld, 1985).

31. Steuerle, *The Tax Decade,* 59–60. See also Pollack, *The Failure of U.S. Tax Policy,* 93–96.

32. Pollack, *The Failure of U.S. Tax Policy,* 120.

33. Janet Hook, "House Passes GOP Proposal to Kill Tax Code," *Chicago Sun-Times,* July 18, 1998, p. 26.

34. The following discussion draws on Timothy J. Conlan and Steven L. Abrams, "Federal Intergovernmental Regulation: Symbolic Politics in the New Congress," *Intergovernmental Perspective* 7 (Summer 1981): 19–26.

35. This discussion borrows from David R. Beam, "If Public Ideas Are So Important Now, Why Are Policy Analysts So Depressed?" *Journal of Policy Analysis and Management* 15 (1996): 432.

36. Steuerle, *The Tax Decade,* 40.

37. Bill Peterson, "Billions in Days: Frenzy on the Hill," *Washington Post,* June 28, 1981, p. D5, quoted in Conlan, *New Federalism,* 119–120.

38. Conlan et al., *Taxing Choices,* 80.

39. Ibid., 245.

40. Douglas R. Sease and Tom Herman, *The Flat-Tax Primer* (New York: Viking, 1996), 19–20, 26.

41. Ibid., pp. xiii–xiv.

42. Maureen Dowd, "There's Something about Bill," *New York Times,* August 2, 1998, p. 15.

43. Witte, *The Politics of Development of the Federal Income Tax,* 244.

44. See Theodore J. Lowi, "American Business, Public Policy, Case Studies and Political Theory," *World Politics* 16 (1964), and "Four Systems of Policy, Politics and Choice," *Public Administration Review* 32 (July–August 1972): 298–310; James Q. Wilson, "The Politics of Regulation," in Wilson, *The Politics of Regulation;* and Paul E. Peterson, Barry G. Rabe, and Kenneth K. Wong, *When Federalism Works* (Washington, D.C.: Brookings Institution, 1986).

45. See Witte, *The Politics of Development of the Federal Income Tax,* 207–217.

46. For detailed analyses of the subsystem concept, see Douglass Cater, *Power in Washington* (New York: Vintage, 1964); J. Leiper Freeman, *The Political Process,* rev. ed. (New York: Random House, 1965); and Randall B. Ripley and Grace A. Franklin, *Congress, the Bureaucracy, and Public Policy* (Homewood, Ill.: Dorsey, 1976).

47. Christopher J. Bosso, *Pesticides and Politics: The Life Cycle of a Public Issue* (Pittsburgh: University of Pittsburgh Press, 1987), 10–11.

48. Eugene Eidenberg and Roy D. Morey, *An Act of Congress: The Legislative Process and the Making of Education Policy* (New York: Norton, 1969), 75, 96, 145.

49. Ibid., 95.

50. Conlan and Abrams, "Federal Intergovernmental Regulation," 19–26.

51. For an insider's account of this process in the case of welfare reform legislation, see David T. Ellwood, "Welfare Reform as I Knew It: When Bad Things Happen to Good Policies," *American Prospect* 26 (May–June 1996).

52. For more discussion of these political changes, which Hugh Heclo has termed "hyperdemocracy," see C. Eugene Steuerle, Edward M. Gramlich, Hugh Heclo, and Demetra Smith Nightingale, *The Government We Deserve: Responsive Democracy and Changing Expectations* (Washington, D.C: Urban Institute Press, 1998), chapter 5.

53. Concerning the counterattack by business, see David Vogel, *Fluctuating Fortunes: The Political Power of Business in America* (New York: Basic Books, 1989), especially chapter 8.

54. Kay L. Schlozman and John T. Tierney, *Organized Interests and American Democracy* (New York: Harper & Row, 1986), 155–157.

55. Robert J. Samuelson, *Washington Post,* May 7, 1997.

56. Conlan et al., *Taxing Choices,* 260.

57. Derthick and Quirk, *The Pollicies of Deregulation,* 53.

58. Ibid., 257.

59. James Q. Wilson, *Political Organizations* (New York: Basic Books, 1973), 344; emphasis added.

60. Mary Ann Glendon, *Rights Talk: The Impoverishment of Political Discourse* (New York: Free Press, 1991), 173.

PART III

Rights Policies

5

Immigration Reform Redux

Peter H. Schuck, *Yale University*

What a difference a year makes—or does it? Immigration policy was utterly transformed in 1996 by new legislation—or was it? My account of immigration politics in *The New Politics of Public Policy* (*NPPP*) has thus been overtaken by events—or has it?[1] My analysis there of the role of ideas in immigration policy is therefore wrong— or is it?

As usual, the truth is much more complicated. To explain why, I must first review the bidding. After summarizing the argument that I advanced in *NPPP,* I describe the events of 1996 that did indeed re-shape immigration policy. I then discuss how these events affect the explanatory power of the analysis that I offered in *NPPP* and which refinements of that explanation seem warranted by these recent de-velopments. Finally, I speculate about the future of immigration policy.

My Argument in *NPPP*

In *NPPP,* I sought to describe and explain a remarkable, far-reach-ing national policy development: the enactment of the Immigration Act of 1990 (which has come to be called IMMACT90). This law, which culminated a decade of exceedingly high-salience immigra-tion politics, was decidedly expansionist. It not only increased au-thorized legal immigration levels by more than 35 percent a year for the indefinite future; it also provided for the legalization of certain categories of previously illegal Cuban and Haitian aliens whose status had remained more or less in limbo for a decade.

I found this expansive immigration policy counterintuitive and thus striking for several reasons. IMMACT90 was adopted at a time of economic recession in the United States, which has historically been associated with immigration restriction. This was also a time in which almost all other immigrant-receiving countries, particularly the European Community states, were in the grip of restrictionist public moods actively exploited by right-wing nativist-nationalist parties. Even Canada, whose admission policies have by some measures been even more liberal than those in the United States in recent years, was having serious second thoughts about these policies. The new law culminated a decade of Republican control of the executive branch and of growing conservative strength in key receiving states like California. The White House, often more proimmigration than Congress, had evidenced little interest in immigration legislation and even less policy initiative or leadership on the issue. A decade of hard-fought battles on immigration reform had left the key policymakers in Congress feeling weary and bloodied; along with Social Security and Medicare policy (but for quite different reasons), immigration reform was widely viewed as a "third-rail" issue, as a "Vietnam of domestic politics" that offered few rewards and much punishment for the foolhardy politicians who chose to take it on. The leaders of the relevant legislative committees, moreover, had not changed much, and the congressional agenda was congested with bitterly contested budgetary and other issues that promised to leave little time for controversial immigration measures. A vigilant, well-connected restrictionist lobbying group, the Federation for American Immigration Reform (FAIR), was lying in wait, eager to derail any expansionist initiatives. Finally, opinion polls then (and now) invariably revealed public concern about immigration and a desire for less of it.

Given these formidable obstacles to immigration expansion, how could I explain the passage of IMMACT90? My explanation included a standard pluralistic account in which organizations gathered information, defined their interests, formed alliances, bargained with other organizations and politicians, sought media coverage, and so forth. This rational choice, interest group model, I argued, could satisfactorily explain much of the expansionist character of IMMACT90. For a variety of reasons, the political perceptions, strategies, and influence exercised by the major interest groups—the growers, business alliances, labor unions, ethnic organizations, human rights advocates—had changed during the 1980s in ways that did indeed seem to shift the balance of power in an expansionist direction. In particular, the unions—the major restrictionist force—had suffered serious political and economic losses, while business interests favoring increased immigration for needed skills and wage competition had prospered during the decade.

Other factors also helped explain IMMACT90's expansionist shape. Class action litigation in which courts constrained the authority of the Immigration and Naturalization Service to deport certain groups of aliens, including large numbers of Central American workers and Chinese students seeking asylum, generated pressure to resolve their cases on a categorical basis by legalizing their status. Political entrepreneurs in both the House and the Senate mobilized both grassroots and elite support for expansion, used creative logrolling to satisfy different groups by authorizing more visas, and skillfully exploited immigration-related symbols. These efforts and other developments succeeded in imparting to immigration issues a much higher profile and salience during the 1980s

But while these interest group and entrepreneurial factors seemed capable of explaining much of what transpired, I suggested, they could take us only so far in explaining how a measure like IMMACT90 could have been enacted under conditions as unpropitious for immigration expansion as those mentioned earlier. Some of these explanatory factors, after all, might as readily militate in favor of immigration restriction or the status quo, not expansion. For example, one might have expected the heightened salience of immigration during the 1980s to galvanize popular fears about high levels of immigration. Liberal court rulings often generate a strong conservative backlash, which in the immigration case would have supported restriction. Political entrepreneurship, especially on the part of rural state conservatives like Alan Simpson, has more commonly created anti-immigration coalitions, not expansionist ones.

What put IMMACT90 over the top, I maintained, was the political mobilization of *ideas*. I acknowledged that because ideas, which I defined as the "values and other generalizations that frame our understanding of the world," simultaneously perform a number of different roles in politics, it was a daunting methodological challenge to distinguish empirically between ideas that are merely epiphenomena of the interest groups that deploy them instrumentally and ideas that may alter political consciousness and hence political outcomes *autonomously*—that is, quite apart from the fact that one or another interest may seek to exploit them tactically. Ideas, I noted, may even obscure the "real" interests that so often lie beneath them. Their relationship is particularly opaque because when interests make their political appeals, they almost always invoke ideas, and not just power; they seek to legitimate their claims by grounding them in a broad public interest justification that transcends (and hopefully masks) their self-interest. At the same time, more disinterested purveyors of ideas (editorial writers, policy professionals, academics) cannot describe their ideas without referring to special or general interests, for ideas (at least policy-relevant ones) necessarily specify changes in the state of the world affecting those interests. Finally, any effort to ascribe an independent causal role to ideas carries the danger of reductionism noted by Peter Hall.[2] That is, the analyst may resort to this causal power of ideas in a desperate effort to bolster weak explanatory theories, using them as an all too convenient tool for explaining the remaining variance in ways that are difficult to operationalize and thus to refute.

Because of the significance of immigration-expanding ideas to my political interpretation, let me take the liberty of quoting from that portion of my earlier chapter that briefly explains and summarizes my argument:

> Ideas can precede interests as well as advance them. They not only help political actors to fulfill their existing political agendas; they also affect how those actors construct their agendas in the first place. Ideas can alter how people perceive the world, decide what to value, and organize to attain it. In this way, they redefine ends and means and may even supply new ones. Immigration politics in the 1980s exemplifies this independent causal role of ideas. Certain distinctive notions about immigration and its effects propelled the reform impulse in directions that were more expansionist than interests, entrepreneurship, and events alone would have dictated.
>
> Among the most important ideas shaping the political debate were the following. Global competition strategy and immigration policy ought to be tightly linked. Ethnic diversity in the United States population should be confirmed and extended. Family unification should continue to be a paramount value. Illegal migration poses a serious threat to social stability and equity. This threat must be reduced before legal immigration is expanded.

Human rights should constitute a major, permanent component of United States immigration policy. The job skills required by the economy and those supplied by domestic workers were seriously mismatched, which immigration policy could and should cure. Civil liberties, civil rights, and due process norms should govern the law's treatment of aliens, even illegal ones. The social benefits of expanded immigration could be achieved at little or no cost.[3]

Seeking to abstract from these specific ideas to the more general uses that are made of them in immigration politics, I identified five such functions: coalition building, belief changing, symbol mobilizing, regime reinforcing, and dissonance reducing. These functions, of course, are intimately intertwined in the real world.

The Road from 1990

IMMACT90, of course, did not end the immigration policy debate; no single law ever does. Still, I argued in *NPPP* that the mix of political forces that shape immigration policy—interests, ideas, external conditions, and the like—had shifted in fundamental respects and that these shifts not only reinforced the high levels of legal immigration that the 1990 law had authorized but also would make it difficult if not impossible to reverse this expansion. Insofar as legal immigration was concerned, the motley coalition of proimmigration forces had effected a new national consensus; they had managed to construct a kind of political ratchet that established a new base capable of resisting future retrogression—at least in the absence of a major economic downturn.

The political history of immigration reform since 1990 appears to confirm my analysis. Despite a number of dramatic developments since 1990 that would seem to have strengthened the political position of the restrictionists, their vigorous assault during the last Congress on the legal admissions system established by IMMACT90 was singularly unsuccessful. This is not to deny that the restrictionists made some gains. In 1996, as discussed below, they succeeded in overhauling the enforcement provisions of the Immigration and Nationality Act (INA), the basic immigration statute, thereby strengthening substantially the INS's authority to swiftly remove aliens who violate the INA. In addition, the 1996 welfare reform law made noncitizens, whether legal immigrants or not, ineligible for a wide range of public cash and service benefits. But welfare reform was supported by a diverse coalition, its strictures applied to citizens as well as aliens, and its purpose was to reduce welfare dependency, not to reduce the number of legal immigrants. Indeed, the public's sympathy for legal immigrants was demonstrated when pressures from the public and from politicians from both parties and at all levels led Congress to restore the eligibility of aliens legally in the United States in August 1996 for many of these benefits. These same pressures caused major immigrant-receiving states to fill in some of the remaining gaps in coverage.

At the end of the day, then, the basic structure of expanded legal immigrant admissions that Congress established in 1990 remained in place and the widespread political support for legal immigrants was reaffirmed. But this outcome was by no means predestined. A tortuous path led from IMMACT90 to the present, a path strewn with perils for immigration advocates favoring the 1990 system and with political opportunities for restrictionists.

The first major threat to the 1990 consensus occurred during the 1992 election campaign, when presidential candidate Pat Buchanan vigorously attacked the new law, with its increased visas and diversity quotas, as a disastrous compromise of Americans' national sovereignty, political identity, and ethnic coherence. Buchanan's views on immigration, however, were linked rhetorically to his condemnation of the North American Free Trade Agreement (NAFTA); the latter position attracted more support than the former.

In the 1994 election campaign, immigration became a central issue in a number of high-immigration states. In California, Governor Pete Wilson made Proposition 187 a centerpiece of his re-election bid. This referendum measure, which proposed to bar illegal aliens from most state-funded social services including public schools, was politically explosive and received enormous media attention not only in California but throughout the country.

The political symbolism and significance of Proposition 187 is not easy to gauge because it was targeted at illegal aliens rather than legal immigrants (although the latter, along with U.S. citizens, would surely be affected by its enforcement). The number of illegal aliens entering California had indeed increased, returning to or surpassing the levels that prompted Congress to adopt employer sanctions in the Immigration Reform and Control Act of 1986 (IRCA), and illegal aliens' use of welfare and social services, especially public hospitals and schools, had increased correspondingly. Wilson's efforts to denounce illegal aliens while praising legal ones did not always succeed in maintaining the distinction and many voters, responding to subtly coded language (the state was being "flooded" by illegals) and provocative images (e.g., Proposition 187 opponents waving Mexican flags), doubtless overlooked it. In the election, Proposition 187 was supported not only by a solid majority of white voters but also by a substantial number of blacks and Latinos, many of whom felt threatened by the influx of illegal aliens who competed with them for jobs, housing, and public services.

Proposition 187–type measures were proposed in other states and adopted in some. Emboldened by Proposition 187's success in California, similar measures were proposed and in some cases adopted in other states. A federal court injunction, however, blocked implementation of the bellwether Proposition 187.

Even before Proposition 187, immigration had become a high-stakes issue for many Republican candidates, but its adoption by a clear majority increased the pressure on them to take public positions on immigration-related issues. This was easy insofar as undocumented workers were concerned; politicians could denounce them at no political cost. But when the question was whether legal immigrants should be denied access to public benefits, the political costs of appearing unsympathetic to them might be greater. After all, many of them would become voters, many of their friends and relatives already were voters, and as a group they enjoyed much support from the general public, whose ancestors were immigrants and who still resonated to the immigrant mythos.

Although the "Contract with America" that helped Republicans win control of Congress in the 1994 off-year election said little on the subject of immigration, restrictionists within the party—especially from some members of its California and Texas delegations—quickly brought immigration issues to the surface. Lamar Smith, a Texas Republican opposed to the high immigration levels authorized by IMMACT90, became chairman of the House immigration subcommittee and scheduled hearings on a variety of immigration reform measures, including proposals to eliminate birthright citizenship for the U.S.-born children of illegal aliens. The Republicans, joined by some Democrats, began moving restrictionist measures through the committees.

These initiatives precipitated deep divisions within the Republican party. On the one hand, restrictionists cited the electoral success of Proposition 187, the popularity of several new books urging severely reduced or even zero-immigration policies, worrisome environmental and demographic trends, welfare abuses by some immigrants, multicultural excesses, a rapid increase in the number of criminal aliens, and other considerations suggesting that anti-immigration positions would be good politics for Republicans as well as sound public policy. On the other hand, many of the party's leaders fervently opposed restriction. Ideological visionaries like Jack Kemp, William Bennett, and William Kristol held that such positions violated the party's deep commitment to free markets, economic growth, and entrepreneurial optimism. Speaker Newt Gingrich spoke glowingly of the contributions that immigrants make to American society. Majority Leader Richard Armey, a libertarian, advocated expanded immigration. These party stalwarts also invoked realpolitik against the restrictionists. Pointing to the Republican leanings of Cuban and many voters from former Iron Curtain and Asian countries, they predicted future Republican gains with other immigrant groups as well if the party could project a proimmigrant image. The voters, they warned, would punish candidates who were seen as hostile to immigrants. These warnings were not heeded. Indeed, the restrictionists in Congress saw new political opportunities in the plunge of the peso, the administration's unpopular fiscal bailout of Mexico, and the continuing increase in illegal migration across the southern border. The Republican-dominated immigration committees in both houses supported legislation that would substantially strengthen INS enforcement authority.

The Transformation of 1996

As the 1996 presidential campaign intensified and Pat Buchanan pressed his nativist ideology in the early primaries, these fissures in the Republican party over immigration widened. In April, the national outrage over the Oklahoma City bombing prompted an immediate, bipartisan response in Congress: the Anti-Terrorism and Effective Death Penalty Act of 1996 (AEDPA). This law contained a number of very stringent criminal enforcement provisions, some of which were aimed at the swift detention and removal—with limited or no opportunity for administrative relief or judicial review—of most asylum seekers and of aliens who had been convicted of crimes in the United States or could be linked to terrorist activity, broadly defined. Congress lifted some of these provisions wholesale from the pending immigration reform bills that had been slowly percolating through the immigration committees when the Oklahoma City catastrophe occurred. These new provisions, however, dealt with the exclusion or deportation of aliens who had violated the immigration laws. None of them was directed at the number or categories of legal immigrants or the system for admitting them.

At their conventions, both parties sought to resolve their conflicts over immigration policy without alienating voters. They did so by focusing on the need for stronger border enforcement, the swift deportation of illegal aliens and criminal aliens, elimination of immigrant abuse of the welfare system, and the like. The Republican platform went beyond these conventional, uncontroversial pieties by also calling for the elimination of future birthright citizenship for the U.S.-born children of illegal aliens, a highly controversial proposal. Even here, however, the party did not call for a reduction in legal immigration.

In August, Congress enacted the welfare reform law, the Personal Responsibility and Work Opportunity Act of 1996. Over the strong objection of President Clinton, who generally supported the law, Congress eliminated the eligibility not only of illegal aliens but also of legal immigrants—except for refugees and asylees in their first five years in the United States, those who had worked in the United States for at least ten years without claiming public assistance, and military veterans—for a wide range of public benefits including Aid to Families with Dependent Children (AFDC), Supplemental Security Income (SSI), and Food Stamps. These restrictions were projected to save more than $22 billion over five years, a substantial fraction of the deficit reductions associated with welfare reform. Nevertheless, Clinton immediately vowed to seek restoration of SSI benefits, at least for already-arrived legal immigrants, and he was supported in this effort by many Republican governors and mayors who feared the state and local fiscal effects of losing the federal benefits and therefore pressed Congress to restore them, which it subsequently did.

In late October just before the election, Congress suddenly enacted the most radical reform of immigration law in decades—or perhaps ever. The Illegal Immigration Reform and Immigrant Responsibility Act of 1996 (IIRIRA) thoroughly revamped the enforcement provisions of the basic immigration statute; it not only incorporated the changes wrought by AEDPA in April but went well beyond them, adopting many of the reforms that the restrictionists had been advocating. Briefly, the new provisions authorized the INS to exclude aliens summarily at the border, made asylum claiming more difficult, limited or eliminated the various forms of discretionary relief that were previously available to aliens, eliminated judicial review of many important INS enforcement decisions, mandated detention of many removable aliens, ended the distinction between exclusion and deportation, enhanced penalties for immigration violations, limited reentry rights for removed aliens, further broadened the category of "aggravated felon" aliens whose rights are severely limited, and made numerous other changes designed to facilitate the exclusion and prompt removal of immigration law violators.

The 1996 reforms should be viewed as a kind of counterrevolution in immigration law. Congress decisively (and in the judicial review provisions, perhaps unconstitutionally) repudiated the liberalization and "proceduralization" of immigration law that the courts had nourished since the early 1980s. Once again, however, the aspect of these changes that is most revealing of the political support for immigration is that they leave legal immigrant admissions policy essentially intact. I do not mean to deny, of course, that the new law will affect some legal aliens. For example, it requires that aggravated felons be detained and bars them from seeking discretionary relief from removal even if they are long-term legal residents. It also toughens the eligibility standards for sponsoring new legal immigrants and makes it easier for the INS to exclude poor ones. Nor am I asserting that Congress will not restrict legal immigration in the future. An economic recession would certainly strengthen the hands of restrictionists, and the final report of the U.S. Commission on Immigration Reform (the so-called Jordan Commission) proposed some reduction in immigration levels and changes in the legal immigration structure that will give ammunition to at least moderate restrictionists. Nevertheless, a decade of relentless criticism and reform of an immigration system widely decried as feckless and permissive has not caused Congress to surrender to the strident demands to restrict the liberal legal admissions policy established by IMMACT90.

The Role of Ideas in Immigration Policymaking, Redux

As we have seen, a lot has happened since 1990 that one would have expected to give aid and comfort to immigration restrictionists. Why, then, have they been unable to exploit these opportunities more effectively? Why have they had to limit themselves to the politically easy project of cracking down on illegal and criminal aliens and asylum seekers rather than reducing the numbers and the ethnic diversity of immigrants entering the United States legally, which is their chief aim? And what light does this pattern, most notable in 1996 and 1997, shed on the power of one part of the explanation—the political functions of immigration-expanding ideas—that I underscored in *NPPP* for the restrictionists' earlier failure in 1990?

At least four answers to these questions are possible. First, I might have been wrong in *NPPP*. There are, of course, a number of different ways in which I could have been wrong. Perhaps immigration-expanding ideas did not in fact play the large role in shaping IMMACT90 that I ascribed to them, or perhaps those ideas did indeed play that role in 1990 but were not structural or embedded enough to play the same role in the years that followed. Second, perhaps I was right about the role that these ideas played in 1990, but the dominant, policy-shaping ideas have changed since then. Third, perhaps I was right about their role in 1990, but the interest group politics changed thereafter, altering the decisive mix of interests and ideas. Finally, perhaps the political outcomes in 1990 and 1996, although similar at one level, were at another, deeper level sufficiently different that different explanations may be called for.

I believe that the truth lies closest to some combination of answers 2, 3, and 4. That is, I was not wrong about the role of ideas in 1990 but some of the ideas affecting immigration policy have changed since then, certain interests have become more salient and powerful, and the policy-relevant ideas about immigration have acquired a new resonance in the light of these changes in the political context. Let me elaborate.

Different Ideas

In a policy field as empirically dynamic and normatively controversial as immigration, there is every reason to expect that the congeries of ideas that (along with interests and events) inform and drive decision makers will change over time. Indeed, such change is in the nature of the market for policy-relevant ideas because, first, the real-world phenomena to which they refer—migration flows, economic conditions, social values—are themselves in flux, even though the rates of change vary and are sometimes too slow to service the needs of impatient policymakers. Second and more interesting, the producers, distributors, and consumers of policy-relevant ideas (these categories overlap, of course) all have an incentive to refine old ideas, combine them in fresh ways, and come up with new ones. Producers such as academics and writers are always searching for something fresh to say; for better or for worse, novelty (so long as it is not demonstrably wrong) is the name of their (our) game. Much the same is true of idea distributors such as media and many government officials, including politicians and political appointees. Ideas that are new—more precisely, ideas that *seem* new (in fact, virtually all "new" ideas have circulated in the public domain in some form and are now being recycled)—are also more likely to catch the attention of idea consumers (the general public and officials), and their attention, of course, is always one of the most precious commodities in politics and is increasingly so.

In 1990 the zeitgeist included a number of important immigration-friendly ideas, which I summarized at the beginning of this chapter. Perhaps the dominant one was the notion that expanding legal immigration was a costless, unequivocal good from which American society and immigrants gained and no one, even low-income domestic workers, really lost. Needless to say, this was a politically attractive idea. Drawing on the work of economist Julian Simon, the editorial page of the *Wall Street Journal,* and other purveyors of this view, industry and ethnic organizations with an interest in increasing immigration pushed it hard. The timing also coincided with the celebration of the hundredth anniversary of the Statue of Liberty and the opening of the new Ellis Island immigration museum. Both events advanced another, cognate idea—that immigration and ethnic diversity had enriched American society immeasurably.

By 1996, these ideas had been eclipsed, although certainly not effaced, by two others. These were hardly novel ideas; indeed, they were as old as the immigration debate itself. But they were now clothed in new garb, promoted by new entrepreneurs (notably, Ross Perot and Patrick Buchanan in 1992 and 1996), and possessed a new political salience. The first of these ideas was the notion that there are good immigrants and bad immigrants, and that the bad ones today are much worse than the earlier waves of immigrants were. When Professor Alex Aleinikoff identified the good immigrant/bad immigrant dichotomy as an important theme of immigration politics in the mid-1980s, the bad immigrants whom he saw being stigmatized were primarily illegal aliens and asylum seekers.[4] These two groups continue to be major foci of immigration enforcement; the 1996 law substantially limited their procedural rights and increased the sanctions against them. But they have now been joined by three other groups, which include many who are permanent legal residents. These are criminal aliens, immigrants on welfare, and nonassimilating immigrants.

Criminal Aliens

The story of how the criminal aliens problem and the policy response evolved is a fascinating and complex one that I (and a coauthor) relate elsewhere.[5] Some bare statistics, however, can help to illustrate the rise in public attention to this problem in recent years. Roughly 75 percent of foreign-born inmates are estimated to be deportable aliens, not citizens. In 1980, there were fewer than one thousand foreign-born inmates in federal prisons, about 3.6 percent of the total federal prison population. By 1988 the number had risen to more than ten thousand (representing 21 percent of that population), and by 1996 the total was almost thirty-one thousand (29 percent). The dynamic was much the same in the state prisons: in 1980 there were eight thousand foreign-born inmates (2.6 percent of their total), while in 1996 the total had grown to seventy-seven thousand (7.6 percent). Foreign-born inmates account for fully 21 percent of California's prison population and 13 percent of New York's. We estimate that in 1996 more than 290,000 deportable criminal aliens were in custody or otherwise under law enforcement supervision nationwide, almost ten times as many as in 1980, occasioning apprehension, custodial, and supervision costs totaling as much as $6 billion each year. Yet even after substantial progress in the last few years, the INS manages to remove well under 20 percent of those already in custody or under law enforcement supervision.

Given the size and trajectory of these numbers, it should come as no surprise that the politics of immigration policy during the 1990s came to be dominated by the idea that criminal aliens posed an enormous social threat and drain on public resources and that they should be mandatorily detained and expeditiously removed. Indeed, the only surprise is that this idea was not more central to policymakers before then and that even now it has not been effectively implemented. Congress had expressed concern prior to 1990 about aliens who commit crimes in the United States and had pushed the INS to act more aggressively to deport them, but it became far more interested in the problem—indeed, the word *obsessed* is not too strong—in the 1990s when the failure of its earlier, largely procedural efforts became manifest with the dramatic increase in the number of criminal aliens in and out of custody. As for the implementation failure, it appears to lie in a federal-state division of responsibility that creates disparate and even inconsistent incentives for officials at different levels of government.

Immigrants on Welfare

Since 1990, much new research has been published on the declining skill levels of many immigrants relative to both earlier immigrant cohorts and natives, with whom they seem to take longer to reach parity.[6] In addition to this work of immigrant "quality," research has also documented the growing use of welfare and public services by immigrants. This research is controversial and difficult to summarize, but it tends to show that although immigrants in the aggregate do not use welfare benefits more than natives do, certain immigrant subgroups use welfare more—sometimes far more—than natives. George Borjas's work on immigrant dependency on welfare has been particularly influential in the policy debate during the last few years, as has the research by the General Accounting Office showing that elderly legal immigrants used SSI at very high rates despite the express commitment of support from the families who sponsored their admission.[7] Responding to this information, Congress in 1996 imposed severe limits on most immigrants' eligibility for public benefits and sought to make the sponsors' support commitments more demanding and enforceable.

Nonassimilating Immigrants

Today, the immigration stream is more racially, ethnically, and linguistically diverse than ever before. Of the ten top source countries, only the Philippines and India have large numbers of English speaking nationals. During the 1990s, bilingual education has become a major curricular battleground in public education, and teaching in dozens of languages has become necessary in many urban school systems. The growing politicization of ethnicity and widespread attacks on the traditional assimilative ideal have magnified long-standing anxieties about linguistic, cultural, and social fragmentation.

These anxieties, which are felt by many on the left (e.g., Arthur Schlesinger) as well as on the right, have led legislatures and public referendums to establish English as the official language in approximately half the states and to support proposals like Proposition 187 to limit the rights of aliens. Many of the newer groups also qualify for affirmative action programs, which has exacerbated tensions among the groups and with American blacks and has further aggravated concerns about national disunity and resistance to cultural integration. Popular commentators like Peter Brimelow, alarmed by projections that Hispanics will soon become the largest minority and that whites may lose their majority status by midcentury, have even argued that the new groups are unwilling and incapable of assimilating to a white, Anglo-Saxon Protestant culture.[8]

The force of this "bad immigrant" idea has been increased by allying it politically to another idea that has become increasingly salient since 1990, one that has supported an argument against the admission of even *good* immigrants. This was the notion that even if immigration does benefit American society and even if those benefits far exceed the costs, the *distribution* of the benefits and costs is unfairly and perversely skewed. Critics have focused on two maldistributions—between levels of government, and between immigrant and native workers—which have become more prominent and salient since 1990.

Intergovernmental Mismatch

First, an acute fiscal mismatch exists between the federal government and state and local governments. Most of the costs of public benefits and services that legal and illegal aliens use (two-thirds, according to state government estimates) are borne by state and local governments, while most of the taxes (again, an estimated two-thirds) paid by those aliens go to the federal government. (The states and localities, however, tend to ignore the likelihood that most of the other economic benefits that aliens generate are received by the local communities in which they live and work.) In the case of illegal aliens, the federal government enjoys a further fiscal advantage; the workers pay Social Security taxes but do not ordinarily claim Social Security benefits. This mismatch between cost bearers and tax receivers became a subject of bitter intergovernmental dispute in the last decade, and the lobbying efforts of state and local governments led directly to Proposition 187, to a spate of state lawsuits against the federal government seeking reimbursement, and to Congress's enactment of an unfunded mandates law in 1995 and its 1996 welfare reform provisions excluding most legal immigrants from eligibility for most public benefits.[9]

Harm to Native Workers

The maldistribution idea also extends to that between native and immigrant low-skilled labor. Opponents of immigration, of course, have always maintained that low-skill immigrants take jobs away from native-born workers, and contemporary restrictionists such as the Federation for American Immigration Reform (FAIR) continue to make this claim. But even though such an effect seems plausible, even self-evident, economists were not able to prove it convincingly; indeed, some would say that they still have not proved it. During the 1990s, however, prominent labor economists began to demonstrate some negative effects of immigration on both the jobs and wages of low-skill native workers, particularly blacks, effects that may have been masked in earlier work by reduced native worker mobility into high-employment labor markets. George Borjas, Richard Freeman, and Lawrence Katz,[10] for example, have attributed to low-skill immigration a significant share of the notorious wage gap between high- and low-skilled workers that seems to have widened since the 1970s, while others have shown that immigrants and natives do not work in different labor markets, thus undermining the common notion that immigrants take only the jobs that natives do not want and will not take. These studies and others, including an influential 1997 report by the National Research Council, buttressed the arguments in favor of the 1996 law's effort to strengthen enforcement against illegal aliens, who compete disproportionately in the unskilled labor market.[11]

In the post-1990 immigration policy debates, then, we can observe a phenomenon that can be found in many other policy domains as well. Under the pressure of events and shifting priorities, political actors annex old ideas and issues to new, renovated, or recycled ones. These ideas and issues often take on a different, amplified resonance and salience in the new context than they had before. Sometimes it is possible to predict these changes in political support, sometimes not. (For example, few would have predicted the spate of anti–managed care legislation in the face of diffuse consumer sentiment and powerful insurance and hospital interests.) In the immigration case, several familiar notions—that immigrants were not simply a costless, wealth-generating amenity but could disadvantage low-income Americans, that the quality and assimilability of immigrants were declining over time, and that the federal government had treated state and local governments unfairly by exploiting a maldistribution of fiscal benefits and costs—became somewhat sharper and more compelling than they had been in the debate over IMMACT90.

Conclusion: The Future of Immigration Politics and Policy

The prospects for increasing legal immigration look very bright. Indeed, barring a serious recession, current levels of legal immigration may operate as a floor, not a ceiling. (Recall that the expansive IMMACT90 was enacted not during a period of economic growth but during the last recession.) The political dynamics within the Republican party on immigration issues is an important force for stability, if not expansion, in legal immigration. Many GOP influentials, who watched with alarm as their party flirted with restrictionist and even nativist political rhetoric in 1994 and 1996, are now outspoken in the view that this course is misguided, futile, and politically self-defeating. Exhibit A in their brief is Pete Wilson's stunning defeat in his reelection bid, a loss widely attributed to his perceived animosity toward immigrants and one that has terminated a once-promising political career. Exhibit B is the success of Republican mayoral candidates' electoral appeals to first—and second-generation Asians and Hispanics in Los Angeles and other cities.

Exhibit C, certainly the most revealing, is the decidedly proimmigration, prodiversity plank in the 2000 Republican party platform. This is hardly surprising as an electoral tactic. The demographic profile of the United States, especially in the key states of California, Texas, New York, New Jersey, and Florida, is one of large and growing immigrant populations with younger and larger-than-average families, high intermarriage rates, and increasing voter registration and political participation. More and more Republican politicians have concluded, with President George W. Bush, that there are more votes to be gained in supporting immigration at more or less current levels (which also appeals to the party's traditional business interests) than in opposing it, and that the party's future success may lie in effectively exploiting the social conservatism and entrepreneurial spirit of many immigrant groups. Bush has assiduously, ostentatiously (he and his Mexican-descended wife speak Spanish on the hustings), and in Texas successfully, courted Hispanic voters, and he is also wooing Asian Americans. Since Al Gore maintained the traditional Democratic party support for immigration, the 2000 presidential campaign turned into a bidding war for the support of recently immigrating ethnic groups. Significantly, Congress has recently enacted several amnesties for hundreds of thousands of undocumented workers from Latin America.

Another important harbinger of future immigration policy is the strong support by both parties for substantial increases in the number of skilled specialty workers, mostly in the computer industry, an effort spearheaded by former senator Spencer Abraham, a Republican. In 1998, he persuaded Congress to expand the H-1B program, which had previously authorized the annual admission of 65,000 such workers for periods of up to five years, to authorize 115,000 of these "temporary" visas for 1999–2000. In 2000, Congress again raised the ceiling—this time to 195,000 a year. (The restrictionist Center for Immigration Studies predicts that in fact this change will result in more than three hundred thousand new H-1B admissions annually.) Many of these workers will eventually adjust their status to that of permanent resident and then become citizens, assuming that the INS can reduce its enormous backlogs of adjustment petitions. At the same time, the permanent employment-based visas enlarged by IMMACT90 have been underutilized, again largely because of INS administrative mismanagement. In a sense, then, the employment-based visa program as a source of permanent skilled workers is gradually being replaced by a much-enlarged H-1B program, which has far greater political support.

Finally, the effect of the 1996 welfare reform, which limited access to benefits not just for immigrants but for American citizens, has changed the terms of the immigration debate. This reform will weaken, if not eliminate, two related restrictionist arguments that have had great political resonance in the past: that many immigrants come to the United States not to be productive members of society but to live off the taxpayers, and that they are not assimilating to core American values of independence and industry. Whether or

not that was true in the past—the evidence is mixed and much depends on what one makes of the numbers—it is hard to see how it
could be true in a world in which few if any new immigrants are eligible for benefits and almost all are employed.

Notes

1. Peter Schuck, "The Politics of Rapid Legal Change: Immigration Policy in the
1980s," in *The New Politics of Public Policy*, ed. Marc K. Landy and Martin A.
Levin (Baltimore, Md.: Johns Hopkins University Press, 1995), 47–87.

2. See, for example, Peter A. Hall, ed., *The Political Power of Economic Ideas:
Keynesianism across Nations* (Princeton, N.J.: Princeton University Press, 1989).

3. Schuck, "The Politics of Rapid Legal Change," 51.

4. T. Alexander Aleinikoff, "Good Aliens, Bad Aliens, and the Supreme Court,"
in *In Defense of the Alien: Proceedings of the Annual National Legal Conference on
Immigration and Refugee Policy, Vol. 9*, ed. Lydio F. Tomasi (New York: Center for
Migration Studies, 1986), 46.

5. Peter H. Schuck and John Williams, "Removing Criminal Aliens: The Pitfalls
and Promises of Federalism," *Harvard Journal of Law and Public Policy* 22 (1999):
367–463.

6. See, for example, George J. Borjas, *Friends or Strangers: The Impact of
Immigrants on the U.S. Economy* (New York: Basic Books, 1990).

7. Ibid.

8. Peter Brimelow, *Alien Nation: Common Sense about America's Immigration
Disaster* (New York: Random House, 1995).

9. Interestingly, the 1996 welfare reform law, even after the restoration of benefits
to pre-August 1996 permanent resident aliens, has in some ways exacerbated this
intergovernmental conflict rather than remedying it. By restricting aliens' access
to federal benefits, the law in effect forces states and localities to defray the costs
of indigent aliens through their general assistance and other programs, which are
politically unpopular. And although the 1996 law bars the states from providing
certain benefits to some aliens who are not legal permanent residents, they must
continue to provide certain other benefits. These include the very costly
Medicaid program, significantly expanded in 1997, to certain favored categories
of aliens such as veterans, refugees, and those who have worked in the United
States for more than ten years. The major immigrant-receiving states have responded by restoring some of the benefits Congress eliminated.

10. George J. Borjas, Richard B. Freeman, and Lawrence F. Katz, "How Much
Do Immigration and Trade Affect Labor Market Outcomes?" Brookings Papers
on Economic Activity (Washington, D.C.: Brookings Institution, 1997): 1–90.

11. National Research Council, *The New Americans: Economic, Demographic, and
Fiscal Effects of Immigration* (Washington, D.C.: Author, 1997).

6

Republican Efforts to End Affirmative Action

Walking a Fine Line

John David Skrentny, *University of California, San Diego*

Members of the Republican party have told the American people that affirmative action preferences and quotas[1] for racial/ethnic minorities and women are wrong, and they have tried to eliminate any government support for preferences, both from the White House and the Congress. Polls indicate wide public support for antipreference efforts. These efforts, however, have not succeeded. All successes in ending affirmative action preferences have been local, nonpartisan, or court ordered.[2]

Republicans have had many opportunities to end affirmative action, which began its current race-conscious form in the late 1960s.[3] Richard Nixon was both the "father of affirmative action"[4] (he institutionalized and expanded the policy) and the first Republican critic of racial quotas, Ford maintained Nixon's expansions, Reagan's administration tried but failed to rescind the policy while presiding over further expansion, and Bush sought only to limit expansion. Republicans took control of Congress in 1995, talked often about ending preferences, but accomplished almost nothing toward that goal in the 1990s. Republican George W. Bush, elected president in 2000, mostly avoided race issues in his campaign.

This failure is surprising for several reasons. First, the policy benefits groups that one would expect to have meager political power. Afro-Americans,[5] Latinos, Asian Americans, Native Americans, and women are the primary intended beneficiaries of the policy, and few would argue that they constitute a political elite in the United States. These groups are proportionally underrepresented in positions of power, such as corporate boardrooms and the upper echelons of both major political parties.[6]

Also, the resilience of preferences is surprising given that extraordinary circumstances and effort were required to gain even "color-blind" nondiscrimination rights for minorities,[7] and many of the activities that now occur and are labeled affirmative action were political taboos in 1964 and 1965, when the civil rights movement achieved its greatest successes. Legislators wanted Afro-American equality but many were very concerned about preventing racial quotas or preferences, and Title VII of the Civil Rights Act of 1964, prohibiting discrimination in employment, appears to be written so that race or gender preferences or quotas would not be allowed. Legions of conservative commentators and some neutral observers agree that preferences go beyond and contradict what Congress intended with Title VII.[8] Much of what is practiced in the name of affirmative action has no clear statutory basis, and many argue that some programs are unconstitutional.

Furthermore, public opinion polls suggest that the public is on the side of Republicans on preferences. The evidence here is far from uniform—a 1995 CBS/*New York Times* poll showed that as many as a third of Euro-Americans do not even know what affirmative action is, and polls that simply ask whether the public favors "affirmative action" tend to find the public evenly divided.[9] However, questions asking about support for preferences for blacks in hiring and university admissions "because of past discrimination" find Euro-Americans consistently and overwhelmingly rejecting the policy. The numbers vary between 82 and 90 percent opposed for questions on hiring from 1986 to 1994, and from 68 to 76 percent rejection in admissions for those same years. The strength of the economy has no discernible effect on percentages opposed.[10] Other polls find similar results.[11] Focus groups and interviews with working- or middle-class Euro-Americans have also found great anger and resentment over race preferences.[12] Despite this potential public support and rhetoric expressing opposition, Republican presidents and Republican Congresses have not ended affirmative action preferences.

The resilience of affirmative action provides a useful test case for the "new politics" themes of this volume. In the following pages, I briefly describe some recent theories on policy retrenchment and elimination. I then use these ideas and the new politics themes as guides for examining the case of affirmative action. I will focus on the 104th and 105th Congresses (1995–1998), where some of the strongest attempts to end preferences have occurred. Secondary sources are buttressed by interviews conducted in 1998 with several Republican congressional staff members and two leaders of conservative civil rights think tanks.[13]

At first glance, affirmative action politics is quintessential old politics. A race- or gender-conscious, preferential affirmative action survives partly because there is no lobbying push to eliminate it. Preferences have low salience for most Euro-Americans, who apparently are not being victimized (or are not aware they are being victimized) by reverse discrimination in large numbers. The regulated businesses are similarly not demanding an end to preferences, and many support them. Republicans are united on the principle of color- or gender-blind law, but most do not want action on the issue. On the other side, program beneficiaries and many Democrats strongly resist retrenchment.

In addition to a lack of "push," however, there are also factors that work as barriers to action and barriers to Republican unity, and these resemble the themes of this volume.[14] The primary barrier to action that is the Republicans want to avoid blame or a negative public image for being unfair, harming minorities, or damaging race relations in the United States. Affirmative action preferences, though not a right, also are buoyed by their close relationship to civil rights laws. These factors give affirmative action supporters their power. While there are strategies to overcome the barriers to retrenchment, thus far Republicans have not shown confidence they can succeed.

Eliminating Policies and Programs: When Is It Possible?

One model of policy rescinding is based on a prominent model of policy making: James Q. Wilson's theory of the political significance of policy cost and benefit distributions.[15] This approach helps explain why there is no demand for policy elimination, even when public opinion supports elimination. The key is the perception of relative concentration or diffusion of a policy's costs and benefits. If a policy's benefits are seen as concentrated, the beneficiaries will believe it worthwhile to fight for the policy, and if that policy's costs are diffused, individuals who pay will find those costs so small that resisting a policy's formation or pushing for its retrenchment is not worth their effort. While losing an opportunity because of a racial preference can cause an individual great pain, the *chance* that a particular Euro-American male would lose an opportunity is small, so affirmative action preferences would seem to fit the model. Though the concentrated benefits–diffuse costs pattern does not explain the great difficulty in developing affirmative action, it is certainly relevant to affirmative action's resilience. Republicans have encountered fierce resistance from civil rights groups, while representatives for the class of white males, presumably the group bearing the costs, have been absent from the struggle.

However, even without lobbying pressure, conservative political elites may move to eliminate policies that are at odds with their ideology. Paul Pierson examined strategies of retrenchment in the cases of the Reagan and Thatcher administrations and welfare policy (defined broadly), arguing that success in retrenchment will be affected by the nature of the policy in question.[16] Policies vary to the extent that they create "lock-in" effects (long-term government commitments, such as Social Security), create high-visibility retrenchment (especially those that offer cash benefits), offer opportunities to divide or weaken the opponents of retrenchment, or (following Wilson) create interest group activity. To understand the failure to eliminate affirmative action programs, then, we must look at the nature of the policy itself: How could retrenchment occur? Would Republican actions produce visible pain? Are there lock-in effects? How does the framework of affirmative action preferences shape interest group activity? Could Republicans divide opponents?

A second study of elite-directed policy retrenchment is Derthick and Quirk's analysis of the successful deregulation of the airline, telecommunications, and trucking industries.[17] They identify several important factors in explaining the success of an effort that occurred despite the powerful forces being opposed. Among the most important was that elite opinion, in both government and the academic world, converged on the idea that reform was desirable. There was agreement across party lines and across disciplines. Second, officeholders in leadership positions took initiative in advocating reform. Last, because some early economic commission and court decisions on deregulation had unsettled the business climate, and because industry leaders were poorly coordinated, the trucking, telecommunications, and airline industries offered limited response. An important lesson for the affirmative action case is the need to look at the role of elites, especially party leaders—was there consensus on a commitment to reform, or division? Furthermore, we need to examine the strategy of regulated industries and the advocates for minority groups—how and why did they respond as they did?

The Nature of the Policy

Republican efforts in affirmative action politics have generally concentrated on eliminating racial and gender preferences and quotas. It is very difficult to describe the "preferences and quotas policy" because government regulations do not specify or mandate preferences or quotas. But many of the regulations do indeed *suggest* preferences and quotas and are very clearly "difference-conscious," and there is much contention over their meaning.

The preeminent affirmative action program has its legal basis in an executive order of the president. Lyndon Johnson signed Executive Order 11246 in 1965, declaring there would be no discrimination in employment in the federal government and by federal government contractors on the basis of race, religion, and national origin, and requiring "affirmative action" to ensure nondiscrimination. The order created an Office of Federal Contract Compliance (OFCC) in the Labor Department that would wield the power to cancel the contracts of noncomplying firms. In 1967, Johnson amended the order to include sex discrimination.

The OFCC's 1969 "Philadelphia Plan" created affirmative action regulations that many in Congress believed required quotas: firms competing for lucrative federal construction contracts would have to promise "good-faith" efforts to hire predetermined percentages of minority workers in specified occupations within specified time periods ("goals and timetables" became the shorthand). In 1970, the OFCC expanded the goals and timetables of the Philadelphia Plan to all government contractors with its "Order No. 4." Contractors with at least a $50,000 contract and more than fifty employees were to make efforts to "correct any identifiable deficiencies" in the utilization of minorities. Utilization was "having fewer minorities in a particular job class than would reasonably be expected by their availability." Order No. 4 required racial hiring goals and timetables, roughly based on "the percentage of the minority work force as compared with the total work force in the immediate labor area."[18] The ambiguity of the regulations has allowed a thirty-year debate: conservatives argue that a goal is really a quota, and nonmeritocratic preferences are required to meet the goal/quota, while liberals deny both claims.

Title VII of the Civil Rights Act of 1964 is also a part of affirmative action policy. Though it explicitly does not require hiring to achieve racial and gender balance, section 706 (g) of the title states that if a court finds intentional discrimination, the court may "enjoin the respondent from engaging in such unlawful employment practice, and order such affirmative action as may be appropriate." Though some believe the affirmative action should be limited to identifiable victims of discrimination, there are many cases in which courts have ordered quota hiring under authority of this title, and consent decrees have also had quota or preference requirements.

Title VII also created the Equal Employment Opportunity Commission (EEOC), which oversees enforcement of prohibition of discrimination in hiring and promotion. The primary mechanism of Title VII is color- and gender-blind; the EEOC investigates individual complaints of discrimination and attempts to conciliate. In late 1965, it began to require larger firms to submit the EEO-1 form, which records hiring data, separated by sex, for "white (not of hispanic origin)," "black (not of hispanic origin)," "Hispanic," "Asian or Pacific Islander," and "American Indian or Alaskan Native."[19] Finding the investigation of individual complaints to be an expensive, time-consuming, and often fruitless task, the EEOC began, in the late 1960s, to use the statistical patterns gathered from the EEO-1 forms to hold public hearings, asking firms with very low percentages of women and minority workers to explain themselves. In 1972, the EEOC gained the power to sue firms suspected of discrimination and sometimes used statistics as evidence of discrimination, usually (though not always) in addition to individual complaints. The EEOC also issues various rulings that sometimes advocate goals and timetables on such topics as ability testing, employee recruitment, and litigation-proof affirmative action plans.[20]

The federal government is, moreover, heavily involved in helping minority-owned businesses. The Minority Small Business and

Capital Ownership Development or "section 8(a)" program allows the Small Business Administration (SBA) to act as prime contractor with the government, and it subcontracts with "socially disadvantaged" firms. The SBA also offers special help with loans and surety bonds for disadvantaged groups. The SBA presumes that firms owned by blacks, American Indians, Latinos, and Asian Pacific Americans are eligible. The law states that nonminorities have to "establish his/her individual social disadvantage on the basis of clear and convincing evidence" to qualify. The "Asian Pacific Americans" category is inclusive, allowing special help for persons with ancestry from Cambodia, China, Guam, Japan, Korea, Laos, Northern Marianas, Philippines, Samoa, Taiwan, the U.S. Trust Territory of the Pacific, and Vietnam. From 1982 to 1989, the SBA added persons with ancestry from India, Tonga, Sri Lanka, Indonesia, Nepal, and Bhutan to the list (though it rejected Hasidic Jews, women, veterans with disabilities, Iranians, and Afghans). In addition, the Business Opportunity Development Reform Act of 1988 ordered annual, government-wide goals in contracting to include 20 percent for small businesses and 5 percent for socially disadvantaged businesses, and in 1994, the Federal Acquisition Act amendments added "small business concerns owned and controlled by women."[21]

Other preferences for minority capitalists exist. By voice vote, Congress established the contract set-aside program in 1977, earmarking 10 percent of a $4 billion public works bill for bidding by "Negroes, Spanish-speaking, Orientals, Indians, Eskimos and Aleuts." The set-asides have been included in appropriation bills in agriculture, banking, communications, defense, education, energy and water development, foreign relations, public works, scientific research, transportation, and space exploration, and they have spread to many state and city government procurement procedures. One important federal set-aside is the Inter-Modal Surface Transportation Efficiency Act of 1982 (ISTEA), which set a 10 percent goal for funds to go to "disadvantaged business enterprises." There is a presumption that firms owned by women and (some) minorities are disadvantaged. Though failure to achieve the goal by a state has not resulted in loss of ISTEA aid, states usually meet the goals. Set-asides allow government funds to go to firms that may not have been the lowest bidders on a particular contract.[22]

Affirmative action is also widely practiced in university and professional school admissions, and is often very clearly preferential. For the most part, these practices are voluntary, though in at least one case (California in 1974), the state legislature created laws to increase the percentage of minority students.[23] There are no federal pressures on university admissions, though the OFCC in the early 1970s put some pressure on universities to be more inclusive in their administrative and faculty hiring.

While usually considered a part of civil rights policy, there is technically no federal statutory "right" to affirmative action, as regulations specify groups and not individuals. The regulations that interpret and implement antidiscrimination laws and executive orders could be rescinded without changing the Civil Rights Act.

Policy Design and Avenues of Policy Retrenchment

How does the legal framework of affirmative action constrain retrenchment efforts? Compared to policies such as Social Security or economic regulation, retrenchment on affirmative action looks easy. There are no "lock-in" effects as in Social Security, no long term promises made on which citizens might be relying for their livelihood.[24] In addition, since affirmative action preferences at their most preferential and quota based have never guaranteed all minorities or women or even any particular individual a job or a government contract, beneficiaries do not know for certain that they have benefited, and could not know that any future blocked opportunities are the result of policy elimination. Ending affirmative action would thus not be as visible to the affected individuals in the same way that ending Social Security or Aid to Families with Dependent Children (AFDC) would be clear and individually devastating.[25] Leaving aside for the moment the issue of interest group activity, we can conclude that there is no inherent quality of affirmative action regulations that should make retrenchment especially difficult.[26]

Republican Congresses have failed to end affirmative action preferences, though they have made halting efforts. Almost immediately after the ground-shaking 1994 congressional election, where Republicans took both houses of Congress, Clint Bolick of the conservative Institute for Justice began developing the bill that became the Equal Opportunity Act of 1995, also known as the Dole-Canady bill, named after new Senate Majority Leader Robert Dole (R-KS) and Representative Charles Canady (R-FL). In the first several months after that election earthquake, President Clinton seemed irrelevant to national politics, and momentum for an antipreference bill was augmented by Republican presidential candidates' enthusiastic search for new issues.[27] In February 1995, Dole asked the Congressional Research Service for a report of federal programs that used racial and ethnic criteria; the results showed 160 different programs.[28] Republican candidates for president began public denunciations of affirmative action preferences and promised to end them. Dole, Governor Pete Wilson of California, and Senator Phil Gramm of Texas were the most outspoken critics of the policy. Even the centrist wing of the Democratic party, the Democratic Leadership Council (DLC), expressed doubts, with chairman Senator Joseph I. Lieberman of Connecticut saying, "We have to find another means" to equal opportunity, and "The current system cannot stand."[29]

Dole introduced his bill on July 10, 1995. It stated that the federal government could not "intentionally discriminate against" or "grant a preference to" "any individual or group based in whole or in part on race, color, national origin, or sex" in connection with federal contracts or subcontracts, federal employment, or "any other federally conducted program or activity." Wilson, aligning himself with the "California Civil Rights Initiative" (CCRI) campaign (a movement to put a referendum similar to Dole's bill ending race and gender preference on the 1996 California ballot), moved to end the executive basis of the policy in his state. Affirmative action seemed doomed.

Very quickly, however, momentum stopped, even reversed, and affirmative action dropped off the Republican agenda. Gramm tried to place Dole's bill as a rider onto an appropriations bill, but Dole resisted. Colin Powell, a black military hero whom many Republicans hoped would be Dole's running mate, gave prominent support to affirmative action.[30] By August 1996, Wilson had dropped out of the presidential race, and the Dole campaign was distancing itself from the CCRI. Newspapers told of anonymous officials close to the Dole campaign predicting (correctly) that "You won't even hear the word CCRI" in their campaign and that "People in the party are scared to death of the issue." Wilson's attempt to get a speaking slot at the Republican convention in San Diego for Ward Connerly, a leader in a successful effort to eliminate racial preferences at the University of California, ended in failure.[31] Powell spoke instead.[32] Though the CCRI referendum (renamed Proposition 209) passed in California,

Dole's antipreference bill, later named the Civil Rights Act of 1997, never made it out of committee.

Explaining Affirmative Action's Resilience, Part I: No Demand

The resilience of affirmative action regulations can be explained in part by standard political variables, especially the presence or absence of interest group activity. There is little public demand for ending affirmative action and little demand from business groups. In addition, the GOP is itself divided on affirmative action retrenchment.

The Public

There is almost no citizens' lobby for repeal of affirmative action in Washington. One staff member emphasized the point to me by reciting a long list of citizen group friends of Republicans who were silent on affirmative action, including the Family Research Council, Christian Coalition, other profamily organizations, property rights groups, low-tax groups, and on and on. There is simply no organized public demand for the repeal of preferences.

Since there is little demand, Republican officials have had to make their own case for reform. Their difficulty in doing so gives insight into *why* there has been so little demand for retrenchment. The diffuse costs of affirmative action to Euro-American males, assuming there are any, are very difficult to identify and measure. Though anecdotes abound, enforcement of the regulations has always been spotty at best.[33] Unlike other policies for which data are plentiful, no one really knows how widespread or "unmeritocratic" racial employment or contract preferences are, and without statistical indicators, it is hard to make a case that a problem exists.[34] The guidelines themselves, even at their most draconian, have only ever required a "good faith" effort to achieve some certain range of percentages of hiring certain groups. Consequently, many firms can get by with mainly symbolic compliance.[35]

Public opinion data also suggest that racial preference is a very minor problem in the lives of Euro-Americans, or perhaps even a "concocted controversy," to use Orlando Patterson's phrase. In a 1990 National Opinion Research Center (NORC) survey, only 7 percent of Euro-Americans asserted that they had personally experienced reverse discrimination, and only 16 percent said they knew someone who had. Less than 25 percent claimed that they had witnessed reverse discrimination or even heard about it at their workplaces. In addition, 70 percent of Euro-Americans believed their employers were doing "about the right amount to hire and promote Black, Latino, and Asian employees," as opposed to too much (8 percent) or too little (9 percent). Nearly identical majorities of Euro-Americans, Afro-Americans and Latinos, and men and women of all groups thought "about the right amount" was being done by their employers for women (varying between 69 and 74 percent).[36] Furthermore, when voters were asked to list their political priorities for the 1996 election, affirmative action was near the bottom.[37]

Given the diffuse costs of the policy, the lack of experience with the issue in Euro-Americans' daily lives, and its low priority, it is not remarkable that there is not a grassroots lobbying push for retrenchment. However, the issue cannot be completely dismissed. A 1990 NORC survey found that despite the lack of evidence and apparent low priority, there is an issue here and some incentive for Republicans to act: over 70 percent of Euro-Americans believed that they were *likely* to be hurt by affirmative action for Afro-Americans, and, as noted previously, even larger majorities think preferences are wrong.[38] Moreover, if there *is* very little minority or women employment preference occurring, this fact could benefit retrenchment efforts as there would be little visibility or harm to be exposed. The antipreference bill could be sold as a salve or insurance for Euro-Americans' worries, and it would not terribly harm minorities and women.

Business Elites

Business leaders are similarly not clamoring for retrenchment. Business groups are fragmented on affirmative action, as they are on many social and regulatory issues.[39] Many business leaders simply do not care, others fear an uncertain legal climate without the policy, and still others say they believe the policy is good for business.

A survey of CEOs of large corporations gathered 127 responses to a question regarding affirmative action procedures, and more than 90 percent said that "numerical objectives" in hiring goals were used partly to achieve "corporate objectives unrelated to government regulations." One hundred twenty-two of 128 said they would continue to use numerical goals to track progress of women and minorities in the corporation even if the government stopped requiring it.[40] Big Business support has continued through the 1990s. A spokesperson for the Business Roundtable's Washington office said in 1995 that "We feel diversity is critical" and explained that "CEOs think it's the right thing to do and it only makes sense."[41] In other words, affirmative action had become institutionalized, a taken-for-granted way of doing things, and had developed its own constituency in many large corporations.[42]

A neglected factor that contributes to preferences' low salience among business and conservative elites generally is that it is relatively cheap for firms and the government to administer. It is a regulatory response to the problem of inequality.[43] Contract set-asides may take business away from some nonminority firms, but not enough to cause a serious threat. For most business leaders, expensive and time-consuming paperwork and court battles are a more important problem than reverse discrimination.[44]

Nearly every Republican that I interviewed said that business groups were absent from the struggle over preferences in the Republican Congresses.[45] One staff member complained that business groups have been "pretty much AWOL"; another said (sounding like an early 1970s liberal) "big business is the enemy of the good." Clint Bolick observed that "business groups, particularly large business groups, have made their peace with preferences." Some also argued that business supports affirmative action for public relations purposes, or because antipreference political activity might be used against them in court if sued for discrimination. Roger Clegg, general counsel for one of those few organizations that is fighting to end affirmative action (the Center for Equal Opportunity), maintains that many firms, especially in retail, also worry about boycotts or a negative "grading" by the National Association for the Advancement of Colored People (NAACP).

The lack of salience among business and conservative citizens' groups suggests a possibility: do Republicans intentionally maintain the affirmative action preferences issue *as a symbol*, as a way of simply distinguishing themselves from the Democrats? Steven Teles has made a similar argument to explain the persistence of the old AFDC welfare regime, which existed for decades despite strong public opinion support (but little lobbying) for work requirements.

In "dissensus politics," Teles argues, "[i]ssues are sought for their symbolic moral value. A single aspect is focused on, and an issue is presented as a matter of acceptance or rejection rather than one of balance in light of other priorities. The issue is not important for its own sake or for the consequences for individuals that it will have but as an indicator of larger ideological patterns."[46]

Though Teles was discussing welfare politics in the 1970s and 1980s, Jennifer Hochschild has made a similar argument in regard to affirmative action and preferences. Pointing out the voluminous literature debating the policy coupled with very few serious empirical studies of affirmative action in practice and its effects, she argues that for political elites, "affirmative action is too valuable as a political weapon in a broader cultural war about what it means to be a good American to be diluted with attention to real-life complexities."[47] This is partly an indictment of academics but also of elected officials and their advisers, who criticize or defend affirmative action based on principles and not a data base. Similarly, after reviewing survey data (cited earlier) which shows how few Euro-Americans see themselves as victims of reverse discrimination, Orlando Patterson argued that "Euro-American fears about affirmative action are a largely invented problem, based in almost all cases not on actual experience but on hearsay, on the by no means disinterested preoccupation of the media on the subject, on the exploitation of the issue by unscrupulous politicians, and on the unrelenting attack on it by conservative intellectuals and pundits."[48]

While the idea that affirmative action is maintained as an issue for political reasons has plausibility, it is difficult to characterize the entire Republican party's relation to this issue in that way. The target of Patterson's ire was politicians who supported affirmative action but then flip-flopped when it appeared (briefly) to be a winning issue. It is clear from the conversations that I had that many are seriously and *morally* concerned about the principle of nondiscrimination, as will be discussed later. In this way, it is not only a symbolic culture war issue or only a rhetorical tool, but it may also be these things.[49]

Republicans Divided

In Derthick and Quirk's study, one of the most important factors in their case of policy elimination was unity among government elites that crossed party lines. This is clearly not the case with race and gender preferences. With a few exceptions, the Democratic party opposes the antipreference effort. Among Republicans, there is almost consensus on the *principle* of ending preferences, at least since Reagan. But on the crucial questions of whether to act, how, and when, Republicans are divided.

This division can be seen in Republican Congress since 1995. While Dole showed important leadership on the issue early on, he seemed to lose his nerve.[50] Both Dole and Gingrich used their power over the Republican agenda to prevent several attempts to use spending bills to end funding for affirmative action.[51] J. C. Watts of Oklahoma, the only Afro-American Republican in Congress after 1996, told the National Coalition of Minority Businesses that "Newt doesn't get credit as a supporter of affirmative action. He was instrumental in slowing the process and thereby saving affirmative action. If he hadn't, then affirmative action would have already been defeated."[52] Divisions continued into 1998. Neither new Senate Majority Leader Trent Lott nor House speaker Newt Gingrich were sponsors of the Civil Rights Act of 1997.

Republican staffers that I interviewed were of two groups: those that strongly supported the antipreference bill in principle and wanted action, and those that supported it in principle but were not interested in moving the bill. While much of what each group said was similar, the character and tone of the interviews were very different. The strong advocates for the antipreference bill emphasized the seriousness and distinctiveness of the issue and their commitment, while the others (more willing to speak on record) often downplayed the distinctive nature of the issue. Horace Cooper, press secretary for Republican House Majority Leader Dick Armey, explained, "There are many issues which have the support of a majority in the public. School prayer, tax relief, deficit reduction, et cetera, have long held majorities with the public. That fact alone hasn't translated into the enactment of these policies." Similarly, Pam Pryor of Watts's office maintained that there was a lot of support for the bill but that it was "an inopportune time" and that the "legislative process takes a long time." In the intraparty debate about preferences, Pryor said that the "people on the other side almost look at us as enemies," quickly emphasizing that "we are for the same thing." The difference is that for many in the GOP, preferences are not even in the top ten of priorities, while others are very passionate about the issue.

Though none of my interviewees mentioned it, there is little doubt that the "fiscalization" of public policy meant that GOP priorities were on higher-cost items.[53] The Republicans came into power promising to balance the budget, and they took much political heat on this issue. For example, Democrats successfully labeled efforts to slow down spending increases on programs such as federal aid for school lunches as program cuts, and some Republican staffers I interviewed mentioned this and the government shutdown in the fight over the 1996 budget as important momentum killers for Republicans. With momentum lost, other retrenchment efforts became more difficult. Since affirmative action was simply a set of regulations and cost very little relative to other programs, it could produce political damage while contributing little to a balanced budget, and remained a low priority with GOP agenda setters.

A final point on division: Derthick and Quirk found unanimity among economists and academic experts in other disciplines on the undesirability of the regulations that were rescinded. Though survey data are not available, such unanimity is obviously not the case with race and gender preferences. Between relevant academic disciplines and within them, there is the perplexing situation of great disagreement on the issue, often heated, and little empirical research to back up opinions.[54] Supporters of preferences wield expert citations and quotations to strongly support their views, and opponents do the same.

Explaining Affirmative Action's Resilience, Part II: Barriers to Retrenchment

A lack of grassroots lobbying and uncertain leadership limits the "push" for Republicans toward greater support of eliminating preferences. However, policies have been eliminated before without great public demand. A complete explanation of affirmative action's resilience must address *why* there is such halting leadership on the issue, and here the story ties in most clearly with the themes of this volume.

Even if lobbying support was present, I believe, leadership would be difficult and many if not most Republicans would still likely not support ending preferences. The primary barrier is the concern of appearing antiminority or, to put it more broadly, the concern of losing moral legitimacy. At times, this concern is expressed only in relation to minorities and tied specifically to votes; appearing racist to racial/ethnic minorities would obviously forfeit considerable minority vote potential. Concerns over appearing misogynist and exacerbating the "gender gap" with women voters is a related though lesser concern. But Republicans also appear to be concerned with their image before the *national* audience or are personally uncomfortable with the whole issue.

The resilience of affirmative action, then, is very much the result of a GOP desire for "blame avoidance,"[55] though to be more accurate, we need to acknowledge that they seek to maintain a positive image as much as avoid blame for a concrete policy result. Republicans do not want to be tied to or blamed for policies or even words that are perceived as mean, harsh, overly intolerant or, in the words of Levin and Landy's introduction to this volume, simply unfair. To some extent, affirmative action also seems to benefit from the moral power of civil rights.[56] Though affirmative action is not a right, its supporters equate it with civil rights enough that any distinction is often lost. Communicating good intentions in the face of countermessages sent by opponents, often in colorful language highlighted by the news media, is a daunting task on any issue, but perhaps especially difficult for affirmative action's would-be retrenchers.

Pierson found a fear of looking unfair, harsh, mean, or uncompassionate to be a factor affecting the Reagan administration's failure to achieve significant retrenchment in welfare policy, and these fears are present in affirmative action politics as well.[57] Affirmative action supporters can skillfully exploit these fears. It is individual politicians' perceived need for a positive moral image and blame avoidance that gives the civil rights groups their leverage. Furthermore, it is this moral issue that makes the variable of "visibility," addressed throughout this volume, an important factor. Republicans must walk a very fine line: tap into voter rejection of preferences, but do not alienate the overwhelming majorities that support "equal opportunity" (98 percent) and an equal chance for jobs regardless of race (97 percent).[58]

Civil rights lobbyists, advocates and sympathizers in Washington and throughout the United States, including the Leadership Conference on Civil Rights, the National Association for the Advancement of Colored People, the National Organization for Women, and various ethnicity or race-based groups watch affirmative action policy developments very closely and register dissatisfaction through letter writing, phone calls, press conferences, and press releases. They convince many Republican officials that retrenchment will be publicly branded as racist and evil, and encourage Democrats to take a stand. Especially notable here was President Clinton's July 19, 1995, speech at the National Archives, during the height of the anti–affirmative action momentum. Clinton declared, "Affirmative action has been good for America." Under pressure from civil rights groups, including a new political action committee made up of the nation's top one hundred Afro-American businesspeople, he explained that most affirmative action programs were fair and flexible, and then he uttered his oft-repeated, Jesse Jackson–esque slogan: "Mend it, don't end it."[59]

Fear of appearing unfair, antiminority, or anti–civil rights, discomfort at being tagged with similar unpleasant labels or more general concerns with party image were usually the first factors mentioned when I asked Republican staff members or think tank operatives why there has been difficulty ending affirmative action.[60] "[R]hetoric can really be manipulated by the other side," one staffer told me. The constant, stinging criticism can create "a really nasty environment in which to function." Another described "the problem of fear," where "they can call us racist[s], bigots." Affirmative action's defenders engage in what this staffer called "rhetorical terrorism." "[T]he fear of being called a racist or a misogynist" is key because this fear "paralyzes people." Bolick stated that "the main deterrent is that anyone who takes a forthright stand in favor of this [antipreference] legislation risks being labeled a racist . . . people understandably recoil from that kind of epithet." He argued that "Charges of racism are almost unique in American politics. It's the kind of label that beyond others, politicians seek to avoid." Even when a staffer dismissed the significance of the racism charge when I asked about it in a specific question ("[Democratic/liberal operatives] are always going to say that, and someone in the press is going to repeat it"), successful communication was still of great importance ("the problem is how that message is going to get carried into some of these communities"). Many Republicans believe that their party's legitimacy on minority issues is already fragile. As one staff member put it colloquially, Republicans "think they have baggage on the race issue." Another argued that women and minorities already think the GOP is against them, an image this staffer found offensive. Moving against preferences would make this situation worse.

The media play a big role, of course, in maintaining the visibility of retrenchment efforts, a fact often noted with palpable frustration by Republicans. The critique of the media is a familiar refrain coming from conservatives on other issues, and it was invoked on affirmative action politics as well. Roger Clegg explained that the "media [are] inclined to report on this area in a way that makes politicians very uncomfortable when they are on the conservative side. . . . It is the case that the media on most issues, on civil rights in particular, are liberal. . . . They slant the coverage in a way that makes people who oppose preferences come across as looking like bigots." Bolick complained that the media ignored congressional hearings featuring Euro-American victims of race preferences. One GOP staffer commented that the media are frequently an accessory to liberal causes, and the GOP has to work harder to "get the media to take our spin on things." Horace Cooper agreed, arguing that the "mainstream media serves as their [the civil rights activists'] echo chamber."

While appearing racist was to be avoided in and of itself ("no one runs on a platform as a bigot"), some Republicans more specifically calculate electoral consequences of appearing antiminority, anti–civil rights, or racist. In a winner-take-all electoral system, politicians must build broad-based majority coalitions. Many Republicans are very concerned about the party's image specifically in the minority community and the striking aversion that the majority of Afro-Americans show toward them. Most see and want to build on vote potential among Latinos and Asian Americans. One staff member argued that it was unwise to repeal preferences in an election year because the Republicans did poorly among Latino voters in 1996, even among Latino Republicans. Though ending preference is "the right thing to do," Republicans "have not gained back enough of the PR ground"; ending preferences "may be something that hurts us so much that we may not be able to recover enough in four years" (for the presidential election).

Why are image politics, fairness, and blame avoidance such salient concerns in this case? Affirmative action may be unique among minority or civil rights issues, and policy issues in general. It is true that public image and information campaigns always matter in modern politics, and terrain is perceived as especially perilous on issues outside of civil rights, as shown in this volume's chapters by Teles and Prinz on welfare, Schuck on immigration, and Derthick on Social Security. The key is the ease with which one side can demonize and thus delegitimize the other; this is clearly more difficult on complex economic policy issues, such as deregulation, or where it is difficult to draw a causal chain connecting the policy to a particular real-world outcome.[61] Affirmative action, however, highlights GOP vulnerability on race issues, and affirmative action may be special among race issues. The public perception of the GOP as the antiblack party began in 1964, and, as discussed previously, this has made party leaders especially timid on affirmative action.[62] Clinton's surprisingly strong stand in defense of the policy did not hurt the Democrats and prevented Republicans from gaining the credibility on the issue that was created on welfare after Clinton sounded a very different message ("end welfare as we know it"). In the latter case, Clinton significantly changed the meaning of the policy and created political opportunity for Republicans, which they seized almost immediately. Meanwhile, the antipreference bill languished.[63]

Furthermore, affirmative action regulations may have a special place in race politics because they apply to so many aspects of life. A Republican staffer who wanted delay on the issue pointed out that what distinguishes affirmative action and the antipreference bill is they "can apply in so many ways." Whereas school, housing, voting, and civil rights issues are relatively specific, affirmative action can go in so many areas, so a party's stance on it shows how it overall views race, and retrenchment says to minorities, "They don't want you in." Affirmative action also creates more diligent interest group activity than other minority policies. Bolick felt that affirmative action preferences were the most difficult of Afro-American–oriented policies to eliminate because there is a large "'diversity' industry" that depends on those programs, while racial gerrymandering for Afro-American political representation only benefits politicians, and "race-balance programs in the public schools are such an obvious disaster that they have little constituency as well."

The Republican attitudes described earlier contrast starkly with the case of Pete Wilson in California, so far the most important site of Republican affirmative action elimination. Wilson ended all California preferential programs within his discretionary authority, he did so in the state with the most affirmative action–eligible residents in America, and he bragged about it loudly and frequently.

Wilson's success highlights two factors. First, California provided a different policy context; Wilson was building on the great voter popularity of Proposition 187, a referendum that denied government benefits to illegal aliens.[64] Second, Republican inaction can be understood as the result of what Wilson Carey McWilliams refers to as the two-tier polity, where policy elites in Washington have their interests, goals, and thus politics shaped by the high density of interest groups in the top tier, cutting them off from the reality of the mass of American citizens in the second tier.[65] In this view, Republican leaders' inaction is based on a top-tier *perception* of the consequences of acting.

Along these lines, Bolick argued that very few Republicans would be defeated because of an antipreference bill, and he put the blame on "a skewed perspective inside the beltway." Yet it is difficult to change such perceptions. One staffer pointed out that Proposition 209 won more votes than Bob Dole did in California, arguing that this and Pete Wilson's actions show that the issue is "not as perilous as Republicans think if it is conducted in the right way." This staff member explained, however, that it is difficult to convince congressional Republicans to support the antipreference bill because they believe they know their districts or states better than an outsider. They could argue that the California case, unique because of its high numbers of both Latinos and Asian Americans and the Proposition 187 politics, may not translate to other states.[66]

Political Strategies to Maintain Image and Avoid Blame

Guided by some the "new politics" variables, extrapolating from work by a variety of scholars,[67] and noting other possibilities, one can identify some strategies that—unless affirmative action supporters are especially vigilant—may be effective at mitigating bad public relations, avoiding blame and allowing for ending affirmative action preferences. Republicans have tried some of these (but not all), and any future success will likely come from one or a combination of them.

Minimize Visibility
Anything is possible if potential opponents do not know about it. A high-visibility strategy is to have a sweeping antipreference bill with hearings, publicity events, and lobbying. Low-visibility strategies would come at the issue more obliquely, such as in riders to appropriation bills or other amendments, decremental retrenchments, or other indirect attacks at the policy basis of preferences. Republicans have tried low-visibility strategies on some occasions, but they have largely failed.

Low-visibility amendments and riders have been crucial to much of the minority rights revolution and to some of the most controversial developments of the American administrative state.[68] Yet this strategy has not worked as well for conservative forces.[69] In March of 1998, Mitch McConnell (R-KY) sought to end one preference program with his amendment to the Intermodal Surface Transportation Efficiency Act (ISTEA). This amendment would have required use of ISTEA funds for encouragement of and outreach to minority- and women-owned businesses, recruitment of businesses located in areas with a poverty rate of at least 20 percent or that use a workforce that is at least 50 percent from such a poverty area, but it would have prohibited preferences on the basis of race, color, national origin or sex in the use of those funds.[70] It seemed a propitious time for an amendment. In the wake of the Supreme Court decision *Adarand Constructors v. Pena*,[71] ISTEA's set-asides became subject to the strictest court scrutiny to pass constitutional standards. The Supreme Court remanded the case to a Colorado district court to make the determination of constitutionality; this court declared one part of the program's set-aside and its implementing regulations to be unconstitutional. Specifically, they were not narrowly tailored to further a compelling government interest. In response, the Department of Transportation proposed a modification of the implementing regulations, though the meaning of the new regulations was ambiguous.

McConnell attacked the various "diversionary tactics" of supporters of preferences, which included disregarding court decisions limiting preferences, claiming that new regulations have eliminated the unconstitutional aspects of the program, and insisting that the program used only a goal and not an unconstitutional quota. He encountered considerable resistance from fellow Republicans, who employed precisely these three tactics, supported by letters from President Clinton's Justice Department. In addition, Republican John McCain (AZ) argued that "the danger exists that our aspirations and intentions will be misperceived, dividing our country and harming our party."[72] Foreseeing a Clinton veto, Republican Christopher Bond insisted that he supported the principle of ending preferences, "But, I will not hold up $3.6 billion for my State of Missouri." The amendment effort failed, as a bipartisan coalition agreed to table it (the vote was fifty-eight to thirty-seven).[73]

Another low-visibility measure is a bill introduced by McConnell that would "establish a Federal cause of action for discrimination and preferential treatment in Federal actions on the basis of race, color, national origin, or sex."[74] The bill could make it easier for victims of reverse discrimination to bring lawsuits. Such a bill touches on preferences in a subtle, oblique way that might lower visibility and offers the possibility of attacking preferences while avoiding blame (discussed later).

Create a Favorable Policy Context
Republicans have tried to manipulate the policy context so as to mitigate the perception that the party is antiminority. The basic strategy is simple: policy initiatives that are clearly to the benefit of minorities and/or women can be propounded at the same time as the antipreference measures.

Congressional Republicans are slowly learning how to manipulate the policy context by creating a positive agenda for minorities to balance the antipreference moves. Newt Gingrich, in June 1997, began to talk seriously about moving ahead with the bill to end affirmative action, timing his comments for President Clinton's unveiling of his new panel to study race problems. Speaking to the Orphan Foundation of America on June 17, Gingrich stated a familiar conservative refrain, "We must make America a country with equal opportunity for all and special privilege for none by treating all individuals as equals before the law and doing away with quotas, preferences and set-asides in Government contract, hiring and university admissions." Gingrich's bold comments were grouped with a ten-point program to help black America. The program gave some old Republican ideas a new spin. For Afro-America, Gingrich advocated vouchers to help pay for private school, a reduction of regulatory barriers that make it difficult to start a business, tort reform, tax cuts, and expanded use of religious charities to operate social programs.[75] He soon dropped the idea, however, and the ten-point program is no longer discussed publicly.

A more direct way to mitigate the racism charge by manipulating the policy context is to put various prominority provisions in the antipreference bill. McConnell's failed ISTEA amendment did just this, by requiring an "outreach" program for minority- and women-owned businesses to take the place of the race and gender set-aside program, and encouraging contractors to employ persons from or locate in poverty-stricken areas. While the struggling Civil Rights Act of 1997 contained a section specifically permitting the government to use affirmative action in the sense of outreach to bring more qualified women and minorities into job applicant pools, discussion ensued among congressional staff in March 1998 to amend the bill to make such affirmative action a requirement.

Republicans with whom I spoke frequently stressed the importance of creating a policy context to preempt the racism charge. This positive agenda was stressed by Clint Bolick both in his 1996 book attacking affirmative action[76] and in his comments to me. The point is simple: Republicans need an alternative. One staff member complained to me that supporters of the antipreference bill "tend to use negative" appeals, neglecting to explain what they are *for*. This was important because "in politics if you [only] say what you're against it creates a negative image."[77] Similarly, others explained their reluctance to support the bill because of inadequate analysis and study of alternatives to preferences.

Controlling the Meaning of Antipreference Policy

Elsewhere I have argued that some affirmative action proponents used a "discourse of tradition" to advocate affirmative action in the late 1960s. That is, their arguments linked the new policy to standard practice and accepted moral rules, in effect denying that anything new or radical was being advocated.[78] Practitioners may refer to this as "spinning" an issue. However it is labeled, most Republicans believe an appropriate discourse is crucial to deflect charges of racism or inhumanity, and they therefore present their antipreference policies as squarely within the civil rights tradition.

It was taken for granted by Republicans in the 1980s and 1990s that to attack affirmative action, they must carefully avoid even the appearance of supporting the pre-1964 arguments against civil rights, such as property rights or states' rights, or arguments even hinting at Euro-American superiority. Republicans therefore mitigate criticism by stressing the idea that affirmative action is both discrimination against whites *and* an insult to blacks.

When Gingrich appeared on the CNBC show "Tim Russert," he stressed a prominority message connecting the idea of racial quotas to harm to blacks. "[Q]uotas and set-asides became the liberal excuse to avoid looking at the tragic failure of inner-city schools which are destroying young people," he claimed. Gingrich added a distinctive switch to the famous Lyndon Johnson metaphor of the unfairness of expecting a suddenly unshackled person to run a race with those never held back, which has long been (erroneously[79]) connected to liberal support for affirmative action: "[Black children] have an impediment, they have a burden . . . they're running a race with a weight on their back called the bureaucracy that's failing them."[80] Similarly, when McConnell introduced his antipreference amendment, he framed it in terms of Martin Luther King Jr.'s famous plea to have Americans judged by the content of their character and not the color of their skin.[81]

Some Republicans believe a few television appearances or speeches will not be nearly enough to get the correct meanings of the antipreference bill communicated through the thicket of the inside-the-beltway "top tier" and out to the people.[82] Representative Charles Canady reported in October that, in *Washington Times* reporter Nancy Roman's words, "the speaker [had] asked him to think of ways to promote the bill nationally—using grass-roots groups, think tanks and hard work—to make sure that they prepare the public before hitting them with an explosive race issue sure to be contentious on the House floor." Gingrich also said in a later speech that he had learned from the GOP's mistake on environmental regulation reform; the party looked simply antienvironment, which was politically costly.[83]

This "hard work" primarily means more repetition of the idea that ending preferences is not an immoral ending of civil rights. Such strategies are played out over and over in the effort to end preferences. The absolute necessity of a positive meaning to actions was a factor stressed by every Republican staff member or conservative intellectual I interviewed. Cooper explained, "People in general only get bits and pieces of information about what we do here in Washington. It's our job to make sure that the information they have puts Republicans and our ideas in their best light." He believed that such public relations was not unique to affirmative action, but most stressed the special nature of this issue. They perceived a need to avoid saying anything that might give "ammunition or fodder" for attacks on their effort. One staff member said that many Republicans in Congress agreed with the antipreference bill but "were unsure how to talk about the issue." Supporters for action on the antipreference bill agreed that "if rhetoric can be delivered in the appropriate way or spun correctly," then even candidates with large numbers of minorities in their districts could hold minority voters.

A most recent attempt to manipulate the meaning of the issue has been to gather information on the presumably wealthy beneficiaries of government contract set-asides. The argument can then be similar to the argument against welfare, which focused on "welfare queens" who did not work but cheated the system out of thousands of dollars. This argument—that affirmative action was corrupt—showed promise when Congress repealed a tax break given to companies selling broadcast licenses to minority-owned firms. A presumptively disadvantaged minority firm was prepared to pay a whopping $2 billion for a license, and the program was scrapped.[84] As Bolick stated, "Focusing assistance on the disadvantaged appeals to core American beliefs that we should give a helping hand to people who need it. It also supports the argument against racial preferences—if you switch to disadvantage-based affirmative action, the only people left out are those who are not disadvantaged. In 1998, no case exists to give special benefits to non-disadvantaged people."

McConnell has used a Government Accounting Office (GAO) study to attack contract set-asides as a waste of taxpayer money (the ISTEA program would cost over $1 billion over several years) and a morally bankrupt handout (most companies did not "graduate" out of the program).[85] McConnell also succeeded with a low-visibility amendment that will have the GAO conduct a study on how the set-aside program of the ISTEA bill really works. The study will ascertain how many Disadvantaged Business Enterprises there are and what percentage actually win contracts. Opponents of preferences hope that these data will prove that companies that get preferences are not disadvantaged and will allow the argument that millionaires are getting preferences.

Divide and Conquer
One possible strategy of policy retrenchment is to go on the offensive, and a standard strategy is to "divide and conquer."[86] Supporters of preferences include members of the Democratic party and a cross-class coalition of civil rights groups representing Afro-Americans, women, Latinos, and other groups, and there are obvious strategies to divide them. Support for preferences could be weakened by taking them from some groups (e.g., women or immigrants, or the wealthy of any minority group) and allowing it for others.

The Republicans with whom I spoke have apparently never considered this strategy. This is true for a variety of reasons. The first and probably most important is that opponents of preferences are arguing for the principle of nondiscrimination and will settle for nothing else. While there are efforts to expose "well-heeled" beneficiaries of affirmative action, this is to change the meaning of the debate and not to drive a class wedge into the pro–affirmative action coalition, though it could clearly do that. Bolick explained, "We don't take a 'divide and conquer' approach because we think race and gender discrimination is wrong, period."[87]

Since affirmative action expanded to include preferences for persons with no historical case of discrimination (e.g., Sri Lankans) and allow preferences for recent immigrants with no public debate,[88] one might assume that Republicans would focus on eliminating these preferences first. My questions to Republicans on this divide-and-conquer strategy, however, generally met with surprise or puzzlement and eventual rejection of the idea. The great variety of thoughts are difficult to summarize. Some thought it was "good" or "interesting," but for most it was not a wise strategy because, for example, most voters do not even know about immigrant or even non-Afro-American minority inclusion in affirmative action, and it would require "voter education" for the rhetoric to take hold, or moving against immigrant preferences would still make Republicans look mean-spirited and would do so among minority voters they believe they have the greatest potential with (Latinos and Asians), or it was an affront to their firm belief that government sponsored discrimination must stop in toto—decrementalism on scope is unacceptable.[89]

Another major cleavage is between racial/ethnic minorities and women, and since Republicans almost always discuss racial/ethnic preferences and not gender preferences, it appears there may be some effort being made to divide the preferences coalition, or at least to lower the visibility of the elimination of preferences for women.[90] Answers to questions on this topic varied considerably, pointing to disorganization even among the strongest Congressional opponents of preferences. Some pointed to polls or focus group studies that suggested it was a good idea to avoid discussing preferences for women, while others argued polls and focus groups showed the opposite and maintained that their race-based arguments were driven only by court cases on the constitutional foundation of preferences, which have been about race. Another said discussion of race and not gender was simply shorthand. A staff member who was reluctant to support the antipreference bill stated that for those "on the go-slow approach, we like that linkage [with women]." Bolick argued that there are "a lot of strategic decisions [on this issue] that can be characterized as damned if you do, damned if you don't." The difficulty here, he argued, was that failing to talk about gender preferences made them look like they were pro–white women at the expense of Afro-Americans, but including women in their critiques brought in more opponents.

The Court Strategy

If Republicans found it politically risky to kill affirmative action preferences themselves, another option could produce the same result while avoiding potential blame: let the courts do it. In the 1980s, there was little chance that the courts would end preferences, however, and the Supreme Court was an important factor in limiting the Reagan administration's attempts. It was not until the 1990s that the court strategy became viable, largely because of Reagan.

It is a routine practice for presidents to appoint persons of consonant ideology to the federal bench. Reagan followed the routine and in his eight years was able to make a mark: nearly half of federal judges by 1988 were appointed by the former governor of California (338 appointments). Ninety-five percent of these were Republicans.[91]

As Hugh Davis Graham has pointed out, the strategy of appointing conservatives to the courts to undo affirmative action can be effective, but it has a delayed payoff.[92] The Reagan appointments strategy would not show its first fruits in the affirmative action area until one year after Reagan left office. The propreference majorities were a slim five to four, and with the retiring of Lewis Powell (author of the famous "diversity" rationale for racial preference in university admissions), his replacement by Anthony Kennedy and the change in views of Reagan appointee Sandra Day O'Connor to one less sympathetic to race preferences, the stage was set for modifications of Court policy. The year 1989 brought *City of Richmond v. J. A. Croson Co.,*[93] *Wards Cove Packing Co., Inc. v. Atonio,*[94] and *Martin v. Wilks,*[95] all of which led to refinements and narrowing of preferences.[96]

Richmond v. Croson was especially important for contract set-asides. Under the Fourteenth Amendment, the Supreme Court struck down Richmond, Virginia's, minority contract set-aside program. Racial categorizations at the state and local level were to be used for remedial situations only. There was no evidence of discrimination in Richmond's minority contracting (especially against the nonexistent Eskimos and Aleuts named in the city ordinance as eligible for preference), and a statistical imbalance was not enough to show that discrimination. This ruling, that all race classifications were inherently suspect, was then expanded to all regulations in a 5–4 decision of 1995, *Adarand Constructors v. Peña*.[97] Also in 1995, a Fifth Circuit court ruled in *Hopwood v. Texas*[98] that the University of Texas Law School's affirmative action admissions program was unconstitutional, rejected the University's "diversity" rationale (the Law School claimed that racial preferences were necessary to maintain a "diverse" student body), arguing that a specific finding of discrimination is necessary for such a program. The court declared, "The law school may not use race as a factor in deciding which applicants to admit." The Supreme Court refused to review the case.

This presents an irony: in the 1980s, antipreference forces could not persuade action because the courts did not agree with them; in the 1990s, they could not persuade action because the courts *do* agree with them. These developments have allowed many Republicans to avoid the issue, and made it more difficult to persuade Congress members to act. The legal developments constraining government use of preferences offer many Republicans concerned about their moral image an excellent opportunity to see their policy preferences fulfilled while avoiding blame. Strong advocates of the antipreference bill now have to argue that Congress still has a duty to act even though the courts are chipping away at preferences, or that Congress must act *because* the courts are acting. Some also note that the antipreference majority in the Supreme Court is but a slim one vote, and future court rulings against preferences are not a certainty.

Conclusion

I have argued that the resilience of affirmative action can be partly explained by reference to the old patterns of politics, specifically the action or inaction of interest groups. There is little organized demand for the repeal of preferences, either from citizens' groups or business groups. There is also no consistent demand from nor unity among Republican party elites. Meanwhile, civil rights advocates strongly support the policies. However, a fuller explanation must account for the lack of demand and explain minority advocates' power. There is much here that fits the patterns of the new politics of public policy as described in this volume. Most important, there are barriers to retrenchment that suggest the concept of blame avoidance. Republicans are concerned that they will be blamed for causing harm to minorities; more generally, they do not want to risk a negative public image of unfairness that could come with affirmative action supporters' charges of mean-spiritedness or an anti–civil rights stance. Pro–affirmative action lobbying is important because of this desire for blame avoidance and image maintenance.

Though I have separated the lack of lobbying from the concerns of being perceived as antiminority, this separation may be artificial. As concerns over party image limit the unity among party leaders, lobbyists themselves may be reluctant to act because of a concern of appearing anti–civil rights. Some Republican staffers argued that the same fear of appearing racist that constrained politicians similarly constrained business leaders, who wanted to promote a positive image. The argument also could apply to increasingly image-conscious groups such as the Christian Coalition. In addition, while some Republicans may desire grassroots lobbying pressure as an indicator that voters would reward an anti–affirmative action bill, another possibility is that some Republicans want that lobbying pressure as a political cover. Outside pressure could serve to justify their action and defend themselves against the antiminority charge. In short, the image-consciousness and the politics of blame avoidance may be implicated in other seemingly independent "old politics" factors that contribute to Republicans' reluctance to act.

The case of the resilience of affirmative action also suggests that other themes of the new politics of public policy described in this volume work together or indeed are different aspects of the same phenomenon. Leaving aside for a moment the issue of interest group activity, one could explain the resilience of affirmative action in the following way.

Again borrowing McWilliams's notion of the two-tier polity, we can see anti–affirmative action Republicans are in the top tier, along with other Republicans, pro–affirmative action Democrats, pro–affirmative action civil rights groups, and political journalists looking for controversy. In the second tier is the public, the majority of which is sympathetic to the antipreference cause, but mostly concerned with other issues and unwilling to support racists or misogynists. The job for the antipreference Republicans is to convince other top-tier Republicans and ideally some Democrats that affirmative action regulations are wrong and it is worth their effort to eliminate them.

This is a tall order, because the risks are high. Image politics have always been important, but communicating image and message are increasingly important. As Landy and Levin describe in their introduction to this volume, parties do not provide the cover that they used to. The stakes of a negative, immoral public image are higher than perhaps ever before because the percentage of voters that can likely be swayed by positive or negative appeals is at its highest point in decades, and perhaps in history. Specifically, the percentage of "independent" voters is twice as high as in the heyday of the New Deal coalition (about 40 percent in 1995 compared to 19 percent in 1937) and greater than the percentage that claim to be Democrats (about 30 percent) or Republicans (about 30 percent).[99] Given the decline in party identification and party organizations in general, the news media has assumed great importance. The decline of parties coincides with the rise of the twenty-four-hour news cycle created by all-news television stations such as CNN and MSNBC.[100] Given the news media's fascination with reporting controversy, charges, and countercharges in neatly packaged sound bites, it has become easier to communicate a negative message and delegitimize a party when it does not have much credibility on an issue. Republicans must communicate to the voters that affirmative action retrenchment is just and good for everyone. Democrats and civil rights groups will label these efforts racist, harmful, and anti–civil rights. To the extent that Republicans will risk taking blame/negative image and press on, they will either do their best to keep their anti–affirmative action moves invisible or utilize any of the strategies described previously to mitigate the charge of racism.

The portrait should not give the impression that liberals and the civil rights forces dominate the Washington scene. They do not, and probably feel weaker than the anti–affirmative action Republicans. The important flip side to Republican inability to end affirmative action preferences is the Democrats' fear of proposing new programs to help minorities. The Democrats have the problem of appearing to be *too* concerned with Afro-American interests especially, which drives away many Euro-American voters.[101] The national electorate is moderate at the turn of the century, and no major policy moves in the civil rights area seem likely unless handled with utmost care.

This suggests a final point on how the affirmative action case illustrates what is new about durability and change in the new politics of public policy. At least since the 1970s, the American public has accepted many liberal goals, including the guarantee of equal opportunity for minorities and women in jobs and schools,[102] while simultaneously rejecting liberal means to those goals.[103] With some exceptions, the conservative charges of "big government" and "tax and spend" can still shoot down many policy proposals, and charges of "racial quota" or "reverse discrimination" will hamper new liberal initiatives to help minorities. Democrats have adapted by pushing small-scale programs not targeted to race. On the other hand, Republican efforts to end liberal policies or promote conservative ones meet the liberals' charges of "mean-spirited," "anti–civil rights," or "racist" and are aborted because the public responds to these charges as well. It is still an open question whether the Republican party will sincerely and honestly address the popularity of liberal policy goals. A positive image of fairness and respect for civil rights before the national electorate requires that the Republicans— and the Democrats as well—walk a fine line on the affirmative action issue.

Notes

1. Whether or not preferences and quotas are a part of affirmative action is a very contentious issue, as will be discussed later.

2. Pete Wilson, governor of California; Jeb Bush, governor of Florida; and Mike Foster, governor of Louisiana, acted to eliminate race and gender preferences in their respective states. Also in California, the California Civil Rights Initiative (CCRI), a grassroots group, succeeded in getting a referendum on the 1996 ballot to end race and gender preferences. The referendum, Proposition 209, won by a vote of 54 percent to 46 percent. Though funded in part by the Republican party, CCRI was officially nonpartisan. The state of Washington followed suit in 1998, passing its own antipreference referendum. Beginning in 1989, federal courts began to limit the use of race and gender preferences, and have ended some programs in cities and states.

3. John David Skrentny, *The Ironies of Affirmative Action: Politics, Culture and Justice in America* (Chicago: University of Chicago Press, 1996).

4. Hugh Davis Graham, "Richard Nixon and Civil Rights: Explaining an Enigma," *Presidential Studies Quarterly* 26 (1996): 93–106.

5. I follow Orlando Patterson in using the terms *Afro-American* to denote American-born persons of African ancestry (as distinct from African or Caribbean immigrants) and *Euro-American* to denote persons of non-Spanish European ancestry. *Latinos* refers to persons with ancestry in Spanish-speaking countries. Such terms, Patterson points out, avoid reifying racial distinctions that have no clear biological basis. See his *The Ordeal of Integration* (Washington, D.C.: Civitas, 1997). The terms also allow one to avoid the cumbersome "non-Hispanic white" and "non-Hispanic black" labels.

6. Richard L. Zweigenhaft and G. William Domhoff, *Diversity in the Power Elite* (New Haven, Conn.: Yale University Press, 1998). Zweigenhaft and Domhoff do find improvement in these groups' representation over the past several decades.

7. Philip Klinkner with Rogers Smith, *The Unsteady March: The Rise and Decline of America's Commitment to Racial Equality* (Chicago: University of Chicago Press, 1999).

8. See for example, Michael I. Sovern, *Legal Restraints on Racial Discrimination in Employment* (New York: Twentieth Century Fund, 1966), Michael Evan Gold, "*Griggs'* Folly: An Essay on the Theory, Problems, and Origins of the Adverse Impact Definition of Employment Discrimination and a Recommendation for Reform," *Industrial Relations Law Journal* 7 (1985): 429–598.

9. Jennifer Hochschild, "Affirmative Action as Culture War," in *The Cultural Territories of Race: White and Black Boundaries,* ed. Michèle Lamont (New York: Russell Sage Foundation and Chicago: University of Chicago Press, 1999).

10. Paul M. Sniderman and Edward G. Carmines, *Reaching Beyond Race* (Cambridge, Mass.: Harvard University Press, 1997), 28–30.

11. For a question that asks for views on whether jobs and places in colleges should be based solely on ability as determined by test scores or allow preferential treatment for women and minorities, 81 percent of men and 84 percent of women supported ability. In a 1991 *Newsweek*/Gallup poll, 72 percent of Euro-Americans disagreed that qualified Afro-Americans should get preferences for jobs and college over equally qualified Euro-Americans. Forty-two percent of Afro-Americans disagreed, and 48 percent agreed. Skrentny, *Ironies of Affirmative Action*, 4–5. Views vary by racial/ethnic category. While 45 percent of Euro-Americans believe "affirmative action for blacks is unfair to whites" (31 percent disagree, and 24 percent say neither), 34 percent of Asians agree (31 disagree), 30 percent of Latinos agree (37 disagree) and 18 percent of Afro-Americans agree (65 percent disagree). Lawrence Bobo, "Race, Interests and Beliefs about Affirmative Action: Unanswered Questions and New Directions," in *Color Lines,* ed. John D. Skrentny (Chicago: University of Chicago Press, 2001), 191–213.

12. Stanley B. Greenberg, *Middle Class Dreams: The Politics and Power of the New American Majority* (New York: Times Books, 1995), 39–44; Alan Wolfe, *One Nation, After All* (New York: Viking, 1998), 216–218; Carol M. Swain, Kyra R. Greene, and Christine Min Watipka, "Understanding Racial Polarization on Affirmative Action," in Skrentny, *Color Lines,* 214–238.

13. I relied on staff members because I believed they would be more likely to give honest and informal "behind the scenes" views of intraparty politics, especially given the sensitive nature of the issue. Most of them spoke on the condition that they be quoted anonymously. Two exceptions were Pam Pryor of J. C. Watts's (R-OK) office, and Horace Cooper, press secretary for House Majority Leader Dick Armey (R-TX). The two think tank leaders are Clint Bolick of the Institute for Justice and Roger Clegg of the Center for Equal Opportunity. I also interviewed Ken Masugi, assistant to Clarence Thomas when Thomas was chair of the Equal Employment Opportunity Commission, and Eugene Volokh, legal adviser to the Proposition 209/California Civil Rights Initiative Campaign.

14. See chapter 2 by Eric M. Patashnik for a similar point on the simultaneous workings of both old politics and new politics factors.

15. The theory is elaborated in James Q. Wilson, *Political Organizations* (New York: Basic Books, 1973), chapter 16; Wilson, *American Government: Institutions and Policies* (Lexington, Mass.: Heath, 1980), Part IV; and Wilson, "The Politics of Regulation," in *The Politics of Regulation,* ed. James Q. Wilson (New York: Basic Books, 1980), 366–372.

16. Paul Pierson, *Dismantling the Welfare State? Reagan, Thatcher and the Politics of Retrenchment* (New York: Cambridge University Press, 1994).

17. Martha Derthick and Paul J. Quirk, *The Politics of Deregulation* (Washington, D.C.: Brookings Institution, 1985).

18. Quoted in Hugh Davis Graham, *The Civil Rights Era* (New York: Oxford University Press, 1990), 342–343. In 1971, the OFCC's Revised Order No. 4 added women to the goals and timetables requirement.

19. From the 1993 EE0-1 form. The categories had different names but denoted the same groups in 1965. The categories are broken down for Officials and Managers, Professionals, Technicians, Sales Workers, Office and Clerical, Craft Workers (Skilled), Operatives (Semi-Skilled), Laborers (Unskilled) and Service Workers.

20. Alfred W. Blumrosen, *Modern Law: The Law Transmission System and Equal Employment Opportunity* (Madison: University of Wisconsin Press, 1993), 242–245.

21. Hugh Davis Graham, "Affirmative Action for Immigrants? The Unintended Consequences of 1960s Reforms," in Skrentny, *Color Lines,* 53–70; Charles V. Dale, "A Brief Legal Overview of Federal Affirmative Action Statutes and Executive Orders" (Washington, D.C.: Congressional Research Service, March 8, 1995).

22. Graham, "Unintended Consequences"; W. Avon Drake and Robert D. Holsworth, *Affirmative Action and the Stalled Quest for Black Progress* (Urbana: University of Illinois Press, 1996); Dale, "Brief Legal Overview." See the debate in *Congressional Record,* March 5, 1998, pp. 1395–1493, and March 6, 1998, pp. 1481–1496.

23. John Douglass, "Anatomy of a Conflict: The Making and Unmaking of Affirmative Action at the University of California," in Skrentny, *Color Lines,* 118–144.

24. Such a lock-in is apparent in contract set-asides, in which firms doing competent work but at non-competitive prices may be nurtured by the government for years. The policy is different from an entitlement, however, because it is expected the firm will not need the preferences for very long and no preferences are guaranteed to any specific firm.

25. On a group level, ending preferences can be highly visible and obvious in higher education, as was clear in the case of the University of California. For example, when the Berkeley campus's law school ended preferences, the percentage of Afro-American and Latino students among all students accepted dropped from 9.2 percent (1996) to 1.8 percent (1997) in the case of Afro-Americans and from 9.6 percent to 4.9 percent for Latinos. See *Sacramento Bee*, May 15, 1997. Republicans in Washington, however, have not proposed policies to end affirmative action in higher education, and it is unlikely such visibility— or even similar declines—would be as obvious in employment and would be less morally objectionable in contract set-asides.

26. Pierson discusses the possibility that policy retrenchment may result in "program irrationalities," where stripped-down programs function in a way that undermines other programs or ideological or political goals. Pierson, *Dismantling the Welfare State?* 24–26. There is a potential problem for Republicans in that ending affirmative action usually means relying on a strengthened difference-blind law. For example, Senator Robert Dole and Representative J. C. Watts (R-OK) wrote in the *Wall Street Journal* criticizing preferences, "[W]e must conscientiously enforce our antidiscrimination laws" and argued for more investigation powers for the EEOC (July 27, 1995; quoted in Ken Masugi, "Modern Law versus Ancient Liberties: The Origins of Affirmative Action," *Political Science Reviewer* 25 [1996]: 313). What is usually not addressed is that this reliance on government investigation of discrimination complaints is also very bureaucratic, expensive, and burdensome to business—all factors that are anathema to most conservatives. However, no Republicans whom I interviewed were at all concerned about the "big government" or litigation explosion possibilities that may result from affirmative action retrenchment with EEOC augmentation. For a critical analysis of the effect of individual claims of discrimination on the American workplace, see Philip K. Howard, *The Death of Common Sense: How Law Is Suffocating America* (New York: Random House, 1994), 133–142.

27. Steven V. Roberts, "Affirmative Action on the Edge," *U.S. News & World Report*, February 13, 1995, pp. 32–33, 35, 37–38; Richard Lacayo, "A New Push for Blind Justice," *Time*, February 20, 1995, pp. 39–40.

28. Stephen Thernstrom and Abigail Thernstrom, *America in Black and White: One Nation, Indivisible* (New York: Simon & Schuster, 1997), 454; Clint Bolick, *The Affirmative Action Fraud: Can We Restore the American Civil Rights Vision?* (Washington, D.C.: Cato Institute, 1996), 14.

29. Holly Idelson, "Pressure Builds for Retreat on Affirmative Action," *Congressional Quarterly Weekly Report* 53 (June 3, 1995): 1578, 1580.

30. Lydia Chávez, *The Color Bind: California's Battle to End Affirmative Action* (Berkeley: University of California Press, 1998), 69.

31. *Chattanooga Free Press*, August 9, 1996.

32. Chávez, *The Color Bind*, 122.

33. One rare empirical study of affirmative action (though strongly critical) sought to show the abuses of the policy but had to rely on newspaper accounts of particular incidents rather than any comprehensive data. Frederick Lynch, *Invisible Victims: White Males and the Crisis of Affirmative Action* (New York: Greenwood, 1989), chapter 3 ("An Affirmative Action Sampler"). For evidence of the uneven enforcement of civil rights laws in general, see Barbara A. Bergmann, *In Defense of Affirmative Action* (New York: Basic Books, 1996), 52–61.

34. John W. Kingdon, *Agendas, Alternatives, and Public Policies* (Boston: Little, Brown, 1984), 95.

35. Lauren Edelman, "Legal Ambiguity and Symbolic Structures: Organizational Mediation of Civil Rights," *American Journal of Sociology* 97 (1992): 1531–1576.

36. Orlando Patterson, *The Ordeal of Integration* (Washington, D.C.: Civitas, 1997), 148–153. Fifty percent of Afro-Americans and 63 percent of Latinos believed their employers were doing "about the right amount" to help minorities.

37. Given a list of ten issues, only 2 percent of Californians polled in 1996 said that "addressing affirmative action" is their top priority, while another survey giving a list of possible priorities for the 1996 presidential race showed Californians listing it at twenty-sixth among twenty-seven issues. See *USA Today*, October 22, 1996. These results are almost certainly pushed downward by the use of the term *affirmative action* rather than *racial or gender preference*. Still, one Republican staffer I spoke to mentioned a similar poll result as a reason for inaction.

38. Patterson, *Ordeal of Integration*, 148–153.

39. Cathie Jo Martin, "Mandating Social Change: The Business Struggle Over National Health Reform," *Governance* 10 (1997): 397–428.

40. Fisher, "Hiring by Numbers." On business's fascination with race- and gender-conscious hiring, also see Frederick R. Lynch, *The Diversity Machine: The Drive to Change the "White Male Workplace"* (New York: Free Press, 1997); Erin Kelly and Frank Dobbin, "How Affirmative Action Became Diversity Management," in Skrentny, *Color Lines*, 87–117; and Alan Wolfe, "Affirmative Action, Inc.," *New Yorker*, November 25, 1996, pp. 106–115.

41. Idelson, "Pressure Builds," 1578. A 1994 poll found that only 2 percent of 641 responding government contractors complained of preferences or quotas. See Hochschild, "Affirmative Action as Culture War." Roger Clegg, however, pointed out in an interview that firms that want lucrative government contracts are not likely to make trouble by complaining to the source of those contracts.

42. Also see Kelly and Dobbin, "How Affirmative Action Became Diversity Management."

43. On the tendency in American politics to use regulations rather than social provision to address inequality, see Theda Skocpol, "Conclusion," in *Social Policy in the United States* (Princeton, N.J.: Princeton University Press, 1995).

44. Daniel Seligman, "Affirmative Action is Here to Stay." *Fortune* April 19, 1982.

45. Gary L. McDowell, "Affirmative Inaction: The Brock-Meese Standoff on Federal Racial Quotas." *Policy Review* (1989): 32–37.

46. Steven M. Teles, *Whose Welfare? AFDC and Elite Politics* (Lawrence: University Press of Kansas, 1996), 15.

47. Jennifer Hochschild, "Affirmative Action as Culture War," 343–369.

48. Patterson, *Ordeal of Integration*, 149.

49. While by no means agreeing with the prior arguments, at least one Republican staff member I talked with believed that affirmative action had political usefulness. This staffer agreed that it was "something we should always be pushing" as a tool to define the GOP, but congressional action on the issue was another matter, as this mobilized opposition. Republicans, this staffer felt, "shouldn't lose [preferences] as a rhetorical device." Another staff member, however, expressed doubt on the utility of such a strategy. Pam Pryor, of J. C. Watts's office, asked rhetorically, "Where else does that [white male] vote go?" She pointed out that the more important strategy is to shore up support among those voters whose support is less certain.

50. Dole's ambivalence is a major theme in Chávez, *The Color Bind*.

51. *USA Today*, October 4, 1995.

52. *Set-Aside Alert*, July 4, 1997.

53. See Paul Pierson's chapter 3 in this volume.

54. Hochschild, "Affirmative Action as Culture War."

55. R. Kent Weaver, "The Politics of Blame Avoidance," *Journal of Public Policy* 6 (1986): 371–398.

56. Thomas F. Burke, "On the Resilience of Rights," chapter 7 in this volume.

57. Pierson, *Dismantling the Welfare State?* 127.

58. Ninety-eight percent of Americans agree with the statement "Everyone in America should have equal opportunities to get ahead." Herbert McClosky and John Zaller, *The American Ethos: Public Attitudes toward Capitalism and Democracy* (Cambridge, Mass.: Harvard University Press, 1984), 83. When asked, "Do you think Negroes should have as good a chance as white people to get any kind of job, or do you think white people should have the first chance at any kind of job?" 97 percent of white respondents said, "As good a chance" in 1972, an increase of 52 percentage points from 1944. Howard Schuman, Charlotte Steeh, and Lawrence Bobo, *Racial Attitudes in America: Trends and Interpretations* (Cambridge, Mass.: Harvard University Press, 1985), 74–75. For public opinion on the American support of a legal guarantee of equal opportunity for Afro-Americans, see Paul Burstein, *Discrimination, Jobs and Politics* (Chicago: University of Chicago Press, 1985).

59. Linda Faye Williams, "Race and the Politics of Social Policy," in *The Social Divide: Political Parties and the Future of Activist Government*, ed. Margaret Weir (Washington, D.C.: Brookings Institution, 1998), 417–464, 442–443; Thernstrom and Thernstrom, *America in Black and White*, 457.

60. It should be noted that strong opponents of preferences were the most emphatic that it was fear of appearing racist that held back Republicans, while others usually did not use these terms but more general ideas about concerns over party image. On media portrayals of conservatives as racist, see Roger Clegg, "Civil Rights and the News Media," *Nexus* 3 (Spring 1998): 37–60.

61. On this latter point, see R. Douglas Arnold, *The Logic of Congressional Action* (New Haven, Conn.: Yale University Press, 1990).

62. Polls conducted by the National Election Studies show that, in 1962, the question of which party "is more likely to see to it that Negroes get fair treatment in jobs and housing?" revealed essentially no difference in the public's perceptions of the Republicans and the Democrats. Specifically, 22.7 percent of respondents identified the Democrats, 21.3 percent identified Republicans, and 55.9 percent said that there was no difference. Response to the question radically changed by late 1964, however. In response to a similar question on party support for fair treatment for blacks in job opportunities, only 7 percent identified the Republicans as offering more support, while 60 percent said it would be the Democrats, and 33 percent said no difference. In a separate question on support for blacks and whites attending the same schools, the figures were 7 percent, 56 percent, and 37 percent, respectively. See Thomas Byrne Edsall and Mary D. Edsall, *Chain Reaction: The Impact of Race, Rights and Taxes on American Politics* (New York: Norton, 1992), 37.

63. Republican opportunism could have led to a "Bill to Mend Affirmative Action" that actually ended preferences. This could have been labeled as in accordance with the President's wishes, but no Republicans moved on this strategy.

64. This is a clear theme in Chávez, *The Color Bind*.

65. Wilson Carey McWilliams, "Two-Tier Politics and the Problem of Public Policy," in *The New Politics of Public Policy*, ed. Marc K. Landy and Martin A. Levin (Baltimore, Md.: Johns Hopkins University Press, 1995), 268–276; McWilliams, chapter 16 in this volume.

66. See Douglass, "Anatomy of a Conflict," for analysis of how this complexity, especially the overrepresentation of Asian Americans in university admissions, may have aided the ending of affirmative action at the University of California.

67. Pierson, *Dismantling the Welfare State?*; R. Kent Weaver, "The Politics of Blame Avoidance," *Journal of Public Policy* 6 (1986): 371–398; Frank R. Baumgartner and Bryan D. Jones, *Agendas and Instability in American Politics* (Chicago: University of Chicago Press, 1993); Margaret Weir, *Politics and Jobs* (Princeton, N.J.: Princeton University Press, 1994).

68. For example, Title IX of the Education Amendments of 1972, prohibiting sex discrimination by educational institutions receiving federal funds, revolutionized education for women and girls, most controversially in the area of intercollegiate athletics. Title IX passed without hearings or lobbying. John David Skrentny, "Uncontentious Politics: Title IX and Women's Equality in Education," presented at the Workshop on Contentious Politics, Columbia University, April 7, 1998; Joyce Gelb and Marian Lief Palley, *Women and Public Policies* (Princeton, N.J.: Princeton University Press, 1982), chapter 5. Section 504 of the Rehabilitation Act of 1973 similarly barred discrimination, in this case against the handicapped and not limited to education. It also passed with-

out lobbying, debate, or hearings. Richard A. Scotch, *From Good Will to Civil Rights* (Philadelphia: Temple University Press, 1984), chapter 2; Robert A. Katzmann, *Institutional Disability: The Saga of Transportation Policy for the Disabled* (Washington, D.C.: Brookings Institution, 1986), 44–49; Thomas F. Burke, "On the Rights Track: The Americans with Disabilities Act," in *Comparative Disadvantage? Social Regulations and the Global Economy,* ed. Pietro S. Nivola (Washington, D.C.: Brookings Institution, 1997), 242–318, 250–251.

69. The Republicans did succeed in slipping a provision into an appropriations bill that allowed for the logging of old-growth forests. President Clinton later said he would not have signed the bill (the 1995 Omnibus Appropriations and Rescissions Act) had he known the meaning of this provision.

70. *Congressional Record*, March 5, pp. 1465–1467. The Clinton administration had considered a similar approach. Williams, "Race and the Politics of Social Policy," 444.

71. 515 U.S. 200 (1995).

72. Democrat Dick Durbin of Illinois challenged that the amendment "runs counter to this country's dedication to civil rights and humanitarianism."

73. See the debate in *Congressional Record*, March 6, 1998, pp. S1481–S1496.

74. S. 952, 105th Congress, First Session, introduced on June 24, 1997.

75. *New York Times*, June 19, 1997; *Washington Post*, June 19, 1997.

76. Bolick, *The Affirmative Action Fraud.*

77. While this may be true, the fact remains that Republicans killed the Clinton health care plan in 1994 by making only negative claims. The idea that a positive is needed may be true only on some types of issue, or in the case of policy retrenchment, or in cases that do not have a massive public relations campaign, as the Republicans had with health care.

78. Skrentny, *Ironies of Affirmative Action*, chapter 6.

79. Johnson's famous speech, given in 1965 at Howard University's commencement, did discuss the need for the federal government to help black Americans compete fairly, but there is no evidence that Johnson or the speech writers were thinking about affirmative action. They preferred Great Society programs such as Head Start. See Gareth Davies, *From Equal Opportunity to Entitlement: The Transformation and Decline of the Great Society* (Lawrence: University Press of Kansas, 1996).

80. CNBC News Transcripts, *Tim Russert*, July 13, 1997.

81. Republicans do not invoke the memory of King nearly as often as do Democrats. Between 1993 and 1997, only 34 Republicans mentioned King on the House or Senate floor, compared with 122 Democrats during the same period. Francesca Polletta, "Legacies and Liabilities of an Insurgent Past: Remembering Martin Luther King Jr., on the House and Senate Floor," *Social Science History* 22 (1998): 485.

82. On the notion of the "two-tier polity," see chapter 16 by Wilson Carey McWilliams in this volume.

83. *Washington Post*, June 19, 1997. Also see Holly Idelson, "Clinton Comes to Defense of Affirmative Action," *Congressional Quarterly Weekly Report* 53 (July 22, 1995): 2194.

84. Bolick, *Affirmative Action Fraud*, 66.

85. Congressional *Record*, March 6, 1998, 1483.

86. Pierson, *Dismantling the Welfare State?* 22–23.

87. At three points in his book, Bolick states that there is no middle ground on preferences, that either the government should have the power to discriminate or it should not. Bolick, *Affirmative Action Fraud*, 118 (twice), 124.

88. In a much-discussed switch, former affirmative action critic Nathan Glazer wrote an article for *The New Republic* defending preferences for Afro-Americans—but he called the bureaucratic expansion of the program to include other groups "mindless." Nathan Glazer, "In Defense of Preference," *The New Republic*, April 6, 1998, p. 20.

89. In support of his amendment to ISTEA ending contract set-asides, McConnell displayed a map of the world with markers showing each country whose immigrants could receive preferences. He scored rhetorical points, and produced some discussion as to whether or not the Sultan of Brunei ("the richest monarch in the world") was eligible for preference. But McConnell's amendment would have ended all preferences. See *Congressional Record*, March 5, 1998, 1418; and March 6, 1998, 1486–1487.

90. Chávez shows that affirmative action supporters believed talking about women as beneficiaries made the policy more popular in California. Chávez, *The Color Bind*, 95, 137.

91. In comparison, Carter's appointments showed similar partisanship—they were 90 percent Democrat. Walter F. Murphy, "Reagan's Judicial Strategy," in *Looking Back on the Reagan Presidency*, ed. Larry Berman (Baltimore: Johns Hopkins University Press, 1990), 210; and Shull, *Kinder, Gentler Racism?* 122–124.

92. Hugh Davis Graham, "The Politics of Clientele Capture: Civil Rights Policy and the Reagan Administration," in *Redefining Equality,* ed. Neal Davis and Dave Douglas (New York: Oxford University Press, 1998), 103–119.

93. 488 U.S. 469 (1989).

94. 490 U.S. 642 (1989).

95. 490 U.S. 755 (1989).

96. In 1989's *Wards Cove v. Atonio* (490 U.S. 642 [1989]), the Court limited use of statistics in charging a firm with discrimination, but Congress cut back on the decision in the Civil Rights Act of 1991 by reducing the burden of proof on plaintiffs.

97. 115 S.Ct. 2097 (1995).

98. 78 F.3d 932 (1996). However, a federal district court has upheld admissions preferences in Michigan (*Gratz v. Ballinger,* 122 F.Supp. 2d 811 [2000]), and a district court has done so in *Smith v. University of Washington Law School* (233 F.3d 1188 [2000]).

99. The increase in independents really began in earnest in 1991. See the data in Ben J. Wattenberg, *Values Matter Most* (Washington, D.C.: Regnery, 1995), 118. On the decline of the parties, see A. James Reichley, *The Life of the Parties: A History of American Political Parties* (New York: Free Press, 1992), 6–12.

100. For an analysis and critique of the rise of the media and the decline of parties, see Thomas E. Patterson, *Out of Order* (New York: Knopf, 1993). In the mid-1970s, it was argued that "the extension of a national communications complex" was connected to party decline. See, for example, Everett Carl Ladd Jr. and Charles D. Hadley, *Transformations of the American Party System* (New York: Norton, 1975), 336.

101. Edsall and Edsall, *Chain Reaction*; Paul Frymer, *Uneasy Alliances: Race and Party Competition in America* (Princeton, N.J.: Princeton University Press, 1999). Women's issues do not follow this pattern, since the gender voting gap is not nearly as large as the Afro-American voting gap, and women's interests are more ideologically diverse than those of Afro-Americans, at least as perceived in Washington. On the distinctiveness of Euro-American and Afro-American political values, see Seymour Martin Lipset, *American Exceptionalism: A Double-Edged Sword* (New York: Norton, 1996).

102. I know of no poll data on contract set-asides or minority business help.

103. A *New York Times* story trumpeted this point, based on a CBS News/*Times* poll that found majorities of Americans rejecting preferences but supporting affirmative action that does not involve preferences, such as special outreach programs. "In Poll, Americans Reject Means but Not Ends of Racial Diversity," *New York Times*, December 14, 1997.

7

On the Resilience of Rights

Thomas F. Burke, *Wellesley College*

Beginning sometime in the 1960s, what has been called a "rights revolution" transformed American public policy.[1] Civil rights law, more or less comatose since Reconstruction, was revived, and its benefits eventually extended beyond African Americans to additional beneficiaries—other racial minorities, religious minorities, women, the aged, people with disabilities, and eventually gays and lesbians. "Due process" in various forms was provided to welfare recipients, schoolchildren, criminal suspects, prisoners, and the mentally ill. A host of consumer and environmental laws were advertised as creating rights to clean air and water, and safe and effective products. New constitutional rights, most prominently the right to privacy, came into being. A bunch of fiscal "entitlements"—welfare, disability, and medical support programs—became obligations of the federal government.[2]

This brief recitation suggests the variety of policy mechanisms commonly lumped under the heading of "rights." Some of the rights in the rights revolution grew out of the Constitution, others out of statutes, others through regulatory processes. Some were justified by concerns about equality; others were animated by notions of autonomy, or social decency, or procedural fairness, or a combination of all these things. Some of these rights solely governed public officials; others were aimed at reshaping the behaviors of businesses and individuals.

Given this variety of origins and effects, it's not clear why all these disparate policies have been lumped together—or why any analyst would hope to make generalizations about them. Yet generalizations are frequently made, usually by critics of the rights revolution. Among the most common criticisms of rights is that they are too strident and inflexible. Communitarian critics of rights argue that rights impose hard and fast rules where give and take is needed instead. Claims of interests, they say, can be compromised, but rights claims are inherently intractable.[3] For example, the political theorist Charles Taylor argues that debate over abortion has become polarized in part because it has become a debate over rights, either the privacy right of the woman or the right to life of the fetus: "[J]udicial decisions about rights tend to be conceived as all-or-nothing matters. The very concept of a right seems to call for integral satisfaction, if it's a right at all; and if not, then nothing."[4]

Mary Ann Glendon, in her influential analysis of the rights revolution, focuses her ire not so much on rights themselves, but on the strident, absolutist rhetoric that accompanies them: "in its simple American form, the language of rights is the language of no compromise. The winner takes all and the loser has to get out of town. The conversation is over."[5]

This emphasis on the stridency of rights claims is common among both academic and popular commentators.[6] It gets to the heart of what many find so troublesome about rights: their tendency to overwhelm other considerations, to flatten and simplify discourse over public policy. Yet this focus leaves certain puzzles.

First, although rights rhetoric is often absolutist, in practice rights are constantly being compromised against other concerns—rights are almost never "trumps" that overcome all competing claims.[7] So while in form rights might seem strident and absolutist, in function they turn out to be much more pliant. Even the right to an abortion has turned out to be more flexible than previously imagined, a point pursued later.

Second, though rights are sometimes considered beyond politics, the recognition of a right rarely ends the struggle among competing forces. It simply changes the rules. The result is a "politics of rights," a continuing battle over the implementation of rights.[8] And the politics of rights often looks a lot like the politics of other forms of public policy.

These two observations raise the main questions of this chapter. If, despite the absolutist rhetoric of rights, a struggle over rights continues in American politics, what is likely to be the fate of the rights revolution? The question is sharpened by conservative gains in all the institutions of government in recent years, particularly the federal courts, which have resulted in challenges to nearly every component of the rights revolution. In this environment rights appear uniquely vulnerable. Despite their rhetorical power, many of the rights in the rights revolution were built on shaky political foundations. They were crafted by ephemeral coalitions of policy entrepreneurs and public interest groups, bound more by the power of their ideas than by highly mobilized constituencies. If even "iron" triangles could be dissolved, what should we expect will happen to rights policies when they are attacked? In sum, how *resilient* should we expect rights policies—especially those of the rights revolution—to be? This chapter seeks to answer these questions, drawing on recent developments in rights politics and on academic analyses of the politics of public policymaking.

Rights as Entrenchments of Duty

First it is important to define exactly what I mean by "rights." Wesley Hohfeld, in his classic exposition on the nature of rights, concludes that they have one defining feature: they correspond with duties.[9] To say that someone has a right, Hohfeld maintains, is to say that the person has a just claim that a duty be performed by another. Indeed, Hohfeld implies that legal duties *always* correlate with rights. For example, the law against homicide correlates with a right not to be murdered. Or, to take an example from the rights revolution, a duty not to pollute water correlates with a right to clean water.

Critics of Hohfeld have taken issue with the notion that duties always correlate with rights, in part because they have a more expansive definition of rights than he did.[10] For the rights of the rights revolution, however, Hohfeld's assertion seems uncontroversial: this brand of rights quite clearly always involves duties. Civil rights statutes told government officials they had a duty to treat people equally and to punish those outside the government who did not follow suit. Environmental protection statutes authorized the government, in protecting the rights of the public to clean air and water, to punish polluters. Due process rules told governmental officials that they had to do certain things—hold meetings, develop records, listen to testimony—before making a decision. Welfare rights forced government officials to provide benefits to eligible recipients. The new rights mostly committed the government to action rather than inaction.

The relationship that Hohfeld suggests, of right to duty, is not merely a conceptual nuance. Indeed, I believe it most helpful to think about the growth of rights in American politics as an establishment of new duties. Contrary to the declamations of some critics, then, the proliferation of rights is best understood as an expansion of, rather than a diminution of, social responsibility. The new rights are more about telling people what to do than telling them to do whatever they wish.

Rights do their work by *entrenching* duties. By this I mean that they create a presumption that the duty will be fulfilled, even over countervailing considerations. "Entitlements," for example, are privileged over other budget items, making the process of cutting Social Security much more difficult than, say, cutting the Tennessee Valley Authority. Similarly, the goals of clean air or clean water are privileged in environmental statutes against considerations such as the cost of pollution abatement. The Supreme Court has interpreted the Equal Protection Clause of the Fourteenth Amendment to command that government's duty to treat citizens of different races equally is outweighed only by a "compelling interest." Under the Americans with Disabilities Act, the right of people with disabilities to "reasonable accommodation" at a work site can be displaced, but only if an employer can demonstrate "undue hardship."

So rights create a presumption about duties, and to overcome this presumption one must do more than "the usual." We can say that the more one has to do to displace a presumption of duty, the more *legally entrenched* it is.

But there's another kind of entrenchment, one that comes from a sense that connected with the mechanisms in the law is a larger *moral* obligation. The civil rights movement was in part aimed at convincing Americans that they owed blacks equal treatment, just as the disability rights movement aims to convince Americans that they owe people with disabilities accessible buildings. When a principle becomes morally entrenched, it creates the presumption one has to have more than "the usual" reason for displacing it. For example, the fact that the United States has a national debt is not by itself generally viewed as a sufficiently compelling reason to eliminate guaranteed payment of Social Security or Medicare, though it has been considered a reason to slice other programs. To the extent that the public believes that one has to have more than "the usual" reason for displacing a presumption, the more *morally entrenched* it is.

Legal entrenchment and moral entrenchment need not go together. A law can legally entrench a duty, but no sense of moral entrenchment need attach to it. In the area of entitlements, for example, public opinion data suggest that few people really thought that taxpayers had a duty to provide an unending stream of AFDC (Aid to Families with Dependent Children) benefits to eligible recipients.[11] Similarly, it seems there is no widespread belief that immigration officials must provide extensive hearing procedures to certain categories of illegal immigrants whom they deport.[12] Policy entrepreneurs who advance rights laws desire to develop an accompanying sense of moral entrenchment, but moral entrenchment is neither a prerequisite for nor a necessary consequence of legal entrenchment.[13]

When duties are both morally and legally entrenched, they are safe from abolition, but they are still subject to various forms of diminution. Despite the popularity of Ronald Dworkin's metaphor, rights are never really trumps, after all.[14] Rights simply tell judges and other policymakers that there's a presumption against displacement of duty by other considerations. Policymakers who are unsympathetic will lower the presumption. For example, the Rehnquist Court decided that states need not come up with a "compelling interest" when displacing (through a law neutral on its face) the duty to protect the free exercise of religion.[15] This example could be multiplied many times, across many policy realms and areas of law. The struggle over the implementation of legally entrenched duties is a major feature of American politics, one which undercuts the notion that rights are all-powerful in the United States. Yet as I will suggest later, the flexibility of rights can also be a source of strength.

Why Rights Have Proliferated

On my account, the "rights revolution" consists of two distinct but related phenomena: the proliferation of legal entrenchment and the proliferation of moral entrenchment.

I'm more certain about the proliferation of legal entrenchment in American public policy over the last thirty years than moral entrenchment. True, American society has taken on a lot of new moral obligations lately, attempting to ensure that all kinds of groups are treated fairly and equally, and that, as Lawrence Friedman put it in his book *Total Justice*,[16] no one suffers too much from things that are not his or her fault. But we should not forget that there are also moral obligations that have gone out of style during this period— for example, that we should protect people's property, that we should protect the autonomy of community decision making, that we should protect parents' rights, that we should protect traditional Christian morality. There's clearly been a *shift* in moral entrenchment, but it's not so clear that there's been growth, at least on the scale that labels like the "rights revolution" suggest. In any case, I want to bracket off the issue of the growth of moral entrenchment, since it is far beyond the scope of this chapter. Instead I will suggest some of the mechanisms by which, even in the absence of moral entrenchment, legal entrenchment might be expected to grow, particularly in an era of divided government.

To understand the causes of the growth of legal entrenchment, we must consider the factors that create incentives for policymakers to cast their desires in the form of rights. Four such factors have been identified by students of public policy: nationalization, cost shifting, venue shifting, and distrust.

Nationalization

As Robert Kagan has argued, federalism encourages activists to advance rights-based arguments as a way of nationalizing policymaking. Kagan provides a vivid example of this phenomenon, drawn from public policy regarding policing, a realm in which federalism posed a profound obstacle for reformers.[17] In most nations police officers belong to a single national agency, so it is comparatively simple for would-be reformers to gain authority over them. In the United States, a federalist system, those who wanted to reform the police had to somehow reach the practices of local police departments across the nation. The solution to this problem lay in the judicial branch. Faced with the difficulties of redirecting thousands of localities, police reformers turned to the Supreme Court, which expanded old constitutional rights and developed new ones in such areas as search and seizure, right to counsel, and interrogation of suspects.[18] These rights became the mechanism by which the practices of police were brought under control. A similar phenomenon is seen in civil rights law, in which the proliferation of rights is at least in part an effort to control local and state officials. In a federal system, changing policy often requires getting states and localities to do your bidding. Aside from bribery, in the United States the only sure way to do this is through the entrenchment of duties. Thus, policymakers who seek to nationalize policy in a federal system will seek new rights.

Cost Shifting

Another motivation for the entrenchment of duty is to push the costs of a policy off onto others. It is a commonplace observation that policymakers like to create "unfunded mandates"—laws that require the private sector and other levels of government to fulfill some duty. The policies of the rights revolution typically involved such mandates. For example, the pioneering environmental statutes pushed costs of compliance off onto private actors, along with states and localities. If a policy initiative is characterized as a social goal, then it follows that the costs of the policy should be socialized. But if the initiative is characterized as a matter of rights, then every individual has a duty and should bear on her own the costs of fulfilling this duty. Thus, the rhetoric of rights is attractive to policymakers who want to take public action without dipping into their budgets.

Venue Shifting

Activists frequently turn to courts when they cannot obtain satisfaction in other venues. The civil rights movement is the most prominent example, but there are many others.[19] Shep Melnick and Steve Teles, for instance, both point to the importance of venue seeking in the evolution of the welfare rights movement.[20] As Frank Baumgartner and Bryan Jones have observed, the venue one chooses shapes the claims one puts forward.[21] To engage courts and judges, one must speak their language, and rights are a primary constituent of that language. So wherever activists turn to courts, they will cast their demands in the form of rights.

Distrust

In a system of separation of powers, policymakers in one branch have good reason to distrust the intentions of actors in the other branches. In a system of federalism, policymakers at one level of government have good reason to distrust the intentions of actors in the other levels. In a political culture whose hallmark is distrust of government authority,[22] individuals at least believe that they have good reason to distrust the intentions of *all* government officials. A common response to all these forms of distrust is to entrench duties on others, and so distrust plays a role in many policies from the rights revolution. For example, the strict statutory guidelines written into the major environmental statutes reflected in part the distrust of Democrats in Congress, who feared that Richard Nixon's Environmental Protection Agency (EPA) might be less than vigilant in policing industry. The early gains of the welfare rights movement reflected judicial distrust of local welfare officials: judges interpreted welfare eligibility rules so as to reduce the discretion of these officials.[23]

These efforts to entrench duties would seem unexceptional if not for an interesting feature of American political history: In much of the first half of the twentieth century, leaders of the majority party in Congress often trusted government agencies to use their discretion wisely, either because they accepted the idea of neutral expertise or because they expected those who staffed the agencies to have their same views. Once this trust evaporated, activists of all stripes had a strong incentive to create legal entrenchments that could be enforced in court. The importance of distrust in the enactment of rights is a story told by many scholars of public policymaking.[24]

If all these factors work as students of public policymaking suggest, the fact that activists attempt to entrench their presumptions in law is deeply unsurprising. What needs to be explained instead is the exceptional case when those who want the government to do something *neglect* to entrench their presumptions. The opposite of rights is discretion, and the delegation of discretion needs to be analyzed along with the entrenchment of duties. The grand delegation of discretion and funds to agencies and local government in the New Deal era seems in retrospect to be the exception, not the rule. Legal entrenchment, because it serves the interests of distrustful policymakers in a federalist, separation of powers system, seems the natural condition of American politics. So the proliferation of legal rights, at least in American politics, appears almost a necessary consequence of the growth of government.

The Counterattack

Nonetheless, attempts have been made to curb or reduce the range of rights. At the level of rhetoric, conservatives have responded to the rights revolution by emphasizing countervailing values, for example, of community order and individual responsibility. These themes have more recently found a place in the writings of the communitarian movement. "The Responsive Communitarian Platform," written in the early 1990s and signed mostly by liberal academics, urges attention to "the responsibilities that must be borne by citizens, individually and collectively, in a regime of rights."[25] It is easy to make fun of academics with their manifestos, but once in a while these documents do presage developments in politics. In this case, communitarian rhetoric has filtered down from academic journals, with their precise discussions of civic republicanism, to the Democratic party, where "rights *and* responsibilities" has become a common theme.

The debate over welfare reform featured much more of the former than the latter. This debate was a rare example in which a right—the right of eligible recipients to AFDC—was curtailed.[26] Many Democrats and liberal organizations opposed welfare reform, but few of them did so on the principle that Americans have a right to welfare. This suggests, as I have argued earlier in this chapter, that the AFDC entitlement was entrenched legally but not morally and thus vulnerable to challenge.

Besides AFDC, the other forms of rights that have been eliminated are mainly procedural. In the wake of the Oklahoma City bombing, President Clinton signed the Anti-Terrorism and Effective Death Penalty Act, a law that takes away the habeas corpus rights of death-row inmates, leaving them only "one bite of the apple." The Supreme Court has upheld the constitutionality of this restriction.[27] The Prison Litigation Reform Act, similarly, reduces the ability of inmates to sue for violations of their rights. As part of a series of immigration bills, Congress has recently restricted the right of noncitizens to challenge their deportation.[28] Tort reform laws passed in many states restrict the ability of individuals to sue for personal injuries they have received.

Much more common than elimination, however, is the diminishment of rights during implementation. After all, not even the most cherished constitutional rights are entrenched beyond challenge. States can pass laws violating freedom of speech, discriminating between individuals on the basis of race, and curbing religious freedoms, though only if they can demonstrate that a "compelling interest" requires this. The strength of a right—its level of entrenchment—is based on how strong the countervailing consideration must be to overcome it. The strength of rights is continually being adjusted, and much of the conservative attack on the rights revolution has taken the form of demands to adjust presumptions downward. So, for example, in *Planned Parenthood v. Casey,* the Supreme Court upheld the basic right to an abortion but downgraded the level of presumption. Where before only a "compelling interest" could justify restricting first-term abortions in any way, after *Casey* any regulation which does not pose an "undue burden" on the right is acceptable.[29] Similarly, in statutory interpretation, the Republican-dominated federal judiciary in the late 1980s interpreted civil rights laws so as to lower the duty of employers in defending policies which have a "disparate impact" on racial minorities. Congress in turn responded by raising these duties back to their original level with the 1991 Civil Rights Act.[30] The adjustment of rights is the primary strategy of attack against the rights revolution.

Another strategy is the promotion of counterrights, a method by which conservatives seek to beat liberals at their own game. For example, victims' rights policies have spread throughout the states, with Bill Clinton even endorsing a constitutional amendment on the subject. Similarly, "Megan's Law" and other such "right to know" policies have been promoted to counter what many consider the excessive civil liberties of convicted sex offenders. To counter environmental rights, property rights laws have been promoted in Congress and enacted in several states. To counter the Internal Revenue Service, everyone's favorite villain, a "taxpayer's bill of rights" has become law.

The fact that conservatives have been driven to create their own rights as a supplement to, or even substitute for, the attack on the rights revolution suggests just how resilient the revolution has been. The result is a kind of population explosion of rights: New rights are continually being born, but old rights have not for the most part died.

Generic Causes of Resilience

What factors might help us understand the resilience of rights policies? First, rights may be resilient for the same reasons that other types of policies are resilient. Rights, like any kind of policy, create what Paul Pierson has called "policy feedbacks," mechanisms by which the existence of the policy shapes future choices.[31] I want to consider briefly the relevance of three general types of policy feedback to rights.

Settled Institutions/Expectations/Commitments

Institutions and actors often make their plans based on their assumption that a public policy is settled, so unsettling the policy threatens great disruption. This creates what Pierson calls "policy lock-in."[32] The most familiar example of this phenomenon is the Social Security program. Any change to the program potentially disrupts the life plans of millions of people who have come to expect payments when they retire, so would-be reformers face a heavy political burden. The political consequences of such disruptions depend, of course, on the political power of those constituencies whose lives are affected: reformers who sought to abolish the AFDC entitlement generated comparatively weak opposition when they explicitly vowed to disrupt the lives of AFDC recipients along with the operation of those agencies that aid them. Lock-in effects don't seem to generally affect attempts to weaken or eliminate civil rights or civil liberties. Eliminating such rights, as some justices acknowledged in *Casey*, can greatly upset some members of the public and even undermine the legitimacy of the Supreme Court.[33] But this is not the strong form of lock-in suggested by the example of Social Security, in which abolition would cause not only consternation but disruption of long-settled life plans. Chief Justice Rehnquist has argued, in *Payne v. Tennessee*, that concerns about expectations—in law this is called "reliance"—are "at their acme in cases involving property and contract rights," but much less important for other forms of rights.[34] Thus, while the weight of expectations and earlier commitments does seem to be a factor in the fate of the rights revolution, it rarely reaches the level of importance that the "lock-in" terminology would suggest.

Settled Interests/Constituencies

Policies often create constituencies that in turn defend the policies from attack. The archetype of this pattern is the iron triangle, in which agencies, their constituent interest groups, and members of Congress exchange benefits and work together to protect their arrangement. With the obvious exception of entitlements, rights policies don't develop clienteles in precisely the way iron triangles do, but they do attract constituencies. The most obvious constituency is the lawyers who employ rights in litigation, and in fact attorney groups and public interest groups who bring lawsuits often lobby against changes in rights.[35] This, however, is a rather limited constituency. It does not include the potential *beneficiaries* of rights, who often remain unorganized. In the area of due process, for example, there is little organization of potential beneficiaries. In part this is because many of the beneficiaries lack resources and political power: prisoners, immigrants, welfare recipients, and criminal suspects are the prototypical weak claimants, so it's not surprising that they have not organized effectively. (It's also unsurprising that the few rights that have been wholly eliminated have been associated with these politically weak claimants.)

Another factor, however, also leads to low level of organization of beneficiaries: most people don't worry much about rights until they need them. For example, plenty of nonpoor, nonminority people every day find they have a strong interest in the rights of the accused, but too late to do much about this.[36] Because the beneficiaries of many rights are an amorphous group, rights may be less protected by their constituencies than other forms of public policy.

Settled Ideas/Meanings

Policies often create a conceptual framework for understanding a social problem which is not easily uprooted. Baumgartner and Jones call this a "policy image." They note, for example, that nuclear power for many years had a positive policy image, involving the control of nature for human gain by well-respected experts. This image was, of course, dislodged by the environmental movement.[37] But policy images often have a staying power, and this may be particularly true with rights—once a problem is identified as an issue of rights, it seems especially hard to think about it in another way. As Marc Landy has observed, once environmental policy was considered a matter of rights, "there simply was not readily available repository of intellectual discourse that both displayed sympathy for claimants, proposed to help them, and yet rejected their rights claims."[38] I have noted a similar pattern in disability policy.[39] Where rights are involved, debate often becomes polarized between those characterized as "for" and those "against" or, even more commonly, between supporters and those who favor competing rights. It is hard to break out of these ways of thinking once they are established. Rights limit the scope of policy debate, and this in turn protects them from some forms of attack.

The Particular Resilience of Rights

Beyond these generic causes of policy resilience, two characteristics of rights may contribute to their durability: they are at once *entrenched* and *flexible*.

The first point, about entrenchment, is tautological, since I have defined rights as entrenching duties. Entrenchment is, in fact, the main feature that separates rights from other policies. Rights entrench duties in rules (legal entrenchment) and in attitudes regarding social obligations (moral entrenchment). By definition, then, it takes more than the usual effort to eliminate a right. Opponents of an entitlement can't simply cut a budget item; opponents of a constitutional right can't simply pass a law overturning it. Opponents of a statutory right can repeal it but often don't—in part because of the difficulties of passing any law, but also because a statutory right often comes to be seen as a social obligation rather than a policy choice. These barriers can be overcome. Ideas about social obligations change over time, so that even rights entrenched in both law and public attitudes can on occasion be swept away. The turn of the 1930s Supreme Court on issues of economic regulation is a particularly dramatic example. The entrenchment of rights, though, generally makes them difficult to attack.

Yet while rights are entrenched, they are also surprisingly flexible. Like a program budget, which can be adjusted from year to year based on fiscal constraints, rights are far from dichotomous: they can be moved "up" and "down" depending on the political mood, as I've suggested. Rights, remember, are never really trumps but instead presumptions about duties. The strength of those presumptions is always being adjusted. Consider, for example, one of the most famous rights given to criminal defendants as part the rights revolution, the *Miranda* rule. This rule excludes from trial confessions illegally obtained by police officers who neglect their duty to advise suspects of the right to remain silent and to obtain an attorney. Contrary to the predictions of some observers, the Burger and Rehnquist Courts failed to abolish *Miranda*. In the recently decided *Dickerson v. United States*, Justice Rehnquist's majority opinion held that *Miranda* was so entrenched that it could not be repealed: "*Miranda* has become embedded in routine police practice to the point where the warnings have become part of our national culture."[40] Yet while the Supreme Court has upheld the basic rule of *Miranda*, it has at the same time chipped away at its application. The Court, for example, has limited the range of circumstances in which Miranda warnings must be given and allowed confessions from unwarned suspects to be admitted at trial in some instances.[41]

As the example of *Miranda* suggests, the flexibility of rights invites a piecemeal attack rather than a frontal assault: Opponents rightly calculate that the strategy of adjustment has a greater likelihood of payoff—and lower cost—than a campaign for repeal. Overturning *Miranda* would have created a furor, but diminishing its application incrementally has had little fallout. A frontal attack on rights is likely to be highly visible and so attract determined opposition; an attempt to adjust rights downward is routine and often all but ignored.[42] For this reason, adjustments to rights are common, but the wholesale elimination of a right is a rare event, rarer even (I suspect) than the elimination of a federal program or agency.

Conclusion: The Rubberiness of Rights

The main theme of this chapter, and the book in which it resides, is resilience. This is ironic, since *The New Politics of Public Policy* was aimed at demolishing an older picture of resilience, a vision of interest group pluralism in which the possibilities for political change were sharply restricted. Seeking a metaphor for this resilience, scholars and journalists seized on the image of an "iron triangle," and, later, of "gridlock." *The New Politics of Public Policy* took issue with this vision of resilience on two counts. First, it demonstrated that there was nothing particularly ironlike about iron triangles—interest groups could be beaten under certain circumstances. Iron triangles were, in fact, vulnerable to outside actors, even actors armed mainly with the power of their ideas, as, for example, in the case of the 1986 Tax Reform Act. Second, *The New Politics of Public Policy* showed that political entrepreneurs, using such weapons as litigation and the formulation of new rights, had belied notions about "gridlock" by enacting new policies. Moreover, these entrepreneurs, operating in an era of demobilized politics, often lacked the interest group support considered so significant by earlier generations of political scientists. Thus, the stability of interest group pluralism, the book concluded, was overstated.

In this volume, the theme of resilience is applied in a new setting: this book ponders whether the creations of the political entrepreneurs *The New Politics of Public Policy* celebrated and criticized are themselves resilient in the face of a conservative attack. I have offered some reasons to suggest that at least one subset of these creations, the rights revolution, is likely to be resilient. Students of public policy labeled the agency/client/Congress relationship an "iron" triangle. Rights might be best likened to an entirely different material: rubber, whose pliability is a source both of strength and weakness. Rights are not easily eliminated, but, like rubber, they can be stretched and molded in new directions. Thus, the politics of rights is far more flexible—more rubbery—than the rhetoric of rights would suggest.

This rubbery quality of rights is likely to become an increasingly prominent aspect of American politics, since we are witnessing, even several years after the glory days of the Rights Revolution, a continuing accretion of rights. The right to be free of a hostile workplace environment now competes with the right to speak in whatever way one chooses. The right of victims to have a say in the disposition of their attackers competes with the right of defendants to a fair trial. Each new rights claim is layered on top of older claims: environmental rights on top of property rights, victim's rights on top of defendant's rights, nonsmoker's rights on top of smoker's rights. It seems much easier to create new rights than it has been to get rid of old ones. Thus, American politics seems destined more and more to be a politics of rights.

Notes

1. Although the term *rights revolution* is widely used, it's not at all clear that those who use it have exactly the same phenomenon in mind. Some commentators see the rights revolution as a purely legislative enterprise, whereas others emphasize the increasing activism of the post-*Brown* judiciary. According to Cass Sunstein, the rights revolution involves "the creation, by Congress and the President, of a set of legal rights departing in significant ways from those recognized at the time of the framing of the American Constitution"; see

Sunstein, *After the Rights Revolution* (Cambridge, Mass.: Harvard University Press, 1990), v. Mary Ann Glendon, on the other hand, seems to identify the rights revolution as primarily a judicial production, a product of increasing judicial activism following *Brown v. Board of Education*; see Glendon, *Rights Talk* (New York: Free Press, 1991), 7.

2. Aaron Wildavsky defined entitlements as "legal obligations that require the payment of benefits to any person or unit of government that meets the eligibility requirements established by law." Wildavsky, "The Politics of the Entitlement Process," in *The New Politics of Public Policy*, ed. Marc K. Landy and Martin A. Levin (Baltimore: Johns Hopkins University Press, 1995), 143.

3. This preference for interest claims over rights claims contrasts sharply with Theodore Lowi's argument in *The End of Liberalism*. Lowi's book, written in the midst of the rights revolution, can be seen as an argument against "interest" claims and in favor of rights claims. Lowi excoriates the grand delegations of discretion to agencies and localities that facilitated "interest group liberalism." As suggested later, Lowi's argument against delegation is in fact an argument in favor of rights policies, since the defining characteristic of rights is that they impose duties rather than delegate discretion. See Lowi, *The End of Liberalism*, 2d ed. (New York: Norton, 1979).

4. Charles Taylor, "The Dangers of Soft Despotism," in *The Essential Communitarian Reader*, ed. Amitai Etzioni (Lanham, Md.: Rowman & Littlefield, 1998), 52.

5. Glendon, *Rights Talk*, 9. Glendon recognizes that there is little relationship between the absolutist rhetoric of rights in the United States and the reality; she titles her second chapter "The Illusion of Absoluteness."

6. Consider, for example, the approach of Patrick Garry, a lawyer and author of *A Nation of Adversaries*, one of many recent popular commentaries excoriating Americans for their excessive rights consciousness. What concerns Garry is the individualism promoted by rights: "Their power is supreme and they trump all social considerations." Lawrence S. Connor, "Litigation in 'A Nation of Adversaries'" (review), in *Indianapolis Star*, June 28, 1997, p. A11.

7. R. Shep Melnick, in his chapter on the Education for All Handicapped Children Act in *The New Politics of Public Policy*, found that in case of disability policy "rights were more than symbols but less than 'trumps.'" This seems a good generalization about all the rights in the rights revolution. Melnick, "Separation of Powers and the Strategy of Rights," 26.

8. This insight was elaborated by Stuart A. Scheingold in his book *The Politics of Rights* (New Haven, Conn.: Yale University Press, 1974).

9. Hohfeld criticizes those who use "rights" more broadly; he argues that many legal relations wrongly termed "rights" (or what he calls "claim-rights") are really "privileges," "powers" and "immunities," none of which involves a correlative duty. See Wesley Newcomb Hohfeld, "Some Fundamental Legal Conceptions as Applied in Legal Reasoning I and II," in *Fundamental Legal Conceptions and Other Legal Essays*, ed. Walter Wheeler Cook (New Haven, Conn.: Yale University Press, 1923), 23–114.

10. For a review of this argument, see Peter Jones, *Rights* (New York: St. Martin's, 1994), 26-32. Jones's book is an invaluable guide through contemporary theories and controversies about rights among moral and legal philosophers, and my chapter benefits considerably from his insights about rights theories.

11. Steven Teles, *Whose Welfare? AFDC and Elite Politics* (Lawrence: University Press of Kansas, 1997), 41–59.

12. Peter H. Schuck, *Citizens, Strangers, and In-Betweens: Essays on Immigration and Citizenship* (Boulder, Colo.: Westview, 1998), 139–148.

13. It is also possible for a right to be morally entrenched but not legally entrenched. The right to education may be one example. I suspect, without any poll data to support my claim, that the public would consider education a moral right. Courts have, however, resisted finding such a right in the U.S. Constitution, though some state courts have this right in their state constitutions. (For two cases in which the Supreme Court backed off from finding a right to education in the Constitution, see *San Antonio Independent School District v. Rodriguez*, 411 U.S. 1 [1973], and *Plyler v. Doe*, 457 U.S. 202 [1982].) There also may be a moral right to nutritional sustenance among Americans, though legally there is only a patchwork of local laws and policies governing emergency aid.

14. Indeed, it's not at all clear that Dworkin himself meant that *in practice* rights act as trumps. He simply claimed, "Rights are best understood as trumps over some background justification for political decisions that states a goal for the community as a whole." Ronald Dworkin, "Rights as Trumps," in *Theories of Rights*, ed. Jeremy Waldron (New York: Oxford University Press, 1989), 153.

15. *Employment Division, Department of Human Resources of Oregon v. Smith*, 494 U.S. 872 (1990).

16. Lawrence Friedman, *Total Justice* (Boston: Beacon, 1985). This book has greatly influenced my view of American legal culture, and I refer readers interested in the phenomenon of widening moral entrenchment to it.

17. Robert A. Kagan, "Adversarial Legalism and American Government," in Landy and Levin, *The New Politics of Public Policy*, 111.

18. Craig M. Bradley maintains that the Constitution allows Congress to create a national code of criminal procedure binding on local police, so that reformers have an alternative to court-created rights. Whether or not he is right as a matter of law—the current Supreme Court, with its emphasis on local rights, would clearly find his argument unpersuasive—Bradley neglects to explain how Congress could be persuaded to take up a thankless task such as this one. See Bradley, *The Failure of the Criminal Procedure Revolution* (Philadelphia: University of Pennsylvania Press, 1993), 144–161.

19. Indeed, the turn to rights in American public policy is closely related to the turn to courts, which I analyze in *Litigation and Its Discontents: The Struggle Over Lawyers, Lawsuits and Legal Rights in American Politics* (Berkeley: University of California Press, 2002). Yet there are aspects of the rights revolution that are not court centered—for example, the growth of entitlements. Thus, the rights revolution is even broader than the turn to courts and so merits separate analysis.

20. R. Shep Melnick, *Between the Lines: Interpreting Welfare Rights* (Washington, D.C.: Brookings Institution, 1994); Teles, *Whose Welfare?* 98–118.

21. Frank Baumgartner and Bryan D. Jones, *Agendas and Instability in American Politics* (Chicago: University of Chicago Press, 1993), 32.

22. In a concise and convincing review of the literature, John Kingdon concludes that distrust of governmental authority is in fact a central feature of American political culture. See Kingdon, *America the Unusual* (New York: Worth, 1999), 23–56.

23. See Melnick, *Between the Lines,* 48.

24. See, for example, Melnick, "The Courts, Congress and Programmatic Rights," in *Remaking American Politics,* ed. Richard Harris and Sidney Milkis (Boulder, Colo.: Westview, 1989), 188–214; Kagan, "Adversarial Legalism and American Government," in *Who Guards the Guardians?* ed. Martin Shapiro (Athens: University of Georgia Press, 1984).

25. "The Responsive Communitarian Platform: Rights and Responsibilities," in Etzioni, *The Essential Communitarian Reader,* xxv.

26. Indeed, the welfare reform bill included a kind of entrenchment in reverse: it entrenched on state and local welfare officials a duty *not* to provide welfare benefits after certain set points, though it appears there are many loopholes in this requirement.

27. *Felker v. Turpin,* 518 U.S. 651 (1996).

28. Schuck, *Citizens, Strangers, and In-Betweens,* 14–15.

29. *Planned Parenthood of Southeastern Pennsylvania v. Casey,* 505 U.S. 833 (1992).

30. In *Wards Cove Packing Company v. Atonio,* the Supreme Court ruled that defendants in civil rights suits no longer had to prove that employment policies which had a disparate impact on minorities were justified by "business necessity." Instead, plaintiffs had to show that such policies weren't justified by business necessity. This seemingly small, technical change in the burden of proof in practice greatly diminished the duty of employers to eliminate policies which have a negative impact on racial minorities. *Wards Cove Packing Company v. Atonio,* 490 U.S. 642 (1989). This part of *Wards Cove* was reversed by the 1991 Civil Rights Act, which explicitly restored the law to the interpretation that governed on June 4, 1989, the day before *Wards Cove* was handed down.

31. Paul Pierson, *Dismantling the Welfare State? Reagan, Thatcher, and the Politics of Retrenchment* (New York: Cambridge University Press, 1994), 39–50.

32. Ibid., 42.

33. *Planned Parenthood v. Casey,* 505 U.S. 833 at 865.

34. *Payne v. Tennessee,* 501 U.S. 808 (1991) at 828. The "swing" justices who wrote the lead opinion in *Planned Parenthood v. Casey* argued that *Roe* also created reliance because "people have organized intimate relationships . . . in reliance on the availability of abortion in the event that contraception should fail"; 505 U.S. 856.

35. This form of political activity is detailed in Burke, *Litigation and Its Discontents.*

36. This is one of the major bases for Marc Galanter's analysis of "Why the Haves Come Out Ahead" in legal disputes; see Galanter, "Why the Haves Come Ahead: Speculations on the Limits of Legal Change," *Law and Society Review* 9 (1974): 95.

37. Frank R. Baumgartner and Bryan D. Jones, *Agendas and Instability in American Politics* (Chicago: University of Chicago Press, 1993), 25–27.

38. Landy, "The New Politics of Environmental Policy," in Landy and Levin, *The New Politics of Public Policy,* 211.

39. Thomas F. Burke, "The Americans with Disabilities Act: On the Rights Track," in *Comparative Disadvantages? Social Regulations and the Global Economy,* ed. Pietro Nivola (Washington, D.C.: Brookings Institution, 1997), 242–318.

40. *Dickerson v. U.S.,* 120 S.Ct. 2326 (2000) at 2336.

41. See *New York v. Quarles,* 467 U.S. 649 (1984), and *Harris v. New York* 401 U.S. 222 (1971).

42. This view parallels Paul Pierson's observations about attacks on the welfare state. He finds that opponents of the welfare state often avoid frontal attacks in favor of low-visibility, gradual strategies. See generally Pierson, *Dismantling the Welfare State?*

PART IV

Social Welfare Policy

PART IV

Social Welfare Policy

8

The Evolving Old Politics of Social Security

Martha Derthick, *University of Virginia*

Social Security is the grandmother of entitlement programs. For more than half a century, it has shown the way to government benefits guaranteed by right. And, from the mid-1970s to the mid-1990s, the public's sense of entitlement—in combination with the overwhelming size of the program, an active and well-organized constituency of retired persons, and party politicians' fear of one another—kept Social Security off the political agenda except when impending insolvency of the Social Security trust funds inescapably put it there. In a time of severe fiscal constraint, dominated by sharply partisan debate over how to deal with the deficit, to talk about Social Security at all would perforce have meant talking about how to control its costs. Most politicians preferred not to.

It therefore came as a surprise in the late 1990s when political talk about Social Security erupted. There is a new politics of Social Security, which arises from proposals to "privatize" the program by giving individuals discretion to invest a portion of their Social Security payroll tax. Politicians who not long ago were loathe to touch Social Security—the "third rail" of American politics, because to touch it was to die—have been venturing forth with proposals for significant change.[1]

I will argue that the new politics of Social Security is an old politics of large public expectation, being played out, however, in a drastically changed political and programmatic context. The public is not offering to give up its entitlement. Nonetheless, with a lot of prompting from elite critics of the program in think tanks, universities, and conservative media, some portion of the public may want to switch to what could be a better deal.

The Growth of Entitlement

Originating in executive design of the Social Security Act in 1935, the entitlement developed over many decades and ultimately was confirmed by Congress in financial rescue packages of the late 1970s and early 1980s.

Unlike much in public policy, the public's entitlement to Social Security benefits did not occur by accident or stealth. It was planned, and by no less than the president. Franklin D. Roosevelt hated the dole—that is, support to the needy financed by general revenues. And, like any shrewd designer of a public program, he wanted to bind his successors. Together, these two considerations led him to insist in 1935 on a program of old-age insurance that would be financed out of earmarked payroll taxes on employers and employees and that would secure for citizen participants the government's solemn guarantee of their benefits.[2]

Social Security administrators' public presentation of the program stressed the guarantee. This was "insurance." Hence, the law effectuating the payroll tax became the Federal Insurance Contributions Act (FICA). Taxpayers were entitled to the insurance payments because they had paid for them through work and sacrifice (although the relation between tax payments and benefits, which was initially designed to be close, was very much diluted after 1939). Social Security was hardly even to be thought of as a government program. It was a way to help people save for their own futures. The use of a trust fund stood for the sanctity of the guaranty.[3]

It took a while for the legislature to grasp the political advantages of this construct. In 1935, Congress was a largely passive and not altogether comprehending respondent to an executive proposal, the benefits from which lay in the future. What Congress understood best at that time was grants in aid to the states, a familiar device, which would flow right away to the needy aged. Congress signed on to old-age insurance and began to make the program truly its own only with Social Security Act amendments in 1950 that extended coverage, increased benefits by 77 percent, guaranteed that insurance would surpass means-tested assistance in importance, and confirmed exclusive reliance on payroll tax financing.[4]

Through the 1950s and 1960s, the program grew incrementally as Congress periodically increased benefits and tax rates, in keeping more or less with the biennial schedule of elections. In an era of easy finance and with a program still not mature, credit was to be claimed from repeatedly increasing the benefits. An important milestone was the addition of disability benefits in 1956. Another was the addition of Medicare in 1965, attached to the program yet not quite of it. It has its own payroll tax and trust fund, and its own distinctive politics.

The next milestone in construction of the entitlement to benefits was amendments of 1972, which increased them by 20 percent *and* indexed them, tying increases for the already-retired to the consumer price index with an annual cost-of-living adjustment (COLA). The wage base—that portion of wages and salary that is subject to the payroll tax—was also indexed. Indexing took effect in 1975. If Franklin Roosevelt had managed to tie the hands of successor politicians in 1935, policymakers of the early 1970s doubled the knot. The program was on autopilot, and members of Congress would henceforth be obliged to provide whatever benefits the interaction of the indexed formula and the economy and demography of the United States produced—or stand ready to explain why not.

Indexing originated with a paradoxical combination of conservatives who hoped that an end to politically rewarding biennial benefit increases would contain the growth of the program and liberals who perceived that indexing would be beneficial in a mature program whose costs were on their way to being fully revealed. They judged that indexing would make Social Security more secure. As it happened, this hugely significant policy change marked the beginning of the end of politicians' love affair with Social Security. Credit claiming had indeed come to an end, as the conservatives wished. Henceforth, there would be only blame avoiding. And there would be far more of that than anyone anticipated in 1972.

The first blow to Congress came with the realization that the indexed formula of 1972 had been faulty and in an inflationary economy produced benefit promises both erratic and excessively generous. In amendments in 1977, Congress corrected the formula and injected large amounts of additional revenue into the program, promising a fix far into the future.

The next financial crisis, however, was only a few years away. Because of slow growth, accelerating inflation, and more unemployment than expected, Congress had to enact a rescue again in 1983, this one involving a combination of tax increases and barely disguised benefit cuts. Taxation of benefits was introduced; scheduled increases in taxation were accelerated; tax rates for the self-employed were raised; the age of eligibility for full benefits was raised in a distant (twenty-first century) future; and one automatic cost-of-living increase was delayed for six months.[5] Most of the contents of this package were worked out in an eleventh-hour negotiation in which members of the Reagan administration met with former Social Security commissioner Robert M. Ball, who was representing the House Democratic leadership. The increase in the age of eligibility was added on the House floor, under the sponsorship of Jake Pickle, chairman of The Social Security subcommittee of The Ways and Means Committee.[6]

Viewed dispassionately, Congress's actions of 1977 and 1983 confirmed the entitlement. Politically, Social Security had passed tests of fiscal stress. A stalwart and frightened Congress had for the most part made good the government's promises.

Beyond that, the political costs of making cuts were dramatized by the experience of the Reagan administration in 1981. Ironically, Reagan in March privately rejected a proposal of Republicans in the Senate Budget Committee to save $25 billion in five years with a COLA cut. Within the committee, at least, there was bipartisan support for this. Reagan, with prompting from his chief of staff, James Baker, said he could not agree because he had promised in the campaign not to cut Social Security.[7] Reagan had private doubts about the program but for political reasons had refrained from attacking it. His political advisers lived in fear that he would do so.

In May 1981, Reagan approved an ill-considered measure put to him by Office of Management and Budget Director David Stockman, who proposed to make a sharp reduction right away in the benefits of early retirees. At least hypothetically, this was a step toward phasing out early retirement, which began at age sixty-two. In place of the existing 20 percent penalty for such retirees, Stockman's plan would have imposed a 45 percent penalty, and it would have taken effect on January 1, 1982. Thus, a worker planning to retire then and expecting to receive $469 in monthly benefits would get $310 instead. The Senate promptly repudiated this patently unfair and politically senseless proposal by a vote of 96–0.

With a bipartisan hue and cry, Congress sent the administration into embarrassed retreat.[8]

Congress did give the Reagan administration a modest short-lived victory by eliminating in July 1981 the $122 minimum monthly payment for Social Security recipients, only to have the president reverse himself in September in response to protests. "It was never our intention to take this support away from those who truly need it," Reagan said. Congress restored the minimum benefit in December.[9]

It was this dramatically failed effort at cutting Social Security that clinched its reputation for being untouchable, though an administration with more common sense might have succeeded better. In the midterm election of 1982, Democrats kept Republicans on the defensive for their assault on the program. Politicians' ensuing fear of touching it was repeatedly demonstrated in the budget negotiations that became the centerpiece of American national politics in the 1980s and 1990s. Paul Pierson has argued the centrality of deficit politics in policymaking in recent decades.[10] And central to deficit politics was a ritual of declaring Social Security to be off the table.

One more valiant effort at cost reduction by fiscal conservatives in the Republican Senate met defeat. When Majority Leader Robert J. Dole and Budget Committee Chairman Pete Domenici tried in 1985 to balance the budget with the help of a COLA freeze—a replay, more or less, of the senators' effort in March 1981—they got no support from either their president or their party in the House of Representatives.[11]

Dole and Domenici achieved a melodramatic victory on their budget bill in the Senate, with a one-vote margin provided by Vice President Bush, after a tie had been secured by bringing an ailing Republican, Pete Wilson of California, into the chamber on a gurney. Several months later, President Reagan sacrificed this effort in a deal cut directly with House Speaker Thomas P. O'Neill Jr. In his 1984 campaign against Walter Mondale, Reagan had again boxed himself in with a promise not to touch Social Security.[12]

The Rise of Public Disillusionment

Though abundantly entitled, today's public is showing signs of dissatisfaction. It still supports the program, in that it overwhelmingly opposes a reduction in Social Security spending and, by smaller

majorities, favors an increase in spending.[13] Dissatisfaction is manifested in two ways. One is a declining confidence that benefits will
be paid at all; the entitlement is not fully credited. The other is a
growing dissatisfaction with rates of return. The program, even if
promising to pay, is not paying "enough."

Declining Confidence

Declining trust in government is a general phenomenon, and Social
Security only a particular instance of it. The causes of the general
phenomenon I will not take up here; they are the subject of a growing academic literature.[14] The specifics of the Social Security case are
evident from polls.

According to poll data, public confidence fell when the successive
fiscal crises of the late 1970s and early 1980s occurred. Asked in 1975
whether they were confident in the future of the Social Security system, 65 percent answered that they were "very confident" or "somewhat confident." By 1982, the proportion expressing confidence had
fallen to 32 percent. It got as high as 52 percent in 1990, but most of the
time since the mid-1980s, it has been below 50 percent. In 1996, 32 percent said they were confident, 30 percent said they were "not too confident," and 32 percent said they were "not at all confident."[15]

In light of the policy outcome of the crises, this outlook may
seem perverse. Why should the public be afraid that the program
will not pay benefits if politicians have so obviously been committed to assuring that it will? Apart from the generalized public distrust of anything and everything politicians do, probably two
answers address this question.

One is that, however politicians may have acted in the case of
Social Security or in budget negotiations, there has been an urgent
concern among policymaking elites, including some leading mem-
bers of Congress, that entitlement spending should be curbed.
Starting in the early 1970s, entitlement programs, including above all
Social Security and Medicare, took an ever larger share of the budget.
Interest on the debt, another nondiscretionary item, also increased.
Defense spending plummeted as a budget share, while discretionary
domestic spending held fairly steady. Many people in and close to
government see a problem in this loss of budgetary discretion.[16]

Although officeholders could not agree what to do about it
(other than to abolish grants to state governments for AFDC in

1996, which politicians offered as proof that they could control entitlements), there were signs that at least a few responsible policymakers wanted to do something. In the early 1990s, President Clinton appointed the Bipartisan Commission on Entitlement and Tax Reform, cochaired by Senators J. Robert Kerrey and John C. Danforth. The commission could not agree on recommendations, but in transmitting its report Kerrey and Danforth stated, "Left unchecked, the Federal government's long-term spending commitments on entitlement programs . . . will lead to excessively high deficit and debt levels, unfairly burdening America's children and stifling standards of living for this and future generations of Americans."[17] This was a prevalent view among elites, widely publicized. It did not breed confidence among the public.

It is also pertinent that a few cuts in Social Security were in fact made in the early 1980s. Although the Reagan administration was roundly defeated in its attempt to reduce benefits for early retirees and to eliminate the minimum benefit, it did succeed in eliminating survivors' benefits for college students between the ages of eighteen and twenty-two. This may not have been momentous, but it was a cut. And the rescue legislation of 1983 was a mixed affair, containing reductions in benefits as well as tax increases.[18] Perhaps of greatest significance, the age at which full benefits will be paid was scheduled to start rising gradually in 2000 for persons born after 1938, eventually reaching the age of sixty-seven for everyone born after 1960.

The second reason for the public's declining confidence is less obvious and more interesting. The financial fix of 1983 was so successful in the short run that it had perverse results. The Social Security program quickly began running big surpluses.[19] Also, payroll taxes increased as a share of government receipts, given the commitment of both politicians and the public to sustaining Social Security, and given rising resistance to the income tax. Tax receipts from Old-Age, Survivors, and Disability Insurance (OASDI), which were 46 percent of individual income tax receipts in 1980, stood at 61 percent of them in 1994. And because the Social Security surpluses were being used to finance activities other than Social Security, the public grew increasingly skeptical of the promise symbolized by the use of trust funds. A large proportion of the public—on the order of two-thirds—attributes Social Security's financial problems to this diversion.[20]

That Social Security is generally conceded to have financial problems is a final and compelling reason for lack of confidence. Although the trust fund surplus is large and growing, projections of the Social Security Administration (SSA) actuary published in 2000 anticipate that after 2015, annual outlays will exceed annual revenue and that the old-age and disability trust funds will be depleted by 2037. Thereafter, revenues will meet only about 72 percent of benefit obligations.

Falling Rates of Return

For most of the history of Social Security, there has not been a commonly accepted benchmark for judging the fairness or adequacy of benefits. In the halcyon days of the program before the mid-1970s financial crisis, the question did not have to be faced. In the policy debates of 1976–1977, "replacement rates" emerged as a touchstone—that is, the relation between the Social Security benefit and preretirement earnings. Replacement rates have since become a standard indicator. They appear often in public documents and scholarly analysis.

More recently, under the impact of conservative criticism, a different measure has acquired currency: rates of return, which measure investment yield.[21] Held currently to this standard, Social Security invites disappointment. Rates of return, which in an immature program were extremely high, have fallen steadily as people spend more years as taxpayers and pay at higher rates than their predecessors. Not only is it easy to show that today's recipients do less well than their predecessors, it is also easy to make the case that they could do better in the stock market. Over time stocks have had a higher rate of return than government bonds, in which Social Security tax receipts are invested.

The declining rates of return feed the conviction of younger persons that they will not do well as participants. Polls done for Third Millennium, an organization that purports to represent young adults, show that more than 80 percent of respondents in the age group 18–34 do not believe that the Social Security system will be able to finance benefits for them upon retirement. A comparably large majority in this age group expects to get less from Social Security than they would get if they invested the money themselves. This is a well-publicized finding. What has not been publicized is that 62 percent of the respondents in this age group also believe that people now on Social Security are getting back less than they paid into the system—a belief wildly at odds with fact.[22] If these results are to be credited, young adults today think that the government program has not been fair to anyone.

What is often interpreted in the press as antagonism between generations is actually a difference between generations in attitudes toward government. An NBC News/*Wall Street Journal* poll done by Hart and Teeter late in 1987 showed large differences among age cohorts in their expectations of what Congress would do about Social Security. Interviewees were given three choices: (1) "Congress will fail, system goes broke"; (2) "will make changes unfair to recipients"; (3) "will make the necessary changes." A plurality of the young—44 percent of those eighteen to twenty-nine—thought that Congress would fail and the system would go broke, whereas only 21 percent said that Congress would make the necessary changes. At the other end of the age spectrum, sixty-five and over, only 10 percent said Congress would fail, whereas 60 percent said it would make the necessary changes. Confidence rose directly with age.[23]

Criticism

The public's discontent with Social Security has been fed by hostile critics, libertarians who see an opportunity fundamentally to revise if not actually dismantle the New Deal program. Social Security has become so complicated that ordinary persons are bound to need help with benefit computations, rates of return, replacement rates, and the like.

There has been no shortage of such help. Critics have cast doubt on the reliability of benefit payments, both by pointing to the benefit cuts that have occurred and by pointing out that, despite the existence of a trust fund on the government's books, current taxes finance current benefits. Social Security benefits depend on political decisions, they argue, implying that for that reason they are uncertain. Future benefits depend on the willingness of future taxpayers to finance them.

Libertarians' interest in privatizing Social Security goes back to the 1960s, the advocacy of the free-market economist Milton Friedman, and Barry Goldwater's campaign for the presidency, which however did not get the cause off to a promising start.

Ronald Reagan, as Goldwater's heir, privately shared Goldwater's preference for a more voluntary system but for political reasons refrained from voicing it.

Yet the cause did not die, and Reagan's election agitated it. Since the early 1980s, intellectual and other critics of Social Security have produced a stream of books, articles, op-ed pieces, technical papers, briefs, and Web pages. These critics are to be found in the economics faculties of major universities, think tanks, financial institutions, publications such as *Forbes* and *Human Events*, pension consultants and managers, and the Concord Coalition, a fiscal watchdog. Just as President Roosevelt saw the Social Security Act as his principal domestic achievement, today's advocates of laissez-faire see fundamental change in it as potentially theirs.

Probably the most active and single-minded of all of the critics has been the Cato Institute, a libertarian think tank. Its publications mapped out a radical attack and plans for privatization as early as 1980. The attack gained strength after the legislation of 1983, a measure that angered Reagan's ideological following. This alleged believer in a voluntary system had presided over a new law that promised to secure the existing government program for generations to come.[24]

The opponents vowed not to give up. They plotted—publicly plotted, that is—a "Leninist" strategy for destroying social security. This would entail expanding alternatives to Social Security such as Individual Retirement Accounts (IRAs), exposing the myths on which trust fund financing rested and weakening the support of specific constituencies by arguing that the program was biased. Thus, they would divide its base of support as well as build a focused coalition for change, to include banks, insurance companies, and others that would gain from privatization.[25]

Ideas for policy change, even if thickly and persistently planted, need to be watered and fertilized by favorable circumstances. Time was on the critics' side. As it passed, the population changed. Those who had experienced the trauma of the Depression and remembered Franklin Roosevelt as a savior were being removed by death. Those reaching voting age had no such experience or memories, and shared instead a distrust of government. They began modestly to engage in organized political activity that contributed to the critique of Social Security. Third Millennium, an organization of Generation X-ers, sponsored a poll from which came the much-publicized finding that more young adults believed in UFOs than expected to receive their Social Security benefits.[26]

Also as time passed, the program, in fact, became more vulnerable to criticism as rates of return fell. Time also tended to increase alarm over the financial condition of Social Security. Although the legislation of 1983 had produced a financial surplus in the near term, official projections of the SSA actuary soon began to show a long-term deficit. Until the late 1990s, when the estimates turned up a bit under the impact of a surging economy, they grew worse with each passing year. This occurred in part merely because the future was that much closer and the number of projected deficit years in the seventy-five-year estimating span that much greater.[27]

Finally, time also produced foreign examples of privatization to point to. A Chilean privatization plan began to be implemented in 1981 and thereafter stirred interest in the United States. Under Prime Minister Margaret Thatcher, old-age pensions were partially privatized in the United Kingdom in the mid-1980s. A bit more time produced the observation that public old-age pension systems were experiencing difficulty throughout the developed world. As of the mid-1990s, a World Bank team of economists had assembled data from more than one hundred countries, concluding, "Almost all existing programs are in serious trouble." Reform of public pensions was on the agenda in many countries, a consequence of adverse demographic change (more retirees in relation to workers) and declining wage growth.[28]

If time was on the critics' side, so, more fortuitously, was the performance of the stock market, which enjoyed a record-setting bull run in the 1990s. Americans were participating in it in unprecedented numbers, principally through the purchase of mutual fund shares. A survey done by Peter Hart for the National Association of Securities Dealers in 1997 found that 43 percent of Americans owned stock, as opposed to just 21 percent in 1990. An NBC News/*Wall Street Journal* survey in the same year found that 51 percent of respondents owned at least $5,000 worth of common stock or mutual funds, either individually or through a retirement savings program. Whereas most Americans had most of their wealth in residential housing in preceding decades, by 1997 a majority had more wealth in stocks. When they opened their newspapers, they were now turning to the financial pages as well as the sports and the comics. Magazines on investing appeared in supermarket racks side-by-side with *People* and sensational tabloids.[29] This gave privatization of Social Security a plausibility that it could not have had in an earlier time, when the stock market was perceived as a risky venture suitable only for very rich men.

The Politicians Join In

Politicians were not quick to take up the critics' cause. For them to do so required that it cease being only a factional cause and acquire more general endorsement. For this, the Social Security Advisory Council of 1994 to 1996 was crucial.

This council was created by law, the last in a series that had precedents as far back as 1935. Beginning in 1939 and extending through the critical year of 1972, advisory councils had been a medium through which leaders of the Social Security Administration tested policy proposals and built consensus before taking them to Congress. The councils were staffed by the SSA. Initially informal and ad hoc, councils after 1956 were authorized by statute and constituted regularly.[30] When the SSA was made independent of the Department of Health and Human Services in 1994, the periodic advisory councils were abolished in favor of a standing one that is not likely to have comparable significance.

By the 1990s, the councils were no longer much influenced by the SSA. The council created in 1994 was at liberty to strike out on its own. Its thirteen members, their report long delayed, eventually divided into three factions.

Five members favored the creation of privately held "personal security accounts" (PSAs) through which Social Security payroll taxpayers would be allowed to invest most of their tax payments (5 percentage points of the total of 6.2 percentage points of the employee tax that prevailed at the time of the report). A flat benefit for all workers would survive as a bottom tier, financed out of the remaining portion of the payroll tax (the employer's share plus 1.2 percentage points of the employee's share).[31]

Two other members endorsed the creation of publicly held individual accounts, to be financed with an increase of 1.6 percent in the employee payroll tax. Individuals would have a limited choice of investment options, to include indexed bond funds and indexed stock funds.[32]

The other six members, a plurality, favored an approach called "maintenance of benefits" that embraced the existing benefit and tax structure essentially unchanged but envisioned, "after a period of study and evaluation, the possibility of a large-scale investment of OASDI Trust Fund monies in the equity market in order to help bring the program into balance and to greatly improve the money's worth ratios for young workers and future generations."[33] Robert M. Ball, a retired commissioner of Social Security and head of this faction, had asked rhetorically, "Why should the trust fund earn just one-third as much as common stocks?"[34]

That an official panel had given so much support, even if not unanimous, to creating a tier of individual investment gave respectability and impetus to the idea. The report received extensive news coverage. It was one thing to read of privatization in pamphlets of the Heritage Foundation or Cato Institute. It was another to see it in an official format, even if from the hands of some of the same authors. (For example, Carolyn Weaver, who headed the pension program at the American Enterprise Institute, was a council member and one of the principal authors of the PSA plan.)

Beyond that, for defenders of the traditional program to suggest that the government invest Social Security funds in stocks conceded that there was merit in the privatizers' position. An overview with which the report began, in which all members presumably concurred, was quite forthright about the declining value of benefits: "[F]rom now on many young workers and workers of future generations under present law will be paying over their working lifetimes employee and employer taxes that add to considerably more than the present value of their anticipated benefits. This is the inevitable result of a pay-as-you-go system such as the United States has had, and an aging population."[35]

Still, not much was heard at first from leading politicians. In 1995, two senators, Robert Kerrey of Nebraska and Alan K. Simpson of Wyoming, a Democrat and Republican, respectively, had cosponsored a bill that authorized a private tier. It would have diverted two percentage points of each taxpayer's payroll taxes to a "personal investment plan." As chairman of the subcommittee on Social Security and family policy of the Finance Committee, Simpson held hearings on the bill, but no one paid much attention. In Congress, a Social Security reform caucus was organized, and a handful of Republican backbenchers—Mark Sanford of South Carolina, Nick Smith of

Michigan—took up the issue, but in 1996 it was still not quite the stuff of high politics. What elevated it, in addition to the Advisory Council report, was the discovery in 1997 that the government was going to run a surplus. Deficit politics was suddenly ended and surplus politics was about to begin. This had consequences for Social Security.

In his State of the Union message in January 1998, President Clinton admonished a Republican-dominated Congress to "save Social Security first." It shouldn't be tempted to respond to the surplus with tax cuts. If it did, the Democrats would charge it with failing to save Social Security.[36] The president presented no proposal but instead announced a plan for a series of regional forums at which Social Security would be discussed with the public. This done, a White House conference on the subject and a convening of congressional leaders to craft legislation would both take place.

For the next two years, in the run-up to the presidential election of 2000, proposals multiplied. In the spring of 1998, Senators Daniel P. Moynihan (D-NY) and again Kerrey advanced a plan that would have introduced a voluntary private tier, along with a short-run reduction in the payroll tax. Soon thereafter, Senators John Breaux (D-LA) and Judd Gregg (R-NH) proposed a bill, based on a study sponsored by the Center for Strategic and International Studies, that would have introduced a mandatory private tier using two percentage points of the existing payroll tax. Both proposals also included a mix of benefit reductions and revenue increases—for example, a COLA cut, an increase in the retirement age, lengthening the period on which the computation of benefits is based, extended coverage of state and local government employees—that were designed to bring the program into long-run financial balance.

In addition, the appearance of a budget surplus gave rise to a new family of proposals—coming from Representative John Kasich, the Republican chairman of the House Budget Committee, Senator Phil Gramm of Texas, and Professor Martin Feldstein of Harvard— that would have used the surplus to finance creation of private accounts. Feldstein's plan, for example, called for each worker to deposit 2 percent of his or her earnings, up to the wage-base ceiling, in a personal retirement account and for these deposits to be offset with an income tax credit. For as long as the projected budget surplus lasted, it would be used to finance the tax credits. Thereafter, increased federal borrowing, tax increases, or spending cuts would be required. When workers reached retirement age and began to draw pensions from their personal retirement accounts, their Social Security benefits would be reduced by $3 for every $4 withdrawn. In effect, the benefits promised by the current Social Security program would become a floor under pensions.[37] This was an ingenious proposal that built on Social Security, taking advantage of its popularity while purporting to replace it with a more private alternative financed at public expense.

As these proposals were being advanced, defenders of the existing program—Robert Ball and the Brookings economists Henry Aaron and Robert Reischauer, most prominently—were trying to stem the tide for a private tier and make the case that no fundamental change was necessary. Social Security, they argued, was still the safest, fairest, and *best* investment when all of its advantages were considered, including progressivity of benefits and benefits for people with disabilities, survivors, and spouses. With modest reductions in benefits and increases in taxes—and with authority for the government to invest trust fund reserves in stocks and corporate bonds, a crucial feature of their position—Social Security could be made solvent for the long run.

As months passed and the surplus grew, the debate subtly shifted. It focused less on what to do about Social Security and more on how to use the surplus. This gave Democratic protectors of the existing system a wholly new opening, which President Clinton moved to exploit in his State of the Union message in 1999. He proposed to credit a large portion of the surplus, more than 60 percent a year for fifteen years, to the Social Security trust fund. In combination with a proposal to invest up to one-fourth of the trust fund in stocks and corporate bonds, this was expected to keep the trust fund solvent until approximately 2055, an extension of twenty years or more. To counter proposals for a partial privatization of Social Security, the president proposed to induce private saving with a new program of individual accounts to which the government would make matching grants. Larger matches would go to individuals with low incomes.

No action followed. It was the season of impeachment, not an auspicious moment for bipartisan collaboration even if any were otherwise possible. Instead, rhetorical jockeying ensued over which party was doing more to save Social Security. As they worked on the budget, congressional Republicans boasted of putting the Social Security surplus—the excess of payroll tax revenues over benefit spending—into a "lockbox" rather than spend it, as had been customary in the era of deficits. This surplus was $133.7 billion in 1999 and $153 billion in 2000.

The critique of Social Security, followed by the unanticipated appearance of budget surpluses, had widened the range of policy options. In the spring of 2000, George W. Bush, the presumed Republican nominee for the presidency, endorsed partial privatization, saying that he favored permitting individuals to invest a portion of their Social Security payroll tax.

The political sky did not fall on him. A CBS News/*New York Times* poll found that 51 percent of respondents thought that individual investment of a portion of the payroll tax was a good idea, while 45 percent thought it a bad one. Several weeks later, after Bush's Democratic opponent, Al Gore, had denounced the proposal as risky, a CNN/*USA Today*/Gallup poll found that 59 percent of 1,059 adults polled favored it. Strongest support came from respondents under fifty. Over age sixty-five, two of three persons were opposed.[38]

At the same time, polls showed that voters had more trust in Gore to "protect Social Security."[39] He was advancing proposals similar to those offered by Clinton early in 1999. He promised to use the budget surplus to reduce the government's debt and to credit to the Social Security trust fund the resulting savings on interest payments. In effect he was promising, as did Clinton, to use general revenues to cover the deficit anticipated in Social Security later in the twenty-first century. Just as Bush's plan for partial privatization was a sharp break with traditional practice, so was Gore's plan for introducing general revenues. Historically, Congress had relied exclusively on an earmarked payroll tax as a way of disciplining the demand for benefits.

Gore also proposed government-subsidized individual savings accounts that he called "Social Security plus" to differentiate them, by implication, from "Social Security minus," the approach he imputed to Bush. Whereas Clinton's proposal called for the government to match individual savings with grants, Gore's called for a subsidy through tax credits. Like Clinton's, it would be more generous at lower levels of income.

As of the summer of 2000, then, it appeared that free-market critics of Social Security had scored a victory in enabling a Republican presidential candidate to propose a narrowing of the purely public program. In a political breakthrough, this had become a legitimate and defensible position to take. But the Democratic candidate's response, rather than concede merit in privatization, called for enlarged public commitments to the established program, along with a new program of publicly subsidized private saving.

This articulation of interparty differences had the merit of giving the electorate a choice, insofar as it might care to choose between the candidates based on this issue. It also made continued stalemate over Social Security likely if party control of the government were divided and no immediate fiscal crisis in the program was at hand. Fifteen years, which as of 2000 was the projected duration of Social Security surpluses, is an eternity in political time.

Conclusion

At sixty-five years, Social Security is an old program, and old programs do not generate an entirely new politics. Old programs become institutions, the central features of which have a strong tendency to persist. At the same time, they are not immune to political, economic, and demographic changes around them. Interactions of old programs with new contexts can create new issues.

Much about policymaking for Social Security has changed since the late 1970s. The institutions of policymaking have changed. The arena is more open, not to say chaotic. Twenty years ago I described a stable and relatively constricted set of actors—program proprietors, as I called them—with the leadership of the Social Security Administration and of the Ways and Means Committee at its core. Policy initiation was dominated by executive leaders of the program, working in close collaboration with Ways and Means and with organized labor's specialists in Social Security.[40]

That set of arrangements has disintegrated. To some extent, it was deliberately destroyed by presidencies seeking to assert control over the program. The Social Security commissionership, once a stable office occupied for long periods by individuals whose careers were devoted to constructing the program, became a revolving door for political appointees who did not necessarily have any experience with it. The Ways and Means Committee, which once had dominated Social Security policymaking in the House, lost much of its power when Wilbur Mills departed the chairmanship and its role was reduced in the mid-1970s wave of congressional reform.[41]

No stable alternative set of arrangements has emerged in place of the old one. Through the 1980s and 1990s, Social Security has recurrently been the subject—or agreed nonsubject—of budget negotiations among the president and leaders of the House and Senate. When it had to be dealt with, as in the fiscal crisis of the early 1980s, the Reagan White House improvised a decision-making instrument in the form of the Greenspan Commission, which itself then dissolved at the last minute into an improvised inner core of decision makers.[42]

Policymaking in regard to privatization has likewise been ad hoc. Prime movers were outside of the government but managed to move partway inside through the statutory advisory council. When President Clinton stepped forward to put Social Security on the national agenda, he chose to invite discussion through regional forums that were to be organized by competing interest groups—the Concord Coalition and the American Association of Retired Persons. In all of this, the Social Security Administration has been conspicuous for its absence, except that its Office of the Actuary is invariably called on to estimate the financial consequences of proposed changes.

The ideational underpinnings of the program have also changed as a result of broad shifts in American politics and in the population. The Democratic party's dominance of the presidency came to an end, tentatively with the election of Eisenhower, more certainly with the election of Reagan. Republican Senates were elected more often and in 1994, a Republican House of Representatives. The proportion of the population identifying with the Democratic party declined. Trust in government generally declined. Although there was no wholesale reduction in government activity, there was an increased willingness to hold the line on expansion, to examine alternatives to public financing of social programs, and to restore the historic American presumption in favor of markets and private, voluntary action. Events elsewhere in the world had something to do with this. If capitalism was not everywhere rising, at least its principal competitor, communism, was falling.

Finally, calculations of interest changed—or were initiated on the basis of new information. It is unlikely that Social Security recipients had any idea until very recently what their rates of return were. In the 1990s, prompted by the program's critics and a rapidly spreading familiarity with investment in stocks, the younger part of the population began looking at Social Security more critically than most persons had ever looked at it before. This development, in combination with the projected long-term deficits, began to induce fear of *not* acting on Social Security—hence, the embrace of some degree of privatization, at least as a proposal seriously to consider.

In sum, changes in institutions, ideas, and interests conjoined to raise the possibility of significant policy change in a program that had long seemed impervious to it. The outcome remains uncertain. Depending on the balance between the major parties and the financial condition of the government, a renewed dynamic of expansion in Social Security may prevail over the critics' attempt to trim. The entitlement that Franklin Roosevelt built remains a mighty fortress.

Notes

1. For example, see Michael Barone, "Voters Are Ready for Social Security Reform," *Wall Street Journal,* May 7, 1998, p. A22; and Clay Chandler, "Hill Weighs Policy Shift for Retirees," *Washington Post,* April 27, 1998, p. A1.

2. Frances Perkins, *The Roosevelt I Knew* (New York: Viking, 1946), 284–285; Arthur J. Altmeyer, *The Formative Years of Social Security* (Madison: University of Wisconsin Press, 1966), 11, 29; Edwin E. Witte, *The Development of the Social Security Act* (Madison: University of Wisconsin Press, 1963), 72–75, 147–151.

3. Martha Derthick, *Policymaking for Social Security* (Washington, D.C.: Brookings Institution, 1979), 5 and passim. On the significance of trust fund financing, see Eric M. Patashnik, "Trust Funds and the Politics of Precommitment," *Political Science Quarterly* 112 (Fall 1997): 431–452; and Patashnik, *Putting Trust in the U.S. Budget: Federal Trust Funds and the Politics of Commitment* (Cambridge: Cambridge University Press, 2000).

4. Derthick, *Policymaking for Social Security,* 43–47.

5. John A. Svahn and Mary Ross, "Social Security Amendments of 1983: Legislative History and Summary of Provisions," *Social Security Bulletin* 46 (July 1983): 3–48.

6. The definitive account of the 1983 negotiations is Paul Light, *Artful Work: The Politics of Social Security Reform* (New York: Random House, 1985).

7. Lou Cannon, *President Reagan: The Role of a Lifetime* (New York: Simon & Schuster, 1991), 243–248.

8. Ibid., 248–251, and Laurence I. Barrett, *Gambling with History: Ronald Reagan in the White House* (New York: Penguin, 1984), 155–159.

9. *Congress and the Nation: Vol. 6. 1981–1984* (Washington, D.C.: Congressional Quarterly, 1985), 646–647.

10. Paul Pierson, "The Deficit and the Politics of Domestic Reform," in *The Social Divide: Political Parties and the Future of Activist Government*, ed. Margaret Weir (Washington, D.C.: Brookings Institution and Russell Sage Foundation, 1998), 126–178.

11. George Hager and Eric Pianin, *Mirage* (New York: Times Books, 1997), 131–145. See also Richard Fenno Jr., *The Emergence of a Senate Leader: Pete Domenici and the Reagan Budget* (Washington, D.C.: Congressional Quarterly, 1991), 62.

12. Warren B. Rudman, *Combat: Twelve Years in the U.S. Senate* (New York: Random House, 1996), 76–81.

13. Lawrence R. Jacobs and Robert Y. Shapiro, "Myths and Misunderstandings about Public Opinion toward Social Security," in *Framing the Social Security Debate*, ed. R. Douglas Arnold, Michael J. Graetz, and Alicia H. Munnell (Washington, D.C.: National Academy of Social Insurance, 1998), 355–388.

14. For example, see Stephen C. Craig, *The Malevolent Leaders: Popular Discontent in America* (Boulder, Colo.: Westview, 1993), and Joseph S. Nye Jr., Philip D. Zelikow, and David C. King, eds., *Why People Don't Trust Government* (Cambridge, Mass.: Harvard University Press, 1997).

15. Jacobs and Shapiro, "Myths and Misunderstandings."

16. For analyses, see Pierson, "The Deficit and the Politics of Domestic Reform," 129–137, and C. Eugene Steuerle, Edward M. Gramlich, Hugh Heclo, and Demetra Smith Nightingale, *The Government We Deserve* (Washington, D.C.: Urban Institute Press, 1998), chapter 4.

17. Bipartisan Commission on Entitlement and Tax Reform, *Final Report to the President* (Washington, D.C., January 1995), ii.

18. Just how tax increases and benefit reductions netted out is a bit problematic. In estimating the effects of the 1983 amendments, raising the age of normal retirement to sixty-seven in the next century accounted for the biggest single gain to the system: 0.83 percent of payroll. The second biggest gain (0.81 percent) came from reallocating revenue from the disability trust fund to the old-age insurance trust fund, which was pure accounting sleight of hand. Taxing benefits gained an estimated 0.56 percent; delaying a COLA increase for six months, 0.28 percent; covering new federal employees, 0.26 percent; and increasing the tax rate on self-employed persons, 0.17 percent. Other changes were minor by comparison. See Svahn and Ross, "Social Security Amendments of 1983," 44.

19. For an optimistic assessment of the program's financial condition, see *Long-Term Status of the Social Security Trust Funds*, Hearing before the Committee on Social Security and Family Policy of the Senate Finance Committee, 100th Congress, 2d Session (1988), part 1.

20. Robert J. Blendon, John M. Benson, Mollyann Brodie, and Flint Wainess, "America in Denial: The Public's View of the Future of Social Security," *Brookings Review* (Summer 1998): 46.

21. Some economists prefer to use the term "implicit rate of return" for Social Security, inasmuch as there is no actual investment. The participant does not acquire assets on which to earn a true rate of return. See Martin Feldstein, "A New Era of Social Security," *The Public Interest* (Winter 1998): 106.

22. "Social Security: The Credibility Gap," unpublished analysis of Third Millennium public opinion survey by Frank Luntz and Mark Siegel, September 1994. I am indebted to Richard Thau for providing me with a copy of this document. The findings of this poll in regard to confidence levels by age group are consistent with those of other polls. CBS News/*New York Times* polls done in the 1990s have consistently found that no more than 25 percent of respondents between the ages of eighteen and twenty-nine and thirty to thirty-nine are confident that they will get benefits. Confidence is high—70 to 80 percent—only at the upper end of the age spectrum (over sixty), a cohort most of whom are already receiving Social Security.

23. *Wall Street Journal,* December 12, 1997, p. R6.

24. See Richard Darman, *Who's in Control? Polar Politics and the Sensible Center* (New York: Simon & Schuster, 1996), 119.

25. Stuart Butler and Peter Germanis, "Achieving a Political Strategy for Reform," in *Social Security: Prospects for Real Reform,* ed. Peter J. Ferrara (Washington, D.C.: Cato Institute, 1985), 159–169. Since 1995, the Cato Project on Social Security Privatization, directed by Michael Tanner, has published a book, Peter J. Ferrara and Michael Tanner, *A New Deal for Social Security* (1998), and a series of papers, among which Tanner's "'Saving' Social Security Is Not Enough," May 25, 2000, SSP No. 20, is a good summary of Cato's position.

26. The poll contrived the question "Do you think UFOs exist?" The response was 46 percent yes; 43 percent, no; and 11 percent, "don't know" or declined to answer. The published interpretations of the results, issued by Third Millennium, then asserted that more young people believed in UFOs than believed they would get Social Security benefits (28 percent). This was an accurate statement of poll results, but it should be noted that the poll did not frame a question comparatively. It did not ask whether the existence of UFOs or payment of Social Security benefits was more probable.

27. Reports on the financial condition of the system may be found on the SSA's website, www.ssa.gov.

28. Estelle James, "Social Security around the World," in *Social Security: What Role for the Future?* ed. Peter A. Diamond, David C. Lindemann, and Howard Young (Washington, D.C.: National Academy of Social Insurance, 1996), 181–208. This essay by James was based on a book, World Bank, *Averting the Old Age Crisis: Policies to Protect the Old and Promote Growth* (Oxford: Oxford University Press, 1994). On foreign experience, see also R. Kent Weaver, "The Politics of Pensions: Lessons from Abroad," in Arnold et al., *Framing the Social Security Debate,* 183–229; Martin Feldstein, ed., *Privatizing Social Security* (Chicago: University of Chicago Press, 1998); and John Myles and Paul Pierson, "The Comparative Political Economy of Pension Reform," in Pierson, *The New Politics of the Welfare State* (Oxford University Press, forthcoming).

29. Barone, "Voters Are Ready for Social Security Reform."

30. Derthick, *Policymaking for Social Security,* chapter 4.

31. *Report of the 1994–1996 Advisory Council on Social Security: Vol. 1. Findings and Recommendations* (Washington, D.C.: Government Printing Office, 1997), 30–33.

32. Ibid., 28–29.

33. Ibid., 25–27.

34. Peter Passell, "Investing It: Can Retirees' Safety Net Be Saved?" *New York Times,* February 18, 1996, p. F1.

35. *Report of the 1994–1996 Advisory Council on Social Security: Vol. 1,* 12.

36. Democrats rose from their seats with a roar when the president said, "Save Social Security first." "It was, to my mind, the most incredible moment of this Presidency," a presidential speechwriter later told a reporter. "Not so much because Clinton had managed to outthink and outflank the Republicans in the midst of the Lewinsky scandal but because in that moment you could just see one trillion dollars moving from their side of the ledger to ours, from tax cuts to Social Security." Joe Klein, "Eight Years: Bill Clinton and the Politics of Persistence," *The New Yorker,* October 16 and 23, 2000, p. 191.

37. My account of Feldstein's proposal and others draws on Henry J. Aaron and Robert D. Reischauer, *Countdown to Reform: The Great Social Security Debate* (New York: Century Foundation Press, 1998), chapter 7. Far from a newcomer to Social Security reform, Feldstein had written on the subject for nearly a quarter-century. An early essay was "Toward a Reform of Social Security," *The Public Interest* 40 (Summer 1975). A more recent one, "A New Era of Social Security," appears in *The Public Interest* 130 (Winter 1998).

38. Richard W. Stevenson, "Challenges to Bedrock of Retirement," *New York Times,* May 16, 2000, p. A19; Richard Benedetto, "Poll: Most Back Bush Retirement Proposal," *USA Today,* June 9–11, 2000, p. 1A.

39. Dan Balz, "Bush Still Leads Gore in Poll," *Washington Post,* June 13, 2000, p. A22. See also the results of an NBC News/*Wall Street Journal* poll in the *Journal,* June 23, 2000, p. A1, which showed both that voters preferred Gore to Bush (42 percent to 35 percent) on Social Security overhaul and that more backed Gore's plan than Bush's plan (51 percent vs. 38 percent).

40. Derthick, *Policymaking for Social Security.*

41. Martha Derthick, *Agency under Stress: The Social Security Administration in American Government* (Washington, D.C.: Brookings Institution, 1990), 192–200.

42. Light, *Artful Work,* 178ff.; Darman, *Who's in Control?* 116–117.

9

The Politics of Rights Retraction

Welfare Reform from Entitlement to Block Grant

Steven M. Teles, *Brandeis University*
Timothy S. Prinz, *United Hospital Fund of New York City*

In 1996, an entitlement was eliminated. This simple sentence was virtually unimaginable just a few years ago, when the social policy literature treated structural change in the welfare state as next to impossible. The dominant paradigm of policy studies argued that radical policy change is exceedingly rare and that the policy process was more likely to be driven by incremental change.[1] At first glance, there is little reason to expect welfare policy to be any different. In *The New Politics of Public Policy,* Aaron Wildavsky observed that Aid to Families with Dependent Children (AFDC) is "resistant to direct cuts and thus expands in the face of disapproval."[2] Landy and Levin argued that once programs have attained the status of a right, "they are exempt from a full and probing evaluation of their merits and their costs."[3] AFDC muddled along, seemingly impervious to all efforts at structural reform, be they in the direction of expansion or contraction. All we knew suggested that, despite its unpopularity, AFDC was an entitlement, a right, and as such it was here to stay.

Yet, after two presidential vetoes, Congress passed and the president signed a welfare bill rescinding AFDC's entitlement status in 1996. Tellingly, the bill stated, "This part shall not be interpreted to entitle any individual or family to assistance under any State program under this part."[4] Somehow, a right disappeared. An entitlement was turned into a block grant. How did this happen? And, more important, what can this process of "rights retraction" tell us about the nature of the policy process?

To understand how AFDC lost its entitlement status, it is critical to view the program in its historical context. Most social programs consolidate their support over time. They become rooted in people's expectations and choices, as interest groups develop to protect them and as mechanisms for low visibility retrenchment become more difficult to find.[5] But AFDC never really became a fully entrenched entitlement. Despite the fact that its rights status was protected by the courts and overseen by federal bureaucrats, its protected status was always tenuous. What is more, small changes in the institutional structure of the program in the early 1980s, which seemed unimportant at the time, set in motion a new policy path, which in the end undermined the one sought by advocates and established by the courts.

Clearly, rights and the courts that enforce them matter and provide an avenue for policy development sharply divergent from that of the classical model of the policy process.[6] But the establishment of programmatic rights[7] does not end politics but transforms it by changing the political conditions on the ground. In some cases, the new "right" is uncontroversial, boring, inexpensive, or inoffensive to any highly focused group. In this case, its rights status remains stable, its politics are low in salience, and the policy drops out of sight, protected by an interest group/courts/bureaucratic shield. In other cases, the right may be unstable or politically vulnerable. Welfare's political shield turned out to be weak and subject to revision once new actors and new ideas entered the policy arena. The story of welfare policy illustrates the importance of taking the longer view when it comes to the establishment of programmatic rights.

This chapter, therefore, attempts to link the policy process literature to historical institutionalism.[8] The key insight in historical institutionalism is what we might call "institutional stickiness."[9] Institutions, including public policies, are sticky because they have mechanisms of self-preservation. On the one hand, policies create new interests, are frequently embedded in rules that make changes very difficult (one of which is "rights status") and, in some cases, such as pay-as-you-go (PAYGO) old-age pensions, create large transition costs to move to alternative systems. On the other hand, policies and institutions can be sticky because they condition actors into a particular understanding of their interests. Moreover, policies not only structure interests but in so doing also limit the alternatives available to challenge the status quo. This insight allows us a certain

degree of advance knowledge about the resilience of different programs. Means-tested welfare benefits, unlike PAYGO pensions, do
not create large transition costs, but they do condition political actors
into particular understandings of the political costs and benefits of innovation. In the period that we examine here, they were also associated with institutional protections that made innovation by
state-level actors seem blocked by legally entrenched rights or bureaucratic intransigence. These rigidities help explain why welfare
rights persisted even as public opinion turned against the program.

If this argument is correct, then it suggests an area of politics that
is understudied: the efforts of political actors to enhance or diminish
the institutional stickiness of public policy. A great deal of politics is
the process of, on the one hand, entrenching particular policy designs
and, on the other, attempting to keep alternative policy paths alive.
AFDC has been relatively easier to attack both because the policy's
programmatic features created few transition costs to innovation but
also because conservatives were more successful in creating alternative paths to compete with the welfare rights model.[10] The establishment of "waivers" introduced new actors and new ideas into
the welfare field and therefore kept alive a competitor to the rights-
oriented model of welfare established by the courts.

However, it was not just the actions of conservatives that undermined the model of welfare rights but also the process by which
they were established. AFDC became a right as a result of the intervention of the Supreme Court, driven by lawyers and welfare rights
activists, many of whom were deeply suspicious of public values
and hostile to a program they saw as a reflection of those values. A
welfare right was conceived as a way to protect vulnerable poor
people from a political system that was inherently oppressive and
ungenerous. The vision was one of the state as guardian, defending
the poor from the effects of an impersonal economic system and a
welfare state dominated by hostile administrators, politicians, and
the public itself.

Such a strategy requires that the right, once established, generate retrospective acceptance. But the establishment of welfare rights
did no such thing. Instead, the transformation of welfare into a right
led to a public backlash. Welfare reform was in part a reaction by
the public to the establishment of a programmatic right.

The story this chapter tells shows that a new category of political processes must be introduced into the policy literature, what we

might called competing or parallel paths.[11] As John Kingdon has taught us,[12] when "windows of opportunity" open up for policy change, not every alternative to the status quo is taken seriously. Only those that are considered to be "ripe" are considered, where ripeness has intellectual ("Is it well thought through?"), political ("Who supports it?"), and policy ("Has it been done before and did it work?") components. This process of keeping an alternative alive is what we mean by the creation of a parallel path. The American political system is especially open to the establishment of rival policy paths, due to the existence of strong subnational political institutions where those who lose at the national level can put their preferred policy alternative into practice. In fact, as we shall see, different parts of the national government, if they can prevent the other branches from stopping them, can actually encourage challenges to existing policy and, in doing so, attempt to mobilize or activate interests and encourage innovation. In addition, the government may fund "experiments" (often as a form of logrolling to break political impasses) that serve as a standing challenge to the dominant approach.

Policy entrepreneurs connected to the dominant approach are involved in a continuing process of entrenching existing policies by preventing the maturation of alternative paths, while rival entrepreneurs attempt to open up space for new policy approaches to evolve. Policy change occurs when the internal contradictions of the dominant approach become visible, an alternative path is sufficiently well developed to overtake the dominant one, and space for the issue in question appears on the political agenda. As we shall show, this competing path approach sheds new light on the politics of welfare reform, and may be a useful concept in other policy areas as well.

The Court's Intervention and the Creation of a Quasi-Right

To understand how the Personal Responsibility and Work Opportunity Act (PRWORA) came to be, it is critical to begin the story with the establishment of a partial welfare right, in the late 1960s. Much of the politics of welfare reform is best viewed as a series of political and policy debates, framed by reactions to, defenses of, and attempts to undermine this rights status.

Prior to the Court's intervention in welfare, AFDC was a program riddled with discretion. In 1967, only 42 percent of those families that were financially eligible for assistance were actually on the welfare rolls.[13] The low participation rate in AFDC was the consequence of a number of factors, both individual (welfare "stigma") and institutional (in particular, high levels of administrative discretion).[14] Prior to the involvement of the Court, much of the work of eligibility determination in AFDC was not done explicitly, through legislation, but implicitly, through the dispersed activities of what Michael Lipsky has called "street level bureaucrats."[15] These determinations, based as they were on the idiosyncratic preferences of thousands of welfare offices, were unclear, inconsistent, and arguably unjust.

This pattern was not wholly an accident. Congress had intended when it wrote the Social Security Act that states would be able to use their discretion to provide welfare to "good" mothers and keep it out of the hands of "bad" mothers. The committee reports and other congressional documents on the Social Security Act made it clear that a state could "impose such other eligibility requirements—as to means, moral character, etc.—as it sees fit."[16] In the South, those few blacks that managed to get on the welfare rolls were often removed at harvest time.[17] Despite what many Democrats argued in 1995 and 1996, when Aid to Dependent Children was created in 1935, no programmatic right was established. While parts of the Social Security Act created specific "entitlements" to assistance (e.g., Old Age Insurance), welfare was not one of them. States had the discretion to provide assistance to who they wished, subject to only the most minimal of federal controls.

For much of the first quartercentury of ADC's history, the federalism story was one of very gradual evolution of national control, but through quite circuitous means. The Department of Health, Education, and Welfare continually pushed for a more "modern" social work approach to ADC, and the development of modern schools of social work (which often funneled their graduates into state welfare administration) provided the opportunity for a slowly evolving modernization of welfare administration.[18] But even advocates of modern social work did not consider welfare a "right"—administrators were supposed to possess substantial discretion to assist their clients, although that discretion was meant to be exercised in support of "scientific" principles rather than local knowledge and prejudice.[19]

It was this edifice of discretion that advocates of welfare rights encountered when they began to mobilize in the early 1960s. In contrast to the "War on Poverty" understanding that poverty in America was aberrant, unintended, and therefore easily eradicated by well-meaning liberal policymakers,[20] advocates of a court-centered strategy argued that poverty served essential functions in American society, dividing the very poor from the working class and undermining opposition to capitalism.[21] The poor were poor for a reason.

This group of activists and scholars believed that the decentralized, stigmatizing structure of AFDC had to be undermined through essentially nonpopular mechanisms, since the views of average Americans were largely the problem. At the core of their strategy was the notion of transforming welfare from a privilege into a "right," enforceable by the courts. Frances Fox Piven and Richard Cloward observed that welfare recipients had been "inhibited from asserting claims by selfprotecting devices within the welfare system: its capacity to limit information, to intimidate applicants, to demoralize recipients and arbitrarily to deny lawful claims."[22] Rights, it was thought, would provide clients a weapon against the welfare bureaucracy. They would be the power of the powerless.

The advocates of welfare rights hoped that stripping bureaucracies of their discretion would lead to a flood of women onto the AFDC rolls, one so huge as to drive state governors to Washington to demand that the program be nationalized in the form of a Negative Income Tax. And they almost succeeded. A line of Supreme Court cases—the most important of which were *King v. Smith*, *Shapiro v. Thompson*, and *Goldberg v. Kelly*—undermined the mechanisms states had previously used to keep women off the welfare rolls. And these decisions, combined with a supportive national bureaucracy, had an effect: almost overnight, the participation rate in AFDC went from 42 percent in 1967, to 64 percent in 1970, to 87 percent in 1983. As a result, the welfare rolls exploded. Had the participation rate stayed at its 1967 level, the welfare rolls would have gone up by 60 percent between then and 1983.[23] As it was, the rolls increased by an astounding 299 percent during this period, while the U.S. population rose by a mere 19 percent and the poor grew by approximately 37 percent.

What is more, the increase in the rolls had the effect Piven and Cloward expected: it helped put the Negative Income Tax (NIT) on the national agenda (although, perversely, it was the efforts of the welfare rights movement that defeated the NIT proposed by the Nixon administration). It also gave birth to the era of dissensus politics in AFDC, in which welfare became a proxy for a range of "regime level issues," those that concern how the polity organizes itself politically, socially, and economically, how it reproduces itself, and how it distributes rights and obligations.[24] Many advocates of welfare rights wanted to use welfare to challenge the dominant American creed, with its emphasis on work, family, and social reciprocity.[25] In the short term, they were able to get the Supreme Court to join their battle. But in the longer term, they created a counterreaction. Welfare became increasingly unpopular with the American public. Whereas at the beginning of the 1960s, less than 10 percent of the public thought that America was spending too much on welfare, by the mid-1970s over 60 percent did.[26] This intense programmatic unpopularity was only exacerbated by many liberals' staunch support of welfare rights, a notion that did not sit well with the public's attachment to the idea of a welfare state governed by the notion of reciprocity.[27]

As a result, welfare quickly became a key part of the conservative countermobilization against liberalism, a powerful totem in the cultural politics that emerged in the 1970s and 1980s. This suggests something important about the role of rights in the "new" politics of public policy. Something may be considered a right in two senses.[28] The first is institutional: rights shift the venue of politics, from those that are popular/democratic low-visibility confrontation and resolution among interest groups, bureaucracy, and courts. Welfare was partially entrenched as a right in this sense, at least where eligibility was concerned (an affirmative right to welfare, as opposed to a ban on certain forms of removal from the rolls, was never created by the courts[29]).

But there is a second sense in which something may be considered a right, and that is moral. A right in this sense is widely understood to be legitimately set apart from ordinary politics, whether or not it is governed by different institutional procedures, such as trust funds. Social Security, Medicare, and perhaps environmental protection are rights of this sort.[30] Welfare, on the other hand, never attained moral status as a right. If anything, the institutional entrenchment of welfare rights exacerbated opposition to AFDC. This suggests that in determining policy durability, moral and cultural beliefs are just as important as institutional processes and design.

Welfare, therefore, was vulnerable almost from the moment it attained rights status. The politics of AFDC from the early 1970s to the present has been the story of the unpopularity, and then the gradual erosion, and finally the outright retraction, of welfare rights.

The Reaction against Welfare Rights

The first step in this process was the unpopularity of welfare. Unlike other new politics interventions, the establishment of welfare rights was not imposed by a unified, technocratic elite. Rather, it was established by one part of a divided elite, in a conflict that was symbolic rather than technocratic.[31] For both the creators of welfare rights and their opponents, the welfare debate was about larger political ideas, the arrangement of rights and responsibilities in a democratic republic, and the role of government in society. As such, the politics of AFDC has always been more politically volatile than other policy areas, since it is weighed down by ideological significance far beyond that of the policy itself.

Like all of the rights that were created in the 1960s and 1970s, welfare seemed, in the early 1980s, to be highly resistant to change. Despite their ideological self-confidence in the early and mid-1980s, conservatives were frustrated at their inability to attack any of these programmatic rights. As a result, they adopted a more circuitous route to undermining welfare rights. In the case of Social Security, they hunkered down for a long struggle, laying the foundations for a future attempt to privatize the program through the creation of publicly subsidized savings (IRAs and the like) and by engaging in a public relations campaign to erode faith in the program.[32] In the case of AFDC, they adopted a similar strategy of laying time bombs that, they hoped, would go off when the environment permitted and that would allow them to continue the symbolic politics of welfare, which proved an effective tool for attacking liberalism.

In AFDC, the time bombs were waivers. In 1986, the Reagan White House's Domestic Policy Council published a report titled *Up from Dependency*. The report noted, "State leaders told the Working Group [which wrote the report] that they would be willing to propose and implement more comprehensive experiments, if only federal laws allowed them to do so." But the truth was somewhat different. The states had shown only a limited willingness to propose anything beyond narrow administrative changes in the program, and they certainly were not chewing at the bit to do so. The White House had to engage in strenuous efforts to encourage the states to do anything ambitious: the states had internalized the political gridlock that rights encourage.[33] While there were good reasons to create a political mythology that decentralization in welfare policy was created by a pull from the states, the truth is that it was created by a push from Washington.

While the states were initially resistant, so was the Health and Human Services (HHS) bureaucracy. It too had become quite comfortable with the bureaucratic/interest group/court nexus that the welfare right had created, especially since it gave HHS substantial power to maintain program stability, a primary interest of any bureaucracy.[34] To break HHS's stranglehold on welfare and its ability to limit state autonomy, the Reagan administration had to create a new nexus of power. It did so by centralizing programmatic control within the executive branch in a White House office, the Low Income Opportunity Advisory Board (LIOAB). This consolidated control over welfare waivers in a single place (waivers often required changes in food stamps, Medicaid, and other programs) and took power out of the agencies (where decisions were based more on the interests of program maintenance and stability) and into the hands of the ideologically motivated. As Chuck Hobbs, who was assistant to the president in the Reagan administration, described the meetings that resulted from the new structure, "HHS would always show up with a couple of appointed people who made sense, and a bunch of bureaucrats who sometimes made sense and sometimes were obstreperous. But since they were sitting in the back of the room, and the debate was going on among appointees, we began to get much more of an influence on the policy end of the thing."[35]

The first step in undermining welfare rights, as we have seen, was undercutting their institutional foundation. The creation of the LIOAB served to inject generalist political figures into a process that had been dominated by specialists, and in doing so it took power away from those with a stake in the existing welfare system and transferred it to those who had none. This process complemented the overall intent of the waiver strategy, which was to induce governors into becoming more interested in welfare reform and therefore implicitly to take power away from those at the state level who had a commitment to the existing welfare system.

The aggressive action of officials associated with the LIOAB succeeded in spurring a number of states to propose waivers, although most were relatively small in significance compared to what came later. But they did succeed in changing the way governors thought about their role in welfare. Previously, if governors thought about it at all, they were primarily concerned with how to get more money for AFDC out of the federal government or to get them to take it off their hands altogether. Few saw any returns from investing their time and effort by encouraging innovation in their welfare program. With a few exceptions (such as then-governor Ronald Reagan in California), few Republican governors applied their more conservative predilections to the issue. Where the average governor, Democratic or Republican, was concerned, welfare was a political minefield, to be avoided if at all possible.

Waivers changed this dynamic, setting in place a new political and policy path. The waiver policy rearranged the politics of AFDC, by shifting power from the old courts/bureaucracy/interest group nexus to a White House/states nexus and introducing new political incentives. Governors soon realized through experience that "moving people from welfare to work" was an effective mechanism for increasing their popular support, and one that could be achieved at low political and financial cost to themselves and the state. Waivers were a strategy that paid increasing returns[36]: governors in one state could see those in other states riding the welfare issue to increased popularity, and this led to replication and mimicry. This is why, when it became clear that HHS would approve a particular change in welfare in one state, large numbers of other states followed with the same or similar change. Innovation in one state drove down the information costs and experimentation risk to all other states' governors, creating a virtuous (in the analytical sense) cycle.

Despite the fact that they were originally justified as "experiments" (which is the only justification that existed in law[37]), the waiver strategy was not intended to make AFDC more effective but to undermine its overall structure. Stuart Butler, who in various positions in the Heritage Foundation in the 1980s and 1990s helped steer conservative policy on the welfare state, says of waivers, "It was an under-the-radar strategy, and therefore we didn't find it necessary [to be too explicit]. You didn't want to say too much about it. And that fitted into the idea of saying, Let's actually set up something, and let's see if we can find one state that will do this; let's do it, and let's make sure its done adequately so we have a real model, and that will help us to achieve what we want."[38] The authority to create waivers, which was not expected to be a very substantial power when it was created in 1962, was gradually expanded, as states tested the federal government's willingness to allow them discretion, and as they began to "think outside the box." As Ron Haskins, head of the Republican staff on the House Ways and Means Human Resources subcommittee, argues the motivation for waivers was that "[a]llowing states to experiment and to develop unique programs would also have the desirable political effect of showing that they were capable of actually thinking up innovative policies and implementing them. Equally important, once states got a taste of independence from federal red tape, they would be motivated to fight for still more freedom from Washington."[39] It seems undeniable that the waiver strategy was not a case of minor tinkering or seat-of-the-pants improvisation but the key element in a long-term strategy to unravel the AFDC entitlement.

For most of President George H. W. Bush's first term in the early 1990s, welfare remained off the policy agenda, as did most domestic policy issues, and power began to drift back to HHS. It was only at the end of his term that Bush recognized the necessity of developing a broadbased domestic agenda, driven in large part by the recognition that he would face then-governor Bill Clinton, who was making "ending welfare as we know it" a central plank in his presidential campaign. Without the time, imagination, or inclination to come up with a substantial welfare reform plan of his own, Bush reached out for the strategy that was already on the shelf: waivers. The Bush administration did two things of critical significance. First, it permitted states to meet the "cost neutrality" requirement for waivers over the entire life of the experiment, rather than year to year. This allowed states to make investments up front and then recoup their costs later, permitting them to propose much more aggressive changes than they could under the old standard. But the most important thing Bush did was to reinvigorate the White House/state nexus, making it clear that the White House would protect state proposals once they arrived in Washington. These two changes, along with the experience state governors were acquiring as to the political efficacy of welfare reform, broke the back of the old welfare structure. Proposals for time limiting welfare, requiring work, imposing family caps, and the like, all of which would have been utterly unimaginable under the old rights understanding of welfare, flooded into Washington.

Waivers turned governors into a political constituency for devolution. They introduced into the politics of AFDC a powerful "old politics" actor with a strong interest in overturning the new politics. To use the terminology of Baumgartner and Jones, the introduction of wide waiver authority was a way of "governing through institutional disruption."[40] Republican administrations in the 1980s changed the future direction of welfare policy through institution shaping rather than policymaking. By investing political capital in mobilizing previously "slack resources," the Reagan and Bush administrations did more to change the long-term direction of welfare policy than if they had attempted to change policy directly.[41]

A Path Not Taken

In retrospect, the last chance to thwart the competing welfare path established by the Reagan and Bush administrations came in 1993. President Clinton had run on reforming AFDC at the national level, advocating strong new work requirements accompanied by additional resources for training and education. By the time the Clinton welfare team proposed its plan, it contained a politically balanced blend of new federal work requirements and substantial state discretion in meeting them. Had the administration actually passed such a plan, it almost certainly would have short-circuited the move for greater state autonomy, for two reasons. First and foremost, it would have taken the welfare issue off the political agenda, thereby denying conservatives the opportunity to push for full-blown devolution. Second, it would have set in motion a new set of institutional relationships, with "experimentation" more thoroughly regulated to conform with nationally established goals than it had been under waivers. Given that the Clinton plan would have slowed and possibly ended the movement for devolution, it is worth examining why the administration failed to pass legislation when it was in a strong position to do so, and why this failure led to the president being forced to sign a bill in 1996 that diverged sharply from the approach he had advocated in the 1992 campaign.

Welfare reform rose to the top of the issue agenda in the summer of 1992, when presidential candidate Bill Clinton promised supporters he would "end welfare as we know it." Most Americans agreed that welfare was broken and needed to be fixed, and the welfare issue symbolized a generic dissatisfaction with the limits and failings of government in Washington. The selection of welfare reform as a leading issue fit well the image Clinton was trying to create and appears to have contributed to his success as a presidential candidate.

After Clinton's election in 1992, the approach he advocated in the election was accepted as the core of welfare reform by nearly all of political Washington, with the exception of small fringes at the edges of each party. To a degree, this reflected a lack of imagination: Workfare was the only approach available that was seen to respond to the public's desire for change. Furthermore, increasing national work standards on welfare recipients worked within an existing bipartisan legislative tradition, established just a few years earlier by the Family Support Act (FSA) of 1988. FSA offered states more federal money to develop programs to move welfare recipients into work and established minimal federal standards for participation in work and training programs. While fraught with loopholes, FSA amounted to an extension of federal control, in the name of a new contract with the poor. In retrospect, the interesting question is why this path, which seemed to have such strong momentum, was not followed in the next round of welfare reform, and the path established by waivers won out.

The Clinton administration's critical mistake was its failure to cement the work-oriented consensus in legislation before substantial opposition to the approach developed and thereby to end the welfare debate before it lost control of it. The most important missed opportunity was Clinton's first budget. David Ellwood recalls, "Until just before it was sent to the printer, the first Clinton budget included several billion dollars for its future welfare reform proposal. If that line had remained in the budget, the administration would have been forced to submit its welfare reform package by late spring 1993 rather than the summer of 1994. With the money taken care of, we could have avoided a search for dollars that ultimately consumed much of our energy."[42] Without the pressure that inclusion in the budget would have induced, other priorities continually slowed down welfare reform.

The most important competing priority was health care. Especially among a number of strategically placed House liberals, such as Representatives Robert Matsui and Jim McDermott, welfare reform was considered not only undesirable on the merits but as agenda competition for health care, which was their priority. As a congressional aide to Matsui told Teles, "You had a bunch of these guys who were really focused on health care, and that's what everybody had run on. Bill Clinton had run on welfare, but they hadn't, . . . and they felt that health care was really what they had to do. Bob Matsui didn't like the president's [welfare] bill: he thought that was where we should have ended up, not where Democrats should have started out."[43] The health care–welfare timing issue, which apologists for the administration would later describe as a kind of unavoidable mistake, was driven as much by substantive disagreement on the desirability of Clinton-style welfare reform as it was by strategic considerations.

The 103rd Congress failed to act on Clinton's plan or any other welfare reform proposal. In fact, a welfare bill never made it to the House floor for a debate or a vote, despite the pleas of a White House now desperate for some action on a major domestic policy issue. This is an outcome the Democrats would later come to regret. Even moderate Republicans generally refused to lend their effort to welfare reform in the waning days of 1994 (despite the fact that they had been supportive earlier in the administration). No one could have foreseen the sweeping GOP landslide that later occurred, but Republicans were willing to bide their time and see how the political landscape changed following the 1994 elections. Thus, action on welfare reform—or the failure to act—in the 103d Congress set the stage for 1995.

Welfare politics was hit in the fall of 1994 with what, in the jargon of social science, would be called an "exogenous shock." The Republican party won a resounding victory in the 1994 elections, and the political landscape immediately changed. Welfare devolution quickly went from a rival approach to an unstoppable force. Ironically, it overwhelmed conservatives, as well as liberals, both of whom looked to the welfare debate as an opportunity to enforce their preferred programmatic approach to reform. Looking back at the politics of welfare policy in 1995 and 1996, what sticks out is the victory of institution shaping over policymaking.

The Republican ranks were sharply divided between those who supported an approach that focused more on work and those who were more concerned with illegitimacy. Ultimately, neither side prevailed, for two reasons. The first is that both sides in this debate

were part of the same political party. This meant that they had incentives for conflict avoidance despite their ideological differences
as to the ultimate purposes of welfare reform. Both the president
and the Republicans in Congress were locked into the need to pass
some form of legislation, and both feared they would be blamed by
the public for the failure of welfare reform. The status quo was not
an option. Devolution provided a politically viable mechanism for
the Republicans to produce legislation while maintaining party cohesion, by diverting controversial programmatic questions to a different venue, the states.

The second reason both sides failed was that more than a
decade of waivers had given state governors a newly privileged status. Each side's programmatic points could therefore be trumped by
the claim that any strong national standards would suggest that
they did not "trust the governors to do the right thing." What is interesting about the power of this argument is that it could not have
been deployed a decade before. The "trust" that the governors
claimed for themselves, the legitimacy of their claims to autonomy,
was the outcome of a waiver process that allowed them to engage
in experimentation in the first place. Had they not had the experience of actually implementing welfare reform and reaping the political benefits that it brought, the governors would not have had the
inclination to ask for additional autonomy, nor would they have
had the legitimacy ("they made it work in practice") that led other
actors to view their claims as credible. As we argued earlier, constructing this legitimacy was the result of conscious planning, not
spontaneous evolution.

The new Republican majority began its search for a viable welfare reform strategy largely where the 103d Congress had left off:
work requirements. Over time, however, the GOP position on the issues changed as their thinking evolved and as fissures within the
party emerged. Soon, two new rival notions emerged to compete
with the dominant work-oriented approach to reform. The first was
the problem of illegitimacy. A number of prominent Republicans
(and some Democrats) argued that the mission for welfare reform
was to stem the rising tide of out-of-wedlock births in this country.
This approach had the virtue of offering a distinctively conservative
approach to welfare that distinguished the Republican position from
that of Clinton. The problem, however, was that this approach offered few if any concrete policy solutions. Aside from outright denial

of benefits à la Charles Murray, very few policy instruments along these lines were available. This approach also divided hardline conservatives from the moderates in the party, reducing the possibility for a winning coalition on the welfare issue.

The second option was devolution. As we argued earlier, the expanded use of HHS's waiver authority created a political dynamic which was very difficult to rein in, once it was let loose. Governors applied for evermore dramatic waiver authority and, upon finding that experimentation in this area yielded political returns, were drawn to ask for even more. This dynamic drove the debate increasingly away from policy questions (How do we get more people into work? What happens after the time limits? How much will this cost?) to questions of intergovernmental relations (How much supervision of state policies is necessary?). From a political standpoint, this made devolution an attractive option, since it was relatively easier to address these federalism issues and leave aside the tough questions such as what to do about illegitimacy or how to move families from welfare to work.

The Republicans ultimately did not choose among the work, illegitimacy, or devolution approaches but split the difference, promising to deal with all three concerns. Soon, however, devolution eclipsed the other two alternatives. Block grants helped Republicans address many of their major goals and concerns—in particular, cutting spending by predictable amounts while concealing who would be hurt and why. In contrast with illegitimacy, for instance, devolution fit well with the consensual Republican philosophy of smaller government and less power to the federal government, without making any of the ideological decisions that would open up party fissures. Senator Moynihan's chief adviser on welfare at the time, Paul Offner, observed, "The thoughtful people within the Republican coalition realize the last thing they want to do is get bogged down in a [shouting] match about teenage mothers and kids born to mothers on welfare. That really was a battle that would just drag them down into the gutter."[44] A senior staff member of the Ways and Means Committee further explained, "There is no question—none—that returning power and money and authority to the states in the form of block grants does allow you a kind of intellectual dishonesty, that you can avoid all the substantive issues and say that is a state issue." It was this political necessity for conflict avoidance that drove, for example, Senator Packwood's argument "We don't want to substitute conservative mandates for liberal mandates." The stronger the mandates, the more they threatened to tear apart Republican unity and drive GOP moderates into a coalition with Democratic moderates.

Devolution was also attractive because it largely trapped Bill Clinton in a web of his own rhetoric. As a longtime supporter of state autonomy, he could offer very little resistance to the devolutionary approach. Furthermore, Clinton had in the summer of 1995, on the advice of Dick Morris, agreed to abandon the federal entitlement to assistance. Since he could not object to this version of welfare reform on programmatic grounds, Clinton was forced to work on the margins to improve the welfare bill.

In the end, devolution prevailed over alternative policy approaches because it solved political problems that none of its rivals could. The Republicans' approach could be sold as "radical reform" and therefore as a politically viable response to the public's desire for substantial change in welfare policy. Devolution fit the larger Republican agenda of reducing the size of government but didn't force the party to agree on the substance of policy change. It not only promised to reduce the deficit, but to do so in a manner consistent with the way that budget cuts were "scored" by the new fiscal institutions introduced in the era of deficit reduction. Finally, and most important, it was equipped with a strong, "old politics" constituency in the nation's governors, who as a result of a decade of experimentation had attained a strong claim to autonomy in welfare policymaking.

Getting to Yes

Not surprisingly, welfare reform went off largely without a hitch in the House; majority control in the legislature and the prior commitment of the majority to the Contract with America meant that welfare reform faced relatively smooth sailing in the House. Democrats complained long and loud over a bill they argued was "tough on kids and soft on work," but in the end they were powerless to stop the Republicans from having their way. The politics of welfare reform in the Senate were a bit more complicated, as ideological divisions within the Republican party surfaced that the Senate leadership was relatively powerless to contain. As a result, the

Senate took much longer to pass welfare reform, and in the end it took a bipartisan agreement between Republicans and Democrats to nudge welfare over the top and gain successful passage.

The Congress's welfare story has been told elsewhere,[45] but several details of that story are worth recounting here. The unique combination of divided government and the politics of blame avoidance combined to propel the welfare bill over several bumps on the road to final passage. No one, it seemed, wanted to be against welfare reform: opposition at the level of principle to some major restructuring of welfare had passed out of the realm of legitimate discourse. The crucial issues, then, were often over the details of how welfare should be reformed, not whether reform should occur at all.

This created a dilemma for congressional Democrats. What had begun as a Democratic issue raised by a Democratic presidential candidate became an important part of the Republican efforts to usher in a new era in the role of government in society. Unaccustomed to their new role as the minority in the House, and lacking strong leadership from the White House, Democrats were ill prepared (and largely unwilling) to stand in the way of what soon became a Republican welfare juggernaut. In addition, Democrats lacked a viable alternative to the Republican approach and as a result were left defending the status quo, attacking the GOP approach, or arguing on the margins of the GOP proposal. Even Democrats' successes had a Janus face: their brief victory in March 1995 on food stamps and child nutrition only made the Republicans appear more moderate once they pulled back from these cuts.

The political dynamic begun by waivers played a prominent role in the passage of welfare reform in the Senate. The upper chamber saw the worst of the ideological divisions within the Republican party, and a sometimes fierce battle between devolution and other options (most notably illegitimacy) slowed the progress of welfare reform in the Senate. Indeed, the fact that Majority Leader Bob Dole delayed bringing welfare reform to the Senate floor several times provides a clear indication of just how difficult the politics of welfare reform were in the Senate.

Majority Leader Dole had to negotiate not one but several major dilemmas in order to pass welfare reform. The first of these difficulties was dissension within the ranks of his own party over the direction of welfare reform in the Senate. Conservative Republican senators wanted tough welfare reform similar to the House bill; moderates, on the other hand, were concerned about reductions in child care and other support services that would help move welfare recipients into the work force. The more collegial structure of the Senate makes center-out legislative strategies a persistent threat to more partisan approaches, so Dole had to be on watch against pushing moderate Republicans into a bipartisan coalition. Finally, Dole had to deal with the threat of a presidential veto. Given his desire to succeed on welfare reform, Dole knew that at the end of the day he had to produce a bill that could be signed by the White House, or at least be defensible against possible criticisms from the president. In short, Dole was caught between several contending and potent positions on the welfare issue. As he put it at one point during the floor debate in the Senate, "I am getting hit by the White House on the one side and my friend from Texas [Phil Gramm] on the other" (S11758).

Ultimately, Dole was able to surmount these difficulties, largely by playing both sides against each other. When conservatives threatened to defect, he let them have their day on the Senate floor, and ultimately the more conservative options failed to win support. In the end, Dole was able to work with moderates and Democrats to craft a bill that passed the Senate by a substantial margin.

Following the 1994 elections, Clinton sought to define a middle path between liberals in his own party and conservative Republicans. Welfare reform became one of the centerpieces of this new effort and an icon for both parties in their efforts to make reality conform to their rhetoric.

In the midst of the internecine struggles between the White House and Congress, the nation's governors also sought to make their mark on the ongoing welfare debate. The governors had been involved in welfare reform from the outset, but in this instance they sought to set the agenda for the Congress's reconsideration of welfare. A number of Republicans in Congress had indicated that they would seriously consider any proposal approved by the governors, and in early February, the National Governor's Association announced that they had reached agreement on a bipartisan proposal on Medicaid and welfare reform. The governor's proposal would convert both Medicaid and welfare to a block grant, saving billions of dollars in the process. While an ambitious proposal, the decision by the governors to combine both welfare and Medicaid probably doomed the proposal from the outset. While a questionable political strategy, Republicans seized the initiative and quickly sent this version to Clinton for a signature. Block-granting both welfare and Medicaid—while clearly attractive to the governors and Republican members of Congress seeking to reduce the federal budget—raised the hackles of too many advocates and too many groups concerned about the impact of the changes on children, the elderly, and people with disabilities. From an administrative or budgetary standpoint, packaging the changes to the two programs made sense, but politically the move proved disastrous. Too many interests and too many objections ensured that the proposal died of a thousand small cuts. Once again, Clinton sent the bill back with a veto message, and with convenient political cover from the thousands of children whose health insurance coverage the president claimed would be threatened by the measure. In a pattern reminiscent of congressional Democrats' earlier fight against the Republicans' plans on child nutrition, vetoing the legislation largely on the basis of its Medicaid provisions left Clinton little room to maneuver when Republicans agreed to send him a "clean" (i.e., AFDC-only) bill.

Once Congress had completed its final version of welfare reform—one very similar to the Senate bill the president had supported—the president was caught in a bind. As a candidate, he had promised voters he would end welfare as we know it, and now that Congress had produced welfare reform, it would be exceedingly difficult for him to reject the welfare bill without appearing to renege on that promise. And with the 1996 elections looming on the horizon, the last thing Bill Clinton wanted to do was to hand the Republicans an issue that could be used against him. Nonetheless, if he signed the bill, he put himself at odds with his own party and especially its liberal wing. As one Senate Democrat put it, "If Congress sends him the Senate bill, that would be the worst situation in the world for Clinton. It would really put him in an untenable position."[46] Ultimately, congressional Republicans went just far enough in the president's direction that a veto became, in the minds of his more politically minded advisers, politically impossible. By signing the bill, those advisers believed, he would take away the Republicans' most powerful weapon in the coming election. At least where narrowly political considerations were concerned, they were right: Dole was unable to get any ideological traction, in large part because of the evaporation of the welfare issue. The question of whether Clinton's acquiescing in the victory of the devolution alternative, to save his grip on the presidency, was a bargain worth making is one that historians a decade hence will be better able to evaluate than we are now.

Conclusion

For good or for ill, the old politics of welfare policy has passed away. What was once a right has now become, once more, a gratuity, to be distributed by the states as they see fit. The new politics of welfare will have its successes and its failures, but whatever else it will be, it will be *new*, radically different from the politics we have described in this chapter. During each period of welfare policy change, the alternative to the existing policy seemed impossible; and then once in place, inevitable; and then when challenged, obviously vulnerable. Those who venture predictions with a high degree of specificity about the future of welfare policy should probably be chastened by this cycle. Although political actors in the future will be constrained by the rules and institutions that characterize the new welfare regime, that is not the same as saying their choices have been determined.

Investing political capital in a long-range project of carving out an alternative policy path worked for the opponents of welfare rights, despite the fact that they had to operate within a highly constrained environment of judicial review and bureaucratic opposition to innovation. The waiver strategy worked because conservatives had developed institutions of their own—in particular, think tanks like the Heritage Foundation, which facilitated long-range thinking. They succeeded at moving policy in their direction in large part because they had longer time horizons than their opponents, and therefore they were able to view each issue in the light of its implications for their long-range strategy. The future of welfare policy will, in large part, be determined by whether liberals develop similar institutional capacities for long-range strategy and whether the strategic decisions they make are wise. If there is one final lesson to be learned from the experience of welfare reform over the last thirty years, it is that political resources are less important than whether they are used well or poorly, that political capital is most valuable when it is invested for the long term.

Notes

Parts of this chapter draw on Steven Teles, *Whose Welfare? AFDC and Elite Politics* (Lawrence: University Press of Kansas, 1996). He would like to thank the press for the right to use this material. Prinz would like to acknowledge the support of the Robert Wood Johnson Foundation Scholars in Health Policy Program for work on this project. We would also like to thank Melissa Bass, Thomas Banchoff, Alan Deacon, Martha Derthick, Marc Landy, Lawrence Mead, Robert Mickey, Paul Pierson, and Robin Rogers-Dillon for their very helpful criticism.

1. Incrementalism has a long tradition in the policy literature, starting with Charles Lindbloom, "The Science of Muddling Through," *Public Administration Review* 19 (1959): 79–88. This way of thinking about the policy process was discussed and critiqued in volume 1 of Marc K. Landy and Martin A. Levin, eds., *The New Politics of Public Policy* (Baltimore, Md.: Johns Hopkins University Press, 1995), especially chapter 1.

2. Ibid., 173.

3. Ibid., 295.

4. Personal Responsibility and Work Opportunity Act, Section 401(b).

5. Paul Pierson, *Dismantling the Welfare State? Reagan, Thatcher, and the Politics of Retrenchment* (Cambridge: Cambridge University Press, 1994).

6. See especially Landy and Levin, *The New Politics*, chapters 2, 4, and 8, and R. Shep Melnick, *Between the Lines* (Washington, D.C.: Brookings Institution, 1994).

7. When we use the term *programmatic rights*, we mean to suggest rights to specific social resources distributed by government agencies, rather than rights to protection from government or private actors. Of course, at the margin, there is no distinction between programmatic rights and "negative rights," since the latter require social resources as well: a right not to have one's house broken into requires positive action and deployment of social resources on the part of government. But the programmatic rights we are discussing are not borderline cases, and as such the term, we think, has descriptive value.

8. Some of the major works in historical institutionalism are Susan Steinmo, Kathleen Thelen, and Frank Longstreth, *Structuring Politics: Historical Institutionalism in Comparative Analysis* (Cambridge: Cambridge University Press, 1992); Peter Hall, *Governing the Economy* (Oxford: Oxford University Press, 1986); Pierson, *Dismantling the Welfare State?*; Theda Skocpol, *Protecting Soldiers and Mothers* (Cambridge, Mass.: Belknap Harvard, 1992); Steven Skowronek, *The Politics Presidents Make* (Cambridge, Mass.: Harvard University Press, Belknap, 1993); John David Skrentny, *The Ironies of Affirmative Action* (Chicago: University of Chicago Press, 1996).

9. A policy or institution is "sticky," as we use the term, to the degree to which it is unresponsive to changes in either public or congressional preferences, much as the price of labor in Keynesian analysis is "sticky," in that it is slow to respond to the demand or supply of labor.

10. Skocpol offers a similar analysis, particularly concerning the relative vulnerability of welfare as compared to Social Security. See Theda Skocpol, *Social*

Policy in the United States: Future Possibilities in Historical Perspective (Princeton, N.J.: Princeton University Press, 1995).

11. This argument draws upon, but is not identical to, the model of politics discussed in Frank Baumgartner and Bryan Jones's *Agendas and Instability in American Politics* (Chicago: University of Chicago Press, 1993).

12. John Kingdon, *Agendas, Alternatives and Public Policies*, 2d ed. (New York: Addison-Wesley, 1995).

13. Patricia Ruggles and Richard Michel, "Participation in Aid to Families with Dependent Children: Trends for 1967 through 1984," unpublished manuscript, Urban Institute, April 1987.

14. Joel Handler and Ellen Hollingsworth, *The "Deserving Poor": A Study of Welfare Administration* (New York: Academic Press, 1971).

15. Michael Lipsky, *Street Level Bureaucracy* (New York: Russell Sage Foundation, 1983).

16. See U.S. Congress, Senate, 74th Congress, 1st session, 1935, S. Rep. 628,29.36; U.S. Congress, House, 74th Congress, 1st session, HR Rep. 615, 18, 24.

17. A good discussion of the southern welfare system as it impacted black Americans can be found in Richard Sterner, *The Negro's Share: A Study of Income, Consumption, Housing, and Public Assistance* (New York: Harper & Row, 1943).

18. Martha Derthick, *The Influence of Federal Grants: Public Assistance in Massachusetts* (Cambridge, Mass.: Harvard University Press, 1970).

19. Andrew Polsky, *The Rise of the Therapeutic State* (Princeton, N.J.: Princeton University Press, 1991).

20. See, for example, Gareth Davies, *From Opportunity to Entitlement* (Lawrence: University Press of Kansas, 1996).

21. Frances Fox Piven and Richard Cloward, *Regulating the Poor* (New York: Pantheon, 1971).

22. Reprinted in Richard Cloward and Frances Fox Piven, *The Politics of Turmoil* (New York: Pantheon, 1972), 95.

23. Teles, *Whose Welfare?* 20.

24. Ibid., chapter 1.

25. Ibid., chapter 5.

26. Ibid., 44. An analysis of trends in public opinion on welfare at the height of welfare reform noted that "one of the most stable elements of American public opinion in the United States is the unpopularity of 'welfare.'" It is important to note as well that public opinion has demonstrated a streak of ambivalence on the welfare issue that at times makes it difficult to gauge. R. Kent Weaver, Robert Y. Shapiro, and Lawrence R. Jacobs, "The Polls-Trends: Welfare," *Public Opinion Quarterly* 59 (1995): 606–627. See also R. Kent Weaver, *Ending Welfare as We Know It* (Washington, D.C.: Brookings Institution, 1999), chapter 6.

27. Weaver, *Ending Welfare as We Know It*, chapter 3. Jose Harris describes this mind-set well: "full citizen rights should be attached to some kind of tangible foothold in the body politic," a foothold that in the American context is provided

by labor. José Harris, "Contract and Citizenship," in *The Ideas That Shaped Post-War Britain*, ed. David Marquand and Anthony Seldon (London: Fontana, 1996). On work as the basis for citizenship, see Judith Shklar, *American Citizenship* (Cambridge, Mass.: Harvard University Press, 1991). For more on the norm of reciprocity and its connection to welfare reform, see Mickey Kaus, *The End of Equality* (New York: Basic Books, 1995), and Lawrence Mead, *Beyond Entitlement* (New York: Basic Books, 1985).

28. This argument benefits from several conversations with Tom Burke.

29. Melnick, *Between the Lines*, chapter 6.

30. It should be noted that this is the status of these programs at the time of publication: conservatives have (without much success) been attempting to reverse the rights status of Social Security and Medicare as well as AFDC for some time.

31. Teles, *Whose Welfare?* chapter 4.

32. Stuart Butler and Peter Germanis, "Achieving a Leninist Strategy," *Cato Journal* (Fall 1983).

33. Teles, *Whose Welfare?* chapter 7.

34. Matthew Holden, *Continuity and Disruption* (Pittsburgh: Pittsburgh University Press, 1996); William Niskanen, *Bureaucracy and Representative Government* (Chicago: Aldine, Atherton, 1971).

35. Teles, *Whose Welfare?* chapter 7.

36. See Paul Pierson, "Increasing Returns, Path Dependence, and the Study of Politics," *American Political Science Review* (June 2000).

37. Public Welfare Amendments of 1962, PL No. 87-543, title 1, at 122, 76 Stat. 172, 192 (codified as amended at 42 U.S.C. at 1315 [1988]).

38. Interview with Stuart Butler, March 12, 1998.

39. Ron Haskins, "Liberal and Conservative Influences on the Welfare Reform Legislation of 1996," unpublished manuscript, 1998.

40. Baumgartner and Jones, *Agendas and Instability*, chapter 12.

41. Evidence indicates that a similar institution-shaping rather than policymaking approach also characterized the Reagan administration's strategy toward pensions. See Steven M. Teles, "The Dialectics of Trust: Ideas, Finance and Pensions Privatization in the US and UK," paper delivered at the Max Planck Institute, Cologne, Germany, June 1998.

42. David T. Ellwood, "Welfare Reform as I Knew It: When Bad Things Happen to Good Policies," *The American Prospect* 26 (May–June 1996): 22–29 (http://epn.org/prospect/26/26ellw.html).

43. Teles, *Whose Welfare?* 154.

44. All quotes in this paragraph are from Teles, *Whose Welfare?* 161.

45. Weaver, *Ending Welfare as We Know It*.

46. Robert Pear, "GOP May Revive a Welfare Plan to Snare Clinton," *New York Times*, January 30, 1996, p. A1.

10

The New Politics of the Working Poor

Christopher Howard, *College of William and Mary*

The spectacular failure of the Clinton health plan in 1994 (see chapter 11 in this volume) and passage of welfare reform in 1996 (see chapter 9) had several points in common. Both were high-profile, high-temperature debates between the two major parties and within the Democratic party. Both were resolved in favor of those who wanted the national government to do less rather than more in social policy.

The recent history of the Earned Income Tax Credit (EITC) has followed a different path. The EITC has managed to garner bipartisan support and experience significant expansion. In the early 1980s, the EITC benefited 6.5 million families at a total cost of about $2 billion. In 1998, the government estimates that it paid $29 billion to over nineteen million families through this program. The maximum EITC benefit in 1984 was $500; in 1999, it was more than $3,800.[1] No other social program, not even Medicare or Social Security, experienced growth of such magnitude during this time.

Over the last two decades, the Earned Income Tax Credit has become one of largest and most popular means-tested programs in the United States. The EITC flourished during a period of record budget deficits, divided government, widening partisan differences within Congress, and the ascendance of highly conservative Republicans like Ronald Reagan and Newt Gingrich. Practical experience and much scholarship suggests that these conditions should be associated with gridlock or cutbacks, not rapid expansion. The purpose of this chapter is to explain why the EITC has been such an anomaly.

Before analyzing the politics of the EITC, we should know how it operates. The EITC is an income transfer to the poor and near-poor, implemented through the tax code. For most eligible individuals, the EITC is large enough to offset their entire income tax obligation and entitle them to a refund check from the U.S. Treasury. Though monthly payments are an option, almost all recipients collect once a year after they submit their income tax returns. Benefits vary by income and family size. As of 1999, the maximum annual credit of $3,816 was available to taxpayers who earned between $9,500 and $12,500 and had two or more qualifying children. It was phased in across earnings of $0 to $9,500 and phased out between $12,500 and $30,850. That year, the official poverty line for a family of four was $16,700, meaning that a substantial number of families above the poverty line were potentially eligible. The maximum credit for individuals with one qualifying child was lower ($2,312) and the phase-out range ended at $26,900. Individuals with no children could claim at most a $347 credit and were still eligible until their earnings reached $10,200.

The Argument in Brief

Many analysts explain policy outcomes in terms of explicit demands by organized groups. This approach does not work here. The working poor have not taken to the streets in protest, forcing policymakers to increase the EITC, or Food Stamps, or the minimum wage. And despite the proliferation of interest groups since the 1960s, those eligible for the EITC are conspicuously absent from pressure politics. A "National Organization of the Working Poor" simply does not exist. To the extent that organized labor has helped the working poor, it has been by trying to increase the minimum wage. More often, labor has worked to protect existing health and pension benefits for its own members.

A second type of explanation attributes policy outcomes to political culture. This explanation is harder to dismiss in this case. According to many of the program's chief advocates, the EITC's popularity and growth can be attributed to the program's consistency with core American values.[2] The EITC is available only to individuals who are employed. It rewards work, not indolence. Its beneficiaries have a legal and a moral claim to public assistance.[3] Moreover, the program upholds the value of limited government. Individuals determine their own eligibility and compute their own benefits based on instructions accompanying existing tax forms. Recipients never have to visit a local welfare office; the entire process is handled through the mail. In this account, widely shared beliefs about good public policy led policymakers to expand the Earned Income Tax Credit, and those same beliefs explain later cuts to Aid to Families with Dependent Children (AFDC), Food Stamps, and Supplemental Security Income (SSI) in 1996.

If one reads transcripts of the relevant congressional hearings or journalistic accounts of the program, one will find these values invoked over and over—especially the need to "make work pay" for families with children. Nevertheless, this explanation has definite limits. One problem is that such broad and powerful values should have broad and powerful effects, yet some programs for the working poor have fared far better than others. The clearest contrast is between the EITC and public spending for employment and job training, which has been cut substantially since 1980. In addition, making a clear causal link between values and public policy is difficult. While opinion polls are often cited as the best evidence of national values, analysts have long known that small differences in question wording can have a large impact on the results of opinion polls, and in some cases (e.g., homelessness), the government has consistently not done what citizens wanted.[4]

A final and more telling problem is that the Earned Income Tax Credit has led two lives. From its creation in 1975 until 1985, it had all the hallmarks of a typical means-tested program: the total cost of the EITC *shrank* in real dollars, as did the value of the average tax credit; hardly anyone in or out of government sang its praises. Since the mid-1980s, the politics and trajectory of the EITC have changed dramatically. There is little evidence that the values of wage work and limited government became more powerful during the 1980s, thereby reversing the program's fortunes.[5]

The key questions, then, are (1) why policymakers suddenly developed a keen interest in expanding the EITC, after a decade of not-so-benign neglect, and (2) what sustained their interest and the program's growth from the mid-1980s to the present?

Part of the answer hinges on party competition. Led by Ronald Reagan, Republicans captured the White House and the Senate in

1980 and talked boldly about the end of the New Deal order and the beginning of a Republican regime. Democrats tried to develop a politically attractive alternative to the incipient "Reagan revolution." Both parties in the 1980s tried to preserve their base while appealing to voters whose party ties were weak. One of the more mobile blocs of voters was the working poor.

While voters earning less than $12,500 consistently voted Democratic in the 1980s, a majority of voters earning over $25,000 routinely voted Republican. Those earning between $12,500 and $25,000—a good approximation of the working poor—were less predictable. Traditionally, the working poor voted Democratic: Jimmy Carter, for instance, carried this group by a 55–43 margin in the 1976 presidential election. Reagan helped narrow the Democrats' lead to 46–44 in 1980 and was reelected in 1984 with a clear majority (57–42). By the 1988 presidential election, the parties were essentially even. In the 1984 and 1986 congressional elections, Republicans won 46 and 47 percent of these voters, respectively, a substantially better showing than in previous elections. Comprising roughly twenty percent of voters, the working poor represented a substantial target of opportunity.[6] Whichever party broadened its appeal to the working poor most convincingly might win enough votes to swing many (if not most) elections for national office. Not surprisingly, policymakers became more attuned to the plight of the working poor and more supportive of the EITC at this time.

It is important not to overstate the role of party competition. Prior to Bill Clinton in 1992, few politicians invoked the Earned Income Tax Credit by name during their campaigns. No one, however, wanted to appear insensitive to the working poor. As Arnold has observed, politicians constantly worry about how their actions will be perceived in the next election. The last thing they want to do is give an important bloc of voters a reason to vote against them.[7] Opposing the EITC was politically risky. Initially, then, party competition over the EITC consisted of a few individuals promoting expansion as good public policy and a large number of reelection-minded politicians supporting expansion in order to prevent their opponents from capturing the hearts and minds (and ballots) of the working poor. Over time, evidence indicates that some of the latter individuals came to view a larger EITC as good policy.

Policy entrepreneurs capitalized on the opportunities created by these electoral shifts. Foremost among these was Robert

Greenstein, founder and director of the Center on Budget and Policy Priorities (CBPP). Established in 1981, the CBPP is a research and advocacy organization specializing in issues affecting the poor and near-poor. It is financed largely by foundation grants and labor unions; it is not a mass membership organization. During the 1980s and 1990s, the center gained a reputation for quick, thorough, and objective analysis of taxing and spending proposals, and in 1996 Greenstein won a MacArthur Foundation "genius" grant for his work. The CBPP became the single most important advocate for the Earned Income Tax Credit. Other notable entrepreneurs included Wendell Primus, a senior staff member on the House Ways and Means Committee who later served in the Clinton administration and then joined Greenstein's staff at the CBPP; and C. Eugene Steuerle, a professional economist who, while in the Treasury Department under Reagan, helped bring about the first major expansion to the EITC.

To develop broad support for the EITC, policy entrepreneurs took advantage of the program's malleability. As an open-ended tax expenditure, not linked to consumption of any specific good or service, the EITC could be linked to a wide variety of problems affecting the working poor. The EITC could not be pigeon-holed as tax relief, welfare reform, or family policy; it could be all of these and more. This malleability enabled political elites to attract a broad array of supporters, who defended the program for distinct reasons.

These policy entrepreneurs also benefited from the fiscalization of policymaking described by Pierson. In the omnibus packages of legislation increasingly favored by Congress, increases to the EITC appeared to be relatively minor. During each episode of expansion, there were no floor votes specifically on the EITC; the congressional debates tended to focus on other, larger issues. Increasing the EITC was particularly attractive for public officials who worried about the distributional equity of these omnibus bills. Unlike most tax expenditures that benefit the middle and upper classes (e.g., the home mortgage interest deduction), the EITC transfers revenue to the less affluent.[8] A larger EITC helped inoculate officials against the charge that they were assembling complex tax and budget bills simply to conceal the overall direction of policy change in favor of the well-to-do. The rest of this chapter chronicles how party competition, policy entrepreneurs, and the program's distinctive design combined to expand the Earned Income Tax Credit.

Tax Reform and the Working Poor

The Tax Reform Act (TRA) of 1986 was the most sweeping overhaul of the tax system in decades. Two fine books, *Showdown at Gucci Gulch* and *Taxing Choices,* have demonstrated in rich detail the importance of party competition to this Act.[9] Both parties believed that TRA could determine the allegiance of lower- and middle-income voters for years to come. In the words of one Reagan adviser, "passage of tax reform . . . will erase the cartoon of our party as defender of the rich and privileged. The dramatic relief . . . would reflect well on . . . all Republican candidates for the next generation."[10] For their part, Democrats fought hard to prove that their "roots [still lay] with working families all across the country."[11]

Among its many remarkable features, TRA effectively removed many low-income families from the income tax rolls, primarily through the largest single increase in the EITC since its enactment. Between 1985 and 1987, the maximum annual benefit increased from $550 to $851, the income ceiling for eligibility rose from $11,000 to over $15,000, and the total cost of the program increased by 50 percent. Just as important, benefits were indexed for inflation.[12] In the process, debates over tax reform reconfigured political support for the EITC.[13]

"Fairness" was a central theme of tax reform, one that had been invoked frequently in connection with Reagan's taxing and spending policies. Several Democratic candidates for the House used the fairness issue to defeat their Republican opponents in 1982. Other Democrats directed the General Accounting Office (GAO) and Congressional Budget Office (CBO) to study the distributional effects of Reagan's policies, and those studies provided ample evidence that the administration's cuts were wreaking havoc on the poor and near-poor.[14] Even Reagan stalwarts such as Arthur Laffer and the American Enterprise Institute publicly criticized the distributional impact of the administration's policies, particularly on the working poor.[15]

Democrats followed up with a series of congressional hearings concerning tax reform. These hearings marked a turning point for interest groups representing the poor and near-poor. Previously, these groups had restricted their lobbying and research activities to traditional social programs like AFDC and Food Stamps. Select Democrats on the Ways and Means committee, as well as committee staff, made a conscious effort to demonstrate the importance of tax policy to these groups and to elicit their support for tax reform—a classic instance of government officials mobilizing interest groups around a specific policy.[16] According to Wendell Primus, then a senior staffer on Ways and Means and a key participant in this effort:

> Prior to the tax reform debate, these groups displayed almost no interest in tax policy. A simple model developed by the [Ways and Means] committee staff was used by Congressman Rangel [D-NY] and other members to persuade these groups to invest heavily in the tax reform debate.
>
> The model calculated the tax burden of a given hypothetical family (for example, a mother with two children or a two-parent family with two children) with earnings equal to the poverty threshold. It demonstrated the large increase in federal taxes paid by families with incomes at the poverty threshold during the 1980s.
>
> The interest groups agreed that it was clearly more saleable to urge a $100 per month decrease in federal taxes, than to gain a $100 increase in additional food stamps or other benefit for families near the poverty threshold.[17]

The tactic worked. Since 1984, a number of organizations have supported tax reductions for low-income workers and expansion of the EITC, as well as increases in direct social spending. Of these groups, the Center on Budget and Policy Priorities has become the most active and influential supporter of the EITC.[18] In a personal interview, CBPP Director Robert Greenstein confirmed that Primus first brought the EITC to his attention. The two had known each other since the late 1970s when Primus worked for the House Agriculture Committee and Greenstein administered the Food Stamps program for the Agriculture Department.[19] These hearings also helped educate legislators about the impact of seemingly small changes in the tax code—not only the EITC but also the personal exemption and standard deduction—on low-income workers.[20]

Fearing that Democrats would make fairness and tax reform central issues of the 1984 campaign, White House Chief of Staff James Baker urged Reagan to seize the initiative. Reagan announced in his 1984 State of the Union message that the Treasury Department would conduct a major study of tax reform.[21] Aided by economic recovery and the Democrats' failure to capitalize on the issue, Republicans relegated fairness to a minor theme in the 1984 campaign. Reagan's landslide victory included record levels of support from the working poor.[22]

Republicans were less successful in controlling the subsequent direction of tax reform. The Treasury study, nicknamed Treasury I, was an economist's dream and a politician's nightmare. In exchange for lower tax rates, greater equity, and simplicity, it eliminated or reduced most tax expenditures. The proposal's combination of concentrated costs and diffuse benefits was a poor recipe for political success.[23] Treasury I posed particular difficulties for Republicans given that many of their constituents (i.e., corporations and the affluent) benefited considerably from tax expenditures.

One tax expenditure spared the Treasury knife was the Earned Income Tax Credit. While conceding that the EITC added "considerable complexity to the system, especially for those least able to understand it," the architects of Treasury I justified an increase based on equity considerations.[24] The impetus for expansion came from Gene Steuerle, economic coordinator of the Treasury study. Steuerle had been studying the growing tax burdens of low-income families for years and believed that government had an obligation to reduce these burdens. Reagan's call for tax reform and the growing attention to tax fairness presented him with a window of opportunity.[25] Of the available options, the EITC was the most attractive because it targeted tax relief as efficiently as possible.[26] Steuerle helped insert a larger, indexed EITC into Treasury I.

Predictably, Treasury I generated intense opposition from groups threatened with the loss of tax benefits. In contrast, "of all the proposals that led up to the Tax Reform Act of 1986 . . . the suggestion to increase the EITC received almost no public or formal opposition from the day it was first put on the table."[27] This is not to say that the EITC was ignored. In fact, before passage of the final Act, the EITC was quietly enlarged beyond what Steuerle and the Treasury Department had proposed.

Democrats and Republicans agreed that any tax reform package had to produce few if any changes to the distribution of tax burdens. Democrats did not want a regressive bill similar to the Economic Recovery and Tax Act of 1981. But, with the Senate and White House in Republican hands, Democrats could not expect a highly progressive bill. Preserving the distributional status quo was not a bad compromise as far as Republicans were concerned, for it solidified changes made in the early 1980s and softened their image as the party of greed.

This agreement meant that anyone interested in amending the tax reform bill in favor of more affluent taxpayers had to add an equal benefit for low-income taxpayers. Several times legislators turned to the EITC as a relatively cheap way of preserving distributional neutrality. Unlike increases in the personal exemption or standard deduction, every dollar added to the EITC program went exclusively to taxpayers at the lower end of the income distribution. Policymakers were thus able to support expansion of the EITC for different reasons.

New Linkages, Greater Support

As policymakers debated tax reform, some Democrats attempted to expand the EITC under the rubric of welfare reform.[28] The Family Economic Security Act, introduced in 1985, combined higher AFDC benefits with several measures designed to move welfare recipients into the workforce, including a larger Earned Income Tax Credit indexed for inflation.[29] The act was in part a signal to voters that Democrats could no longer be accused of coddling the poor.[30] As with tax reform, Reagan officials tried to preempt the Democrats by making welfare reform a top domestic priority. In his 1986 State of the Union speech, Reagan called for a study of the entire welfare system and recommendations for change. In Congress, Republicans managed to reshape the Democrats' proposal enough to share credit for the final product. After considerable debate and partisan jostling, Congress passed the Family Security Act in 1988. Proposed changes to the tax system, including the EITC, were dropped once the Tax Reform Act passed in 1986.[31] Nevertheless, the episode gave policymakers another reason to support the EITC—as welfare reform— and continued the pattern of party competition.

After Republicans lost control of the Senate in 1986, Democrats began to raise issues that had long been in disfavor. For example, congressional liberals, backed by organized labor, civil rights, women's, and church groups, introduced the Minimum Wage Restoration Act in 1987.[32] This act would have gradually increased the minimum wage from $3.35 to $4.65 by 1990 and later indexed the minimum wage to 50 percent of the average hourly wage.

Proponents pointed out that the minimum wage had lost one-quarter of its purchasing power since 1981 and linked its erosion to the growing number of working poor families.[33] Not surprisingly, this proposal generated strong opposition from Republicans and trade associations, particularly those representing low-wage industries (e.g., the National Federation of Independent Business, American Hotel and Motel Association, American Farm Bureau Federation). These opponents did not offer any alternative; the choice was simply whether or not to increase the minimum wage.

Representative Thomas Petri (R-MN) suggested substituting an increase in the EITC for an increase in the minimum wage. No fan of the minimum wage, Petri nevertheless recognized that the key House committees were stacked with liberal Democrats, and he agreed with them that the government should do more to help the working poor.[34] He believed that some increase was inevitable and attempted to minimize its size. Petri tried unsuccessfully to amend the act so that it would include a small increase in the minimum wage, a large increase in the EITC, and an adjustment in the EITC for family size. He had more luck in helping persuade fellow Republicans to endorse the EITC in their 1988 platform: "As an alternative to inflationary—and job-destroying—increases in the minimum wage, we will work to boost the incomes of the working poor through the earned-income tax credit."[35] Simultaneously, key elements of the print media began editorializing against raising the minimum wage and in favor of enlarging the EITC.[36]

This approach appealed as well to the Democratic Leadership Council (DLC), a newly formed coalition of moderate and conservative Democrats. DLC members believed that their party had become too closely associated with special interests like organized labor and welfare recipients. The party's policies, in their view, had yet to catch up with the rightward shift of the electorate. Mondale's drubbing in 1984 was clear proof in their minds that the party had to change. They created an organization outside the Democratic National Committee to appeal to voters who were more concerned about economic growth than redistribution. These were the New Democrats.[37]

An increase in the minimum wage was precisely the type of issue that DLC members wanted to avoid. It further tied the Democratic party to organized labor, fueled the party's image as antibusiness and antigrowth, and was economically inefficient. For DLC Democrats, the EITC was "a sparkling opportunity to show that their party [was] no longer in thrall to old ideas and the labor Left."[38] They joined Republicans in opposing the bill and favoring instead an increase to the EITC.[39] Supporters of the bill replied that both a higher minimum wage and a larger EITC were needed.[40] They failed, at least initially. DLC Democrats and Republicans prevented the minimum wage bill from coming to a vote on the floor of either chamber by the end of the 1988 session.

Ultimately, Congress did enact new minimum wage legislation, though the increases were smaller than originally proposed and were coupled with a new training wage. Passage required exclusion of any extraneous matter, including the EITC, from the final bill. Nevertheless, the minimum wage debates mobilized conservative support for the EITC much as debates over tax fairness prompted liberal groups to support the program a few years earlier. The program gained support among congressional Republicans, the Bush administration, and key business groups (e.g., the U.S. Chamber of Commerce) as an alternative to a higher minimum wage. Moderate and conservative Democrats embraced the EITC as part of a larger strategy to move the party in a more centrist direction. And the program generated widespread media attention for the first time in its history. By 1990, the *New York Times* was calling the EITC "the best means available for lifting the working poor out of poverty."[41]

These trends continued as policymakers began linking the EITC to family policy in general and child care in particular. Much as they did with tax fairness and welfare reform, Democrats and Republicans competed over who would be the profamily party in the 1980s.[42] Republicans stood for "traditional" family values, indicating their opposition to abortion, busing, and homosexuality and support for school prayer. This position was calculated to appeal both to conservative Republicans and to working-class Democrats. Democrats responded in the mid-1980s by charting a decidedly centrist course, with heavy emphasis on larger personal exemptions in the tax code, larger and more targeted child care tax credits, parental leave, flextime and job sharing, more job training, and portable corporate pensions.[43] They placed as much emphasis on changing business practices as on government programs, as much on tax-based solutions as on additional spending. They made no mention of divisive issues like abortion and homosexuality. Many liberal Democrats distanced themselves from the party's official position, though they still recognized the importance of helping families.

Debate in Congress centered on the Act for Better Child Care (ABC), which proposed additional spending on child care programs and increased government regulation of child care providers. With the exception of Senator Orrin Hatch (R-UT), the ABC bill was clearly associated with liberal Democrats and liberal interest groups. The bill's Democratic supporters expected that ABC would highlight an important policy difference between the two parties in an election year. They did not bank on highlighting fissures within their own party as well. DLC Democrats worried about the program's cost and about favoring two-income families who purchased child care over more "traditional" families in which one parent stayed home. ABC struck them as more of the same old Democratic politics—throwing money at social problems. Republicans generally shared these concerns and objected as well to what they saw as excessive regulation of child care providers. A number of legislators submitted alternative child care bills, almost all of which relied heavily on the tax code, either by expanding the EITC and dependent care tax credit or by creating a new tax credit for parents of young children. Critics of their approach argued that tax credits would do little to improve the quality of child care or make child care more affordable for the poor and near-poor.

Democrats were unable to reach a consensus position concerning the right mix of tax incentives, direct spending, and regulation. Though many House Republicans preferred tax credits to ABC, and some saw the EITC as a way of attracting traditionally Democratic voters, enough Republicans were troubled by the size of the Ways and Means bill ($16 billion over five years) to withhold their support. As a result, no child care bill passed Congress in 1989. Proponents of the ABC approach subsequently resigned themselves to some combination of tax credits and direct spending. They simply did not have the votes, and the EITC continued to receive favorable press. Their acceptance of a tax-based approach paved the way for compromise in 1990. The House and Senate agreed on a package that included $18.3 billion of tax credits aimed at low-income working families with children and $4.3 billion for direct child care subsidies. Roughly half of the total cost was due to expanding the EITC.[44]

Still, the legislative journey was not over. At the last minute these child care provisions were folded into the Omnibus Budget and Reconciliation Act of 1990 (OBRA-90).[45] OBRA-90 included almost $500 billion in tax increases and spending cuts over five years, marking it as the first substantial deficit reduction measure in years. One objective in adding child care and the EITC was to mute opposition from liberal Democrats, who objected to sizable spending cuts elsewhere in the budget. As in 1986, the EITC was used to enhance the distributional equity of a much larger bill. Declared a Ways and Means staff member, "'the working poor were made better off by this agreement than by any other piece of legislation passed in the 1980's.'"[46]

The 1993 Budget Accord

The last major expansion of the EITC occurred in 1993. Because the process echoed that of 1990, it can be summarized quickly. The increases were incorporated as part of the Clinton administration's first budget, which reduced the projected deficit by more than $430 billion over five years. Specifically, the Omnibus Budget and Reconciliation Act of 1993 raised the maximum EITC benefit, extended the phase-out range, and made individuals without dependent children eligible for the first time.[47] The total cost of these changes was approximately $20 billion. Compared to the "furor over . . . the higher gasoline taxes that all Americans will pay and higher individual tax rates for the wealthy and small businesses . . . debate over the earned income tax credit . . . was remarkably low-key."[48] Again, the Center on Budget and Policy Priorities took the lead in lobbying for an increase.

The impetus for expansion came during the 1992 presidential campaign.[49] As a candidate, Bill Clinton made two powerful promises: to "end welfare as we know it" and to "make work pay" for all Americans. Politically, this was a shrewd combination, for it enabled Clinton to appeal to Old and New Democrats alike. Apart from time limits, candidate Clinton was rather vague on the specifics of welfare reform. He said more about how he would alleviate the economic insecurity of ordinary citizens. No one who worked full-time and had children, Clinton declared, should be in poverty. He identified health insurance, investment in human and physical infrastructure, a higher minimum wage, and a larger EITC as top priorities for his administration. These themes struck a responsive chord among voters. In particular, Clinton found that "the tax credit had been one of his best applause lines during the campaign. 'I've never seen a program for working poor people be so enthusiastically supported by the middle class and in the suburbs.'"[50]

Turning those promises into policies proved quite difficult. Clinton won less than half the popular vote, and Democrats enjoyed smaller majorities in the House and Senate than they had under President Carter. Ross Perot's strong showing (winning 19 percent of the popular vote) persuaded Clinton to make deficit reduction a top priority, which in turn limited the possibilities for additional spending. Congressional Republicans united as the opposition party, vowing to oppose all legislation on which they had any substantial disagreement.

Democrats would have to govern alone, yet they remained divided over how to reshape their party. Clinton's closest aides and key members of the House tended to come from the party's liberal wing; indeed, the 1992 congressional elections produced a record number of women and racial minorities in Congress, almost all of whom were liberal Democrats. They placed less emphasis on deficit reduction than new spending initiatives, and wanted to rely more heavily on tax increases on the rich and corporations to achieve any deficit reduction. On the other hand, Clinton appointed a number of fiscally conservative Democrats to key administration posts (Treasury Secretary Lloyd Bentsen, OMB Director Leon Panetta) and had to deal with a number of equally conservative Democrats in the Senate. These officials viewed deficit reduction as the government's top priority and favored greater reliance on spending cuts, particularly of social programs, to achieve that goal.

Shortly after the election, Clinton decided not to push an investment package and postponed efforts to increase the minimum wage. With health reform still in the planning stages, the administration placed great weight on expanding the Earned Income Tax Credit. The EITC was one item that both wings of the Democratic party could enthusiastically support. Those on the left viewed the administration's proposed five-year, $28 billion increase in the EITC as a clear sign that Clinton genuinely meant to make work pay. Senator Kennedy (D-MA) called it a "lifeline for the working poor," and a representative of the Children's Defense Fund declared that the EITC was "wonderfully effective" and "one of the few ways this country gives a boost to the working poor and near-poor families."[51] The fiscally conservative wing tended to view a larger EITC as much needed welfare reform and liked the program's ability to increase take-home pay without imposing costs on business.

The budget passed in the House left Clinton's proposed changes in the EITC largely intact. The Senate was another story. Democrats there were more intent on reducing spending and limiting tax increases than their colleagues in the House, and they were especially hostile to the proposed BTU (energy) tax. They limited the EITC to taxpayers with dependent children and scaled back the total increase. These legislators forced Clinton to capitulate on several key points, such as larger cuts to Medicare. He, in turn, insisted that Congress expand the EITC further and extend benefits to childless workers. Once Clinton agreed to replace the BTU tax with a more regressive gasoline tax, expanding the EITC acquired an additional justification. Because administration officials wanted to ensure that no one earning less than $30,000 would pay additional taxes, they used the EITC to enhance the overall fairness of the budget. Expansion thereby enabled Democrats to counter charges that they had passed the largest tax increase in history by pointing out that millions of ordinary Americans would not have to pay higher income taxes.

The Threat of Cutbacks

Even as these changes were effected, political support for the EITC started to erode.[52] For the first time, elected officials started to criticize the program's objectives and performance. For the first time, the program was targeted for substantial cutbacks. Where and why did the EITC fall in disfavor? Answering where is easy—among conservative Republicans in Congress. To answer why, one might start by noting the growing numbers of new GOP legislators, many of them quite conservative, starting in 1990 and peaking in 1994. Because they were not Washington insiders during the 1980s, many of these new members did not think of the EITC as an integral part of tax reform, welfare reform, or family policy. In their eyes, the EITC stood out as one of the fastest-growing parts of the budget and one of the largest income transfers to the poor. Repeated expansion of the EITC since the mid-1980s had cost the program its low visibility.[53] In their quest to produce a balanced budget without raising taxes, congressional Republicans took dead aim at the Earned

Income Tax Credit. The Senate in 1995 recommended cutting the program by $43 billion over seven years, roughly twice what the House proposed.

Taking on the EITC was made easier by studies showing that the program suffered from high error rates. A significant fraction of people applying for the EITC claimed too large a credit or were ineligible. Although many of these appeared to be honest mistakes, driven by the difficulty low-income individuals have in dealing with complicated tax forms, there were also cases of deliberate fraud.[54] Critics therefore claimed that the EITC was growing out of control and plagued by waste and abuse. If Clinton officials were serious about deficit reduction and reinventing government, they argued, then the Earned Income Tax Credit had to be cut back.

The other important change to note concerned voting behavior and party competition. Beginning in the early 1990s, Republicans became less interested in using the EITC to win over the working poor. After drawing even in the 1980s, Republicans started to lose these voters to the Democrats in the 1990s. In the 1992 elections, Clinton won the working poor by a 46–34 margin over Bush, which was larger than his overall margin of victory. Democratic candidates for Congress that year won the working poor by a similar margin (57–43). In 1994, the year of the Republican tsunami, a clear majority of voters earning less than $30,000 still favored Democrats in Congress.[55] At the same time, Republicans started shifting their party's overall strategy, stressing economic issues to business interests and more affluent individuals and cultural issues (abortion, prayer in school) to less affluent individuals, and framing any painful spending cut or tax increase as deficit reduction. Some Republicans were less worried, in short, about what voters might think about any cuts to the EITC.

The EITC weathered the first round of attacks largely because Republicans made strategic errors and overreached in 1995. To produce a balanced budget and pay for tax cuts, Republicans had to make substantial cuts to a number of spending programs that Clinton and the Democrats held dear. High on that list was the Earned Income Tax Credit. Since the fall of the Clinton health plan, protecting the EITC had gained even greater importance, for it was one key campaign promise that Clinton had kept. It could be portrayed both as welfare reform and as a way to make work pay. Clinton vetoed the Republican budget, and opinion polls showed strong support for the president's actions, forcing Republicans to submit a revised budget without cuts to the EITC.

The EITC was targeted for cutbacks again in 1996 and 1997, and both times the Clinton administration refused to budge. Having weathered severe criticism for his support of welfare reform in 1996, Clinton had to defend the EITC as a crucial means of helping families come off welfare and stay off. As part of the major welfare reform bill, the House version passed in July 1996 included a $1.75 billion cut to the EITC and the Senate version included a $5 billion cut.[56] The final package signed by the president in August included truly minor modifications to the EITC, such as decreasing from $2,350 to $2,200 the amount of income individuals might exclude when determining their eligibility. Clinton also forced Republicans to exclude the EITC from the Taxpayer Relief Act of 1997, when they were looking for ways to pay for a new child tax credit and lower taxes on estates, capital gains, and Individual Retirement Accounts.

GOP leaders again took aim in 1999 and again failed. When House Republicans tried to defer EITC refunds to free up monies for other spending priorities, they were roundly attacked. The deciding blow came from fellow Republican George W. Bush, then governor of Texas and the leading candidate for president in 2000, who said, "I don't think they ought to balance their budget on the backs of the poor." A few days later, House Republicans dropped the idea. In the process, Governor Bush had bolstered his credibility as a moderate Republican and as someone who would not kowtow to Congress.[57]

By the end of the 1990s, the EITC was a much larger program while spending for Food Stamps and SSI had been cut, and AFDC had been converted from an entitlement to a block grant. Previous increases to the EITC proved durable, even in the face of motivated and powerful opponents. Clearly the Clinton administration's commitment to the program, which became (partly by default) one of its major domestic policy achievements, was instrumental. The EITC was an incentive to move people off welfare, a way of injecting equity into the tax system and major revenue bills, and an alternative to increases in the minimum wage. Clinton repeatedly refused to sign legislation if it appeared to increase the tax burdens of working families across the country.[58] A second factor working in its favor was that there was a documented history of conservative support for the program. It was President Reagan, after all, who had once called the EITC "'the best antipoverty, the best pro-family, the best job-creation measure to come out of the Congress.'"[59] Many influential Republicans, including Governors Engler of Michigan and Thompson of Wisconsin, embraced the program as a tool of welfare reform or an alternative to a higher minimum wage. With so many possible incarnations, the Earned Income Tax Credit offered something for almost everyone to like.

Future Prospects

One might think that because the EITC managed to grow during a time of record budget deficits, then present forecasts of record budget surpluses ought to make the program's future even brighter. Indeed, as of the summer of 2000, another EITC increase was being debated. President Clinton proposed a $2 billion per year increase in his last budget, with most of the money going to higher benefits rather than expanded coverage. In particular, the Clinton administration wanted to channel more money to families with three or more children and reduce the marriage penalty embedded in the EITC. If passed by Congress, it would be the largest expansion since 1993.

A number of policymakers sympathetic to the program, however, are debating a complete overhaul. They are worried about the work disincentives in the phase-out range of the tax credit and about the hodgepodge of tax benefits aimed at low-income workers. One alternative is to combine the EITC, the dependent exemption, and various tax credits for families with children into a single program, with simplified eligibility rules. The idea for such a "universal unified child credit" has been developed by the liberal Economic Policy Institute and endorsed by Gene Steuerle, and it is supposed to be introduced in Congress by a bipartisan team of legislators.[60] One ancillary benefit of such a move would be to reduce the program's error rate, a lightening rod for critics. Responding to evidence that benefits were being distributed too freely, as well as pressure from GOP legislators, the Internal Revenue Service has recently started to target EITC recipients for formal audits. In a program touted for its lack of bureaucratic intrusion into recipients' lives, this is not a welcome development.

Politically, advocates still have reasons to be concerned. The EITC is now one of the largest income transfers to the poor and will continue to be scrutinized more closely than when it was a small, anonymous tax expenditure. The working poor are voting more consistently Democratic than they did in the 1980s, so that Republicans may be less likely to compete for their support. Nevertheless, Democrats disagree over whether their base consists of voters with below-average or above-average incomes.[61] There could come a time when neither party will try very hard to win the support of the working poor. Moreover, the working poor still lack a strong organized presence outside of the two parties and still must rely on groups like the Center on Budget and Policy Priorities—groups without a mass membership or deep pockets—to defend their interests.

Whatever the outcome of these conflicting pressures, the meteoric rise of the Earned Income Tax Credit will remain one of the more interesting and hopeful chapters in the history of U.S. public policy. Clearly, the EITC is one case in which divided government did not produce gridlock; indeed, key episodes of expansion in 1986 and 1990 were the product of divided government, as elected officials tried not to lose, and often to win, the votes of the working poor. Indirectly, we have also seen two other examples—welfare reform in 1996 and tax cuts in 1997—in which substantial change occurred under divided government. The EITC is also a case of top-down policymaking at its best. A few policy entrepreneurs, working on behalf of a large group of citizens lacking in political resources, gradually built the EITC into a large cash transfer benefiting millions of families. Their arguments were powerful in part because elected officials realized that their desire to win reelection dovetailed nicely with their desire to make good policy. While there may be reasons to become discouraged about policymaking at the dawn of the twenty-first century, this is not one of them.

Notes

This chapter is a revised and updated version of Christopher Howard, *The Hidden Welfare State: Tax Expenditures and Social Policy in the United States* (Princeton, N.J.: Princeton University Press, 1997), chapter 7. Michael Cassidy provided valuable research assistance concerning developments in the 1990s.

1. U.S. Congress, Committee on Ways and Means, *Overview of Entitlement Programs* (Washington, D.C.: Government Printing Office, 1996), 804–809; U.S. Congress, Joint Committee on Taxation, *Estimates of Federal Tax Expenditures for*

Fiscal Years 1999–2003 (Washington, D.C.: Government Printing Office, 1999); Robert Cherry and Max B. Sawicky, "Giving Tax Credit Where Credit Is Due," briefing paper (Washington, D.C.: Economic Policy Institute, 2000).

2. David T. Ellwood, *Poor Support: Poverty in the American Family* (New York: Basic Books, 1988); Isaac Shapiro and Robert Greenstein, *Making Work Pay: A New Agenda for Poverty Policies* (Washington, D.C.: Center on Budget and Policy Priorities, 1989).

3. By "legal claim," I mean that the EITC is a budgetary entitlement with no annual ceiling on expenditures. Everyone who meets the eligibility criteria is entitled to benefits.

4. R. Kent Weaver, Robert Y. Shapiro, and Lawrence R. Jacobs, "Poll Trends: Welfare," *Public Opinion Quarterly* 59 (1995): 606–627.

5. Benjamin I. Page and Robert Y. Shapiro, *The Rational Public: Fifty Years of Trends in Americans' Policy Preferences* (Chicago: University of Chicago Press, 1992); Weaver et al., "Poll Trends: Welfare."

6. Harold W. Stanley and Richard G. Niemi, *Vital Statistics on American Politics*, 3d ed. (Washington, D.C.: CQ Press, 1992): 107–110; Seymour Martin Lipset, "The Significance of the 1992 Election," *PS: Political Science and Politics* 26 (March 1993): 7–16.

7. R. Douglas Arnold, *The Logic of Congressional Action* (New Haven, Conn.: Yale University Press, 1990), especially chapter 4.

8. Howard, *The Hidden Welfare State*, chapter 1.

9. Jeffrey Birnbaum and Alan Murray, *Showdown at Gucci Gulch* (New York: Vintage, 1987); Timothy J. Conlan, Margaret T. Wrightson, and David Beam, *Taxing Choices: The Politics of Tax Reform* (Washington, D.C.: Congressional Quarterly, 1990).

10. Mitch Daniels quoted in David R. Beam, Timothy J. Conlan, and Margaret T. Wrightson, "Solving the Riddle of Tax Reform: Party Competition and the Politics of Ideas," *Political Science Quarterly* 105 (Summer 1990): 201.

11. Ways and Means Chairman Dan Rostenkowski (D-IL), cited in Conlan et al., *Taxing Choices*, 94.

12. U.S. Congress, Committee on Ways and Means, *Overview of Entitlement Programs*, 804–809.

13. For the connections between the EITC and tax reform, see Beam et al., "Solving the Riddle of Tax Reform"; Birnbaum and Murray, *Showdown at Gucci Gulch*; Dom Bonafede, "Democratic Party Takes Some Strides Down the Long Comeback Trail," *National Journal* 15 (October 8, 1983): 2053–1055; Conlan et al., *Taxing Choices*; Linda E. Demkovich, "Fairness Issue Will Be Campaign Test of Reagan's Record on Budget Policies," *National Journal* 16 (September 8, 1984): 1648–1653; Karlyn H. Keene, "Who's the Fairest of Them All?" *Public Opinion* 7 (April–May 1984): 47–51; Robert Pear, "Budget Study Finds Cuts Cost the Poor as the Rich Gained," *New York Times*, April 4, 1984, p. A1; Wendell E. Primus, "Children in Poverty: A Committee Prepares for an Informed Debate," *Journal of Policy Analysis and Management* 8 (Winter 1989): 23–34; Susan Smith, "New GOP Leadership Readies Grassroots Organizing

Effort," *Congressional Quarterly Weekly Report* 41 (March 12, 1983): 519–522; C. Eugene Steuerle, "Tax Credits for Low-Income Workers with Children," *Journal of Economic Perspectives* 4 (Summer 1990): 201–212; U.S. House of Representatives, Committee on Ways and Means, Oversight Subcommittee, *Federal Tax Treatment of Low-Income Persons*, April 12, 1984; U.S. Senate, Finance Committee, *Tax Reform Proposals—IV (People below Poverty Line)*, June 17, 1985; and personal interviews with Robert Greenstein, Wendell Primus, Gene Steuerle, and Randy Weiss.

14. According to the CBO, the good news was that the average family had $840 more in income in 1984 as a result of cuts made in 1981. The bad news was that these benefits were skewed in favor of the affluent. Families earning less than $10,000 per year actually *lost* $390 in income, and those between $10,000 and $20,000 basically broke even. Those making more than $80,000 per year, however, pocketed an additional $8,270.

15. According to Jack Mayer of the American Enterprise Institute, "the working poor are 'an egregious example of people who have been hurt' by the Administration's social policies . . . 'I am very much in favor of the austerity Reagan advocated . . . but I do not think he distributed it fairly.'" As a remedy, Mayer suggested greater cuts in middle-class entitlements. Quoted in Demkovich, "Fairness Issue," 1651.

16. Such actions are sometimes referred to as reverse lobbying. Cathie Jo Martin describes a similar process in *Shifting the Burden: The Struggle over Growth and Corporate Taxation* (Chicago: University of Chicago Press, 1991).

17. Primus, "Children in Poverty," 30. Primus was the Ways and Means staff economist. President Clinton later appointed Primus to be deputy assistant secretary of human services at the Department of Health and Human Services.

18. Other groups in this category include Bread for the World, Catholic Charities USA, the Children's Defense Fund, Coalition on Block Grants and Human Needs, the Lutheran Council, the NAACP, and the American Federation of State, County, and Municipal Workers (AFSCME).

19. Personal interview with Robert Greenstein. The CBPP later became instrumental in coordinating a nationwide campaign to publicize the Earned Income Tax Credit in poor communities.

20. See, for example, the testimony of Joseph Minarik, then an economist with the Brookings Institution, and of Robert Greenstein. U.S. House of Representatives, Committee on Ways and Means, *Federal Tax Treatment of Low-Income Workers*. Greenstein estimated that the real value of the EITC in 1985 would be less than one-half its original value in 1975 unless Congress acted.

21. Birnbaum and Murray, *Showdown at Gucci Gulch*; Conlan et al., *Taxing Choices*. The latter authors argue (46–49) that Reagan did not view tax reform simply as a defensive maneuver to hold the Democrats in check. Reagan also equated tax reform with further reductions in tax rates.

22. Mondale tried to make fairness a key theme of the 1984 presidential election. He referred to Republicans as the party "of the rich, by the rich, and for the rich" (cited in Demkovich, "Fairness Issue," 1648), and appealed directly to

Reagan Democrats on grounds of economic self-interest. Many voters found it difficult to square Mondale's commitment to fairness with his pledge to raise taxes and avid courtship of special interest groups. Moreover, to many white, working-class ears, "fairness" was a code word for affirmative action and preferential treatment of minorities.

23. James Q. Wilson, *Political Organizations* (New York: Basic Books, 1973), chapter 16.

24. U.S. Department of the Treasury, *Tax Reform for Fairness, Simplicity, and Economic Growth* (Washington, D.C.: U.S. Department of the Treasury, 1984), 71.

25. For a discussion of how problems, solutions, and politics come together to form "policy windows," see John Kingdon, *Agendas, Alternatives, and Public Policy* (Boston: Little, Brown, 1984).

26. Less efficient options included increases in the standard deduction and personal exemption, which would benefit all taxpayers regardless of need. Personal interview with Gene Steuerle.

27. Gene Steuerle, "The Integration of Tax and Transfer Systems Part 2: A Negative Earnings Tax (NET)," *Tax Notes* 50 (January 7, 1991): 8990.

28. "After Years of Debate, Welfare Reform Clears," *Congressional Quarterly Almanac 1988* (Washington, D.C.: Congressional Quarterly, 1988), 349–364; *Congressional Record*, May 22, 1985, S6861-75; U.S. House of Representatives, Committee on Ways and Means, Subcommittee on Public Assistance and Unemployment Compensation, *Welfare Reform*, March 13, 1987; U.S. Congress, Joint Committee on Taxation, "Federal Tax Treatment of Individuals Below the Poverty Line," in Senate Finance Committee, *Tax Reform Proposals—IV (People below Poverty Line)*.

29. The act also tried to move more AFDC recipients into the labor force by extending their Medicaid coverage, making permanent the WIN and WIN Demonstration programs, and increasing the standard deduction and personal exemption.

30. On the salience of welfare reform to working-class whites, see Thomas Byrne Edsall with Mary D. Edsall, *Chain Reaction: The Impact of Race, Rights, and Taxes on American Politics* (New York: Norton, 1991).

31. However, the Family Support Act of 1988 did require states to disregard the EITC when calculating AFDC eligibility and benefits.

32. Timothy B. Clark, "Raising the Floor," *National Journal* 19 (March 21, 1987): 702–705; Nadine Cohodas, "Minimum Wage Getting Maximum Attention," *Congressional Quarterly Weekly Report* 45 (March 7, 1987): 403–407; "Minimum-Wage Impasse Finally Ended," *Congressional Quarterly Almanac 1989* (Washington, D.C.: Congressional Quarterly, 1990), 45: 333–340; "Minimum Wage Increase," *Congress and the Nation: Vol. 7, 1985–1988* (Washington, D.C.: Congressional Quarterly, 1990), 705–706; Macon Morehouse, "Senate Opens Debate on Minimum-Wage Hike," *Congressional Quarterly Weekly Report* 46 (September 17, 1988): 2587; Jonathan Rauch, "Paycheck Politics," *National Journal* 21 (July 8, 1989): 1746–1749; personal interview with Joe Flader, legislative assistant to Representative Tom Petri.

33. The minimum wage had equaled between 45 and 60 percent of the average hourly wage since the late 1940s. It slipped from 48 percent in 1981 to 38 percent in 1987. Clark, "Raising the Floor."

34. Petri was a member of the moderate Ripon Society and had a reputation as a maverick and innovator. Phil Duncan, ed., *Politics in America, 1990: The 101st Congress* (Washington: CQ Press, 1989): 1643–1645. Tom Tauke (R-IA) was another advocate of expanding the EITC rather than the minimum wage.

35. Cited in Rauch, "Paycheck Politics," 1747.

36. Howard Banks, "A Better Way to Help the Low-Paid," *Forbes* 141 (June 27, 1988): 43; "Better Than $3.35, $4.25 or Even $5.05," *New York Times,* July 11, 1988, p. A16.

37. E. J. Dionne Jr., "Democrats Fashion Centrist Image in New Statement of Party Policy," *New York Times,* September 21, 1986, pp. 1, 28; Jon F. Hale, "Party Factionalism in Congress: A Study of the Democratic Leadership Council's Membership in the House," paper presented at the annual meeting of the American Political Science Association, Washington, D.C., August 28–September 1, 1991; Janet Hook, "Officials Seek Moderation in Party's Image," *Congressional Quarterly Weekly Report* 43 (March 9, 1985): 457; Robert Kuttner, *The Life of the Party: Democratic Prospects in 1988 and Beyond* (New York: Viking, 1987).

38. Rauch, "Paycheck Politics," 1746.

39. Representative Buddy MacKay (D-FL), "Raise the Minimum Wage? No, There's a More Sensible Approach," *Washington Post,* May 5, 1988, p. A23; Robert J. Shapiro, "Work and Poverty: A Progressive View of the Minimum Wage and the Earned Income Tax Credit," Progressive Policy Institute, *Policy Report No. 1* (June 1989). The Progressive Policy Institute is the research arm of the DLC.

A Gallup poll taken in 1987 indicated across-the-board support for an increase in the minimum wage from $3.35 to $4.65 per hour, phased in over three years. Seventy-seven percent of all respondents favored such an increase, including 66 percent of Republicans, 78 percent of independents, and 79 percent of those earning between $15,000 and $25,000 per year—some of the very groups targeted by DLC Democrats. George Gallup Jr., *The Gallup Poll: Public Opinion 1987* (Wilmington, Del.: Scholarly Resources, 1988): 125–128.

40. Robert Greenstein and Isaac Shapiro, "A Higher Minimum Wage *Would* Help the Poor," *Washington Post,* August 15, 1989, p. A19.

41. "A Better Idea on Tax Credits," *New York Times,* July 3, 1990, p. A16.

42. This discussion of the EITC and family policy is based on "Child-Care Bill Dies Amid Partisan Sniping," *Congressional Quarterly Almanac 1988* (Washington, D.C.: Congressional Quarterly, 1989), 44: 365–368; Jason DeParle, "Poor Families Gain under Tax Accord," *New York Times,* October 31, 1990, p. A20; Dionne, "Democrats Fashion Centrist Image"; Thomas B. Edsall, "Consensus Builds to Expand Aid for Working Poor," *Washington Post,* August 21, 1989, p. A1, A10; "Families Gain Help on Child Care," *Congressional Quarterly Almanac 1990* (Washington, D.C.: Congressional Quarterly, 1990), 46: 547–551; Elaine Ciulla Kamarck and William A. Galston, *Putting Children First: A Progressive*

Family Policy for the 1990s (Washington, D.C.: Progressive Policy Institute, 1990); Julie Kosterlitz, "Family Fights," *National Journal* 22 (June 2, 1990): 1333–1337; Julie Rovner, "Congress Shifts Its Attention to the Working Poor," *Congressional Quarterly Weekly Report* 47 (February 18, 1989): 326–328; Julie Rovner, "Consensus Grows on Dual Path to Boosting Child-Care Aid," *Congressional Quarterly Weekly Report* 47 (April 22, 1989): 902; William A. Schambra, "Turf Battles: The Parties Clash over Community," *Public Opinion* 11 (July–August 1988): 17–19+; U.S. House of Representatives, Committee on Ways and Means, Subcommittee on Human Resources, "How to Help the Working Poor, and Problems of the Working Poor," February 28, March 21, and April 27, 1989; and personal interviews with Helen Blank, David Ellwood, Robert Greenstein, Wendell Primus, Nancy Reeder and Madlyn Morreale, and Michael Scheinfield.

43. Many of these policies were also justified in the name of improving American competitiveness in the world economy, another site of interparty competition in the 1980s.

44. At the insistence of Lloyd Bentsen (D-TX), chairman of the Senate Finance Committee, Congress created a new tax credit for health insurance for children of working poor families. That tax credit, plus a new tax credit for families with children less than one year old (deemed nonnegotiable by White House chief of staff John Sununu), came at the expense of the EITC, whose increases were scaled back.

45. "Budget Adopted after Long Battle," *Congressional Quarterly Almanac 1990* (Washington, D.C.: Congressional Quarterly, 1990), 46: 111–166; Lawrence Haas, "Treasure's Buried in the Budget Deal," *National Journal* 22 (November 20, 1990): 2543–2545.

46. Quoted in DeParle, "Poor Families Gain under Tax Accord," A20. The staff member was referring as well to increases in Medicaid eligibility passed as part of the same budget package.

47. Though the maximum benefit was small, this last change had the potential to increase substantially the number of individuals, and hence potential voters, receiving the EITC.

48. James Risen, "Credit for Working Poor Exemplifies Tax Burden Shift," *Los Angeles Times,* August 10, 1993, p. A12.

49. This discussion of expansion in 1993 draws on material from "Deficit-Reduction Bill Narrowly Passes," *Congressional Quarterly Almanac 1993* (Washington, D.C.: Congressional Quarterly, 1994), 107–124; Guy Gugliotta, "How to Aid 'Working Poor'?" *Washington Post,* April 15, 1993, p. A1; Marshall Ingwerson, "Tax Credit Geared for Working Poor Stays in Budget Mix," *Christian Science Monitor,* August 5, 1993, p. 8; Steven Mufson, "Clinton's Social Safety Net: A Bigger Tax Credit," *Washington Post,* March 6, 1993, p. A1+; Timothy Noah, "Program to Help Working Poor with Bigger Tax Credit Is Urged," *Wall Street Journal,* February 18, 1993, p. A10; Timothy Noah and Laurie McGinley, "Advocate for the Poor, Respected on All Sides, Secures a Pivotal Role in Expanding Tax Credit," *Wall Street Journal,* July 26, 1993, p. A12;

Paul Pierson, "The Deficit and the Politics of Domestic Reform," in *The Social Divide: Political Parties and the Future of Activist Government,* ed. Margaret Weir (Washington, D.C.: Brookings Institution, 1998), 126–178; Paul J. Quirk and Joseph Hinchliffe, "Domestic Policy: The Trials of a Centrist Democrat," in *The Clinton Presidency: First Appraisals,* ed. Colin Campbell and Bert A. Rockman (Chatham, N.J.: Chatham House, 1996), 262–289; Risen, "Credit for Working Poor Exemplifies Tax Burden Shift"; R. Kent Weaver, "Ending Welfare as We Know It," in *The Social Divide,* 361–416; and Bob Woodward, *The Agenda: Inside the Clinton White House* (New York: Simon & Schuster, 1994).

50. Clinton quoted in Woodward, *The Agenda,* 128.

51. Both quoted in Mufson, "Clinton's Social Safety Net," A12, A13.

52. Evidence for this section is drawn from David Cloud, "Clinton Looking to Tax Credit To Rescue Working Poor," *Congressional Quarterly Weekly Report,* March 13, 1993, pp. 583–587; Pierson, "The Deficit and the Politics of Domestic Reform"; Alissa Rubin, "Low-Income Workers' Tax Credit among GOP Budget Targets," *Congressional Quarterly Weekly Report,* October 7, 1995; Jeff Shear, "The Credit Card," *National Journal,* August 12, 1995, pp. 2056–2060; and Weaver, "Ending Welfare as We Knew It."

53. The leading critics were Senators Nickles (R-OK), Pressler (R-SD), and Roth (R-DE) of the Senate Finance Committee.

54. The creation of two new tax credits in 1990, whose eligibility and benefits were linked to the EITC, added to this complexity. This problem was solved in 1993 with the elimination of those other credits.

55. "Who Voted for Whom in Congress on Nov. 8," *National Journal,* November 12, 1994, p. 2631; "Who Voted for Clinton, Dole and Perot," *National Journal,* October 9, 1996, p. 2407.

56. These cuts may seem to undermine welfare reform, considering that the EITC helped pull people off AFDC, until one remembers that one objective of the welfare reform bill was simply to lower spending.

57. Lee Walczak, "Bush's Declaration of Independence," *Business Week,* October 18, 1999, p. 58; see also Michael Barone, "Going against Type," *U.S. News & World Report,* October 18, 1999, p. 36.

58. Recent studies of the 1996 election show how important less educated and lower-income voters were to Clinton's reelection and thus how rational it was to protect the EITC. Ruy Teixeira, "The Real Electorate," *The American Prospect* 37 (March–April 1998): 82–85.

59. Cited in Shear, "The Credit Card," 2056.

60. Cherry and Sawicky, "Giving Tax Credit Where Credit Is Due"; Burt Solomon, "The Cutting Edge," *National Journal* 32, no. 21 (May 20, 2000): 1630; Gene Steuerle, "Combining Child Credits, the EITC, and the Dependent Exemption," *Tax Notes,* April 24 and May 1, 2000, pp. 567–568, 703–704.

61. See, for example, the debate among leading party advisers in "Why Did Clinton Win?" *The American Prospect* 31 (March–April 1997): 12–22 and Teixeira, "The Real Electorate."

11

Dead on Arrival?

New Politics, Old Politics, and the
Case of National Health Reform

Cathie Jo Martin, *Boston University*

In September 1993, Bill Clinton captured the imagination of the television audience when he promised to create a new right for all Americans, the right to health coverage, embodied in a red, white, and blue plastic card he described as the "health security card."[1] A poll taken by Robert Blendon on the night of the viewing found 80 percent of voters willing to pay more in taxes to make health care universal and to contain escalating costs.[2] Clinton appointed his own wife to lead the health care reform crusade, and for a few flushed weeks Hillary Rodham Clinton was universally hailed as the lady of the hour.[3] Health care reform seemed imminent and irrepressible. Yet by late winter of 1994, the president's reform bills were languishing in critical congressional committees. Even before its legislative demise in the summer of 1994, the reform episode was admitted by friend and foe alike to be the perfect example of how *not* to conduct public policy.

It is striking that a policy initiative enjoying such popular will and moral force could have met with an egregious demise, and volumes have been dedicated to explaining national health reform's downfall.[4] It is not my purpose to contribute to this vast literature; rather, I propose to use the sad plight of national health reform to reflect on differences in policymaking campaigns—the caustic conflicts of a high-salience, interest-driven legislative battle versus the more quiet negotiations of ideas-driven policymaking described in the *New Politics of Public Policy*.[5]

In some ways one might have anticipated legislative success for health care reform. The initiative sought to establish a new right of the strongest kind: grounded on moral imperative rather than legal code. A compelling idea, managed competition, offered to end the political stalemate that had divided market and regulatory approaches to health care reform in the past. The legislation would be financed with a hidden tax, the employer mandate, that seemed to side-step the constraints of deficit reduction. The major beneficiaries of the bill would be large employers and the working poor, the latter being the same deserving swing-voting constituents advantaged by the Earned Income Tax Credit.[6]

Ultimately, however, the health initiative gained high political salience and was overwhelmed by intense interest group conflict. As other authors in this volume have noted, legislation often passes more easily when ideas are strong, interests are weak, political salience is low, and the public is otherwise engaged. Although technical-rational ideas originally drove health care reform, actively engaged interests, partisan ambitions, and high political salience quickly transformed the reform effort from a technical fix by policy experts into a high-stakes game of political brinkmanship. As McWilliams writes in chapter 16 of this volume, the administration's effort to gratify the convoluted array of organized interests ultimately produced a "Dungeons and Dragons of policy" that satisfied none.

This essay uses the health care reform case to address two major themes of the volume: the power of ideas and the impact of political salience. First, the chapter testifies to the importance of ideas by showing how new conceptions of health care reform brought the issue to the national agenda and how health care reform faltered when interest groups managed to supplant the technical-rational ideas about policy with broader ideological conflict. The push for reform grew out of the increasing conviction of experts in *both* the public and private sectors that the system was profoundly disturbed. Granted, experts disagreed about the best solution, being rather evenly divided among single-payer, play-or-pay, and market reform plans. But in the early stages decision makers fixed on managed competition as a way out of this bind. Managed competition neatly combined elements of both the play-or-pay and market reform plans and, therefore, seemed to offer a promising compromise to the expert debate over ideas. Later during the health care reform legislative cycle, the fragile consensus over managed competition fell apart as the contradictions in the proposal emerged. At the same time, technical-rational ideas about policy were subsumed in a larger debate over the role of government in society, as vested interests opposing health care reform managed to refocus the public's attention.

The health care reform case also suggests quite a bit of interplay between ideas and interests. Ideas were quite critical to societal actors' perceptions of their own interests in health policy. Even the allegedly most material of actors—business managers—found their interests transformed by ideas. Technical experts within the firm brought companies in line with the thinking of technical experts elsewhere.

In reciprocal fashion, interests influenced both the generation of and public reception to the ideas underlying reform. Health care reform came to be based on managed competition not only because the idea was compelling but because it protected companies' vested interests in the employer-based system. At the same time, the ultimate demise of health care reform reflected the ability of its opponents to reframe the managed competition idea as antithetical to the interests of both employers and the broader public. The leaders of the opposition engaged in "spin control," selective polling, and other tactics to cast a rightist tint on the policy initiative.

Second, the health care reform case illustrates how high political salience can diminish the role of technical expertise, distort the public's perception of policy tools, and reduce a bill's likelihood of passage. Although political salience may be manipulated by political entrepreneurs as a strategy for building political will, salience may also increase the likelihood of interest group conflict and decrease the power of political experts. Before the reform legislative cycle, quiet, major changes were taking place in the organization of the health care system, which James Morone has categorized as "slouching toward national health reform."[7] Similar major changes in the postreform period might be characterized as hurtling toward managed care. During the congressional debate, however, political salience dramatically distorted the very managed competition initiatives that were subsequently adopted by the market.

Of course, as Schattschneider notes, interest groups recognize the political power of salience and often manipulate scope to increase or to suppress salience.[8] These groups may work to increase the political salience of an issue to move it out of the technical-rational realm and to recast it in more ideological terms. When issues gain visibility, it becomes more difficult for policy entrepreneurs to retain control and to pursue an ideas-driven legislative strategy.

In the case of national health reform, one sees political entrepreneurs *both* deliberately manipulating salience and responding to interest group efforts to increase the visibility of the issue. Clinton's decision to increase the salience of health care reform by identifying it as the major initiative of his first term reflected the realpolitik conflict of party politics and a conflation of a new president's political ambitions with policy needs. The politics was transformed as the two parties made the issue a test for party identification and control, and the outcome may have been different if they had chosen a different vehicle for this partisan conflict.[9]

The Clinton administration also chose the high-salience route because it believed that true reform would require a tremendous amount of political will. Health policy is an area with deeply entrenched interests. The patchwork pattern of public/private provision in health made for a very intricate mix of interests growing out of current benefits and privileges on both the supply and demand side. These interests invested enormous resources to change the terms of the health care reform debate. The policymakers within the administration were well aware of the drawbacks of increasing the salience of the issue, but they felt that increased salience through a class-based mobilization was necessary for action, even though this mobilization would distort the policy process and detract from expert power.

Thus, the case of health care reform reveals the paradoxical nature of political salience. A key reason for increasing political salience is to generate political will, but ironically salience pushes action and at the same time delimits it. Political will can, in fact, inhibit policy legislation, and policy entrepreneurs may achieve more where there is a policy vacuum without much public demand. But in issue areas such as health care in which entrenched interests block action in the absence of political will, comprehensive change may be impossible without full-scale interest mobilization and high political salience.

Ideas in Policy Change: The Rise and Fall of Managed Competition

The health care reform case strongly confirms the volume's emphasis on ideas as a powerful determinant of policy: ideas brought health care reform to the national agenda, and the supplanting of technical-rational ideas with broader ideological conflict ultimately killed reform. Ideas were an initial powerful support for comprehensive overhaul of the health system. Although national health reform had been traditionally viewed as a socialist's dream, in the late 1980s the concept became associated with cost control and system rationalization. A pivotal constituency for reform in this early period was experts from both the public and private realm who believed the health system to be highly irrational and profoundly disturbed. As Mark Peterson has argued, it was this consensus of expert opinion, even drawing supporters from the medical and business communities, that radically changed the prospects for national health reform.[10]

Agreement about the problem did not translate into consensus about the solution; indeed, over the years a chasm had existed between advocates of market solutions and those desiring regulatory change. Health care reform advocates were divided among those wanting a single-payer plan, a regulatory approach called play-or-pay, and incremental market reforms, the most comprehensive being the Heritage Foundation plan.

The single-payer approach would create a single pool financed by taxes that would negotiate with hospitals and doctors; many plans would abolish private insurance and depend on public administration.[11] Woolhandler and Himmelstein argued that a Canadian-style system would save $69 to $83.2 billion in administrative costs.[12] Critics retorted that the Canadian national debt is twice as high as that of the United States per capita and that the Canadian federal government is shifting costs to the provinces.[13] Others worried that the national government would not be competent to administer the plan and that quality would decrease without competitive market pressures.

The play-or-pay system was a mixed public-private system that offered global budgets to limit costs, regulated rates to reduce inequities, and employer mandates to expand coverage. Supported by many congressional Democrats, the play-or-pay feature meant that employers would either *play* and offer health insurance or *pay* a new payroll tax of 5 to 8 percent, used to expand the public program.[14] Critics worried that play-or-pay would create a new burden on business, increase the hourly cost for workers receiving the minimum wage by up to $0.80, and precipitate a loss of jobs.[15] Some saw play-or-pay as a first step toward a single-payer system, especially after the proposal to set the "pay" rate at 7 percent of payroll when many company health costs are as much as 14 percent of payroll.[16]

The Heritage Foundation tax credit or voucher system sought to reintroduce competition into the health care market. The plan would change all employment-related benefits into direct wages, and workers would pay for premiums directly. All heads of households would be required to buy at least catastrophic insurance, but state mandating of specific benefits would be illegal.[17] In its pure form, the Heritage plan entailed almost as much government monitoring as play-or-pay, although it left the reform process to the private market.[18] President George H. Bush's plan adopted pieces of the Heritage approach without a realistic funding strategy, and critics worried that this plan would fail to meet the needs of the very ill.[19]

Considerable disagreement divided supporters of these three plans; no technical consensus pointed the way to easy legislation. But a new idea, managed competition, briefly offered a means for reconciling market and regulatory approaches.[20] Managed competition, based on work by Alain Enthoven, sought to change the market incentives for both providers and consumers by aggregating consumers into large purchasing cooperatives. A national board would determine a standardized benefit package; only plans that provide the package would be certified as "accountable health plans."[21] Advocates argued that managed competition could accomplish dramatic changes in the health-financing landscape without excessive government intervention.[22]

The Clinton administration proposal borrowed from both play-or-pay and managed competition plans. In keeping with the spirit of play-or-pay, Clinton proposed that all employers be mandated to provide health benefits to their employees. To contain costs, Clinton proposed a national board to set spending targets for the amount to be spent on health care. Combined with these regulatory efforts to contain costs was the market-oriented managed competition proposal. Employer-paid premiums would be aggregated into non-government purchasing cooperatives that would coordinate coverage and restrain costs.[23]

The concept of managed competition appealed to the New Democrats and to President Clinton, as fitting with the president's efforts to rewrite the boundaries between the market and the welfare state. Although social initiatives are usually viewed as a drag on economic growth, the Clinton administration sought to reconcile the ancient antagonism between social welfare and accumulation by organizing social policy to support economic growth and by using markets to achieve social ends. Clinton argued that markets alone are insufficient to spur growth and international competitiveness; instead, government must assist industry through incentives strategically calculated to maximize America's competitive advantage. Thus, health joined labor market initiatives to guarantee a productive workforce for the postindustrial future. At the same time, the mandate offered a means of achieving social ends without threatening the private health-financing market. Employer mandates were the epitome of a new social philosophy that sought not to create expanded public programs but to correct the functioning of the private markets.

Political feasibility also made the managed competition idea seem attractive. The administration recognized that big business and large insurance companies were attracted to the idea (discussed later). Managed competition also claimed to be more fiscally viable than plans requiring greater government intervention. As Patashnik and Pierson point out in this volume (see chapters 2 and 3, respectively), our national obsession with budget deficits combined with the politician's fear of bearing the tax responsibility burden greatly constrain the development of new government programs. Managed competition avoided this conundrum with a hidden tax in the form of an employer mandate and thus could claim to offer wonderful benefits with very little fiscal costs.

Something happened to the ideas informing health care reform; namely, the technical-rational ideas of bureaucrats became lost in a broader ideological conflict over the role of government. At this point experts could no longer control the debate, and the fortunes of health care reform declined. In a few pages we will consider how this substantial shift in the ideas underlying health care reform occurred, but first let us look at another important way that ideas shaped the health care reform process—in their impact on business managers' perceptions of their own interests.

Linking Ideas and Interests:
Employer Support for Reform

In emphasizing the power of ideas, one runs the danger of neglecting interests or of drawing overly stark comparisons between ideas and interests. In fact, the two are deeply connected: ideas shape interests and interests shape ideas.

The enormous impact of ideas on interests in the case of national health reform can be documented with the transformation in the thinking of corporate purchasers of health. By the late 1980s and early 1990s, most business managers seemed accepting of both systemic reform and employer mandates. In my study of randomly sampled Fortune 200 companies, over half of the business respondents (54 percent) supported mandates, and another 19 percent felt mixed on the subject.[24] In 1991 a Harris poll found two-thirds of a corporate sample at least somewhat accepting of a mandated standard benefits plan.[25] Membership polling within the major umbrella associations supported the findings of academic business surveys. In a 1992 study, 55 percent of National Association of Manufacturers (NAM) members favored a play-or-pay approach (complete with employer mandates) as part of overall system reform.[26] A NAM survey in 1993 found a majority supporting mandates and health alliances for firms with more than five hundred employess.[27] A June 1994 Washington Business Group on Health survey of large firms showed 72 percent supporting a requirement for all companies to offer insurance, 59 percent wanting firms to pay a portion, and 71 percent objecting to an arrangement that allowed small business to escape the mandate.[28] As one lobbyist put it, "Business from the far right has moved to the center in saying that the federal government needs to be involved."[29]

Business supporters of health care reform were motivated by complicated reasons. Economic circumstance was certainly important. For many years employers have been major providers of health benefits, covering almost two-thirds of the nonelderly population in the United States.[30] But in recent times health costs have grown enormously, claiming 8.3 percent of salaries and wages by 1989.[31] In the age of multinational trade, export-oriented firms wanted to keep labor costs low. Corporate supporters of health care reform wanted government to force their competitors to offer benefits and to end cost shifting. Some big corporate spenders (often with fast commitments to their unions, such as auto and steel firms) wanted, like the government, to bail them out by assuming some of the costs of social provision. Finally, many firms believed that a coherent health policy could rationalize the current system.

But material conditions are insufficient to explain managers' preferences for reform; rather, one must investigate the new ideas about the role of human resource investments in competitive strategies. Some managers following a laissez-faire approach continued to believe that spending cuts in both the private and public realms were necessary to be competitive because these cuts would reduce labor costs and to free up investment capital.[32] Yet others bought into the high-performance workplace logic that recommended rationalizing, targeting, and often expanding social investment spending by governments and/or firms in order to develop a competent, productive workforce. Many business managers agreed with Jim O'Connell (Ceridan) that the interest in social issues reflected concerns about productivity: "Companies not only have a conscience, but in addition there's a profitability motive."[33]

The importance of ideas in managers' perceptions of their interests is illustrated in my study of firm preferences for health care reform. Companies that supported employer mandates in health care reform had an institutional capacity to grasp the technical-rational ideas underpinning national health reform, a quality I have labeled *corporate policy capacity.*[34] Three institutional factors enhanced companies' corporate policy capacity: private-sector policy expertise, the political organization of managers, and social policy legacies within business. First, the expansion of private policy expertise within the firm affected how business managers thought about their interests and increased their receptivity to the ideas underpinning health care reform. Thus, the companies in my study with institutionalized policy expertise in the form of Washington government affairs offices were significantly more likely to support mandates. Oddly, these firms began forming Washington, D.C., government affair offices in the 1970s to fight the expansion of government regulations. Yet meeting with public sector regulators and congressional staffers over time exposed them to technical policy arguments and brought them to view social problems from a more technical and less ideological perspective than others in the business community.[35] Government affairs positions came to be staffed by experts with considerable professional training in their substantive fields, who were then able to influence top management's perceptions of their firms' interests.[36]

Second, business support for health care reform was shaped by prior corporate experiences with private benefits.[37] When private welfare plans failed, firms often moved toward government solutions. Many managers described their path to systemic reform as one of increasing frustration with firm-level efforts to change provider behavior.[38]

Finally, the firms that developed their preferences collectively in group settings were significantly more likely to accept employer mandates. The collective exploration of health problems exposed respondents to a range of new information that expanded their perspectives and transformed their thinking.[39] Managers developed their preferences in various types of groups, even those with no national policy focus. For example, area coalitions were formed before health care reform became an important issue, were created to try to control local markets, and were originally oriented to market solutions. Yet this community activism at the local level led to activism at the national level. A participant of a trade association task force explained that the deliberative process radically altered her perspective: "On most issues I am a hard-core Republican, but I'm radical on this issue. I generally don't believe in regulation, but regulation should be when the market breaks down, and it has in health care. I know that I sound like a bleeding liberal, but we need to know that each person will be accounted for. Maybe employers will have to pay more, but at least it will be explicit."[40]

The Impact of Interests on Ideas

Just as ideas inform interests, interests also influence both the generation of and public reception to ideas. For example, the emergence of managed competition as a central organizing principle of health care reform reflected the policy legacies of the employer-based system and managers' vested interests in the status quo. Market approaches tend to enjoy greater ideological acceptability in general, but even more important, the managed competition plan was built on market changes already afoot in the business community. Since the 1980s, many companies had been securing provider services through managed care networks, such as point-of-service (POS) plans, and had used their large patient pools to secure advantageous rates for their customers.[41] In 1992, Foster Higgins found nearly three-fourths of the firms sampled offering a managed care option (either POS or HMO).[42] The cognitive step from managed care to managed competition promised to be a small one, and policymakers believed that business managers would be instinctively drawn to a national solution that was close to what they were already doing at the microlevel.

The policy choice of managed care was consistent as well with the business coalition movement that had developed to increase purchaser power at the local level; this institutional innovation provided a model for the consumer purchasing groups in the managed competition plan. Managers had been quite impressed by the Enthoven concept of community-based purchaser coalitions to reinstate market rationality into the health system, and important corporate forums such as the Jackson Hole group and the Managed Health Care Association were devoted to the managed competition idea.[43] Finally, the big insurers' move into managed care offered a compelling political draw: these giants hoped to administer the purchaser cooperatives.[44] Thus, interests were important to the original choice of managed competition as a vehicle for reform.

In reciprocal fashion, interests played an important role in the reframing of the Clinton initiative and the recasting of the rights embodied in the proposal. Recognizing that liberals had an advantage in idea generation, conservative think tanks had for some time been creating forums for developing counter-ideas. Think tanks and foundations such as the Citizens for a Sound Economy sought with spin control to change the ideas associated with comprehensive health care reform. Through the use of devices such as the famous Harry and Louise ads, the opponents of reform amazingly transformed a market approach—managed competition—into a symbol of big government intrusion into private lives. The media campaign was actually less interested in affecting public opinion than in affecting how Congress viewed public opinion.[45] As a result, the ads were mainly shown in Washington, D.C., or in districts with uncommitted legislators. But the nightly news greatly increased the circulation: major interest groups received 798 seconds of (free) news coverage about their ads. The Harry and Louise ads alone got 324 seconds of free air time.[46] The Health Insurance Association of America (HIAA) spent $15 million on advertising attacking Clinton in 1994.[47]

The opponents of reform were also able to reframe the rights debate connected to the health initiative. The central ambition of the reform measure was to establish a new right to universal health coverage, packaged by the administration as "security of decent health care for every American family."[48] According to the Schuck typology, this right should have been of the strongest kind, as it was morally based as opposed to legally based and grounded in natural law. Yet this new right was too vulnerable to withstand the opposition, when naysayers countered with an opposing right—the right to choose—thus adding an odd inverse of the language of abortion to the debate. Rather than questioning the right to health, health care reform's detractors argued that the solution proposed would threaten other rights. In this vein, Tod Lindberg wrote, "'Universal coverage'—something Americans supported in the abstract—suddenly paled in importance compared with the loss of certain features of the current system that people had taken for granted (the right to choose their own doctors, for example)."[49] This vulnerability was accentuated by the fact that health access is highly divisible, and most citizens already enjoy this de facto right, making a new initiative problematic especially when it potentially threatened their right to choose. Some feared that the new right would take health access out of the private domain in which it had rested comfortably for many years, and many Americans resisted further government intrusion into the health domain.[50] Thus, President Clinton was told, "Mind your own business," in the *American Spectator*.[51]

The following section on political salience delves more deeply into the strategies used by health care reform's opponents to change the fundamental terms of the reform debate from ideas about fixing the technical problems of the system to arguments about the role of the state.

The Politics of Salience: Party Ambitions and Reform's Demise

Health care reform readily appears to support another theme of this volume: that policy is more easily passed when it is handled by policy experts under conditions of low political salience. Comparing the dialogue during the reform debate to discussion of health policy before and after illustrates how salience removed health policy from the domain and language of experts. Political salience increased enormously during the health care reform battle, and the type of bureaucratic adjustments that were easily made before and after the legislative cycle were suddenly cast as major shifts in the boundary between public and private. The efforts of both parties to increase the political salience of reform harmed the legislation's chances for enactment.

Although physicians and their interest groups traditionally dominated the health policy arena, in the fifteen years before Clinton's health security bill, bureaucrats steadily challenged the medical profession's dominion. These changes were highly incremental, producing a revolution so quiet that even the major players seemed unaware of its implications. Under the guise of cost containment, regulators introduced limits on new medical facilities, rigid reimbursement schemes for Medicare patients, and procedures to monitor physician decisions.[52] Private sector consumers also pursued a range of cost controls that curtailed physician power.

The period following the reform legislative cycle also saw huge changes in health financing. Corporate providers of health have flocked to managed care in droves since the 1980s, despite health care reform opponents' arguments that managed competition attacked consumer choice. HMO enrollment went from two million in 1970 to fifty-one million in 1995.[53] A Foster Higgins survey found that by 1995 managed care networks had come to cover 71 percent of workers who received health benefits through their jobs.[54] The 1996 Kassebaum-Kennedy health insurance legislation made many incremental regulatory changes in the health universe and kiddie care established universal access for a new beneficiary group: the nation's children.

It is true that the recent managed care developments differ from Clinton's managed competition proposal in important ways. National health reform sought both to group providers into managed care networks and to enhance the market power of disadvantaged consumers by aggregating them into purchasing pools. But the changes that are reorganizing the health care market today are largely hurting consumers with the least amount of market power. Rate regulation is being phased out in many states, and while competitive contracting with managed care networks helps large corporate customers, it makes it more difficult than ever for providers to extend charity to the uninsured and to train young doctors.[55] Yet, while these market innovations lack the scope of the Clinton health plan, they add up to fairly profound modifications of the health policy universe.

Political salience is also important to the health story in its impact on the legislative fortunes of reform. Although the initial stages of the health care reform legislative process seemed driven by ideas and bureaucratic experts, both parties struggled to increase the political salience of the issue and, subsequently, damaged reform's chances for enactment. Ira Magaziner and Hillary Rodham Clinton began the health care reform process in the same bureaucratic technical-adjustment mode that influenced many past important health changes. Rather than offer a simple working document for Congress to elaborate, they decided to articulate good policy answers to the host of problems embedded in the goal of reforming our nation's health system.

The administration appointed a task force of more than five hundred members broken down into thirty-four subgroups to develop aspects of the bill. Congressional staffers, agency officials, doctors, economists, administrators, and ethicists met for sixteen-hour days to discuss 1,100 separate policy questions that needed answers. The subgroups were asked to generate possible solutions to each question that could then be presented to the president to decide. [56] President Clinton's subsequent 1,400-page proposal for health care reform reflected this extensive deliberation.

It is rather ironic for our purposes that the administration was subsequently vilified for its bureaucratic approach. Staffers on the Hill felt that the large complicated bill offended almost everyone: "It was not in the interests of anyone to push—everyone's second-best choice was to do nothing." Legislators felt rebuffed by the administration in efforts to shape proposal development. One Democratic House staffer echoed the sentiment of many when he remarked, "The task force was a sham; they knew what they wanted going in. In July 1992, a high-level guy [from the administration] came and told me what they were going to do. There was really no consultation with Congress." Congressional aides also felt that there was an incentive in the administration's game to hold back commitment to the bill until the end of the process that increased. Fewer concessions may have been made to special interests had the administration sent a brief proposal to Congress and allowed legislators to make the deals and work out the thorny issues. [57]

The bureaucratic approach miscarried in part due to contradictions within the plan and within the concept of managed competition. The Clintons failed to provide an adequate financing scheme for its very large benefits package and lost credibility in the process. Some doubted that health care reform could be achieved without a tax hike and some worried that the cost control mechanisms were excessively weak in the president's plan. Many initial business supporters considered the minimum benefits package excessive and worried about losing control over their company plans and being transformed into "check writers."[58] The details of the administration's health alliances prompted widespread concern: because only firms with five thousand employees were permitted to opt out of the public plan, managers worried that few could elude the public pool. Because the public alliances were to span entire regions, companies feared losing their current considerable purchasing leverage over providers. A Foster Higgins model predicted that few companies would find it economical to continue to operate their own plans or would find appealing the option of forming a corporate alliance.[59] Many felt that Clinton's proposal was excessively complicated and despite claims to the contrary, created a new federal bureaucracy. As Rick Smith of the Association of Private Pension and Welfare Plans (APPWP) put it, "Bill Clinton gave mandates a bad name."[60]

The bureaucratic approach also floundered because the Clinton administration was torn between wanting to leave reform under the domain of experts and making reform into a major source of political credit. The credit seekers won out, and the politics was transformed as the two parties made the issue a test for party identification and control. Indeed, the outcome may have been different if they had chosen a different vehicle for this partisan conflict (substantiating Landy and Levin's and Shapiro's arguments about elections in chapters 1 and 18, respectively).

To some extent, Clinton's decision to increase the salience of health care reform reflected the realpolitik conflict of party politics and a conflation of a new president's political ambitions with policy needs. Clinton made health care reform a major point in his campaign and announced that renovating the nation's medical system would be a major initiative of his first term.

Yet the administration's decision to pursue a politics of salience also reflected a realistic appraisal of the interest group world. The administration was caught in a vice grip between rallying the mass public with a populist attack on insurers and providers and working behind the scenes with experts in both the public and private sectors. It opted for populism and decided that drug companies and insurers were perfect for the role of villain.[61] The need to rally mass support also prompted a shift in focus from cost containment to access, but corporate supporters responded best to the administration's plan when the problem was framed as curbing costs. Stan

Greenberg argued for framing the issue as one of access because people would doubt that the government could really curb costs:

> The dominant goal should be health care security: that people will have health insurance and that they will never lose it, never. . . . Health care security has much more power than the cost argument, and it is much more believable: people think we can deliver on security; they are not sure we can deliver on cost control. There is also an emotion in security (lacking in cost) that empowers our rationale for bold changes.[62]

Perhaps deserved, the language of heroes and villains elicited emotional, ideological responses that undercut the business policy experts' ability to portray the issue in technocratic terms and to sell the plan to their firms. Clinton's dealings with business purchasers was also complicated by Democratic legislators' demands in the fall of 1993 that the Clintons "shut down the process" of making deals with interests.[63] Suddenly, after promises to the contrary, the Clintons seemed uninterested in adapting to corporate concerns. The administration quietly reassured groups that their demands were consistent with the administration's own "end-game scenarios."[64] But this behind-the-scenes strategy did nothing to assuage the fears of the groups' mass memberships who could judge the Clinton plan only by its public manifestation. Thus, NAM president Jerry Jasinowski told Magaziner, "I have a problem with some of my members. They're afraid that you're rope-a-doping me." Others told the administration, "[Corporate opponents] say that you're going to roll us and that you won't be flexible. If you made some of the changes that you yourselves admit, even if you don't change employer mandates or benefits, it gives us something to work with."[65]

The Republicans also worked to increase the political salience of health care reform, especially after Republican pollster Bill McInturff told Gingrich that health care reform's defeat could lead to a Republican House.[66] Most Washington observers ultimately concluded that conservative Republicans were determined to block any bill with a Democratic label, even centrist efforts.[67] Supporting this theory was William Kristol's advice to the Republican right:

> The fate of health care reform is now out of the hands of Bill and Hillary Clinton. . . . Acting Presidents Mitchell and Gephardt will unveil a new Democratic health care bill . . . the actual

details of this not-quite-universal-coverage bill don't matter. *Sight unseen, Republicans should oppose it.* Those stray Republicans who delude themselves by believing that there is still a "mainstream" middle solution are merely pawns in a Democratic game. . . . Our enemy is no longer Clinton, it is Congress.[68]

The Republicans' interaction with the big business community is informative. GOP legislators pressured big business to reject reform, directing employers toward incremental alternatives, framing the health debate in larger terms, and capitalizing on the Republican party's historical relations with individual companies. The message to business was that health care reform was "a new entitlement" and "a whole package" and that firms shouldn't sell out for individual benefits. One aide remembered her congressman's admonishment: "'If you want our help in killing the Clinton plan, don't do separate deals on other things.' Again and again we were trying to lay out the big picture for them. 'Maybe you can accept the deal right now, but think about what can be done to you in 10 years.'"[69]

The Republicans also threatened to retaliate in other policy areas if companies joined the Democrats on health care reform, forcing them to choose between health and issues more directly tied to core production activities. Shortly before the Business Roundtable vote, Newt Gingrich told two dozen CEOs that "their interests were best promoted by being principled rather than going for short-term deals." Ameritech, a longtime supporter of health care reform, planned to sponsor a presentation by President Clinton. Republican congressmen on the House Energy and Commerce Committee told the company that if it supported the president, it would be punished in other regulatory areas under the committee's jurisdiction. Caterpillar and several telecommunications companies received similar threats. CEOs were told, "If you are going to come back and ask for help in future areas, you should know that it's not in your interests" to support mandates.[70]

Congressional Republicans take much of the credit for the dramatic policy reversal of the Chamber of Commerce. The Chamber vice president, Bill Archey, worked with the chamber's Health and Employee Benefits Committee to endorse an employer mandate, managed competition, and a standardized benefits package. This position greatly angered the House Republican Conservative

Opportunity Society, who demanded a meeting with the Chamber's president Richard Lesher and Archey and "read them the riot act." Jim Bunning (R-KY) gave a speech against big government, big labor, and big business (causing one participant to wonder whether Bunning knew that the organization included big Fortune companies). John Boehner (R-OH and chairman of the group) sent letters on congressional letterhead to Chamber of Commerce constituents saying that they should cancel their Chamber membership. Dick Armey asked for an opportunity to offer the Republican view to the board before the Chamber took any action. Meanwhile, the National Federation of Independent Business initiated a membership drive against the Chamber. Few members resigned, but the chamber reversed its position on reform.[71]

The Republicans worked closely with business groups opposing health care reform, an effort discussed in greater detail later. On the House side, Billy Pitts (an aide for Bob Michel) ran a Monday morning meeting of congressional aides on the key committees and business representatives from the Health Care Equity Action League and the major small business associations.[72] Pitts would identify the issue of the week, and the group would "brainstorm on strategies, line up key amendments to focus on, and make sure that everyone was pulling in one direction." Participants would identify "who was gettable and who wasn't" and discuss "what kinds of pressures to bring to bear in the districts." A big topic of conversation was "when to put the plug on reform so that it didn't look like the Republicans had pulled the plug."[73]

Political Salience and Interest Groups

The health care reform case certainly shows that political salience killed the measure's chances of sneaking through as bureaucratic reform and that politicians' decisions to make it into a party-defining issue contributed to this fate. But the case also raises the question of whether salience is a cause or an effect of interest group power. Just as salience can work to increase or decrease interest representation, interests work to augment or to suppress salience.

Opposing interests often increase the political salience of issues to remove these issues from the purview of experts and to recast them in stark ideological terms.[74] In these cases, it may be hard for policy entrepreneurs to pursue ideas-driven policymaking. Health care is a classic policy area marked by a high degree of vested interests. The patchwork pattern of public/private provision makes for a very intricate mix of interests growing out of current benefits and privileges on both the supply and demand sides. In such a situation, the freedom of movement available to policy experts is greatly constrained.

Thus, the story of the health care reform struggle is incomplete without reference to the way that reform's opponents struggled both to increase the salience of the issue and to change the terms of the debate. In this section, we explore two critical junctures in the reform saga in which opponents were able to set back greatly the policy's prospects: the campaign to prevent NAM from supporting reform and the struggle to stop the Energy and Commerce Committee from producing a bill.

Although many managers in large companies supported health care reform in the early stages, the major business organizations were unable to deliver an official position to this effect. As has been discussed earlier, the Chamber of Commerce came the closest, but active interference by the House Republicans made the group change course. An active campaign by reform's opponents within the major business associations also played a major role in suppressing support for health care reform. The umbrella organizations were unable to overcome the divisions within their ranks, reflecting the perennial tendency of such groups to sink to lowest common denominator politics.[75]

The experience within NAM exemplified how difficult it was for umbrella organizations with a minority representation of health care providers to exert leadership in health care reform. Nearly all NAM members (99 percent) offered benefits in 1988, and a NAM-commissioned Foster Higgins study found health care costs representing 37.2 percent of employers' profits.[76]

NAM investigated health care reform in a white paper entitled "Meeting the Health Care Crisis," cosponsored with the Washington Business Group on Health a symposium to consider legislative issues, and formed a health care task force to develop a NAM policy.[77] Some of the task force companies (GE, Allied Signal, and Motorola) were drawn to a managed care approach; others (Southern California Edison and Chrysler) favored regulation. Ultimately, the task force supported a play-or-pay plan much like that of the

National Leadership Coalition's. The NAM newsletter was to brag that "NAM policy initiatives will help maintain the association's continuing key role in the health debate, broadly representing the business community."[78]

The NAM board debated the task force recommendations from February until October of 1991. The association's tax task force, which viewed play-or-pay as a corporate tax, opposed the recommendations; providers and insurers also lobbied hard against health care reform.[79] Finally, in October the board voted down the task force proposal and instead endorsed a set of principles that were essentially a reiteration of long-standing policy. One task force member complained, "Last September NAM received the Lewin report claiming that $11.5 billion has been cost-shifted onto its members. NAM should have been outraged but has done nothing with that. Isn't there some responsibility of the leadership to rattle chains, rather than giving in to Aetna and the pharmaceuticals?"[80]

After its 1991 failure, the health care reformers within NAM commissioned another Foster Higgens survey of NAM members on health care issues. Insiders hoped that solid member support would move the board toward comprehensive health care reform.[81] The study showed 55 percent of the members favoring a play-or-pay approach (complete with employer mandates) as part of overall system reform.[82] An NAM survey in the late summer of 1993 found a clear majority of its members backing mandates and health alliances for firms with more than five hundred employees.[83]

The Clinton administration hoped to gain NAM support and met with the association a number of times throughout 1993. NAM tried to remain open to the variety of health proposals on the legislative table and gave the president kudos for putting the issue on the congressional agenda. According to Magaziner, NAM president Jerry Jasinowski was one of the first individuals to see the draft in the summer of 1993. An informal deal was struck: Jasinowski agreed to a resolution that he would take before the board; the administration would fix five issues troubling to large employers. In reference to a September 1993 press release praising the Clinton plan, Jasinowski wrote, "I avoided any mention of mandates in order to imply that they may be a cost that business has to pay to get comprehensive reform; and to signal that mandates are not likely to be a top priority concern to manufacturers."[84] The administration felt that with NAM and the Chamber of Commerce on board and the Business Roundtable divided between its insurer constituents and large employer purchasers of health care, it might be able to push through a reform package.

But renewed efforts to push NAM toward supporting a comprehensive health care reform were stymied by providers and fast-food magnates on the board. Opponents circulated a letter to members in advance of the February 1994 board meeting, framing the Clinton health plan in very different terms from the technical fix that its supporters advocated and emphasizing the political salience of the measure. Opponents also highlighted the Clinton administration's promise to assume some of the costs of early retiree coverage (a boon to the automobile and steel industries), a move that divided the supporters of comprehensive reform within the organization. NAM staff reported going into the board meeting having "good things to say about the Clinton bill" and watching the board do an 180-degree turn.[85]

Another critical juncture in the health care reform episode was the failure of the House Energy and Commerce Committee to report out a bill, and interest group opponents were largely responsible for this omission. The committee's chair, John Dingell, was highly motivated to enact reform; his father had been a sponsor of national health reform in 1943. But the committee was rich with representatives from rural and southern areas, helpful to the chair in his conservative positions on environmental regulation but obstructive when it came to his more liberal views about health care. The conservative Democrats were worried about getting "BTUed," as when Clinton moved away from the energy tax in the stimulus package that he had earlier urged conservative Democrats in the House to back. Jim Slattery (D-KS) was running for governor and wanted to maintain good relations with the small businessmen in his state.

Dingell made many concessions to the conservative Democrats: making alliances voluntary in order to allow insurers to stay in business, introducing community rating slowly, and exempting small businesses from mandates. He promised legislators that he would not publicly identify plan supporters before he had lined up all of the votes. The Democratic leadership worried about pressures on conservative members during Easter recess but ultimately felt that all but Slattery had made a firm commitment. Shortly before the break, Dingell's staff leaked a compromise plan to the press "in order to show the members that there was movement on some issues that were giving them heartburn. The expressed purpose of the leak was to let the legislators on the fence know that headway was being made."[86]

The leak backfired when the opposition mobilized against Clinton *and* the compromise plan. The Republicans and their small business allies targeted Slattery and other conservative Democrats to keep the committee from passing a bill. NFIB sent action alerts to all of its members in the ten districts with swing legislators and faxes to about 10 percent of its members. The organization contacted all eight thousand members in the state of Kansas and as part of the Coalition on Jobs and Health Care held a press conference the day before Slattery was to appear with President Clinton in Topeka.[87] NFIB also did action alerts in a series of moderate Republicans' districts as a kind of preventative measure. The association compiled the list from the Republicans who had voted for the family leave act. Meanwhile, Pizza Hut, headquartered in Topeka, wrote to all of the local Chambers of Commerce in Kansas. Denny Hastert worked closely with a group to resist the mandate that included the National Restaurant Association, JCPenney, and Pepsico, among others. The National Restaurant Association developed a formula for members to evaluate the economic impact of mandates on their enterprises. Hastert also arranged for the restaurateurs to fax their legislators en masse from a national meeting in Chicago.[88] The object of these activities was to convey that the Dingell compromise was unacceptable: "We wanted to create an atmosphere for the Slatterys of the world where they thought that they were doing a back-room deal on the Dingell plan that was quite new, and then they had small businessmen in their districts come up and say, 'Vote no on Dingell.'"[89]

Ultimately Slattery reversed his position on the mandate, even though he had been strongly inclined to support his former mentor, John Dingell. NFIB was thrilled with Slattery's about-face. In early March, he had told a group of NFIB representatives that he was going to endorse a mandate and that there was no way out of it. One participant said that the legislator was very defiant about backing mandates: "he was very bold; it was a brave performance."[90]

The impressive show of force of the bill's opponents, many of whom came from the small business community, is illustrated by the large concessions developed by legislators to try to buy off the small business opposition. The bill increasingly benefited small business interests; for example, legislators gradually expanded the size of firms to be excluded from a mandate. A Wyatt study showed that under a partial mandate (exempting firms with fewer than one hundred employees), large employers would cover 14.7 million more individuals than they would under a full mandate.[91] By the end of the legislative cycle, the bill that initially attracted big business because it could reduce cost shifting was shifting more costs than ever.

The intensive effort to change the public perception of the Clinton health plan largely succeeded. By May 1994 Clinton's public approval rating had dropped to 48 percent, with a 44 percent disapproval rating; this undoubtedly reflected dissatisfaction with his health plan.[92]

Conclusion

The case of national health reform bolsters two themes of this volume related to ideas and political salience in policymaking. Ideas were critical to placing health care reform on the public agenda and to bringing even employers to support comprehensive system overhaul. The power of ideas is heartening to those who desire governmental activism; even under conditions of divided government and the widely touted stalemate between branches and parties, innovation is possible.

Health care reform also reveals that political salience, especially as it enhances interest mobilization, can be an obstacle to policy legislation. Although conventional wisdom suggests that political will is necessary to create space and resources for policy initiatives, political entrepreneurs are often most successful when they offer policy based on strong ideas in areas with little public demand for action. A comparison of health care reform to other cases in this volume demonstrates an irony in the strategy of augmenting salience to increase political will: salience pushes action and at the same time delimits it.

At the same time, health care reform raises important questions about the power of ideas and the use of political salience as a policy strategy. The health legislative episode suggests that some categories of public policy are more amenable to idea-driven policymaking than others. New ideas are most likely to change the policy landscape when they are consistent with the distributional status quo and not threatening to entrenched interests.

New ideas and new rights find ready acceptance when they are consistent with the distributional status quo. Thus, Baumgartner and Jones note that the "buttressing" ideas of policy monopolies are usually connected to core political values, which limit the possible range of policy change.[93] Rights that purport to redistribute resources are more difficult to create. The right to universal access to health care, for example, had many redistributive consequences, not only between the haves and have-nots but between cost bearers and cost shifters.

Policy initiatives driven by ideas are also more likely to succeed in the absence of entrenched, opposing interests; otherwise, putting the issue on the public agenda may require an enormous amount of countermobilization. Thus, most of the agenda-setting and social movement literature is not relevant to ideas-driven policymaking, because it describes a politics of change that depends on the mobilization of political will. Ultimately it may be very difficult for new policy ideas to succeed in issue areas where entrenched interests block action in the absence of political will. Comprehensive change in interest-intensive areas such as health care may be impossible without full-scale interest mobilization and high political salience.

Notes

1. Marcus, Ruth and Ann Devroy, "Clinton Stamps 'Urgent Priority' on Health Plan," *Washington Post*, September 23, 1997, p. A1.

2. Robert Blendon, "The Public's View of the Future of Health Care," *Journal of the American Medical Association* 259, no. 24 (1988): 3587–3593.

3. Mary McGrory, "Capital Hillary," *Washington Post*, October 3, 1993, p. C1.

4. See, for example, Theda Skocpol, *Boomerang* (New York: Norton, 1996); Mark Peterson, "The Politics of Health Care Policy," in *Social Divide*, ed. Margaret Weir (Washington, D.C.: Brookings Institution and Russell Sage Foundation Press, 1999); Tom Hamburger, Ted Marmor, and Hon Meacham, "What the Death of Health Care Reform Teaches Us about the Press," *Washington Monthly* (November 1994): 35–41; Lawrence Jacobs and Robert Shapiro, "The Politicization of Public Opinion," in Weir, *Social Divide*.

5. *New Politics of Public Policy*, ed. Marc K. Landy and Martin A. Levin (Baltimore, Md.: Johns Hopkins University Press, 1995).

6. For discussions related to these themes, see chapters 1, 2, 3, 5, and 10 in this volume.

7. Jim Morone and A. Dunham, "Slouching towards National Health Insurance," *Yale Journal of Regulation* 2, no. 2 (1985): 263–291.

8. E. E. Schattschneider, *The Semi-Sovereign People* (New York: Holt, Rinehart, & Winston, 1960).

9. For relevant discussion, see chapters 1 and 18 in this volume.

10. Peterson, "The Politics of Health Care Policy."

11. Representatives Marty Russo, Senators Bob Kerrey (D-NE), Tom Daschle (D-SD), Howard Metzenbaum (D-OH), and Paul Simon (D-IL) all sponsored single-payer bills.

12. Steffie Woolhandler and David Himmelstein, "To Save a Penny Two Are Spent," Division of Social and Community Medicine, unpublished paper, Cambridge, Massachusetts, no date, 8.

13. Barry Brown, "How Canada's Health System Works," *Business & Health* (July 1989): 29.

14. The bill was proposed by Majority Leader George Mitchell (D-ME), Edward Kennedy (D-MA), John D. Rockefeller VI (D-WV), and Donald Riegle (D-MI). It imposes a payroll tax of 7 percent. Funds from this tax would be used to create a new public insurance plan called "AmeriCare," which would also absorb Medicaid. Edward Kennedy, "An Affordable Health-Care Plan for All," *Boston Globe*, June 6, 1991, p. 21.

15. Gail Wilensky, "The Real Price of Mandating Health Benefits," *Business & Health* 7, no. 3 (March 1989): 32.

16. See Sheila Zedlewski et al., *Exploring the Effects of Play or Pay Employer Mandates: Effects on Insurance Coverage and Costs* (Washington, D.C.: Urban Institute, 1992).

17. Edmund Haislmaier, "The Principal Culprit in Health Insurance Is the Current Tax Treatment of Benefits," *Roll Call*, May 4, 1992, no page.

18. Michael Kinsley, "Quack," *The New Republic* 206, no. 9 (March 2, 1992): 4.

19. Julie Rovner, "Bush's Plan Short on Details, Long on Ambition, Critics," *Congressional Quarterly* 50, no. 6 (February 8, 1992): 305–307.

20. Theda Skocpol and Jacob Hacker, *Journal of Health Politics, Policy and Law* 22 (April 1997).

21. Jeremy Rosner, "A Progressive Plan for Affordable, Universal Health Care," in *Mandate for Change*, ed. Will Marshall and Martin Schram (New York: Berkley, 1993), 111–115.

22. Edmund Faltermayer, "Let's Really Cure the Health System," *Fortune* 125, no. 6 (March 23, 1992): 58.

23. Paul Starr, "Healthy Compromise: Universal Coverage and Managed Competition under a Cap," *The American Prospect* 12 (Winter 1993): 44–52.

24. Cathie Jo Martin, *Stuck in Neutral* (Princeton, N.J.: Princeton University Press, 2000), chapter 3.

25. "Leaders Look at Health Care," *Business and Health* 9, no. 2 (February 1991): 8–9.

26. Foster Higgins/NAM, "Employer Cost-Shifting Expenditures" (November 1992).

27. Unpublished survey provided by the administration.

28. NAM survey described in interview by Ira Magaziner; "Washington Business Group on Health," paper provided by the administration, no date.

29. Interview with industry lobbyist, May 1991.

30. Marilyn Field and Harold Shapiro, "Summary," in *Employment and Health Benefits,* ed. Marilyn Field and Harold Shapiro (Washington, D.C.: National Academy Press, 1993).

31. Katherine Levit, Helen Lazenby, Suzanne Letsch, and Cathy Cowan, "National Health Care Spending, 1989," *Health Affairs* (Spring 1991): 117, 127–129.

32. Frank Doyle and Anthony Carnevale, "American Workers and Economic Change," Committee for Economic Development, 20–21.

33. Phone interview with Jim O'Connell, May 1996.

34. Martin, *Stuck in Neutral,* chapter 3.

35. Ibid. See also Richard Harris, "Politicized Management," in *Remaking American Politics,* ed. Richard Harris and Sid Milkis (Boulder, Colo.: Westview, 1989), 261–286; James Post, Edwin Murray Jr., Robert Dickie, and John Mahon, "Managing Public Affairs," *California Management Review* 26, no. 1 (Fall 1983): 135–150.

36. For a similar finding, see Edward Handler and John Mulkern, *Business in Politics* (Lexington, Mass.: Lexington, 1982), 8, 27.

37. Ann Shola Orloff and Eric Parker, "Business and Social Policy in Canada and the United States, 1920–1940," *Comparative Social Research* 12 (1990): 295–339.

38. James Morone, *The Democratic Wish* (New York: Basic Books, 1990).

39. Allen Barton, "Determinants of Economic Attitudes in the American Business Elite," *AJS* 91, no. 1 (1985): 54–87.

40. Interview with industry representative, March 1993.

41. J. Jaeger, *Private Sector Coalitions: A Fourth Party in Health Care* (Durham, N.C.: Duke University Press, 1985); Carol Cronin, "Business Wields Its Purchase Power," *Business and Health* 6, no. 1 (November 1988): 4–7.

42. Foster Higgins, "Health Care Benefits Survey: Managed Care Plans," distributed by Foster Higgins (1992), 5.

43. Cronin, "Business Wields Its Purchase Power"; Linda Bergthold, *Purchasing Power in Health* (New Brunswick, N.J.: Rutgers University Press, 1990).

44. Interview with industry representatives, September 1992.

45. Catherine Manegold, "Using TV to Create Skewed Window on Nation," *New York Times,* July 17, 1994, p. 16.

46. Dana Priest, "Health Ads' Big Dividends," *Washington Post,* July 19, 1994, p. A6.

47. Marilyn Werber Serafini, "Turning Up the Heat," *National Journal* 27, no. 32 (August 12, 1995).

48. William Clinton, "Address to a Joint Session of the Congress on Health Care Reform," *Public Papers of the Presidents* 29, Weekly Compilation Presidential Documents 1836 (September 22, 1993).

49. Tod Lindberg, "Beware Magazinerism," *The Weekly Standard* 1, no. 2 (September 25, 1995): 18.

50. Shapiro and Jacobs, "The Politicization of Public Opinion."

51. P. J. O'Rourke, "The Liberty Manifesto," *The American Spectator* (July 1993).

52. James Morone, "Elusive Community: Democracy, Deliberation, and the Reconstruction of Health Policy," in Landy and Levin, *New Politics of Public Policy.*

53. Steven Findlay, "Will Big HMOs Stamp Out Competition?" *Business and Health* 13, no. 10 (October 1995): 52.

54. Milt Freudenheim, "Survey Finds Health Costs Rose in '95," *New York Times,* January 30, 1995, p. D1.

55. Kenneth Thorpe, "The Health System in Transition," *Journal of Health Politics, Policy and Law* 22, no. 2 (April 1997): 340.

56. Dana Priest, "Putting Health Care under a Microscope," *Washington Post,* April 16, 1993, p. A1.

57. Interviews with congressional staffers.

58. Richard Smith, "Getting Business Support for Health Care Reform," *Washington Post,* June 13, 1994, p. A18.

59. Jeannie Mandelker and Steven Findlay, "Truth in Numbers," *Business and Health* 12, no. 1 (January 1994): 25.

60. Interview with Rick Smith.

61. Bob Woodward, *The Agenda* (New York: Simon & Schuster, 1994), 110, 147.

62. Memo to Ira Magaziner from Stan Greenberg, "The Health Care Joint Session Speech," obtained from White House sources, 2.

63. Interviews with Ira Magaziner, July and September 1993.

64. The least optimistic end-game scenario showed phased-in universal coverage, possibly voluntary alliances of one hundred or fewer, less stringent triggered premium caps, a smaller benefits package, lower Medicare and Medicaid cuts, and a cut in the 1 percent corporate assessment. "Passing Health Care Reform: Policy and Congressional Summary" (December 17, 1993, but first draft had been developed in August 1993), 10–14; obtained from the White House.

65. Interview with Magaziner, September 1993.

66. Robin Toner, "Pollsters See a Silent Storm That Swept Away Democrats," *New York Times,* November 16, 1994, p. A14.

67. See, for example, Julie Kosterlitz, "Brinksmanship," *National Journal,* July 9, 1994, p. 1648.

68. Memo to Republican leaders from William Kristol, "Health Care: Why Congress Is Now More Dangerous Than Clinton" (Washington, D.C.: Project for the Republican Future), July 26, 1994.

69. Interview with congressional staffer in leadership role.

70. Interview with congressional staffer in leadership position.

71. Interview with Chamber of Commerce staff.

72. The group included the National Federation of Independent Business, the National Restaurant Association, the National Retail Association, and the Health Insurance Association of America, among others.

73. Interview with participating lobbyist.

74. Schattschneider, *The Semi-Sovereign People*.

75. Martin, *Stuck in Neutral*.

76. Donna DiBlase, "Group Health Bills Equal a Third of Profits," *Business Insurance* 23, no. 22 (May 29, 1989): 37–38.

77. Jerry Geisel, "NAM Proposes Plan to Contain Health Costs," *Business Insurance* 23, no. 22 (May 29, 1989): 39.

78. "NAM Board Considers Health Care Reform Policy," *Employee Benefits Newsline* (Washington, D.C.: NAM, October 1990).

79. Interview with industry representative, June 1992.

80. Ibid.

81. Ibid.

82. Foster Higgins/NAM, "Employer Cost-Shifting Expenditures," November 1992.

83. Unpublished survey provided by the administration.

84. Memo to Magaziner from Jerry Jasinowski, "Administration Health Care Plan," September 15, 1993.

85. Interview with NAM staffers.

86. Interview with staffer, November 15, 1994.

87. The coalition included NFIB, National Retail Federation, National Restaurant Association, Pepsico, General Mills, and JCPenney.

88. Interview with staffer, November 12, 1994.

89. Interview with industry representative.

90. Interview with industry representative.

91. The Wyatt Company prepared for APPWP, "Unintended Consequences of Excluding Small Firms from an Employer Mandate" (Washington, D.C.: APPWP, May 1994).

92. James Barnes, "He's Sliding, but Not toward Home," *National Journal*, May 14, 1994, p. 1152.

93. Policy monopolies with stable institutional structures originate in powerful ideas; these structures are destroyed by interest group access to the policy agenda. See Frank Baumgartner and Bryan Jones, *Agendas and Instability in American Politics* (Chicago: University of Chicago Press, 1993), 7.

12

The New Politics
of the Census

Peter Skerry, *Claremont McKenna College* and
The Brookings Institution

In 1998, Los Angeles led several large cities in opposition to House
Speaker Newt Gingrich's suit to prohibit the Census Bureau from
statistically adjusting the 2000 census. Arguing that the 1990 census
undercount had cost it $12 million annually from programs such as
Community Development Block Grants, Los Angeles anticipated
that the 2000 undercount would result in $180 million in lost state
and federal funds between 2000 and 2010.[1]

A decade earlier, similar proadjustment litigation had been led by
New York City, joined by New York State.[2] That effort failed, but a set
of adjusted numbers was published in June 1991 by the Census
Bureau. Never used for any official purposes, those figures contained
many surprises. For example, many northeastern and midwestern jurisdictions with high undercounts wound up only marginally better
or even worse off with those adjusted numbers. Not coincidentally,
by 1998 New York had relinquished its leadership of the push for
census adjustment.

Herein lies the untold tale of a controversy that pits one of the
U.S. government's oldest, most basic, and until recently most respected functions against the political ethos and institutions of late
twentieth-century America. In January 1999, the Supreme Court
ruled that adjusted 2000 census numbers could not be used to apportion Congress. But the Court left open the question whether adjusted numbers could be used for redistricting.[3]

In March 2001, a committee of Census Bureau experts determined that while the adjustment methodology was fundamentally
sound, it could not produce data reliably more accurate than unad-

justed census numbers within the time constraints posed by redistricting. Secretary of Commerce Donald Evans then seized on this finding to rule, as he had been expected to do anyway, that only unadjusted 2000 census data would be released for redistricting purposes. Almost immediately there were calls for the available adjusted data to be released—at least for inspection and research purposes, as had been done after the 1990 census. There were also demands that adjusted census data be released for such specific purposes as the allocation of federal formula grants. But as this volume goes to press, no adjusted data whatsoever have been released.

Thus, the controversy is hardly resolved and will continue to roil our politics. But even if settled tomorrow, this dispute is worth examining for what it reveals about contemporary American politics and public policy, especially with regard to racial minorities. Particularly worthy of attention are two claims made by adjustment proponents: first, that census adjustment is a matter of scientific expertise; and second, that racial minorities (who have undeniably been undercounted) have a right to be counted.

This controversy abounds with unanswered, often unacknowledged questions. Are the interests at stake as clear cut and substantial as commonly believed? Are rights and science neutral sources of authority transcending the vicissitudes of politics, as claimed by the advocates of census adjustment? And are the opponents of adjustment correct in seeing this controversy as further evidence of the misguided nature of affirmative action and other race-conscious policies? More important, are both sides so enmeshed in the administrative logic of the contemporary welfare state that they have neglected to consider whether minority benefits or political power depend on sheer numbers? Or might adjustment even further disadvantage minorities by shifting decisions that are inescapably political into an arcane administrative realm dominated by experts? Finally, have our political elites become so acclimated to today's demobilized electorate that they prefer arguing over census adjustment to grappling with the genuine social and political problems of disadvantaged minorities?

The Undercount Is Real

There is no gainsaying the undercount. In 1990, the net undercount for Los Angeles was 3.8 percent; for the nation as a whole, 1.6 percent.[4] Moreover, the net national undercount in 1990 was higher than in 1980, when it was about 1.2 percent. The 1990 census was the first since 1940 for which this undercount rate did not improve.[5]

Of course, the controversy is not about the overall undercount but about that of minorities relative to nonminorities. Thus, in 1990 the net undercount rate for non-Hispanic whites was 0.7 percent, compared to 2.3 percent for Asians/Pacific Islanders, 4.4 percent for blacks, 5.0 for Hispanics, and a whopping 12.2 percent for American Indians/Alaska Natives on reservations.[6] And this "differential racial undercount" has been getting worse. For example, while the black undercount rate has improved since 1940, the nonblack undercount rate has improved more, resulting in a black-nonblack differential that has inched upward from 3.4 percent in 1940 to a high of 4.4 in 1990.[7]

To be sure, the 2000 census appears to have reversed this trend. In 2000, the net national undercount was reduced to a low of 1.2 percent. As for the minority undercounts, they were dramatically reduced: down to 1.0 percent for Asians, 2.2 percent for African Americans, 2.9 percent for Hispanics, and 4.7 percent for American Indians/Alaska Natives on reservations. Yet the net undercount for whites remained virtually unchanged from 1990, at 0.7 percent.[8] So the differential racial undercount persists, and demands for statistical adjustment of the census will continue—particularly in light of the political dynamics analyzed here.

How Statistical Adjustment of the Census Would Work

In response to this problem, the Census Bureau in 1990 and again in 2000 followed up the headcount on April 1 with a postcensus survey. This survey is a huge random sample of several hundred thousand individuals conducted several weeks after the actual census. By means of complicated logistical and statistical techniques, the survey results are compared with those of the census to derive estimates of those missed on Census Day. The results are then incorporated into a final set of "adjusted" census totals.[9]

An important but almost universally overlooked point is that census adjustment involves more than just sampling. The controversy has typically been characterized as between enlightened proponents and benighted opponents of "scientific sampling." To be sure, there is a science of statistical sampling, and it obviously figures in the adjustment process. Yet the process also relies on dual-system estimation, a

methodology that involves elaborate, error-prone matching procedures and statistical models that have nothing to do with what was is
commonly understood as sampling. Those procedures do not partake
of the reliability and objectivity suggested by the term *scientific sampling*. Political scientist Thomas Brunell puts it well: "The problem
with the census adjustment process is not conducting a survey of
780,000 people; the Bureau is well equipped to conduct large-scale
surveys. Rather, the problem is matching these 780,000 records with
the correct records from the first phase of the census."[10] Undoubtedly,
this is why the principal opponents of adjusting the 1990 census
within the Census Bureau were not the statisticians but those responsible for the unprecedented logistical effort required.[11]

What Are the Interests at Stake?

Real though the differential racial undercount may be, its impact on
specific jurisdictions is difficult to pin down. Indeed, the interests at
stake are more volatile and contingent, and therefore harder to predict, than generally acknowledged.

Consider New York City again. Adjusting the 1990 data would
have increased its population by 3.0 percent—a gain relative to the
national population, which adjustment would have increased 2.1 percent. Yet a more relevant comparison is with other cities, especially in
the South and West. New York would have benefited less than
Houston, whose population would have increased 5.0 percent with
adjustment. Other cities would have gained absolute numbers but
would have clearly lost relative population shares: Philadelphia's
increase would have been 1.3 percent; Boston's only 0.9 percent—
both well below the national gain of 2.1 percent.[12] Boston's fate
under adjustment would have been particularly ironic, since its
mayor, Ray Flynn, chair of the National Conference of Mayors, was
a highly visible proponent of adjustment.

Adjustment would have had a similar impact on the states. For example, New York's 1990 population would have increased 1.7 percent;
New Jersey's, 1.4 percent—again, absolute gains below the 2.1 percent
national figure, which would have meant relative losses. Indeed, a host
of northeastern and midwestern states such as Massachusetts, Illinois,
Michigan, Pennsylvania, Ohio, and Wisconsin would have been worse
off relative to southern and western states such as California, Texas,

Florida, New Mexico, and Arizona.[13] Once again, these were not the anticipated results of adjusting the 1990 census.

Elusive Fiscal Gains

Similarly counterintuitive are the fiscal stakes. Comments *Wall Street Journal* reporter David Shribman, "When it comes to the census and money, nothing is as simple as it seems."[14] The $180 million that Los Angeles projected losing over the decade 2000–2010 if the census were not adjusted works out to less than 1 percent of the city's annual budget.[15] Moreover, such estimates are invariably inflated by local officials who, because of booster interests that focus on population growth as evidence of economic vitality, find in the census undercount a rare opportunity to respond to the concerns of both local business elites and minorities.

To be sure, census counts are used to allocate substantial federal funds. In fiscal year 1998, federal grant programs relying on census data totaled $185 billion. But analyzing fifteen such programs, which together account for about four-fifths of this dollar total, the General Accounting Office (GAO) concluded that using adjusted 1990 population counts would have reallocated among the states only $449 million, or 0.33 percent.[16]

How can this be? First, as already noted, what matters is not a jurisdiction's absolute population gain but its gain relative to others. Second, population is only one factor in most federal grant formulas, and population increases do not always lead to commensurate funding increases. Some programs, notably Community Development Block Grants, interpret population growth as an indicator of economic health and respond by reducing funding. Finally, total funding for federal grant programs is typically fixed: adjustment means the fiscal pie simply gets cut into more and smaller pieces.[17]

The Apportionment Gamble

The political stakes of the undercount and adjustment may appear more clear cut, as states and other jurisdictions stand to either gain or lose legislative seats. Yet these political outcomes are even less predictable than the fiscal.

Consider the apportionment of Congress, which is after all the constitutional rationale for the decennial census. Since 1940, Congress has relied on the "method of equal proportions" to apportion its total seats among the states. This formula first awards one seat to each state and then assigns the remaining 385 seats sequentially on the basis of descending "priority values." These values are calculated by dividing each state's population by the square root of $N(N-1)$, where N equals the Nth seat (whether the second, fifth, or fiftieth) in a given state's congressional delegation. Thus, the higher a state's population, the higher its priority values.[18]

This relatively straightforward formula has several less than straightforward implications. For example, in 1990 California was assigned its third congressional seat before Texas received its second— because the priority value of the former was higher. Another more important wrinkle is that minor shifts in state population totals can result in the loss or gain of congressional seats. If Massachusetts had only had 12,607 additional residents in 1990 (and if the population of the other states remained constant), it would have held onto the congressional seat it had to forfeit.[19]

The states most affected by such shifts are of course the handful whose priority values hover around the 435th-seat cutoff. But it is tricky to know in advance which states these will be. This is due partly to the notorious unreliability of population projections and partly to the sensitivity of the formula to small changes in the counts. Even without adjustment, the period leading up to any census is marked by uncertainty as to which states will gain or lose seats.

With adjustment, the uncertainty would be exacerbated—because adjusted numbers are themselves only estimates whose imprecision is large enough to affect priority values. Indeed, when the Census Bureau published adjusted counts in 1991, it had several different sets of adjustment estimates to choose from, each based on equally valid assumptions and each potentially leading to a different set of apportionment outcomes.[20]

Having decided which set of adjustments was "official," the Bush administration then decided against using any. In the ensuing controversy, it was widely overlooked that this decision was arguably against the partisan interests of Republicans. One of the few to notice was *Wall Street Journal* reporter Timothy Noah: "Adjusting the 1990 census would appear to favor Democrats over Republicans. . . . But adjusting the 1990 census would likely result in one more congressional seat for Arizona, which is predominantly Republican, and one less for Wisconsin, which is predominantly Democratic."[21] But this judgment hinges on yet another uncertainty: redistricting.

Redistricting Is the Wild Card

Apportionment's reliance on an established formula has obviated many political conflicts and allowed the process to be driven by demographic change. Redistricting, by contrast, is driven less by demography than by myriad political variables: the size of districts, the location of jurisdictional boundaries, the residences of incumbents, and the party affiliations and power of relevant individuals and groups. Redistricting is thus suffused with politics and, given the interaction of these variables, extremely unpredictable. Despite the impression given by the adjustment debate, there is no direct correlation between numbers of individuals counted and seats in Congress or other legislative bodies—and no grounds for assuming either that the undercount disadvantages Democrats and advantages Republicans or that adjustment would do the opposite.

David Butler and Bruce Cain have argued that the partisan stakes in congressional redistricting are exaggerated: "Virtually all the political science evidence to date indicates that the electoral system has little or no systematic partisan bias and that the net gains nationally from redistricting for one party over the other are very small."[22] Granted, the stakes can be high in particular states and localities, as in the contentious California redistrictings of 1980 and 1990. Yet in an era of weakening party loyalties, even the most partisan gerrymandering has become what Butler and Cain call "an inexact science."[23]

It is similarly assumed that Democrats would benefit from adjustment because greater minority populations translate into more minority (i.e., Democratic) districts and elected officials. Yet this overlooks the reluctance of many Democratic leaders to increase the influence of minority Democrats whose demands might alienate nonminority voters. As for Democratic incumbents, their interests may be threatened by adjustment. Recall how, after the 1990 census, Republicans embraced the Voting Rights Act as a way to create *both* majority-minority districts *and* homogeneous white, Republican-leaning districts—both of which undermine white Democratic incumbents.[24] Redistricting is clearly a complex political process whose outcomes are not neatly correlated with population totals.

This analysis hardly reassured Republicans preoccupied during the latter half of the 1990s with holding on to their slim majority in the U.S. House. But their understandable unwillingness to gamble on adjustment hardly justifies the utter certainty with which virtually all commentators continue to assert that adjustment would help Democrats and hurt Republicans.

Minority Concern—and Distrust

As for minorities, they have clear stakes in an accurate census, but their interests in adjustment are not unambiguous. Just as we have seen with cities and states, adjustment could conceivably improve the absolute numbers of minorities, but in terms of population shares leave them worse off relative to nonminorities. In any event, the many litigation battles over adjustment have been waged less by minorities themselves than by nonminority surrogates (cities and states in particular) fighting on their behalf—an indication that minorities are not as enthusiastic about adjustment as generally believed.

Granted, minorities are highly attuned to the undercount, which for African Americans in particular is a hurtful reminder of the Constitution's original stricture that the census count each slave as three-fifths of a person. But minority concern about the undercount has not always translated into minority support for adjustment.

Back in 1968, for example, when black leaders met with census officials to discuss the undercount, they saw no advantage in a complete census. Indeed, as one of the leaders told Dr. Herman Miller, chief of the Census Bureau's Population Division, "If the count of young Negro males on a given city block increased suddenly, the Welfare Department would soon send investigators around to see if they were violating the welfare laws and the draft board would send investigators to try to find draft dodgers."[25] In 1979, some black leaders argued that political power comes from organization not numbers. In the words of Leon Finney, former head of Chicago's Woodlawn Organization:

> I would not delude anybody . . . by saying that because we have an accurate count, Black people and brown people and poor

people are going to get to share those resources that are allocated for them . . . we have to continue to think about organizing ourselves, developing the political muscle . . . sufficient to make sure that when those resources are allocated . . . they just don't go to those same old guys to run the same old games on us.[26]

During the 1980s, misgivings about adjustment surfaced in the Census Bureau's minority advisory committees. As RAND demographer Ira Lowry reports, "Curiously, the committees did not support the Bureau in its plan to compensate for underenumeration of minorities by adjusting the census count."[27] One member of the Committee on the Black Population expressed concern that any preoccupation with adjustment would undercut the Bureau's efforts to do the best possible job on the actual enumeration.[28]

By the early 1990s, of course, black and other minority leaders settled on adjustment as the remedy for the undercount problem they had come to regard as serious. Still, it is worth emphasizing that black leaders were not adjustment's first or most enthusiastic advocates. And throughout the 1990s, minority concerns about the complicated statistical methodologies being proposed, as well as outright distrust of the Census Bureau's motives, continued to surface. After all, minority leaders seemed to be saying, if the government failed to count correctly the first time, why should it be trusted to correct its mistakes?

It's Not Affirmative Action, Stupid!

Opponents of adjustment, many of whom believe that the census should not be collecting racial and ethnic data in the first place, often argue as though individuals who identify as members of protected minority groups on census questionnaires benefit directly or materially from such responses.[29] Yet this is simply not the case. If it were, there would be a strong incentive for minority individuals to cooperate with the census, and minority undercounts would be much lower.

To be sure, *someone* benefits when more individuals claim minority status on the census. Judges and administrators rely on census data to determine affirmative action goals and quotas. Minority leaders understand this and are therefore concerned about the census undercount. Higher census counts do translate, albeit indirectly, into more benefits to individuals *as members of designated minority groups*. But *as individuals* minority group members are free riders: the benefits they derive from affirmative action programs do not depend on how they identify on the census.[30]

Moreover, there is considerable evidence that many minority individuals believe that cooperating with the census works to their disadvantage. A consistent finding in dozens of ethnographic studies sponsored by the Census Bureau is that minority individuals do not evade the census out of some generalized sense of alienation from government but out of quite rational concerns to protect concrete interests. For example, a black mother living in public housing does not complete her census form for fear that the housing authorities will thereby determine that more than the permissible number of individuals live in her apartment. Alternatively, a Salvadoran refuses to open his door to a census enumerator because his apartment is being used as a piecework sweatshop.[31] In other words, many minority individuals perceive their interests in accurate census counts quite differently from their leaders.

It is precisely to overcome these divergent perspectives that minority leaders resort to high-visibility media campaigns urging their rank and file to cooperate with the census. Typically appealing to group identity rather than civic duty, such campaigns are seen by nonminorities as evidence that the United States is balkanizing into exclusive racial blocs. Yet the irony is that if those blocs were all that cohesive, these media campaigns would not be necessary.

Scientific Expertise to the Rescue?

To avoid this confusing and shifting array of interests, adjustment advocates seek ground that is not only firmer but higher. One such foothold is science. Advocates as well as professionals who do not regard themselves as advocates argue that the conduct of the census generally, and adjustment specifically, is a nonpolitical matter properly left to the experts.

Thus, the plaintiffs in the suit to force an adjustment of the 1990 census argued that "the decision whether to correct was a technical one" best left to the Census Bureau director, not the political appointees at the Department of Commerce.[32] Similarly, the American

Statistical Association advocated adjustment on the grounds that "sampling is an integral part of the scientific discipline of statistics."[33] At one session convened by the Census Bureau, a statistician from a prominent midwestern university asked, "There is agreement in the professional community [on adjustment]—so what's the problem?"[34] And finally, the *New York Times* editorialized, "The politics that drives this debate now threatens to undermine what should be a politically neutral government task."[35]

Appealing to science as a source of authority transcending politics harkens back, of course, to the Progressive era.[36] Yet precious little science is involved in the census, especially when it comes to the racial and ethnic data at the heart of the adjustment controversy. Indeed, as the Census Bureau and the Office of Management and Budget emphasize about their own racial and ethnic categories, "These classifications should not be interpreted as being scientific or anthropological in nature."[37]

Moreover, the census itself is not a scientific undertaking. As one high-level demographer at the Census Bureau put it, "We don't do much science around here. Really it's just glorified accounting." Yet neither is the census simply a nose count, which could be achieved by adding up administrative data from birth records, death certificates, and the like.[38] Instead, the census is concerned to situate individuals in three dimensions: social, geographical, and temporal. None of these three dimensions has any natural units. All are calibrated according to certain conventions. And these conventions are derived and agreed on through politics.

In other words, the census is about drawing boundaries. Some of these boundaries are drawn around the nation. For example, it must be decided whether the census includes American citizens living overseas and illegal aliens. Other boundaries are internal— around metropolitan statistical areas, for instance. Still others get drawn between social groups: since the beginning of the Republic, the census has distinguished among whites, black slaves, and American Indians.

This boundary drawing is the quintessence of the census. Indeed, it is the quintessence of politics, certainly as conceived of by Aristotle: the proper ordering of the diverse parts that make up the political community.[39] The Framers understood the inherently political nature of the census, which is not to say that they abandoned it to sheer power politics. Rather, as was their wont, they embedded the census in a structure that would balance one set of political interests against another. Specifically, they made the census the basis for apportioning among the states both representatives *and* direct taxes, the former purpose causing states to maximize their population totals and the latter to minimize them.[40]

Far from intruding on the census from outside, politics inheres in it. To be sure, there are ways in which politics can improperly intrude—for example, the gross manipulation of numbers, which has occurred on many occasions. And there certainly are degrees of "politicization" of the census. Especially since the one-person/one-vote decisions of the 1960s, the census has been subjected to extraordinary scrutiny, particularly the race and ethnicity questions. As two Census Bureau professionals note, "Political pressures, primarily from the Asian and Pacific Islander community, and Congress influenced the Census Bureau's final decision on the 1990 Census race question."[41] Former Census Bureau director Barbara Bryant similarly maintains that political appointees at the Commerce Department have engaged in a "takeover" of this once largely autonomous agency.[42]

Yet to highlight such developments is not to argue that the census has suddenly been overrun by politics. For when those boundaries get drawn, there is simply no avoiding politics. There are correct and incorrect, prudent and imprudent ways to conduct surveys and tabulate data, to be sure. But in terms of providing noncontroversial, apolitical answers to the vexing issues facing the census, science has no special guidance to offer.

A Right to Be Counted?

When adjustment advocates seek higher ground to transcend politics, their other foothold is the "right to be counted." According to former congressman Charles Schumer (D-NY), "The Constitution, of course, guarantees the right of every person residing in the United States to be counted."[43] Even as sober an analyst as Senator Daniel Patrick Moynihan cast the undercount in terms of rights when, back in 1967 as director of the Harvard-MIT Joint Center for Urban Studies, he wrote, "Inasmuch as Negroes and other 'minorities' are concentrated in specific urban locations, to undercount significantly the population in those areas is to deny residents their rights under Article I, Section 3 of the Constitution."[44] Today even opponents of adjustment assert this same right, albeit on behalf of those who are counted in the actual enumeration and whose numbers would be reduced by adjustment.

The problem with the right to be counted is revealed by a brief thought experiment. Virtually all parties to the adjustment controversy concede that if the undercount rates for racial minorities were equivalent to those for nonminorities, then there would be no controversy.[45] But if being counted is a right, how can this be so? This is like arguing that it would be permissible to deny the right of free speech as long as it were done evenly across all sectors of society.

It might perhaps be argued that the right to be counted inheres not in individuals but in groups and that such a right would be satisfied if all groups were equally undercounted. But the right to be counted has been advanced as an individual not a group right. If the differential racial undercount were eliminated, large numbers of individuals would still go uncounted, and their putative rights would be violated. That most of us would tolerate such an outcome suggests that we are not dealing here with anything as fundamental as rights.

Any notion of a right to be counted is further undermined by the fact that cooperation with the census has been construed historically as an obligation required by law.[46] The Framers envisioned no such right. Indeed, their conception of the census drew on classical notions of virtue and civic duty. We have lost sight of this aspect of the census, in part because the direct taxes that the Framers originally intended to be levied on the basis of census totals have fallen into disuse. More generally, our political culture has come to be pervaded by "rights talk."[47]

Rights-based arguments for adjustment have also gained currency due to the racial complexion of the undercount. As Peter Zimroth, one of the attorneys representing New York City in the 1990 litigation, has said, "I always viewed this case primarily as a civil rights case, and I think in fact it is one of the most important civil rights cases in the country today."[48] Yet how does this perspective square with the Census Bureau's ethnographic studies, cited earlier, which just as clearly indicate that many minority individuals have self-interested reasons not to cooperate with the census?

The right to be counted is further sustained—at least rhetorically— by the links between the census, redistricting, and the right to vote.

Indeed, proponents of adjustment argue that because the un-counted are not included in the one-person/one-vote calculations on which legislative district lines are based, such individuals are de-nied representation and even disenfranchised.

But once again, such claims do not withstand scrutiny. If the right to be counted is equivalent to the right to vote, then adjusting the census would be tantamount to rigging an election. For if each individual enjoys the right to be counted, and if this right is cognate with the right to vote, then in jurisdictions where adjustment re-sulted in decreased counts, any previously enumerated individuals thereby eliminated would also be deprived of the franchise.

To be sure, uncounted individuals are not included in the one-person/one-vote calculations used to draw district lines. But to equate the creation of electoral districts with actual representation is to ad-vance an extremely formalistic view of the political process. Can indi-viduals or groups be regarded as represented regardless of their efforts in the political arena—merely by being counted in the census, for ex-ample? I do not believe so. Conversely, can individuals or groups who are not counted in the census vote, engage in political action, and or-ganize others to vote? Most definitely. The argument that adjustment will "empower" minorities may seem persuasive in a society grown accustomed to opting for administrative solutions to political prob-lems. But to equate the undercount with disenfranchisement is to as-sume away any notion of a self-reliant, engaged citizenry.

Adjustment advocates further undercut their rights argument with their frequent assertion that adjustment and its associated sta-tistical methodologies would help reduce the burgeoning costs of the decennial census. But if disadvantaged minorities were truly being denied a right, then costs would surely not be a consideration.

Finally, adjustment advocates invoke the prerogatives of science and the language of rights in tandem. In the words of Mervyn Dymally, former chair of the House Subcommittee on Census and Population, "When we are talking about a guarantee of constitu-tional rights, we should settle for nothing less than the most accu-rate figures modern science will allow us to produce."[49]

When it comes to census adjustment, however, science and rights do not sit comfortably together. For the science in question—statistics—deals not in precision but in probabilities and degrees of uncertainty. As one Census Bureau statistician wore emblazoned on his T-shirt, "Being a statistician means never having to say I'm certain."[50]

But as Congressman Dymally properly suggests, much more rigor is demanded by the uncompromising language of rights. Even statisticians who favor adjustment acknowledge that the outcome would be estimates subject to sampling error that would be closer to the truth *on average*—but not in every case. Adjusted numbers might well be closer to the truth than unadjusted numbers in the majority of cases.[51] But to argue for adjustment on such grounds is to defend the rights of racial minorities by means of an incongruous utilitarian logic: that the interests of the greatest number outweigh those of the *numerical* minority negatively affected by adjustment.

Conclusion

It is unfortunate that the controversy over Lani Guinier's 1993 nomination for assistant attorney general for civil rights obscured her insightful critique of the Voting Rights Act (VRA). In various law review articles, Guinier argues that the VRA has reduced assessments of minority empowerment to mere nose counts of officeholders, in lieu of broader inquiries into minority political mobilization and community organization between elections.[52] Future Lani Guiniers may well write similar critiques of census adjustment as a suspiciously technocratic proposal that crowds out more fundamental examinations of minority empowerment.

Any such critique would undoubtedly draw on the emerging body of research concluding that since the 1960s American political institutions have been more open, more technically proficient—and more alienating and confusing to ordinary citizens. As Richard Harris and Sidney Milkis have noted with regard to regulatory politics, "The irony of the new social regulation is that it is at once more open than traditional forms of regulation, yet it is also more insulated from traditional political channels."[53] Hugh Heclo has similarly observed, "Everyday Americans find their lives entangled in a regime of activist government and activist antigovernment politics that they can little understand, much less sense they are controlling."[54] Those who advocate census adjustment in the name of reaching out to the most disaffected among us would do well to heed such conclusions about contemporary American politics.

Notes

1. Affidavit of Jessica F. Heinz, assistant city attorney for Los Angeles, April 2, 1998, included among Affidavits in Support of Motion to Intervene as Defendants of Intervenors City of Los Angeles et al., in the case of *United States House of Representatives v. United States Department of Commerce, et al.*, United States District Court for the District of Columbia (Case No. 1: 98CV00456-RCL), 9.

2. *City of New York v. U.S. Department of Commerce* (1990, Eastern District, New York).

3. *Department of Commerce v. U.S. House of Representatives*, 525 U.S. 316 (1999).

4. Revised postenumeration survey (PES) data. See Committee on Adjustment of Postcensal Estimates (CAPE), *Assessment of Accuracy of Adjusted versus Unadjusted 1990 Census Base for Intercensal Estimates* (Washington, D.C.: U.S. Census Bureau, August 7, 1992).

5. Howard Hogan and Gregg Robinson, "What the Census Bureau's Coverage Evaluation Programs Tell Us about Differential Undercount," in *1993 Research Conference on Undercounted Ethnic Populations*, ed. U.S. Bureau of the Census (Washington, D.C.: Government Printing Office, October 1993), 9. Note that these numbers are not precisely comparable to those documented in the previous endnote because they are derived through a different method, demographic analysis, which is better suited for providing longitudinal undercount data. This highlights a relevant aspect of the census issue: that several sets of data are available, which can confuse the experts, never mind laypeople.

6. CAPE, *Assessment of Accuracy of Adjusted versus Unadjusted 1990 Census Base for Intercensal Estimates*; Hogan and Robinson, "What the Census Bureau's Coverage Evaluation Programs Tell Us," 18.

7. Again, these numbers are based on demographic analysis; see Hogan and Robinson, "What the Census Bureau's Coverage Evaluation Programs Tell Us," 9.

8. These data are derived from a postenumeration survey after the 2000 census. In this regard, they are comparable to the similarly derived minority undercounts cited in the previous paragraph, though the racial and ethnic categories reported in these two surveys are not precisely the same. See *Report of the Executive Steering Committee for Accuracy and Coverage Evaluation Policy* (Washington, D.C.: U.S. Census Bureau, March 1, 2001), 4–5.

9. This general methodology is explained in David A. Freedman, "Adjusting the 1990 Census," *Science* 252 (May 31, 1991): 1235–1236.

10. Thomas L. Brunell, "Using Statistical Sampling to Estimate the U.S. Population: The Methodological and Political Debate over Census 2000," unpublished paper, Department of Political Science, State University of New York–Binghamton, May 17, 1999, 22.

11. Felicity Barringer, "Decision Today on Adjusting the Census," *New York Times*, July 15, 1991, p. A12.

12. The careful reader will have noted that the 2.1 percent national undercount figure indicated here is different from the 1.6 percent cited earlier. The figures here were those available when the decision to adjust was presented to

Secretary of Commerce Mosbacher in July 1991. These 1991 data (so-called postenumeration survey, or PES, data) were subsequently revised and published by the Census Bureau in 1992. Those revised numbers changed the interest calculations of many jurisdictions with regard to adjustment. For both the 1991 PES and 1992 revised PES numbers, see CAPE, *Assessment of Accuracy of Adjusted versus Unadjusted 1990 Census Base for Intercensal Estimates.*

13. Again, these are 1991 PES data; see CAPE, *Assessment of Accuracy of Adjusted versus Unadjusted 1990 Census Base for Intercensal Estimates.*

14. David Shribman, "Local Politicians Fear Harm Census Data Can Do to Funding, but Their Worry May Be Overdone," *Wall Street Journal,* January 2, 1991, p. A8.

15. In 1995, for example, total expenditures for the city of Los Angeles were $4.4 billion, according to Deirdre A. Gaquin and Mark S. Littman, eds., *1990 County and City Extra: Annual Metro, City, and County Data Book,* 8th ed. (Washington, D.C.: Bernan, 1999), 923. An increase of $18 million through an adjustment would represent only 0.4 percent of the city's annual expenditures, as of 1995.

16. General Accounting Office (GAO), *Formula Grants: Effects of Adjusted Population Counts on Federal Funding to States,* GAO/HEHS9969 (Washington, D.C.: Government Printing Office, February 1999), 4–5.

17. See Barry Edmonston and Charles Schultze, eds., *Modernizing the U.S. Census* (Washington, D.C.: National Academy Press, 1995), 40–43.

18. For an exposition and analysis of this formula and of apportionment more generally, see Michel L. Balinski and H. Peyton Young, *Fair Representation: Meeting the Ideal of One Man, One Vote* (New Haven, Conn.: Yale University Press, 1982).

19. Jeffrey S. Passel, "What Census Adjustment Would Mean," *Population Today* 19 (June 1991): 7.

20. "Recommendations on 1990 Census Adjustment to the Honorable Robert A. Mosbacher from Kenneth W. Wachter, Special Advisory Panel," June 18, 1991, 25–26.

21. Timothy Noah, "Mosbacher, While Admitting Undercount of Minorities, Won't Adjust 1990 Census," *Wall Street Journal,* July 16, 1991, p. A9.

22. David Butler and Bruce Cain, *Congressional Redistricting: Comparative and Theoretical Perspectives* (New York: Macmillan, 1992), 8.

23. Ibid., 9.

24. See Charles S. Bullock, "Winners and Losers in the Latest Round of Redistricting," *Emory Law Journal* 44 (Summer 1995): 943–977.

25. Hyman Alterman, *Counting People: The Census in History* (New York: Harcourt, Brace & World, 1969), 283.

26. Cited in Peter Skerry, "The Census Wars," *Public Interest* 106 (Winter 1992): 28.

27. Ira S. Lowry, "Counting Ethnic Minorities in the 1990 Census," unpublished paper, Pacific Palisades, California, September 1989, 22.

28. Ibid., 22–23. Others, including professionals at the Census Bureau, have also expressed such concerns.

29. See, for example, Dinesh D'Souza, "My Color 'Tis of Thee," *Weekly Standard*, December 16, 1994, pp. 47–48.

30. I develop this analysis in Peter Skerry, "The Affirmative Action Paradox," *Society* 35 (September–October 1998): 8–16.

31. For an overview of these ethnographic studies, see Manuel de la Puente, "Why Are People Missed or Erroneously Included by the Census? A Summary of Findings from Ethnographic Coverage Reports," in U.S. Bureau of the Census, *1993 Research Conference on Undercounted Ethnic Populations*, 29–66.

32. Memorandum of Law in Support of the Plaintiffs' Motion for a Preliminary Injunction; *City of New York, et al., Plaintiffs, against United States Department of Commerce, et al., Defendants*, November 3, 1988, 16.

33. American Statistical Association, *Report of the Census Blue Ribbon Panel*, "Executive Summary" (September 1996), www.amstat.org/outreach/execsummary.html.

34. Dr. Paul Voss, Department of Rural Sociology, University of Wisconsin–Madison, at the 2000 Census Advisory Committee meeting, Washington, D.C., May 16–17, 1996.

35. "Taking Leave of the Census," *New York Times*, January 17, 1998, p. A12.

36. See Kenneth Finegold, *Experts and Politicians: Reform Challenges to Machine Politics in New York, Cleveland, and Chicago* (Princeton, N.J.: Princeton University Press, 1995).

37. See Office of Management and Budget (OMB), "Directive No. 15: Race and Ethnic Standards for Federal Statistics and Administrative Reporting," *Federal Register* 43 (May 4, 1978): 19269.

38. This critical insight has been made by Nathan Keyfitz in "Statistics, Law, and Census Reporting," *Society* 18 (January/February 1981): 5.

39. Arlene W. Saxonhouse, *Fear of Diversity: The Birth of Political Science in Ancient Greek Thought* (Chicago: University of Chicago Press, 1992), 227.

40. Article I, Section 2, of the Constitution: "Representatives and direct Taxes shall be apportioned among the several States which may be included within this Union, according to their respective Numbers." And see "*Federalist* No. 54," in *The Federalist*, ed. Alexander Hamilton, James Madison, and John Jay (New York: Modern Library, 1937), 358–359.

41. Nampeo R. McKenney and Arthur R. Cresce, "Measurement of Ethnicity in the United States: Experiences of the U.S. Census Bureau," in *Challenges of Measuring an Ethnic World: Science, Politics and Reality*, ed. Statistics Canada and U.S. Bureau of the Census (Washington, D.C.: Government Printing Office, 1993), 180.

42. Barbara Everitt Bryant and William Dunn, *Moving Power and Money: The Politics of Census Taking* (Ithaca, N.Y.: New Strategist Publications, 1995), 158–159.

43. See *Proposed Guidelines for Statistical Adjustment of the 1990 Census*, Hearing before the Subcommittee on Census and Population of the House Committee on Post Office and Civil Service, 101st Congress, 2d session (Washington, D.C.: Government Printing Office, 1990), 8.

44. Daniel P. Moynihan, "Foreword," in *Social Statistics and the City*, ed. David M. Heer (Cambridge, Mass.: Joint Center for Urban Studies, 1968), v–vi.

45. See John E. Rolph, "The Census Adjustment Trial: Reflections of a Witness for the Plaintiffs," *Jurimetrics Journal* 34 (Fall 1993): 87: "If the rate of net undercount were about the same across the population, there would be little concern since the basic uses of the census—apportionment, redistricting, and fund allocation—largely depend on population *shares*."

46. 13 U.S.C. 221.

47. The phrase is from Mary Ann Glendon, *Rights Talk: The Impoverishment of Political Discourse* (New York: Free Press, 1991).

48. Peter Zimroth quoted in Richard Levine, "Big Gain Predicted in New York City If Census is Adjusted," *New York Times*, April 20, 1991, sect. 1, p. 25.

49. Decennial Census Improvement Act of 1987, *Congressional Record*, October 20, 1987, p. E4053.

50. Bryant and Dunn, *Moving Power and Money*, 155.

51. See John W. Tukey, testimony in *Oversight Hearing to Review the Progress of Coverage Evaluation Procedures*, Hearing before the Subcommittee on Census and Population of the House Committee on Post Office and Civil Service, 102d Congress, 1st session (Washington, D.C.: Government Printing Office, 1991), 46. Yet not every expert even grants this. See David A. Freedman, "Adjusting the Census of 1990," *Jurimetrics Journal* 34 (Fall 1993): 99–106.

52. These articles are brought together in Lani Guinier, *The Tyranny of the Majority: Fundamental Fairness in Representative Democracy* (New York: Free Press, 1995).

53. Richard A. Harris and Sidney M. Milkis, *The Politics of Regulatory Change: A Tale of Two Agencies*, 2d ed. (New York: Oxford University Press, 1996), 42.

54. Hugh Heclo, "The Sixties' False Dawn: Awakenings, Movements, and Postmodern Policy-making," *Journal of Policy History* 8, no. 1 (1996): 58.

PART V

Foreign Trade

13

The Postwar Liberal Trade Regime

Resilience under Pressure

David Vogel, *University of California, Berkeley*

The more than half a century since the end of World War II marks the longest sustained period of steady, if uneven, trade liberalization in the history of the United States. The Reciprocal Trade Agreements Act of 1934 (RTAA), along with the American ratification of the General Agreement on Tariffs and Trade (GATT) the following decade, fundamentally transformed both the direction of American trade policy and the way it was made. The RTAA allowed the executive to negotiate tariff reductions without obtaining congressional approval, while American membership in the GATT signified the U.S. willingness to play a leadership role in a global, liberal trade regime. These policy departures remain the cornerstone of American commitment to a relatively open global economy.

What is striking about American trade policy over the past several decades is not only the magnitude of the break with the high tariff policies that had reigned since the Civil War but the durability of this policy shift. Despite considerable public uneasiness with the consequences of free trade and periodic downturns in the performance of the economy, both the substance of American trade policy and the way it is made have proven remarkably stable. In 1930, the average American tariff rate was 50 percent, the highest in American history. By 1951, it had been reduced to 12.5 percent, the lowest rate since 1789, and it has since declined to approximately 5 percent. Congress has ratified each trade reduction agreement submitted to it by the executive branch, including most recently a Free Trade Agreement with

Canada in 1988, the North American Free Trade Agreement (NAFTA) in 1993, and the Uruguay Round GATT/WTO Agreement in 1994.

The latter two agreements are of historical importance. NAFTA, by expanding the FTE to Mexico, created a huge, tariff-free, $6.5 trillion regional market with more than 350 million consumers. Never before had the United States approved an agreement that reduced trade barriers between it and a country as poor and as different as Mexico. For its part, the Uruguay Round Agreement, reached after six years of often tortuous negotiations, represented the most comprehensive trade agreement in world history. It not only reduced remaining tariffs by an average of 40 percent but also phased out long-standing worldwide quotas on textile and apparel exports. It was also the first international trade agreement to cover trade-related intellectual property rights, an issue of considerable importance to many American companies.

At the same time, there are signs of a populist backlash against globalization. Since 1994, Congress has refused to reauthorize fast-track authority, thus slowing the pace of further trade liberalization.

A Historical Perspective

The significance of both the stability and liberalism of trade policy during the postwar period clearly emerges when it is placed in historical context. During the first 150 years of U.S. history, trade issues were among the most visible and divisive issues in American national politics. In the seventy-five years following the Civil War, a period when partisan rivalries were especially pronounced, the tariff became highly partisan.[1] The Democratic party supported lower tariffs, reflecting both the historical preferences of its southern electoral base and an effort to cultivate support in the farm states and the northeast by appealing the interests of the "common man." Republican party platforms, in turn, reflected the protectionist preferences of northern industry. Through the 1930s, tariff rates divided the Democratic and Republican parties in Congress more than almost any other issue,[2] and the two parties' presidential candidates frequently offered sharply contrasting views on trade policy.[3]

Due to close linkages between partisanship and trade policy, the broad contours of American trade policy during this period closely reflected the shifting political fortunes of the Democratic and

Republican parties. The protectionist Payne-Aldrich Act of 1909 was passed during the Taft administration, while the election of Woodrow Wilson in 1912 was followed by the lower-tariff Underwood Act of 1913. The Republican ascendancy of the next decade led to the Fordney-McCumber Act of 1922, followed by the even more protectionist Smoot-Hawley Tariff of 1930. Nonetheless, the post–Civil War trade regime was, on balance, highly protectionist. Few Democrats supported general tariff rates below 30 percent, and it was only when they exceeded 40 percent for particular commodities that Democrats challenged them.[4]

Postwar Trade Policy and Politics

Trade policy during the last half century has differed markedly. Most obviously, it has assumed a lower political profile, only intermittently occupying a prominent place on the national political agenda, despite the fact that Congress has either debated or enacted trade legislation in virtually every legislative session since World War II. The reduced salience of trade issues on the agenda of contemporary American politics in part reflects the substantial expansion of the size and scope of the national government since the Great Depression. Prior to the 1930s, the tariff was among the most important sources of federal revenue, and hence tariff policy was central to federal taxing and spending policies. As the income tax became a major source of government revenue in the 1930s and 1940s, trade policy lost its fiscal importance. Debates over the size and purpose of the federal budget are now made with little reference to the tariff, and vice versa.

The lower political salience of American trade policy is also linked to its decline as a partisan issue. Since the mid-1940s, the Republican party has largely shed its commitment to protectionism, while the Democratic party no longer consistently favors free trade. Both parties now contain both proponents and opponents of trade liberalization, though recently congressional Democrats have become more opposed to trade liberalization than congressional Republicans. But recent congressional voting on trade policy has more closely reflected the economic interests of firms and their employees in each district and state than the partisan affiliation of representatives and senators.[5] No Democratic or Republican presidential nominee during the last half century has sought to sharply distinguish his views on trade policy from those of his opponent. Nor, to date, has trade policy figured prominently in the presidential or congressional platforms of either party. In sharp contrast to the half century prior to World War II, voter preferences on trade policy have had no discernible effect on the outcome of congressional or presidential elections. Consequently, trade policy in the postwar period has *not* mirrored the shifting electoral fortunes of the Democratic and Republican parties.

Like foreign policy in general, it has more frequently reflected a bipartisan consensus. Thus, the Republican party's 1994 congressional "platform," while radical and innovative in many policy areas, did not even mention trade policy. Nor was trade policy an issue in either the 1996 or 2000 presidential elections. In this sense, trade policy resembles affirmative action at the national level, another area of public policy in which an elite consensus has been largely insulated from partisan rivalries and shifts in electoral outcomes.

Liberalization Threatened

Nonetheless, the story of American trade policy during the last four decades does read like the *Perils of Pauline:* America's commitment to trade liberalization invariably appears to be in mortal peril, yet somehow it survives, its virtue tarnished but still intact. At any given moment, protectionist forces appear to be threatening the liberal trade consensus. Yet at the end of each decade, the American economy has become more integrated into the global economy.

At the conclusion of the Kennedy Round in 1962, one commentator observed that "the lowering of tariffs has, in effect, been like draining a swamp. The lower water level has revealed all the snags and stumps of non-tariff barriers that still have to be cleared."[6] In 1985, the *New York Times* reported that "industry by industry, the battle to maintain open markets is being lost."[7] A year later, Pietro Nivola wrote that "upbeat descriptions [of the postwar liberalization of American international policy] appear increasingly inappropriate today, considering the extent to which orderly marketing agreements, voluntary export restraints, selective procurement, product standards, and buy America requirements, to name a few, have replaced the old tariffs."[8] He added, "The present atmosphere

in Congress is one of virtually unanimous alarm about the widening trade gap and of bipartisan movement toward protective coun-
termeasures."[9]

I. M. Destler's 1986 book on American trade policy begins, "In
the mid-1980s, American foreign trade policies came under unprecedented pressure from embattled domestic industries."[10]
Destler argued that "industries beset by import competition were
hurting as never before; exporters were demoralized." Accordingly,
"Congress found itself under enormous pressure to 'do something'
about trade."[11] Three years later, Jagdish Bhagwati suggested that
"United States trade policy . . . may have taken a turn for the
worse." He cited in particular "the weakened commitment of the
United States to multilateralism."[12]

In 1992, Laura Tyson's appointment as chair of the President's
Council of Economic Advisers was greeted with dismay by supporters of trade liberalization. In her book *Who's Bashing Whom?* Tyson
had described herself as a "cautious activist."[13] She urged that "the
nation's trade laws be used to deter or compensate for foreign practices that are not adequately regulated by existing multilateral
rules."[14] The *Financial Times* worried that "one consequence of her
views would be to give *carte blanche* to US politicians and lobbyists,
who are itching to have a go at perfidious foreigners, particularly the
Japanese. . . . [The most important result] could well be still more
trade friction as the US adopts a narrowly sectoral and bilateral
focus."[15] Two years later, William Lash III concluded that "the Clinton
tango in trade policy is actually moving the country away from free
trade and free markets." He wrote that "the administration has liberalized trade while simultaneously encumbering markets with new
agencies, development banks and market-distorting moves."[16]

Yet to date each of these fears have proven to be exaggerated.
Protectionist pressures, such as opposition to immigration, may have
been relatively persistent, but they have meet with remarkably little
political success. While the 1980s saw a groundswell of public opposition to "imports" of both people and goods, Congress responded by
enacting legislation that liberalized imports of the former in 1990 and
the latter in 1993 (NAFTA) and 1994 (GATT/WTO). As a result, flows
of both to the United States have steadily increased, though compared to a century ago, America is now relatively less open to the free
flow of people and more open to the free flow of goods.

The Politics of Economic Decline

What is especially remarkable is the political durability of trade liberalization in the face of the erosion of American economic hegemony in the 1960s, the severe economic difficulties experienced by the United States during the 1970s and early 1980s, including oil shocks and double digit inflation, and the substantial trade and budget deficits that characterized much of the 1980s.

American trade policy could not help being affected by the significant erosion in the market share of many domestic industries under the postwar multilateral trade regime. The United States emerged from World War II with a more dominant economic position than any nation in the history of modern capitalism. Like Britain in the previous century, its support for trade liberalization reflected its economic dominance.

During the 1960s, this dominance began to erode. The United States' share of merchandise exports among the fifteen largest industrial nations declined from 25.2 percent in 1960 to 20.5 percent in 1970 and 18.3 percent in 1979. America's share of the combined gross national product (GNP) of these countries stood at 57.1 percent in 1960, but it had declined to 50.2 percent by 1970 and to 38.1 percent by the end of the 1970s.[17] Not surprisingly, the AFL-CIO, which had previously supported liberal trade policies, responded to the rise in imports of manufactured goods such as textiles, footwear, automobiles, steel, and electrical consumer goods during the late 1960s by supporting import quotas.

Between 1980 and 1982, the American economy experienced its most severe economic downturn since the Great Depression. For the first time since the end of World War II, the number of manufacturing jobs declined for three consecutive years. Imports, which traditionally fall during recessions, actually increased: while U.S. manufactured exports declined by 17.5 percent, imports grew by 8.3 percent. Steel imports represented 25 percent of domestic consumption, leading to a nearly 50 percent decline in domestic employment in this historically important industrial sector.[18]

During the remainder of the 1980s, while the American economy grew relatively rapidly, America's trade deficit grew more rapidly still. Buttressed by an overvalued dollar, imports of foreign goods increased by 24 percent between 1983 and 1984 and, by the middle of the decade, totaled more than $300 billion per annum.

Meanwhile, exports either stagnated or declined. Consequently, the United States' current account balance, the broadest measure of the difference between U.S. imports and exports of goods, investments, and services, reached a deficit of $10 billion in 1984. (The last time the ratio of imports and exports had been as negative was in 1864, in the midst of the Civil War.[19]) America's annual current account deficit peaked in 1987 at $160 billion but remained at above $100 billion for six more years.

Throughout the 1980s one country, Japan, accounted for a persistently large share of America's trade imbalance. Its percentage of America's total trade imbalance averaged nearly 40 percent between 1983 and 1989. Even as America's overall trade deficit declined from its 1987 peak, the absolute size of its trade imbalance with Japan remained stable. Many Americans associated this trade deficit with the loss of American high-wage jobs and feared that Japan was replacing the United States as the world's dominant economic power. Worse still, they claimed that Japan was "cheating" as it gained market share in the United States in one high-wage manufacturing sector after another while continuing to keep its domestic market relatively closed to American products.

Each of these developments heightened domestic support for trade restrictions. But in sharp contrast to the seventy-five years prior to World War II, when protectionist forces rarely encountered effective political opposition in the Congress or from the executive branch, during the postwar period they have more often been frustrated.

During the last two decades Congress has been flooded with literally hundreds of pieces of protectionist legislation. Yet only a small number have won approval. For example, when in 1970 the House of Representatives approved legislation that mandated statutory quotas for textiles, footwear, and oil and made it easier for other industries to secure similar redress, the legislation was defeated by a Senate filibuster.[20] During the 1970s, domestic content legislation—which would have severely curtailed Japanese automobile imports—was twice passed by the House of Representatives, but each time it failed to secure Senate approval. Congress also refused to approve the Burke-Hartke bill, which would have frozen the 1967–1969 ratio of imported goods to the production of "similar" domestic goods.[21] In 1985, both houses of Congress approved legislation to severely curtail textile and shoe imports, but the president vetoed the bill. The only industries that have benefited from direct legislative action during the last twenty-five years have been the fishing industry in 1976 and frozen concentrated orange juice producers in 1984.[22]

During the 1970s and early 1980s, the United States did impose restrictions on imports of footwear, television sets, textiles and apparel, sugar, specialty steel, motorcycles, and automobiles.[23] All told, between 1974 and 1990 the International Trade Commission, a federal agency established in 1916 to investigate dumping cases and recommend changes in trade policy, granted some form of protection for fifty-two major (greater than $100 million) industries.[24] The value of imports subject to "special restrictions" increased from $0.6 billion in 1955 to $28.9 billion in 1980 and $67.1 billion in 1984.[25] If automobiles, which were subject to a "voluntary" import quota, are included, then during the 1980s approximately one-quarter of imports into the United States were subject to some form of protection.

But this retreat from trade liberalization must be placed in perspective. The executive branch has consistently given industries less assistance than they have requested and more than half of industry petitions to the International Trade Commission have been rejected.[26] American tariff rates have, moreover, continued to decline. Between 1962 and 1974, the average tariff rate stood at 10 percent; by 1991 it had been reduced to 5.2 percent.[27]

The United States currently has the lowest average tariff rates in the world, averaging approximately 4.5 percent weighted by trade, excepting oil.[28] "The most obvious indicator of the limited impact of American trade barriers is that from 1980 to 1986, the growth in U.S. imports outstripped the growth of world imports seven to one. . . . Clearly, American protectionism has not been as severe or damaging as some have claimed."[29] In addition, "the scope of today's defense against imports is narrower than the all-embracing tariff in effect a half-century ago."[30] Even the expanded use of nontariff barriers such as quotas and "voluntary" import restrictions during the 1970s and 1980s had a limited effect on trade: both global and American trade have continued to expand *more* rapidly than domestic production.[31] And the Uruguay Round Agreement cut American industrial tariffs by an additional 34 percent.[32]

Equally important, the United States has managed to prevent its periodic quarrels with its various trading partners from seriously disrupting trade with them. In spite of the persistent complaints from American firms about their inability to gain access to the

Japanese market, only in the case of semiconductors has the United States insisted on a sector-specific agreement establishing a numerical measure of Japanese market openness. America has restricted imports of a number of Japanese products, most notably automobiles, steel, and motorcycles. But, given the high political visibility of America's trade deficit with Japan and widespread criticism of Japanese trade practices, what is striking is the weakness of American pressures to force Japan to open up its markets.[33] The American economy has remained relatively open to Japanese imports, even as the access of American producers to Japan's has remained restricted.

The fears expressed by numerous commentators that the Clinton administration would aggressively seek to pry open Japan's domestic market to American goods and services, creating a trade war between the world's two largest economies, proved groundless. American-Japanese trade negotiations were frequently extremely tense and often on the verge of collapse. But each time the Clinton administration—like the Bush and Reagan administrations before it—backed away from imposing serious trade sanctions. U.S.–European Union (EU) trade relations have also been frequently strained, and there have been an endless series of "trade wars," mostly over agricultural products.[34] Nonetheless, both parties were able to complete the Uruguay Round negotiations, bringing agriculture—a highly protected and subsidized sector in both regions—within the scope of the newly established World Trade Organization (WTO). Moreover, this agreement significantly strengthened the governance of international trade, not only by bringing a wide array of so-called technical barriers to trade, such as standards and regulations within its scope, but also by making the decisions of its dispute panels binding.

The United States has periodically threatened to invoke the provisions of "Super 301," which permit the president to restrict imports from an entire country, not just a particular industry, if that nation unfairly restricts American commerce. While this has been a persistent source of tension between the United States and other countries, Super 301 sanctions have only been applied three times, against, India, Brazil, and Japan. Since 1962, in response to pressures from environmentalists and some American producers, the United States has enacted thirteen statutes that authorize the unilateral use of trade sanctions to advance environmental or conservation goals.[35]

But with a few notable exceptions, such as bans on imports of tuna from nations whose fishing practices violated American standards for dolphin protection and on shrimp imports from nations that refused to adopt adequate turtle protection measures, they have rarely been imposed.[36] The same pattern holds true for American threats to restrict imports from countries which mistreat or exploit workers. Thus, notwithstanding widespread public concern about China's human rights record, Congress annually voted during the 1990s to maintain China's most favored nation (MFN) status, which permits Chinese goods to enter the United States with reduced tariff rates. And in 2000, Congress enacted legislation that facilitated China's membership in the World Trade Organization.

Explaining the Persistence of Liberal Trade

How can we account for the persistence of the American commitment to trade liberalization even though America's position in the world economy is so radically different than it was in the 1940s and 1950s? Why didn't the relatively poor performance of the American economy during much of the 1970s, 1980s, and early 1990s, which included three recessions, a prolonged period of inflation, as well as a slowdown in the rate of productivity growth, lead to a shift away from liberal trade? Or, to put this question in historical perspective, why did the serious economic distress experienced by the United States during the 1970s not lead to the kind of protectionist spiral that characterized the 1920s, even though the global position of the United States was nearly identical in both decades?[37]

Three factors seem to have been critical: the triumph of free trade as both an economic and national security doctrine among policy elites, the institutional changes in the way trade policy is made, and changes in the trade preferences of American business. These factors have complemented and reinforced one another.

In sharp contrast to its role during the first third of the twentieth century, when the United States shied away from global economic leadership, after its victory in World War II, the United States took the lead in creating a wide network of international economic, military, and political treaties, agreements, and institutions.[38] These arrangements were based on the assumption that international cooperation in a number of policy areas, including trade policy, was in the long-term interests both of the United States and the noncommunist world.

Unlike after World Word I, American economic and political elites emerged from World War II with a strong commitment to international economic interdependence. This commitment had both an economic and national security dimension.[39] According to mainstream economic thinking, it was the unilateral imposition of substantially higher tariff rates by the United States in the early 1930s that turned what would have been a "normal" economic downturn into the Great Depression. While the casual connection between the two events has since been disputed by a number of economic historians, the relationship between a major unilateral increase in trade barriers by the United States and global political and economic chaos remained an important article of faith among policymakers and the economists who advise them. Paradoxically, it was in part the very severity of global economic slowdown of the 1970s that mitigated against an increase in trade barriers by the United States: American policymakers feared that such the unilateral imposition of trade barriers by the United States might well precipitate an even more severe international economic crisis. In this sense, the legacy of Smoot-Hawley continues to haunt American policymakers.

When Joseph Wharton endowed the nation's first business school in 1881, he explicitly stipulated that one of the school's basic missions was to teach students about the importance of high tariffs on manufactured goods for American prosperity. Indeed, throughout the second half of the nineteenth century, few persuasive arguments were advanced for a low-tariff policy: the arguments of British political economist David Ricardo in favor of free trade had little resonance on this side of the Atlantic. But it is hard to conceive of a similar stipulation being attached to a university endowment or any intellectually respectable research institution today. In this sense, free trade has triumphed intellectually among policy elites.

This stands in marked contrast with American policy discourse a century ago, even though on virtually every dimension the world economy was then *more* integrated and interdependent than today. Between 1870 and 1913, there was a single world currency standard, uniform global interest rates, and substantial cross-border movements of goods, capital, and people. "The world was so tied together by trade and investment in the late nineteenth century that, despite the glorious years of growth in trade and GNP from 1950 to

1973, it took most countries nearly 70 years for merchandise trade as a proportion of their GNP to overtake the levels it had achieved in the years before the first world war."[40] Trade as a portion of global production totaled 33 percent in 1913; by contrast, it amounted to only 15 percent in 1980. Yet, informed opinion still considered America as somehow uniquely isolated from the rest of the world. Indeed, as recently as 1930, "the philosophy of autarky seemed firmly in the saddle."[41] While the Roosevelt administration did enact the RTAA in 1934, New Deal economic thinking and policies were largely based on the assumption that the United States was an economically self-sufficient nation, one for whom foreign markets and international competition were largely irrelevant to the recovery of the United States from the Great Depression.[42]

America's commitment to trade liberalization in the postwar period was also reinforced by national security considerations. An important component of American strategy in the cold war was to shore up the economies of noncommunist nations by opening up America's markets to them. Security considerations played a particularly important role in shaping American trade policies toward Japan, the maintenance of whose military alliance with the United States was considered far more important to American policymakers than the complaints of American businessmen about Japanese trade policies. American support for the creation and strengthening of the European Union can also be understood in this context. In this sense, the cold war helped temper protectionist pressures against nations who were both America's political allies and economic rivals; American policymakers consistently allowed the former role to trump the latter.

While NAFTA was approved after the end of the cold war, America's support for a historic agreement to liberalize trade with Mexico—an underdeveloped nation of marginal economic significance to the United States—followed from the same geopolitical logic on the part of the Bush and Clinton administrations. The main purpose of NAFTA was political: it was to lock in the commitment of Mexican political leaders to liberalize their domestic economy, thus promoting both economic growth and political stability in an important neighbor of the United States. In this sense, the negotiation and approval of NAFTA can be seen as a legacy of the cold war.

Another important source of the durability of the America's postwar liberal trade regime was institutional. The experience of American trade policy through the 1930s strongly suggested that as long as trade policy was primarily made in Congress it would be biased toward protectionism. Accordingly, the passage of the 1934 RTAA represented an important institutional shift toward a more liberal trade regime. Acting under its provisions, Presidents Roosevelt and Truman signed twenty-five bilateral trade agreements, and, more important, Truman was able to negotiate the GATT, which remains the principal framework of the world trading system.

The 1974 Trade Act went a significant step further in reducing Congressional authority over the details of trade agreements. It established a legislative procedure known as *fast-track* in order to expedite Congressional approval of trade agreements negotiated by the executive branch. Under this procedure, trade agreements must be voted up or down by Congress within sixty days; they cannot be amended either in committee or on the floor of Congress. This enables American trade negotiators to assure their trading partners that the terms of any agreement will not changed by Congress, thus forcing a potentially endless series of renegotiations. The 1979 Tokyo Round GATT Agreement, NAFTA, and the Uruguay Round GATT/WTO Agreement were all negotiated and approved under fast-track procedures.

Nonetheless, Congress has repeatedly made it easier for industries to seek protection and assistance from the executive branch. Between 1962 and 1986, Congress enacted trade legislation that permitted and, in some cases, required the executive branch to impose quotas or tariffs on foreign producers when imports "cause or threaten to cause substantial injury . . . threaten to impair national security . . . [or] . . . are priced below 'fair market values.' Congress also expanded the scope of the administration's ability to respond to industry complaints by permitting the executive to impose trade restrictions when exports to the United States are unfairly subsidized or when other nations treat U.S. firms in an "unjustifiable, unreasonable or discriminatory fashion."[43]

Under Section 301 of the Trade Act of 1974, enacted in response to growing public concerns about declining American competitiveness, the executive branch was authorized to threaten trade retaliation to induce policy changes by America's trading partners. In 1979, Congress expanded the scope of the private sector's participation in trade policy. Private firms were given the legal right to seek governmental redress from "unfair trade practices," and the federal government was required "to take account of the views of affected industry," in formulating the American response to private petitions.[44] In 1988, Congress, under pressure from industries upset by the fact that the executive branch had repeatedly shied away from trade retaliation, "because of the desire to use trade to barter for other nontrade issues" effectively transferred substantial authority to enforce Section 301 to the office of the United State Trade Representative (USTR), thus hoping to trigger more Section 301 cases.[45]

These legislative provisions have acted as a political "escape valve." They have provided a way for politically powerful private interests to demand and sometime receive either protection or assistance in securing access to foreign markets, without permitting the kind of logrolling among producers that occurred when tariff schedules were set by the Congress. By establishing various administrative procedures for addressing complaints by business firms and displaced workers, Congress has managed to combine redress or assistance for particular sectors without undermining the overall commitment of the United States to trade liberalization.[46] In a sense, these laws have enabled legislators to take credit for redressing the complaints of their constituents about particular American trade policies, without risking being blamed for the collapse of the liberal international trade regime.

A final critical factor underpinning the durability of the postwar American commitment to open trade has been a significant change in the position and preferences of important segments of American business. The protectionist policies of the late nineteenth century reflected the preferences of politically influential American manufacturers, who were for the most part uncompetitive, especially vis-à-vis British firms. Many American industries did become more competitive during the first third of the twentieth century when America emerged as the world's largest industrial economy. But if much of heavy industry no longer needed high tariffs, neither did it have any incentive to reduce them, as their market orientation remained primarily domestic. The Smoot-Hawley tariff led to retaliation by twenty-five nations and reduced American exports by two-thirds in two years. But its domestic impact was modest because American exports were so small to begin with.

The contrast with the participation of American firms in the global economy in the postwar period is marked. Even as the relative size of the American economy to the world economy has declined, American exports have grown in relative importance to the size of the domestic economy. U.S. exports as a percentage of GDP stood at only 4 percent in 1959; by the early 1990s, they had increased to 11 percent. During the 1980s, one-third of American farm production and nearly 20 percent of domestic manufacturing output were exported. During the 1990s, a third of American economic growth was due to overseas sales, while export-related jobs accounted for nearly one-quarter of private sector new-employment growth between 1990 and 1994.[47] Nor is increased participation in international trade confined to large firms: small-firm exports have been growing just as fast as those from the fifty largest companies.

A significant portion of American business is highly competitive globally. These include firms in the rapidly growing service sector—which now constitutes 70 percent of the American economy and includes financial services, construction, entertainment, transportation, communications, insurance, software, and telecommunications—as well as a number of high-technology manufacturers and, as in the past, much of American agriculture. For these firms, an increase in American trade barriers would be extremely costly, since it would make their access to foreign markets vulnerable to retaliation by other countries. These firms have formed the political backbone of domestic support for trade liberalization.

The growth of American investment overseas constitutes another critical difference between the political economy of the pre- and postwar periods. While only 2.6 percent of the assets of American firms were held overseas in 1922, by the 1970s, this figure had grown to 20 percent.[48] During the 1980s, one-third of American exports were brought by American-owned companies abroad while the subsidiaries of American-based multinationals accounted for a fifth of total American imports.[49] Clearly, these large and politically influential firms have a major stake in the continued openness of the American economy, since trade barriers interfere with their ability to manage their international operations.

These changes in the American economy have driven a wedge between the interests of American firms and their employees. In recent years "organized labor has become a driving force in a wide assortment of anti-import campaigns."[50] But the extensive foreign investments of American manufacturing firms means that their interests and those of their American employees are no longer identical. This emerged with striking clarity in the course of the debate over NAFTA, a trade agreement which almost American manufacturing firms supported (with the exception of the textile industry) and their unionized workers strongly opposed.

Another important postwar development has been the growth of foreign direct investment in the United States. (While foreign capital was much more important during the nineteenth century, it primarily took the form of portfolio investment.[51]) Foreign-owned firms now control 9 percent of domestic assets and employ 4 percent of the labor force, including 10 percent of workers employed in manufacturing; they account for 10 percent domestic sales. Equally significantly, they are responsible for about one-third of American imports.[52] These firms and their employees constitute another important political constituency for maintaining trade liberalization, one that did not exist before World War II. In addition, many domestic manufacturers are dependent on components produced by foreign suppliers. And of course many domestic retailers, most notably automobile dealers, have a strong economic interest in liberal trade policies.

In short, the oft-cited confusion over "Who is us?" not only has made the task of organizing a protectionist business coalition more difficult but has created a set of powerful business interests that oppose the classical protectionist position and favor strategic trade policies and market opening measures.[53] The growth of international economic interdependence, both within firms as well as among them, has also made it more difficult to restrict imports without also injuring firms and workers in America.

In part for this reason, many recent American trade initiatives have been directed less at protecting domestic producers than in seeking to open up foreign markets to American exports of goods, services, and agricultural products. Indeed, for many American companies the best strategy for protecting their domestic markets is to liberalize foreign ones. Consequently, a major source of trade friction between the United States and its trading partners has been American efforts to use the threat of retaliation against imports to demand the lowering of trade barriers to American exports.[54]

These efforts, as the recent trade disputes between the United States and the European Union over bananas and beef from cattle that have been treated with hormones, can, of course, be highly disruptive of world trade.[55] But there is an important difference between using the American government to pressure other countries to reduce their trade barriers and in demanding that one's own government to restrict imports. While both may violate the orthodoxy of liberal trade and undermine the dispute settlement procedures established by the WTO, the former reflects economic strength; the latter, economic weakness. The former represents an embrace of international competition; the latter, a retreat from it.

When placed in a historical context, what is especially important is the geographic dispersion of globally oriented firms. During the nineteenth century, both protectionist and export-oriented producers tended to be geographically concentrated. Hence, trade policies and partisan politics were tightly linked. But this is no longer the case: even those states with significant concentrations of producers and employees who favor trade restrictions—such as the textile-producing states in the South or some manufacturing firms in the Northeast and the industrial heartland—now also contain large numbers of firms that have a stake in either keeping the American economy open or increasing access to foreign markets, or both. In sharp contrast to the past, the politics of trade policy no longer divide along geographic or regional lines. All but a handful of senators and representatives are now exposed to pressures from business interests who have a stake in liberal trade policies.

The Contemporary Backlash against Globalization

Yet we are confronted with a paradox.[56] During the 1970s, 1980s, and early 1990s, when the performance of the American economy was highly uneven and American firms were facing increasing strong international competition, trade liberalization steadily expanded. Yet during the second half of the 1990s, a period when the American economy experienced the longest peacetime expansion in history and unemployment levels were at historic lows, opposition to trade liberalization became more politically influential. The clearest expression of this policy shift is the fate of fast-track authority. While fast-track authority was extended by Congress in 1979 and again in 1993, it expired in 1994 and has not been renewed. Indeed, just four years after Congress overwhelmingly approved the Uruguay Round GATT/WTO agreement by a vote of 76 to 24 in the Senate and 288 to 146 in the House, the House of Representatives denied fast-track reauthorization by a vote of 243–180. (Reauthorization was about to pass the Senate.)

Hostility toward free trade is not a new development in contemporary American politics. Throughout the postwar period, various national politicians, including Ross Perot, Tom Harkin, Richard Gephardt, and Pat Buchanan, have campaigned on protectionist platforms. In addition, the trade union movement has become increasingly protectionist. But through the mid-1990s, political forces opposed to free trade were remarkably ineffective in influencing American trade policy. However the refusal of Congress to reauthorize fast-track placed proponents of trade liberalization on the defensive: the executive branch was now unable to negotiate any trade agreement which requires congressional approval. Chile's inclusion in NAFTA was effectively been put on hold, as was the Clinton administration's effort to negotiate a free trade agreement of the Americas.

What makes this development historically significant is that unlike the opposition to trade liberalization through the 1930s, and even during much of the postwar period, the current wave of support for protectionism is *not* being driven by business. With a few exceptions, Congress is not finding itself pressured by business to protect domestic firms from foreign competition. Quite the contrary, the American business community is now more committed to trade liberalization than at any time in American history. All major business lobbies support new trade agreements to increase their access to foreign markets. America Leads on Trade, an umbrella organization of business groups, financed a $3 million media campaign in favor of fast-track.[57] What, then, is driving the contemporary resurgence of protectionism?

Part of the vote against fast-track stems from the growing strength of protectionist forces within the Democratic party. In part because of a shift in corporate campaign contributions to congressional Republicans following the Republican capture of Congress in 1994, congressional Democrats have become increasingly dependent on campaign funds from trade unions. At the same time, another part of the Democratic party's constituency, environmentalists and consumer groups, have become increasingly vocal opponents of trade liberalization. As a result, congressional Democrats have become increasingly protectionist. While 40 percent of House Democrats supported NAFTA, only 20 percent voted in favor of fast-track reauthorization. For the first time in the history of the

United States, the Democratic party is more opposed to trade liberalization than the Republican party.

As these votes suggest, the key to the success of recent trade liberalization initiatives has been congressional Republicans. It is they who supplied the administration with its thirty-four margin of victory in the House in 1993: only forty-three Republicans voted against NAFTA. But in 1998, seventy-one Republicans, one-quarter of the party's representation in the House, voted against fast-track reauthorization. These representatives were responding to the increasingly vocal and influential opposition to trade liberalization on the part not of business but of the grassroots conservative movement. At the same time, they saw the defeat of fast-track as a way to embarrass President Clinton.

Fast-track reauthorization was defeated by a left-right populist coalition that included not only the AFL-CIO, the Sierra Club, and Ralph Nader's Public Citizen but also the National Rifle Association and Phyllis Schlafly's Eagle Forum. These organizations and the constituencies they represent may disagree on many issues, but together they have been able "to puncture the free market internationalist consensus that has dominated American politics since the end of the cold war."[58] As one Democratic supporter of free trade observed, "Labor's hitting us from the left, and the Buchanan wing, the isolationist, nationalistic wing of the Republican Party, from the right."[59] The Clinton administration, its own strength and credibility weakened by scandal, was unable to mount the kind of political effort necessary to secure fast-track approval.

For their part, liberal constituencies blame economic globalization for weakening political support for their domestic social and economic agenda.[60] In their view, the increased international competition fostered by trade liberalization has intensified pressures to weaken environmental standards, lowered wages, and increased economic inequality. What they want is not free trade but "fair trade." Thus, Lori Wallach of the Public Citizens' Global Trade Watch heralded the defeat of fast-track as "signal[ing] a shift to a new trade policy in the United States, a rejection of the NAFTA and GATT model, in which there is a race-to-the-bottom competition where there are no standards of fair play, and the cheapest labor, the most crushed union movement, the most trashed environment becomes the winner."[61]

For many liberal interest groups, the prolonged and bitter conflict over the ratification of NAFTA during the early 1990s represented a kind of political watershed. While specific unions had periodically supported trade restrictions to protect the jobs of their members, NAFTA was the first trade agreement opposed by the entire trade union movement. They feared that opening up American markets to products produced in Mexico would depress American wages and permit American firms to relocate to Mexico. The debate over NAFTA also marked the first time environmental groups had become actively involved in the politics of trade policy.[62] For their part, they argued that trade liberalization would both exacerbate Mexico's already deplorable environmental conditions and make it more difficult for the United States to maintain its own higher environmental standards. While a number of major environmental organizations did ultimately agree to support NAFTA in exchange for the Clinton administration's pledge to add a Supplementary Agreement on the Environment, they were disappointed by the agreement's subsequent inability to improve Mexico's environmental performance.

For conservatives, opposition to trade liberalization reflects the growing strength of economic nationalism among their constituents. In recent years, populist conservatives have become increasingly concerned about the loss of "sovereignty," a term that encompasses their hostility to both federal regulation as well as the World Trade Organization, the United Nations, and the International Monetary Fund. Significantly, many conservative organizations oppose both trade liberalization and favor restrictions on immigration. The cold war helped convert a historically isolationist political party into an internationalist one. With the cold war now over, the Republican party's nationalist wing now appears to have regained much of its strength.

In a sense, if trade liberalization reflected the convergence of ideas and economic interests, then the contemporary backlash against it signifies the triumph of ideas and ideology over economic interests: in the long run few Americans stand to benefit from increased trade restrictions, and most certainly will be worse off if other countries raise their trade barriers.[63] The nation's economic and political elites continue to support free trade principles and policies, but they now confront a kind of populist revolt. Significantly, 54 percent of Americans oppose the congressional renewal of fast-track authority, while two-thirds believe that trade pulls wages down.[64]

Ironically, it is the very triumph of liberal trade policies that has helped spawn public opposition to further trade liberalization.

American trade, as measured by the combination of imports and exports, grew by 1,261 percent between 1970, far exceeding the 566 percent increase in national output. Between 1970 and 1995, the proportion of trade to domestic output—the clearest measure of the openness of the American economy—more than doubled, the largest such increase for any developed economy during this period.[65] And while many American firms are well positioned to take advantage of a more open global economy, many ordinary Americans have come to feel increasingly vulnerable to economic and political forces that they do not understand and that they feel unable to control. Many Americans have come to associate trade liberalization with wage stagnation and declining job security.

In a further irony, the relatively strongly performance of the American economy compared to that of many of its trading partners, especially in Asia, has resulted in a major trade imbalance as the latter's economic difficulties have reduced their demands for American exports. As a result, in 1998, America's trade balance ballooned to more than $250 billion, leading to increased demands for protection from steel producers and other firms hit by a flood of imports. Not surprisingly, many commentators have again become gloomy about the political future of trade liberalization.[66]

However, the contemporary backlash also needs to be placed in perspective. The accomplishments of the postwar liberal trade agenda, symbolized most recently not only by NAFTA and the Uruguay Round Agreement but also the ability of the United States to reach post–Uruguay Round agreements liberalizing trade in three critical sectors of the service economy in 1996 and 1997— namely, telecommunications, information technology, and financial services—remain firmly in place. The postwar American commitment to trade liberalization is not at risk: the United States is not going to abandon NAFTA or withdraw from the WTO. The defeat of fast-track did not imperil any important pending trade negotiations. Nor did it prevent Congress from voting to support China's membership in the WTO.

Indeed, it may well be that after the significant trade liberalization initiatives of the early 1990s, the United States needs some time to "digest" them before moving on to the next round of trade reductions. After all, fifteen years elapsed between the conclusion of the Tokyo Round of GATT negotiations and the approval of the Uruguay Round, while it took almost five years to negotiate NAFTA. Trade liberalization may well follow a pattern similar to environmental protection, subject to periods of advance and retrenchment, but in the long run steadily expanding.[67] Significantly, the newly elected Bush administration has indicated its strong support for a free trade agreement of the Americas.

Notes

1. Judith Goldstein, *Ideas, Interests and American Trade Policy* (Ithaca, N.Y.: Cornell University Press, 1993), 81–136.

2. Pietro S. Nivola, "The New Protectionism: U.S. Trade Policy in Historical Perspective," *Political Science Quarterly* 101, no. 4 (1986): 587.

3. Goldstein, *Ideas, Interests and American Trade Policy*, 94, 164–165.

4 Ibid., 92.

5. Roger Baldwin, "The Changing Nature of U.S. Trade Policy since World War II," in *The Structure and Evolution of Recent U.S. Trade Policy*, ed. Robert Baldwin and Anne Krueger (Chicago; University of Chicago Press, 1984), 15.

6. Quoted in Nivola, "The New Protectionism," 596.

7. Quoted in I. M. Destler, *American Trade Politics: System under Stress* (Washington, D.C.: Institute for International Economics, 1986), xiii.

8. Nivola, "The New Protectionism," 577.

9. Ibid., 589.

10. Destler, *American Trade Politics*, xi.

11. Ibid.

12. Jagdish Bhagwati, "United States Trade Policy at the Crossroads," *World Economy* 12, no. 4 (December 1989): 439.

13. Laura D'Andrea Tyson, *Who's Bashing Whom? Trade Conflict in High-Technology Industries* (Washington, D.C.: Institute for International Economics, 1992), 9–14 and *passim*.

14. Ibid., 13.

15. Martin Wolf, "The View from Silicon Valley," *Financial Times*, January 28, 1993.

16. William Lash III, "The Clinton Trade Tango: One Step Forward, Two Steps Back," Contemporary Issue Series 64, Center for the Study of American Business (St. Louis: Center for the Study of American Business, May 1994), 1.

17. Baldwin, "The Changing Nature of U.S. Trade Policy since World War II," 22.

18. Nivola, "The New Protectionism," 580–581.

19. Destler, *American Trade Politics*, xi.

20. Victor A. Canto, "U.S. Trade Policy: History and Evidence," *Cato Journal* 3, no. 3, (Winter 1984): 683.

21. Ibid., 684.

22. Pietro Nivola, *Regulating Unfair Trade* (Washington, D.C.: Brookings Institution, 1993), 111.

23. Ibid., 111.

24. Ibid.

25. Quoted in David Yoffie, "American Trade Policy: An Obsolete Bargain," in *Can the Government Govern?* ed. John Chubb and Paul Paterson (Washington, D.C.: Brookings Institution, 1989), 116.

26. Baldwin, "The Changing Nature of U.S. Trade Policy since World War II," 19.

27. Goldstein, *Ideas, Interests and American Trade Policy.*

28. Richard Steinberg, "The Uruguay Round: A Legal Analysis of the Final Act," Berkeley Roundtable on the International Economy Working Paper (1994), 8.

29. David Yoffie, "American Trade Policy: Am Obsolete Bargain," in Chubb and Paterson, *Can the Government Govern?* 117–118.

30. Nivola, "The New Protectionism," 577.

31. Helen Milner, *Resisting Protectionism: Global Industries and the Politics of International Trade* (Princeton, N.J.: Princeton University Press, 1988), 11.

32. Steinberg, "The Uruguay Round," 8.

33. See Clyde V. Prestowitz. Jr., *Trading Places: How We Allowed Japan to Take the Lead* (New York: Basic Books, 1988).

34. David Vogel, *Barriers or Benefits; Regulation in Transatlantic Trade* (Washington, D.C.: Brookings Institution, 1998).

35. Elizabeth DeSombre, "Baptist and Bootleggers for the Environment," *Journal of Environment and Development* 4, no. 1 (Winter 1995): 56–59.

36. David Vogel, *Trading Up: Consumer and Environmental Regulation in a Global Economy* (Cambridge, Mass.: Harvard University Press, 1995), 125–128.

37. Milner, *Resisting Protectionism,* 7.

38. John Ruggie, "International Regimes, Transactions, and Change: Embedded Liberalism in the Postwar Economic Order," in *International Regimes,* ed. Stephen Krasner (Ithaca, N.Y.: Cornell University Press, 1983).

39. For the role of ideas in shaping American trade policy, see Goldstein, *Ideas, Interests, and American Trade Policy.*

40. "The Nation State," *Economist,* September 22, 1990, p. 45.

41. Raymond Bauer, Ithiel de Sola Pool, and Anthony Dexter, *American Business and Public Policy* (Chicago: Atherton, 1972), 25.

42. See David Kennedy *Freedom from Fear: The American People in Depression and War* (New York: Oxford University Press, 1999), 375.

43. 1974 Free Trade Act, Section 301, quoted in "Section 301 Law Offers a Big Stick," *Washington Post,* September 22, 1985, p. F2.

44. Susan Sell, "Multinational Corporations as Agents of Chance: The Globalization of Intellectual Property Rights," in *Private Authority and International Affairs,* ed. A. Claire Cutler, Virginia Haufler, and Tony Porter (Albany: State University of New York Press, 1999), 177.

45. Ibid.

46. Destler, *American Trade Politics*, 12–15.

47. Bruce Stokes, "A Geoeconomic Strategy for the 21st Century," in *Trade Strategies for a New Era*, ed. Geza Feketekuty with Bruce Stokes (New York: Council on Foreign Relations, 1998), 164.

48. Ibid., 27.

49. "The Myth of Economic Sovereignty," *Economist*, June 23, 1990, p. 67.

50. Nivola, "The New Protectionism," 583.

51. See Robert Gilpin, *U.S. Power and the Multinational Corporation* (New York: Basic Books, 1975).

52. "The Myth"; see also Robert Reich, "Who Is Us?", *Harvard Business Review* (January–February 1990): 55.

53. See Reich, "Who Is Us?", 53–64.

54. See David Yoffie and Helen Milner, "Why Corporations Seek Strategic Trade Policy," *California Management Review* (Summer 1989): 113–131.

55. "At Daggers Drawn," *Economist*, May 8, 1999, pp. 16–18.

56. For an extended analysis of this observation, see I. M. Destler, "Trade Policy at a Cross Roads," *Brookings Review* (Winter 1999): 27–30.

57. Amy Borrus, "Business Is in a Hurry for Fast-Track," *Business Week*, September 15, 1997, pp. 39–40.

58. Peter Bienart, "The Nationalist Revolt: Fast-track Is Only the Beginning," *New Republic*, December 1, 1997, p. 21.

59. David Hosansky, "Free Trade Doesn't Sell in Congress Anymore," *Congressional Quarterly Weekly*, September 19, 1998, p. 2460.

60. Gary Burtless, "Worsening American Inequality," *Brookings Review* (Spring 1996): 26–31.

61. Thomas Edsell and John Yang, "Whose Side Are They On?", *Washington Post National Weekly Edition*, November 17, 1997, p. 10.

62. See Vogel, *Trading Up*, 234–247.

63. For an analysis of the economic case for trade liberalization, see Gary Burtless, Robert Lawrence, Robert Litan, and Robert Shapiro, *Globaphobia: Confronting Fears about Open Trade* (Washington, D.C.: Brookings Institution Press, 1998).

64. See "Freer Trade Gets an Unfriendly Reception," *Business Week*, September 22, 1997, p. 34; and Ellen Frost, "Gaining Support for Trade from the American Public," in Feketekuty and Stokes, *Trade Strategies*, 69.

65. J. David Richardson, Geza Feketekuty, Chi Zhand, and A. E. Rodriguez, "U.S. Performance and Trade Strategy in a Shifting Global Economy," in Feketekuty and Stokes, *Trade Strategies*, 41, 39.

66. See, for example, Destler, "Trade Policy at a Crossroads," 27–30.

67. See David Vogel, *Fluctuating Fortunes: The Political Power of Business in America* (New York: Basic Books, 1989).

PART VI
Durability and Change

14

Much Huffing and Puffing, Little Change

David R. Mayhew, *Yale University*

Of the merits exhibited by the policy essays in this volume, not the least is the interesting variety among the messages they convey. The story of affirmative action in the 1990s does not resemble that of the Earned Income Tax Credit (EITC), which in turn does not resemble that of welfare reform, and so on. Still, in policy terms the 1990s do seem to have possessed a certain coherence. I believe it is possible to generalize across this volume's various accounts, or at least most of them. On my reading, six generalizations are in order.

First, in terms of successful policy innovation at the national level, the 1990s was rather a fallow decade. That is, in the realm of actual policy change, notwithstanding the ambitious aims often advanced by Bill Clinton, Newt Gingrich, and others during the decade, not a great deal resulted. Not much major innovation occurred. This claim is implicitly comparative, and I have two comparisons in mind. First, during the 1990s the American national government was arguably outpaced in policy innovation by state and municipal governments. Governors Tommy Thompson of Wisconsin and John Engler of Michigan, for example, pioneered in welfare reform; Governor John Kitzhaber of Oregon, in health care reform. The state attorneys general took on the tobacco companies and forced a huge settlement. Mayors Rudolph Giuliani of New York City, Edward Rendell of Philadelphia, Richard Riordan of Los Angeles, and others inaugurated new efficiency-oriented, anticrime policy regimes in the major cities.

The other comparison is across time. It is well to remember, even if today's undergraduate students cannot, that the American federal government is capable of policy démarches that capture the attention of society and significantly affect society. In the 1930s, there was the Works Progress Administration (WPA), Social Security, and the Wagner Act; in the 1940s, the Manhattan Project (that was a government enterprise) and the GI Bill; in the 1950s, the federal highway program; from Hoover's era through Eisenhower's the big dams in the West; in the 1960s, Medicare and the great civil rights enactments; around 1970, the Clean Air, Clean Water, and other acts regulating the environment; in 1981, Reagan's tax and spending cuts.

Against this background, the record of the 1990s looks modest. The chief innovations were arguably the North American Free Trade Agreement (NAFTA) in 1993 and welfare reform in 1996 (see the account by Steven M. Teles and Timothy J. Prinz in chapter 9). (I am using the term *innovation* here, I believe legitimately, to encompass major contractions of state authority such as large tax cuts, deregulation of industries, or devolution of welfare, as well as expansions of authority.) Otherwise, the record of the 1990s was largely one of failed aims, stasis, incremental change (as in the expanding of the Earned Income Tax Credit, which originated under President Ford in 1975; see the account by Christopher Howard in chapter 10), or repeat performances (as with the immigration reform of 1996—which offered certain novelties, to be sure—following on the reforms of 1986 and 1990; see the account by Peter Schuck in chapter 5).

Teles and Prinz's treatment of welfare reform strikingly aside (see chapter 9), modest or no change is a leitmotiv of this volume's essays. Cathie Jo Martin on health care reform in 1993–94 documents a policy failure—a large nonevent (see chapter 11). Martha Derthick on Social Security discusses interesting and important policy changes that may occur but have not done so yet (see chapter 8). In Thomas F. Burke's account, the politics of "rights" stayed alive and well (see chapter 7). In John D. Skrentny's account, national affirmative action policy largely stayed in place (see chapter 6). There was much continuity to report.

A second generalization is that, in policy terms, the 1990s was not a distinctive decade. This is a slightly different point. As Martin A. Levin and Marc K. Landy note in this volume's introductory chapter, certain past decades stand out for their policymaking distinctiveness—the 1860s, the 1930s, the 1960s, even possibly for their own kinds of reasons the 1920s and 1950s. So far as I could discern, none of this volume's authors makes any such claim about the 1990s.

It might have been otherwise. The federal government returned to unified party control as a consequence of the 1992 election, after twelve years of divided control. Arthur M. Schlesinger Jr., applying his cyclical "moods" theory, discerned a new mood of Progressive/ liberal policy activism arriving on schedule. It was to be the 1930s or the 1960s all over again.[1] Later, when divided party control returned in unfamiliar upside-down form as a result of the 1994 election—the Democrats in the White House, the Republicans controlling Capitol Hill—that configuration might have brought on its own distinctive policy effects. Good ideas were available to back up such an expectation.[2] But none of these results came to pass. Certainly the 1930s and the 1960s have stayed safely history. As for unified versus divided control, the subject seems to be dormant—at least for the moment. None of the authors of this volume dwell on any systematic or theoretically arresting effects of unified as opposed to divided party control during the 1990s.

If not the 1990s as a distinctive era, then what? One move made in this volume, particularly prominently in the treatments of taxes, expenditures, and budgeting, is to couple the 1990s with the 1980s, or more broadly with the post-Nixon late 1970s and 1980s, as one long, distinctive policy era. In Paul Pierson's account (see chapter 3), a quarter-century-long "austerity" regime began in the mid-1970s and lasted into the late Clinton years. In Eric M. Patashnik's interpretation (see chapter 2), a centralized, ideologically charged budgeting system driven by a politics of rights-based entitlements set in in the mid-1970s and lasted into the late 1990s. For David R. Beam and Timothy J. Conlan, national politics after 1980 featured one all-encompassing revenue deal after another—in 1981, 1982, 1984, 1986, 1990, 1993, and 1997 (see chapter 4). The flavors of these deals differed, but the 1990s did not itself exhibit a special flavor.

In terms of actual policy in various realms, to cite one particular time juncture, the switch from the Bush years to the Clinton years proved to be notably seamless.[3] Neither president had any luck advancing an antirecession stimulus bill. Campaign finance reform went nowhere under both. Clinton carried Bush's NAFTA drive to completion. Immigration policy was reformed under both presidents.

After Reagan's antiregulatory thrust, regulation of industry and society came into a modest vogue again as Bush signed the Americans with Disabilities Act of 1990, the Clean Air Act of 1990, and the Civil Rights Act of 1991, and Clinton signed the Family Leave Act of 1993. Bush signed a minimum wage hike passed by a Democratic Congress in 1989; Clinton signed one passed by a Republican Congress in 1996. Above all, Clinton's controversial budget package of 1993, once Congress had largely stripped it of certain societal "investments" favored by the White House, came to resemble budgetary products of the Bush and even Reagan eras. In the 1993 package, as in the not less controversial one engineered under Bush in 1990, defense spending was substantially cut, and the EITC was substantially augmented. In the size of its much-advertised five-year, half-trillion-dollar bite out of the national debt, the 1993 package actually ranked slightly behind that of 1990 (controlling for the value of the dollar); in its revenue increases, the 1993 instrument ranked behind the deficit reduction package of 1982 (also controlling for the value of the dollar). Looking back across the two decades, the 1993 settlement was just one more important step along the path between Reagan's deficit-forcing program of 1981 and the eventual balanced-budget deal struck by the White House and a Republican Congress against the background of a booming economy in 1997.

But if these conclusions are valid, how about all that nasty, attention-grabbing conflict that invested Washington, D.C., politics during the 1990s? The third generalization here is that, during the decade, there was a remarkable dissonance between high politics and actually policymaking. That is, anyone focusing on the decade's election results, flashy party programs, and ideological crusades might have missed the actual policy results. It was easy to focus on just the former, since that was where the 1990s proved to be exciting and special. Party politics rose to modern heights of ambition and bitterness. Party cohesion crested on Capitol Hill, as did the authority accorded to House and Senate leaders to advance party causes. Party-controlled "soft money" deployed in elections may have contributed to roll call loyalty in both parties' ranks. Evidently motored by aggressive ideological activists on both sides, the congressional parties drew farther apart on major issues even as each grew more cohesive.[4]

In this context, which seemed to open up policymaking possibilities, both parties occasionally fell victim to the temptation to try to, in the language of spatial modeling, "enact their medians." That is, they tried to enact policies (or to bring about other important political results) favored by their own median members—their own middle-ranking House or Senate members on (ordinarily) a left-right scale—rather than favored by, to draw one contrast, the median members of the entire floor memberships of the House and Senate or, to draw an alternative contrast, the median member of the American public. No doubt this is always a tendency in party operations, and a number of ways of looking at it are possible. Perhaps it is an expected and commendable sort of policy leadership that can be curbed if need be in subsequent elections. But perhaps, in the language of public choice, it is a kind of ideological "rent seeking." In traditional Madisonian terms, which Nicol C. Rae has used to characterize the Gingrich-led policy campaign of 1995, it is perhaps a brand of assertive "factionalism."[5] The Gingrich-led Republicans were in these terms, among other things, a Madisonian "faction."

Dialing backward through the 1990s, we can see three especially aggressive efforts by one party or the other to "enact its median." The Republican impeachment drive of 1998–99, whatever else may be said about it, ran up against a hostile public opinion median. So did the Gingrich-Dole budget drive of 1995–96, which culminated and came apart through "shutting down the government." No less off-median were the Clinton-led Democrats in 1993–94 as they advanced their policies on gays in the military, the expensive "investments" woven into the early version of the 1993 budget package, and their prodigious plan for health care reform.

In the American system, it is not easy to carry off-median projects to completion. At the level of party politics, the storminess of the 1990s brought largely a history of disappointing or failed crusades that have not left major traces in policy.

Still, in general, to move to a fourth generalization, the policy results of the 1990s seem to have reflected public opinion. If the parties did not win victories during the 1990s, who did? In the essays of this volume, one recurrent answer is that public opinion did: Over and over again, actual policy results ended up being in accord with, so far as one can tell, the typical or median view of the American public. Strictly speaking, this is a report of consonance between opinion and policy results rather than in any simple way of opinion causing policy results. Ordinarily, public opinion on policy issues is not stable enough, clear enough, or neatly exogenous enough to elite policy processes, for any such simple causal model to work. But the chapters of this volume relate many accounts of end-state consonance.

In possibly the signal policy result of the decade, welfare reform in 1996 was resoundingly popular (see Teles and Prinz, chapter 9). Yet, the old discredited Aid to Families with Dependent Children (AFDC) program aside, government aid to the poor has enjoyed widespread backing among the American public, and, in accord with this supportive consensus, means-tested programs such as the EITC, Medicaid, food stamps, and Supplementary Security Income (SSI) continued their long course of expansion during the 1990s. No less in consonance with public opinion, the White House's health care plan sagged in the opinion polls in 1993–94 and then died (see Martin, chapter 11). The idea of deficit reduction enjoyed broad public support, as evidenced in Ross Perot's showing in the 1992 election. In the foreign trade area, new presidential "fast-track" authority may have failed in 1997 because of adverse public sentiment (see Wilson Carey McWilliams, chapter 16). The varying wrinkles in immigration reform during the last two decades seem to have corresponded to changing public "ideas" (see Schuck, chapter 5).

An exception to this generalization is affirmative action (see Skrentny, chapter 6), in which national policies stayed on track in the 1990s despite hostile numbers in the polls. In this issue area, as in many others, it may be necessary to consider asymmetrical intensity of views if policy results are to be grounded empirically in public opinion. That is, one side may care more intensely than the other. Note that the state electorates of California and Washington, in referendum processes conducted according to the principle of one person, one view—regardless of the intensities of voter views—rolled back affirmative action policies in the 1990s, whereas the state legislatures of those two states exhibited no such inclination. By instinct, elected politicians tend to weigh and respect opinion intensity.

If policy results generally reflected public opinion in the 1990s— at least in the cases of concrete proposals of the decade tested in actual political processes—how can we account for that? Levin and Landy wrestle with this question in chapter 1. I do not know of a general answer. In particular, there is something mysterious about the way that many means-tested programs for the poor, backed by diffuse public majorities but *not* by highly organized, self-interested constituencies as in, say, agriculture, keep getting expanded.

One interesting answer, however, does emerge from the mainstream congressional scholarship of the 1990s. It is perhaps that scholarship's most interesting recent contribution. What might be called "centrist defecting" is alive and well on Capitol Hill, even in an era of exceptionally strong parties, and the incentive system underpinning it has become better understood. That is, if you are a member of the House, you can gain points in the next election by bolting your party and voting with the opposition party on issues where the opposition enjoys public favor.[6] This may seem obvious, but the effect has been elegantly measured in the 1990s for Democrats of the 103d Congress bolting from party orthodoxy on Clinton's budget in 1993 and on the party's omnibus crime package in 1994; and for Republicans of the 104th Congress bolting from orthodoxy on Contract with America items. In all these cases, as a matter of statistical significance, members of the House majority party who defected on the key roll-call votes performed better in the next election than did their party colleagues from comparable constituencies who had not defected. In the American system, members of Congress *can* bolt (nobody stops them), they can profit electorally from bolting, they evidently know that, and therefore they often do bolt. A frequent result is victorious cross-party congressional roll-call coalitions that reflect public opinion and defeat the aims of majority parties trying to "enact their medians." Such floor majorities in the 1990s included the conservative ones in the House in 1993–94 *defeating* the Democratic majority party's omnibus crime package and its health care reform (which, lacking 218 endorsees, never came to the floor), and the liberal-tilted ones in both the formally Republican-controlled House and Senate in 1996 *enacting* a minimum wage hike and the Kassebaum-Kennedy portability health insurance act. "Centrist defecting" can be a powerful engine of public opinion expression.

Notwithstanding all the above, the essays of this volume fuel a fifth generalization, and a familiar one: There is still room for inventiveness in crafting policies. It can pay, sometimes grandly, to frame a policy or the official procedures for handling one in a way that is at once simple, novel, intuitively appealing, and geared to infusing administrative or judicial processes as efficiently as a virus does a computer. This often-exhibited capacity lends a certain autonomy to the policymaking sector.

To go back three decades for a perfect example, consider the requirement for "environmental impact statements" that was incorporated into the National Environmental Policy Act of 1969. The effects of that clever move are still being felt. In the 1990s, the idea of "rights," probably the most successful of all such defining enterprises during recent decades, continued its career of policy creativeness—as in the Republicans' "taxpayer's bill of rights" of 1997 (see Burke, chapter 7). Newly defined "spending caps" served to constrain federal expenditures after 1990 (see Patashnik, chapter 2). Every expansion of the EITC reinforced the canniness of "tax credits" as a means to expand the welfare state (see Howard, chapter 10). The idea of "waivers," ingeniously contrived by Republicans in the 1980s as a way to allow experimentation at the state level in the area of welfare policy, paid off in the 1990s as state governors more or less took over in that policy realm (see Teles and Prinz, chapter 9).

Not all such devices catch on. The Clinton administration's "health alliances" of 1993–94 did not. The Republicans' "medical savings accounts" are still in play but are not yet a winner. The stakes in this sphere of competitive design can be extremely high, as is shown in the late 1990s in moves by both of the parties to devise and merchandise privatization schemes for Social Security (see Derthick, chapter 8).

As a sixth and final generalization, or perhaps a reflection, the 1990s was a very poor decade for the national public sector—possibly the worst decade of the twentieth century. I intend here a contrast with the country's private sector. At the end of the twentieth century, it is perhaps appropriate to recall just how ambitious Progressive or liberal aims once were for the American national government. This was notably true at the level of "planning," a leading aspiration in the 1930s and 1940s. Then, the country experimented with the National Industrial Recovery Act; the Tennessee Valley Authority as, among other things as noted by Martin Shapiro in this volume (chapter 18), a rehearsal for additional regional planning exercises of that kind; the National Resources Planning Board with its blueprints for the economy; and after that a generation of confident Keynesianism.

Those days are past, but consider the 1990s with this older thrust toward synoptic public "planning" in mind. Across a range of policy realms, the decade was a disaster. Whatever else it might have been, the Clinton health care package of 1993–94 was a vast planning venture that went sour. So was the Republican drive to roll back the government through one comprehensive budget instrument in 1995–96. So was the half-trillion-dollar tobacco plan of 1998, a giant soufflé of taxes, spending, regulations, and lawyers' fees that swelled and then collapsed on Capitol Hill, leaving scarcely a trace a year later. One result of huge failed enterprises like these can be a kind of public inoculation against the very idea of synoptic planning by the national government.

Consider certain other particulars of the 1990s:

- The widespread distrust of government.
- The victory (that's what it was) of health maintenance organizations (HMOs) over government planning in the health care market.
- The drift toward part privatization of Social Security, a politically unvoiceable idea until recently.
- The flight of skilled personnel from the armed forces.
- The congressional assault against the Internal Revenue Service in 1997.
- The surprising displacement of policymaking by scandals.
- The declining hold of labor unions, a pro-government influence, on the workforce—as of early 1999, only 9.5 percent of private-sector employees were unionized, though 37.5 percent of public employees were.
- The shift of the Clinton White House, evidently bereft of other options, to blizzards of micro-initiatives as policy material, a style that makes an uncertain contribution to lasting policy accomplishments. Robert Kuttner has written of minimalist proposals like a Clinton one involving long-term care in early 1999: "They reinforce the message that the government isn't for real. Public programs don't really aim to remedy problems—they're just part of the show."[7]
- The triumph of the idea of "market efficiency" in a sequence of legislative enactments including NAFTA in 1993, telecommunications reform in 1996, banking reform in 1999, and admittance of China to the World Trade Organization (WTO) in 2000. (See the discussion by Levin and Landy in chapter 1.) In fact, these *anti*planning moves, which share with welfare reform in 1996 the property of having been enacted by cross-party

> coalitions, constitute probably the decade's best refutation of this chapter's theme of "little change."

Still, under the rubric of government planning in the 1990s, it may be objected that the Federal Reserve Board under Alan Greenspan and the Treasury Department under Robert Rubin exhibited exactly such instances of government planning and that they were highly successful ones to boot. That is certainly true, in a sense. Yet both those operations seemed to blend into the private economy, there was little social meliorism in them, and elected politicians were not in evidence. Greenspan and Rubin were something like deistic gods in the background. In these policy arenas, an instructive contrast to the 1990s is available in Allen J. Matusow's recent work on fiscal and monetary policy during the Nixon administration, when virtually nothing in this broad policy realm was fixed or settled, and topics as various as deficits, taxes, wages and price controls, unemployment, and the dollar as an international currency kept drifting back to the elected president in the White House for political adjudication.[8]

The opposite of public-sector recessiveness in the 1990s was, of course, private sector efficiency and ebullience. It is a good bet that, in the perceptions of people who ever considered the matter, an efficiency gap was widening in the late twentieth century between the country's public and private sectors. To draw an analogy, just over a century ago in the 1880s, as Alfred D. Chandler Jr., has written, the Pennsylvania Railroad emerged as an astonishing organizational creation—a private-sector enterprise, albeit one involving a public good, that no one then would have thought the American public sector at any level capable of pulling off.[9] For the 1990s, the same story could be told about Microsoft and Netscape, and that has possibly had rub-off effects on attitudes toward government.

Notes

1. Arthur M. Schlesinger Jr., "The Turn of the Cycle," *The New Yorker*, November 16, 1992, pp. 46–54.

2. Gary C. Jacobson, *The Electoral Origins of Divided Government* (Boulder, Colo.: Westview, 1990).

3. See David R. Mayhew, "Clinton, the 103rd Congress, and Unified Party Control: What Are the Lessons?" chapter 10 in *Politicians and Party Politics,* ed. John G. Geer (Baltimore: Johns Hopkins University Press, 1998).

4. Sarah A. Binder, "The Disappearing 'Political Center,'" *Brookings Review* (Fall 1996): 36–39.

5. Nicol C. Rae, *Conservative Reformers: The Republican Freshmen and the Lessons of the 104th Congress* (Armonk, N.Y.: Sharpe, 1998).

6. Gary C. Jacobson, "The 1994 House Elections in Perspective," *Political Science Quarterly* 11 (1996): 203–223; John Ferejohn, "A Tale of Two Congresses: Social Policy in the Clinton Years," chapter 2 in *The Social Divide: Political Parties and the Future of Activist Government,* ed. Margaret Weir (Washington, D.C.: Brookings Institution, 1998).

7. Robert Kuttner, "Clinton's Tokenism on Long-Term Care," *Boston Globe,* January 10, 1999, p. C7.

8. Allen J. Matusow, *Nixon's Economy: Booms, Busts, Dollars, and Votes* (Lawrence: University Press of Kansas, 1998).

9. Alfred D. Chandler Jr., *The Visible Hand: The Managerial Revolution in American Business* (Cambridge, Mass.: Harvard University Press, 1977).

15

Bill Clinton and the Politics of Divided Democracy

Sidney M. Milkis, *University of Virginia*

In their introduction to this volume, Martin Levin and Marc Landy claim that its various chapters and subjects add up to a coherent whole, "to a policy regime dominated by moderation." This essay suggests that the presidency of Bill Clinton offers an important window to evaluate the current state of moderation in American politics. There is a real sense in which the fate of the moderate policy regime that emerges from the pages of this volume hinged on Clinton's uneasy relationship with his own party and, more generally, on the tension between third-way politics and the party system.

Only the third Democratic president to win reelection this century (Woodrow Wilson and Franklin Roosevelt being the other two), Clinton remains an enigma to his party. Whereas Wilson and FDR established legacies that dedicated the Democratic party to protecting individual men and women from the abuses of big business and the uncertainties of the marketplace, Clinton proclaimed that "the era of big government is over." From this perspective, Clinton's presidency may, as Levin and Landy suggest, have confirmed the legacy of Ronald Reagan. Just as Dwight Eisenhower's so-called modern republicanism, which triumphed in the presidential elections of 1952 and 1956, accepted and ensured bipartisan support for Roosevelt's New Deal, so Clinton's New Democratic principles may have signaled the Democrats' full retreat in the face of a conservative political realignment. Eisenhower was a domestic political conservative who had no desire to innovate except in modest, incremental ways, but he believed that the New Deal had become a permanent part of modern American life. When his conservative brother Edgar, impatient with his sibling's compromises with liberalism, criticized him privately for carrying on liberal policies, the president replied bluntly, "Should any political party attempt to abolish social security and eliminate labor laws and farm programs, you should not hear of that party again in our political history."[1] "Above all else," the historian Oscar Handlin wrote soon after Eisenhower left office, "Eisenhower made palatable to most Republicans the social welfare legislation of the preceding two decades."[2]

So Clinton's presidency may have ratified the Reagan "revolution." His willingness to sign the 1996 welfare reform bill, eliminating the entitlement to Aid to Families with Dependent Children (AFDC), abetted a rout of the party's liberal establishment. (On the final vote to repeal AFDC in the Senate, only twenty-one Democrats voted against the measure.) Similarly, Clinton acquiesced to the general objectives of the Republican program to balance the budget by the year 2002, an agreement that included the most significant tax cuts and spending restraints since the heady days of the Reagan revolution.

And yet, as the saying goes, Clinton is no Dwight David Eisenhower. Eisenhower was a military hero who came to the White House "to crown a reputation not to make one."[3] As his love was not for power but for duty, Ike was well suited to the task of bestowing legitimacy on the New Deal. In contrast, Clinton struck most Americans as a charming and talented but irresolute man on the make. Having failed to achieve reform that would guarantee all Americans a comprehensive package of health care benefits, he appeared all too eager to embrace the conservative mood that ushered in the first Republican Congress since 1954. Then, sensing that Speaker Newt Gingrich and the Republicans had overreached, the president pounced on the Republican budget cuts, particularly in Medicare, and blocked their passage. Of Clinton and his relationship to the post–New Deal order, it can apparently be said as the historian Robert Blake wrote of Benjamin Disraeli: "He did not care which way he traveled providing he was in the driver's seat."[4]

That Clinton committed a long train of private and political indiscretions only reinforced the serious doubts about his character. The spectacle of the Lewinsky scandal, which saw Clinton become the first elected president to be impeached by the House of

Representatives, confirmed the public's disrespect for his personal morality. (Andrew Johnson, the only other president to be impeached, had succeeded to the office when Abraham Lincoln died.)

But no less remarkable than the House indictment and Senate trial of Clinton was the president's popularity throughout the ordeal; indeed, his job approval ratings for 1998, which was dominated by the Lewinsky scandal and investigations related to it, were higher than those earned by any previous sixth-year president. The public thus made a remarkable distinction between Clinton the chief executive, whom they approved, and Clinton the man, whom they regarded as immoral and untrustworthy.

In truth, Clinton's presidency displayed the virtues of his defects. Ideological promiscuity and volatility are the story of his political life. Indeed, as governor of Arkansas, as well as president, Clinton's first two years in office were desperately unsuccessful. But this very unsteadiness suits Clinton's "political time," an era of weak partisan loyalties, divided government, and widespread distrust of the political process.[5] Criticized by ardent liberals and militant conservatives for failing to provide a compelling vision of the nation's future, Clinton's extraordinary dexterity often served him well at a time when most Americans resist the programmatic ambitions of both major political parties.

The "two-tier politics" described so penetratingly in this volume by Wilson Carey McWilliams (see chapter 16), issuing in a disjuncture between bitter partisanship in Washington and weakening partisan loyalties outside the beltway, gave Clinton, with his skill in combining doctrines, a certain appeal in the country. Although this eclecticism risked degenerating into rank opportunism, the popularity of programs such as Americorps, "Reinventing Government," and the Earned Income Tax Credit (EITC) suggests that Clinton's "triangulation," as his political consultant Dick Morris termed it, may endure—and restore the vitality of progressive politics. Nonetheless, third-way politics tends to disregard the importance of political associations in a manner that may condemn it to ephemerality. Absent a political party and mass-based constituencies that can routinize his charisma, Clinton's may be remembered, as his Republican critics hope, not as the savior of progressivism but, rather, as the rear guard of the welfare state. More penetratingly, the very nature of third-way politics, in which media-oriented and poll-driven politics threaten to displace partisan debate and resolution, may render impractical the emergence of an enduring policy regime.

The "New" American Party System

Bill Clinton's ascent to the White House and his tumultuous presidency must be understood within the context of a new form of partisanship that emerged during the 1970s and 1980s. Put simply, he won the 1992 presidential election because he presented himself as a "New Democrat," as an "agent of change" who offered the hope of an alternative to both traditional Democratic liberalism and traditional Republican conservatism. In truth, triangulation was not created from whole cloth in 1995 by a desperate Clinton and a scheming Dick Morris—it was there at the beginning of Clinton's quest for power.

Above all, Clinton's third-way politics sought to ameliorate the ideological and institutional confrontations that arose with the recrudescence of partisanship during the 1980s. Since the 1970s, political scientists had kept a death watch over the American party system. Reforms and the mass media had deprived political parties of their limited but significant influence in American politics, scholars and pundits lamented, and there was little prospect of recovery. The declining influence of traditional decentralized, patronage-based party organizations was reflected not only in the presidential selection process but also in the political loyalties of the American people. Institutional changes that deemphasized partisan politics and governance, combining with television's emergence as the most important platform of political action, were "freeing more and more millions of Americans," as Theodore White wrote in 1973, "from unquestioning obedience to past tradition, their union begetting what has been called the age of ticket-splitting."[6] Indeed, for all but four years between 1968 and 1992 (Jimmy Carter's one term in the White House), the voters delivered a split verdict in national elections, handing control of the presidency to the Republicans and Congress, as well as most state and local elections, to the Democrats.

By the late 1980s, however, it appeared that the age of divided government had brought not the decline but rather the transformation of the American party system. Although partisan loyalties in the electorate declined during the late 1960s and 1970s, parties did not simply whither away. Indeed, during Ronald Reagan's presidency, the party system showed at least some signs of transformation and renewal. Reagan, and his successor George H. Bush, supported efforts by Republicans in the national committee and congressional campaign organizations to restore some of the importance of political parties by fashioning them into highly untraditional but politically potent national organizations. The Democrats lagged behind in party-building efforts, but the electoral losses suffered in the 1980 elections encouraged them to modernize the national party machinery, openly imitating some of the devices employed by Republicans.

Even as they have become more national, programmatic organizations (a development that had its origins in the New Deal and the opposition it spawned), the Democratic and Republican parties lost their connection with the American people. Unlike the decentralized parties system that flourished in the nineteenth century and beginning of the twentieth, the politics of the 1960s and 1970s had spawned a form of partisanship that centered on government rather than the electorate. The Democrats and Republicans have become parties of administration—intent on the use of centralized administrative power to further the intractable demands of policy advocates. Moreover, partisan disputes about rights have become increasingly associated with the expansion of national administrative power (even conservatives in the abortion dispute demand governmental intervention to protect the rights of the unborn). The expansion of rights (the attempt to graft programmatic rights onto individual liberties) has further shifted partisan politics away from parties as associations that organize political sentiments as an electoral majority.[7]

A major, if not the main, forum for partisan conflict during the Reagan and Bush years was a sequence of investigations in which Democrats and Republicans sought to discredit one another. In part, the legal scrutiny of public officials was a logical response to the Watergate scandal. But partisan maneuvering by investigations and scandalous revelations was institutionalized by the 1978 Ethics in Government Act, which provided for the appointment of independent counsels to investigate allegations of criminal activity by executive officials.[8] Not surprisingly, divided government encouraged the exploitation of the act for partisan purposes. In the 1980s, congressional Democrats found themselves in a position to demand criminal investigations and possible jail sentences for their political opponents. When Clinton became president, congressional Republicans turned the tables with a vengeance. Consequently, political disagreements were readily transformed into criminal charges. Moreover, investigations under the special prosecutor statute tended to deflect attention from legitimate constitutional and policy differences and to focus the attention of Congress, the press, and citizens alike on scandals.[9]

The Democratic and Republican organizations have raised large campaign war chests and fostered party discipline in Washington. Yet recent developments—virulent institutional clashes between the executive and legislature, the decline of public authority, and the impeachment of a popular president presiding over the most prosperous economy in three decades—have raised serious doubts about the capacity of these emergent national parties to build popular support for political principles and programs.[10] Indeed, as fierce partisan battles were waged within the Washington beltway, the influence of the Democrats and the Republicans on the perceptions and habits of the American people continued to decline. The weak partisan attachments of the electorate were exposed by the 1992 presidential campaign of H. Ross Perot, whose 19 percent of the popular vote was the most significant challenge to the two-party system since Theodore Roosevelt's Progressive party campaign of 1912. Indeed, Perot's campaign, dominated by thirty-minute "infomercials" and hour-long appearances on talk shows, set a new standard for direct, plebiscitary appeals that threatened to sound the death knell of the party campaign. "Perot hints broadly at an even bolder new order," the historian Alan Brinkley wrote in July 1992, "in which the president, checked only by direct expressions of popular desire, will roll up his sleeves and solve the nation's problems."[11]

The New Covenant

Clinton was a master at exploiting the American people's disdain for partisanship; indeed, his third-way politics—originally dubbed a "new covenant"—made Perotism respectable. He dedicated his 1992 campaign to principles and policies that "transcended," he claimed, the exhausted left-right debate that had afflicted the nation for two decades. More particularly, like that of his Democratic predecessor, Jimmy Carter, Clinton's purpose was to move his party to the center and thus prepare it to compete more effectively at a time when the New Deal and Great Society appeared to be losing support in the country. But Clinton appeared to pursue this objective with greater programmatic coherence than had Carter. In 1990, Clinton became the chairman of the Democratic Leadership Council (DLC), a moderate group in the Democratic party that developed many of the ideas that became the central themes of his run for the presidency. As Clinton declared frequently during the campaign, these ideas represented a new philosophy of government that would "honor middle-class values, restore public trust, create a new sense of community and make America work again." He heralded "a new social contract," a "new covenant," one that would seek to constrain, in the name of responsibility and community, the demands for rights summoned by the Roosevelt Revolution. Invoking Roosevelt's Commonwealth Club address, in which FDR first outlined the "economic constitutional order" heralded by the New Deal, Clinton declared that the liberal commitment to guaranteeing economic security through entitlement programs such as Social Security, Medicare, Medicaid, and AFDC had gone too far. The objective of the New Covenant was to correct the tendency of Americans to celebrate individual rights and government entitlement programs without any sense of the mutual obligations they had to each other and their country.[12]

Clinton's commitment to educational opportunity best exemplified the objective of restoring a balance between rights and responsibilities; its central feature, a national service corps, was emblematic of the core New Covenant principle—national community. According to Clinton, a trust fund would be created, out of which any and all Americans could borrow money for a college education, so long as they paid it back either as a small percentage of their life's income or with two years as service by working as teachers, police officers, or child care workers or by participating in other activities that "our country desperately needs."[13]

Clinton's New Democratic message appeared to work. To be sure, his 43 percent share of the popular vote was hardly a mandate. (Indeed, it was roughly the same percentage that losing Democratic candidates had received in the previous three elections.) But support for Clinton was impressively broad. He won a strong 370–168 electoral college majority by sweeping thirty-two states, many of which had not voted Democratic since 1964.

In the congressional elections, the Democrats preserved but did not increase their majorities in both the House and Senate. More than one hundred new members were elected to Congress in 1992, many of them willing to work cooperatively with the new president. Since 1968, the public's striking ambivalence about the parties usually had left the government divided between a Republican president and Democratic Congress. In 1992, however, an exit poll revealed that 62 percent of the voters now preferred to have a presidency and Congress controlled by the same party, in the hope that ideological polarization and institutional confrontation would come to an end.[14]

In truth, Clinton and his allies in the DLC were ambivalent about party politics. Clinton—the first president of the baby boom generation—cut his political teeth during the late 1960s and 1970s when parties were under siege. He rose to national prominence as a luminary of the "new" politics that matured during the 1970s, in which those ambitious for higher office saw no reason to seek the support of old machines and regular organizations. Instead, as a 1984 article celebrating Clinton and other practitioners of the new politics observed, they were "tough, outspoken champions of the movements they [stood] for." Eschewing party politics, they viewed politics as an "exercise in narrowcasting," seeking out people who "shared their vision."[15]

Clinton's disinclination to rely on party organization was reinforced by the tension between the Democratic Leadership Council and the regular party apparatus. The DLC was founded for the most part by elected Democratic officials who believed that the national committee and congressional caucus had become too responsive to liberal constituency groups. In fact, the DLC was divided between those who wanted to reform the party and those who preferred to build a progressive coalition that would transcend parties entirely.[16] Clinton himself appeared to be torn between these two objectives. Even as he styled himself a "new" Democrat who would challenge the liberal orthodoxy of his party, he formed a campaign organization that included many traditional liberals and promised congressional Democrats that he would work in "harness" with them to pursue policies of mutual interest.[17] Clinton's artful fence mending allowed the Democrats to run a unified, effective campaign in 1992; at the same time, his campaign rhetoric was at odds with the majority of liberal activist groups and Democratic members of Congress. The difficulty of reconciling "new" Democratic principles and the traditional commitments of the party would be a constant source of trouble for Clinton, threatening to undermine his authority as a moral leader.

Indeed, Clinton's words and actions during the early days of his presidency seemed to betray his campaign pledge to dedicate the

Democratic party to the new concept of justice he espoused. No sooner had he been inaugurated then Clinton announced his intention to lift the long-standing ban on homosexuals in the military. The president soon learned, however, that there was no prospect that such a divisive issue could be resolved through the "stroke of a pen." To be sure, the development of the administrative presidency since the New Deal gave presidents more power to exercise domestic policy autonomously.[18] Yet with the expansion of national administration to issues that shaped the direction and character of American public life, this power proved to be illusory. Intense opposition from the respected head of the Joint Chiefs of Staff, Colin Powell, and the influential Democratic chair of the Senate Armed Services Committee, Sam Nunn of Georgia, forced Clinton to defer the executive order for six months while he sought a compromise solution. But the delay and the compromise aroused the ire of gay and lesbian activists who had given strong financial and organizational support to Clinton during the election. Most damaging for the new president was that the issue became a glaring benchmark of his inability to revitalize progressive politics as an instrument to redress the economic insecurity and political alienation of the middle class.

The bitter partisan fight in the spring and summer of 1993 over the administration's budgetary program served only to reinforce doubts about Clinton's ability to lead the nation in a new, more harmonious direction. Even though Clinton's budget plan promised to reduce the deficit, it involved new taxes and an array of social programs that Republicans and moderate Democrats perceived as traditional tax and spend liberalism. The Republicans marched in lockstep opposition to Clinton's economic program, especially to his $16 billion stimulus package, which he offered as a partial antidote to the economic contraction that he feared deficit reduction would cause. In April 1993, Senate Republicans unanimously supported a filibuster that killed the stimulus package. Congress did enact a modified version of the president's budgetary plan a few months later, albeit by razor-thin margins and without any support from Republicans, who voted unanimously against it in the House and Senate. Clinton won this narrow, bruising victory only after promising moderate Democrats that he would put together another package of spending cuts in the fall. But this uneasy compromise failed to dispel the charge of his political opponents that Clinton was a wolf in sheep's clothing—a conventional liberal whose commitment to reform had expired at the end of the presidential campaign.[19]

The failure of the Clinton administration and congressional leaders to fulfill their promise of a second round of spending cuts further belied Clinton's claim to be a new Democrat. The Clinton administration linked the prospects for achieving such savings to its "reinventing government" (REGO) initiative. This approach was originally championed by journalist David Osborne and former Visalia, California, city manager Ted Gabler, who argued that the fall of communism and the failure of traditional bureaucracies in the free world to solve basic social and economic problems called for an alternative to standard centralized administration.[20] A prominent feature of Clinton's New Democratic agenda, REGO was the centerpiece of the National Performance Review (NPR), which was commissioned by Clinton and chaired by Vice President Al Gore. Gore's report was issued with much fanfare in September 1993; the administration's public relations campaign included a celebrated appearance by Gore on *Late Night with David Letterman,* in which he mocked the inefficiency of national administrative practices. Such hoopla exploited the public's disdain for big government; in poll after poll, respondents indicated they desired a smaller, less bureaucratic government, even as they expected government to administer large programs such as Social Security, Medicare, and the Clean Air Act. Beyond promising budgetary savings of $108 billion in five years, Gore's report called for "a new customer service contract with the American people, a new guarantee of effective, efficient, and responsive government." REGO would trim 252,000 federal jobs, overhaul federal procurement laws, update the government's information systems, eliminate a few programs and subsidies, and cut bureaucratic tape.[21]

Critics dismissed the promises of government reinvention as hollow rhetoric, and Congress failed to enact Gore's most important recommendations. Nevertheless, as Donald Kettle, a prominent scholar of the American bureaucracy has written, the NPR accomplished far more than critics anticipated: "It energized employees, . . . attracted citizens, . . . drew media attention to government management, . . . and made the point that management matters."[22]

In a major blow to the administration, however, the Congressional Budget Office (CBO) dramatically downgraded claimed savings from the administration's plans to remake the bureaucracy. Unable to come up with an alternative package that satisfied deficit hawks in his party, Clinton nearly suffered a devastating defeat to his economic program. Despite intense administration opposition, a tough bipartisan deficit reduction bill, sponsored by Minnesota Democrat Tim Perry and Ohio Republican John Kasich, lost by only four votes in the House.[23] Sounding an ominous note, Representative Perry complained that the reinventing government initiative was symptomatic of one of Clinton's most serious faults, the tendency to "oversell and underdeliver his programs."[24]

In fact, Clinton said and did little about a New Covenant during the first two years of his presidency. In a February 1993 address to Congress, in which he laid out his administration's goals, Clinton, instead of trumpeting reciprocal obligations between citizens and their government, proposed a new set of entitlements in the form of job training, a college education, and health care. Clinton's proposal to make college loans available to all Americans did include the campaign-touted plan to form a national service corps. But news of the enactment of a scaled-down version of this educational reform program in August was lost amid Clinton's promises to expand the welfare state. In fact, the reciprocal obligation Clinton expected of the beneficiaries of college loans seemed almost apologetic. They will be able to pay the country back with a small percentage of their income, thereby avoiding national service—this option to public service, it seems, greatly dilutes the concept of national community. Indeed, Clinton muddied the message of sacrifice by emphasizing the financial benefit of his reform program to college students.[25]

In this respect, Americorps did not become an "earned entitlement" as the GI Bill had after World War II. "While millions benefitted from the GI Bill," Steven Waldman lamented in the spring of 1999, "only about one percent of 18 year olds have had the AmeriCorps [sic] experience—hardly enough to transform a cultural ethos. While AmeriCorps has established the principle that at least some government benefits should be tied to giving something back to the community, almost all of college aid is still given out according to other criteria, primarily need and academic merit."[26]

The Restoration of Divided Government

The apologetic stance that Clinton displayed in the face of traditional liberal causes was, to a point, understandable; it was a logical response to the modern institutional separation between the presidency and the party. The moderate wing of the Democratic party that he represented—including the members of the DLC—was a minority wing. The majority of liberal interest group activists and Democratic members of Congress still preferred entitlements to obligations and regulations to responsibilities. Only the unpopularity of liberal groups and the emphasis on candidate-centered campaigns in presidential politics made Clinton's nomination and election possible. The media-driven caucuses and primaries that dominate the presidential nomination process gave him an opportunity to seize the Democratic label as an outsider candidate but offered no means to effect a transformation of his party when he took office. Clinton's Democratic predecessor, Jimmy Carter, who intended to be fiercely independent and a scourge to traditional liberal approaches, faced a situation of nearly complete political isolation during his unhappy term in office. To bring about the new mission of progressivism that he advocated during the election, Clinton would have to risk a brutal confrontation with the major powers in the Democratic party, a battle that might have left him even more vulnerable politically than Carter had been.[27] In truth, no president had risked such a confrontation with his party since Franklin Roosevelt's failed "purge" campaign of 1938.[28] It is not surprising, therefore, that Clinton's allies in the DLC urged him to renew his "credentials as an outsider" by going over the heads of the party leadership in Congress and taking his message directly to the people. Most important, the president needed to take his New Covenant message directly to the large number of independents in the electorate who had voted for Perot, DLC leaders argued, so as to forge "new and sometimes bipartisan coalitions around an agenda that moves beyond the polarized left-right debate."[29]

In the fall of 1993, Clinton took a page from his former political associates in his successful campaign to secure congressional approval of the North American Free Trade Agreement (NAFTA). The fight for NAFTA caused Clinton to defend free enterprise ardently and to oppose the protectionism of labor unions, which still represented one of the most important constituencies in the national Democratic party. Clinton's victory owed partly to the active support of the Republican congressional leadership; in fact, a majority of Republicans in the House and Senate supported the free trade agreement, while a majority of Democrats, including the House majority leader and majority whip, opposed it. No less important, however, was the Clinton administration's mobilization of popular support. Indeed, the turning point in the struggle came when the administration challenged Perot, the leading opponent of NAFTA, to debate Vice President Gore on *Larry King Live*. Gore's optimistic defense of open markets was well received by the large television audience, rousing enough support to persuade a bare majority of legislatures in both houses of Congress to approve the trade agreement.[30]

With the successful fight over NAFTA, moderate Democrats began to hope that Clinton had finally begun the task of dedicating his party to principles and policies he had espoused during the campaign. But the defining legislative battle of Clinton's first two years was for the administration's health care program, which promised to "guarantee all Americans a comprehensive package of benefits over the course of an entire lifetime." The formulation of this program appeared to mark the apotheosis of New Deal administrative politics; it was designed "behind closed doors" by the Health Care Task Force, which was headed by the First Lady, Hilary Rodham Clinton, and the president's longtime friend, Ira Magaziner. Moreover, the health care proposal would create a new government entitlement program and an administrative apparatus that would signal the revitalization rather than the reform of traditional social welfare state policy.[31]

Significantly, in his September 1993 speech to Congress on health care reform, Clinton brandished a red, white, and blue "health security card," a symbol of his ambition to carry out the most important extension of social policy since the enactment of social security in 1935. In fact, the Clinton administration's proposal offered an alternative to more liberal and conservative plans. But the president's "third way," which purported both to guarantee universal coverage and to contain costs, resulted in a Rube Goldberg contraption that appeared to require an intolerable expansion of the federal bureaucracy. With its complexity (the bill was 1,342 pages long) and obtrusive bureaucracy, the Clinton proposal was an easy target for Republicans.[32]

Although the administration sounded conciliatory overtures to the plan's opponents, hoping to forge bipartisan cooperation on the Hill and a broad consensus among the general public, the possibilities for comprehensive reform hinged on settling differences over the appropriate role of government that had divided the parties for the past two decades. In the end, this proved impractical—the health care bill died in the 103rd Congress when a compromise measure, negotiated between Senate Democratic leader George Mitchell of Maine and Republican Senator John Chafee of Rhode Island, could not win enough Republican support to break a threatened filibuster.[33] By proposing such an ambitious health care reform bill, Clinton enraged conservatives. By failing to deliver on his promise to provide a major overhaul of the health care system, he dismayed the ardent liberals of his party. Most significant, the defeat of the president's health care program created the overwhelming impression that he had not lived up to his campaign promise to transcend the bitter philosophical and partisan battles of the Reagan and Bush years.

The president and his party paid dearly for these failures in the 1994 election. In taking control of the Congress, the Republicans gained fifty-two seats in the House and eight in the Senate. Moreover, they won dramatic victories at the state and local level: Republicans increased their share of governorships from nineteen to thirty, their first majority since 1970; they also reached near parity in state legislatures, a status they had not enjoyed since 1968. The Republicans achieved this victory in an off year campaign that was unusually ideological and partisan. The charged atmosphere of the campaign owed largely to House minority leader Newt Gingrich (R-GA). Gingrich, his party's choice to be the new Speaker of the 104th Congress, persuaded more than three hundred House candidates to sign a "Republican Contract with America," a "covenant" with the nation that promised to restore limited government by eliminating programs, ameliorating regulatory burdens, and cutting taxes. Clinton's attack on the Republican program during the campaign seemed to backfire, serving only to abet Republicans in their effort to highlight the president's failure to fulfill his promise to "reinvent government." Examining exit polls that suggested that a "massive anti-Clinton coalition came together" to produce the "revolution" of 1994, political analyst William Schneider wrote of the voters' desire for change, "If the Democrats can't make government work, maybe the Republicans can solve problems with less government."[34]

The Republican triumph was especially notable in the South. For the first time in this century, southern Republicans emerged from an election in control of a majority of the governorships, a majority of the seats in the Senate, and a majority of seats in the House.

Republican also gained 119 southern state legislative seats and captured control of three state legislative chambers, the Florida Senate, North Carolina House, and South Carolina House.[35] For the first time since Reconstruction, Republicans elected the Speakers of two southern legislatures. Although white southerners had been rebelling against national Democratic politics since the 1950s, Democratic candidates in the South assumed they could insulate themselves from what southern voters regarded as the most unappealing aspects of the national party.

But Clinton's first two years as president stripped them of this illusion. "Clinton had earned praise as one of the brightest, most agile governors in his region," Dan Balz and Ronald Brownstein wrote after the 1994 elections; "but, as President his policies, from his advocacy of ending discrimination against homosexuals in the military to his economic and health care programs that stressed big-government activism, often seemed like a stick in the eye of his native South."[36] Southerners had expressed a sense of betrayal in their reaction to the progressive policies of Lyndon Johnson and Jimmy Carter; with Clinton, however, their anger spilled over to Democrats in Congress and state government. White southerners' long memories of the Civil War and Reconstruction had helped the Democrats control the Congress for most of the post–New Deal era, even as the South became estranged from the national Democratic party. Now they identified with the Republican party in roughly the same percentages as northern Protestants, the most loyal Republican constituency since the party was founded. As William Galston observed in the wake of this dramatic partisan transformation, "the Civil War is finally over."[37]

The dramatic Republican triumph in the 1994 midterm elections led scholars and pundits to suggest that the nation might be on the threshold of another critical partisan realignment.[38] It remained to be seen, however, whether the New Deal and its aftermath had left room for still another rendezvous with America's political destiny. The emphasis on rights and administrative politics that characterizes contemporary political struggles seems to belie the sort of collective partisan affiliations that have made full-scale party realignments possible in the past. To be sure, the Reagan years showed that party conflict had not withered away, that the New Deal and the opposition it spawned brought a new blending of partisanship and administration, in which administration had become a vehicle for both Democratic and Republican objectives. But the

American people had become alienated from these parties of administration by the 1990s, so much so that the renewal of partisan loyalties in the electorate, let alone a full-scale partisan transformation, seemed unlikely. Indeed, the 1994 elections attenuated the moderate wings of both parties, thus threatening to deepen this alienation. Just as the defeat of southern Democrats strengthened the influence of liberals within the party councils, so the expansion of Republican power in the South deepened the conservative tendencies of the GOP, particularly its commitment to social issues such as school prayer and abortion.

The new Republican majority in Congress and the states was not unmindful of these obstacles to realignment. They promised to pursue a program dedicated to rebuilding the wall of separation between government and society and to cultivating a vital debate about the role of the state in "promoting the General Welfare." Significantly, the Republican Contract with America was silent on the abortion issue. The failure to mention the "rights of the unborn" in this "covenant" with the electorate suggested that some Republican leaders were willing to approach controversial social issues such as abortion more pragmatically. More to the point, this political strategy appeared to signify the determination of some conservatives to moderate programmatic ambitions that presupposed new uses of, rather than a fundamental challenge to, the centralized administrative power created in the aftermath of the New Deal realignment.

The determination of the new conservative majority to challenge the administrative state was also apparent in the sweeping changes that the new Speaker and his allies made in the House rules. House Republicans reduced the number of standing committees and their staffs, limited the tenure of committee chairs, and prohibited closed door hearings and unrecorded votes. These reforms promised to restrain the institutions that had encouraged the House to focus excessively on management of the executive, at the expense of serious public debate about major issues of national policy. Indeed, Speaker Gingrich pledged to Democrats and moderate Republicans a renewed emphases on legislative debate that would "promote competition between differing political philosophies."[39]

Although the new Republican majority promised to rededicate the government to principles of limited government and states' rights, they were hardly unreconstructed Jeffersonians. The Republican contract proposed to strengthen national defense in a form that would require the expansion rather than the rolling back of the central government's responsibilities, and the GOP's proposals to reduce entitlements for the poor and to get government off the back of business demanded the creation of alternative national welfare and regulatory standards.[40] Finally, the Republican party was reluctant to challenge middle-class entitlements such as Social Security and Medicare, which dwarfed the spending of programs that guaranteed a minimum standard of living to the destitute, thus making unlikely a serious reexamination of the core assumptions of the New Deal.[41]

In the absence of a meaningful debate between conservative and liberal principles, the first session of the 104th Congress degenerated into the same sort of administrative politics that had corroded the legitimacy of political institutions since the presidency of Nixon. This time, however, the struggle between the branches assumed a novel form: institutional confrontation between a Democratic White House and a Republican Congress. Amid this struggle, Republicans in the House began to regret, indeed, to reconsider, the institutional reforms they enacted at the beginning of the 104th Congress that reduced the capacity of the legislature to oversee the activities of the executive. The perception that Clinton was an enfeebled president, thwarted at every turn by fierce Republican opposition and unsteady Democratic support, was belied by his aggressive use of the administrative presidency. Beginning in 1995, in fact, the president issued a blizzard of executive orders, regulations, proclamations, and other decrees on matters such as tobacco regulation, labor policy, and environmental protection to achieve his goals, with or without the blessing of Congress. Unlike his initiative on gays in the military, some of these executive orders were well received. But Clinton's actions encouraged the Republican Congress to torment him with investigations and try to "micromanage" domestic and foreign policy, just as Democratic Congresses had assaulted the presidency during the Nixon, Reagan, and Bush years.[42]

Clinton's Resurrection

The battle between Clinton and Congress became especially fierce in a contest over legislation to balance the budget. More than any other idea celebrated in the GOP's Contract with America, Republicans be-

lieved that a balanced budget bill would give them their best opportunity to control Congress for years to come. But their proposal
for a constitutional amendment to require a balanced budget died
in the Senate, where, facing stiff resistance from the president and
his Democratic allies, it failed by one vote to get the necessary two-
thirds support.

With the defeat of this constitutional amendment, Republicans in
the House and Senate put their faith in a bold legislative plan to balance the budget by 2002. The most controversial part of this program
was a proposal to scale back the growth of Medicare, by encouraging
beneficiaries to enroll in health maintenance organizations (HMOs)
and other private, managed health care systems. Rallied by their militant partisan brethren in the House, Republican leaders sought to
pressure Clinton to accept their priorities on the budget by twice
shutting down government offices and even threatening to force the
U.S. Treasury into default. These confrontation tactics backfired.
Clinton's veto of a sweeping budget bill in December 1995, which
would not only overhaul Medicare but also remake decades of federal social policy, roused popular support for the administration.
Most important, Clinton's budgetary stand, signaling his growing
willingness to draw sharp differences between his priorities and
those of the Republican Congress, appeared to preserve the major
programs of the New Deal and its successor, the Great Society. In attacking Medicare and social policies such as environmental programs, the Republicans' militant assault on programmatic liberalism
went beyond what was promised by the Contract with America, thus
giving Clinton the opportunity to take a political stand that was supported by most of the country.

When Congress returned for the second session of the 104th
Congress in January 1996, it was not to Speaker Gingrich's agenda of
reducing the role of Washington in the society and economy, but to
the measured tones of Clinton's third State of the Union message. The
president addressed many of the themes of his Republican opponents, boldly declaring, "The era of big government is over."[43] This
was not merely rhetorical flourish. The National Performance Review
Board's second annual report, issued in September 1995, suggested
that the REGO-spawned budgetary savings and personnel cutbacks
promised by Vice President Gore two years earlier would actually be
achieved.[44] More significant, Clinton withstood furious criticism from
liberal members of his party and signed welfare reform legislation in

August that replaced the existing entitlement to cash payments for low-income mothers and their dependent children with temporary assistance and a strict work requirement.[45]

Clinton conceded that the act was flawed, cutting too deeply into nutritional support for low-income working people and denying support unfairly to legal immigrants. Although he had promised to "end welfare as we know it" during the 1992 campaign, his initiative had called for increased funding for jobs, training, and child care. New Democrats shared with conservatives a commitment to replacing the legal entitlement to welfare with a reciprocal compact linking public assistance to work. But conservative Republicans, disdaining the notion of reinventing welfare as a 1990s version of Harry Hopkins's Works Progress Administration (WPA), incorporated budget savings and strict time limits on adults' receipt of cash assistance into the welfare legislation. Nevertheless, Clinton insisted, by forcing welfare recipients to take jobs, the welfare reform bill served the fundamental principle that he had championed in the 1992 campaign: "recreating the Nation's social bargain with the poor."[46]

By standing for a program that not only required work but also enabled the poor to find decent employment, Clinton and his New Democratic allies claimed the high ground in the welfare debate. Clinton absolved himself of responsibility for the more draconian Republican-sponsored measures of the welfare legislation by taking credit for successfully championing the Earned Income Tax Credit, which was expanded substantially in 1993, and for fending off Republican efforts to scale back support for the working poor during the debate over welfare reform. Characteristically, Clinton tried to have it both ways: he simultaneously appealed to conservatives and moderates by claiming credit for "ending welfare as we know it" while promising liberals that if reelected he would "fix" the flaws in the welfare law.[47]

Indeed, even as Clinton sounded the death knell of big government, his 1996 State of the Union Message called for a halt to Republican assaults on basic liberal programs dedicated to providing economic security, educational opportunity, and environmental protection.[48] Employing Democratic National Committee funds, the White House had orchestrated a national media blitz toward the end of 1995 that excoriated the Republicans' program to reform Medicare and presented the president as a figure of national reconciliation who favored welfare reform and a balanced budget but who also would protect middle-class entitlements, education, and the environment.[49] Clinton's carefully modulated State of the Union message underscored this media campaign, revealing the president as a would-be healer eager to bring all sides together.[50]

Throughout the 1996 election, Clinton held firmly to the centrist ground he had staked out after the 1994 election, campaigning on the same "new" Democratic themes of "opportunity, responsibility, and community" that had served him well during his first run for White House. He won 49 percent of the popular vote to Dole's 41 percent and Perot's 8 percent, along with 379 electoral votes to Dole's 159.

Clinton thus became the first Democratic president to be elected to a second term since Franklin Roosevelt. But his candidate-centered campaign, abetted by a strong economy, did little to help his party. The Democrats lost two seats in the Senate and gained but a modest nine seats in the House, thus failing to regain control of either legislative body. In truth, Clinton's campaign testified to the fragility of the nationalized party system that arose during the 1980s. The president's remarkable political comeback in 1995 was supported by so-called soft money that was designated for party-building activities and thus was not covered by campaign finance laws.[51] But these expenditures were used overwhelmingly to mount television advertising campaigns, such as the media blast of the Republicans during the 1995 budget battles, that championed the president's independence from partisan squabbles. Indeed, Clinton scarcely endorsed the election of a Democratic Congress; moreover, his fund-raising efforts for the party supported congressional candidates only late in the campaign. Adding insult to injury, the administration's questionable fund-raising methods led to revelations during the final days of the election that may have reduced Clinton's margin of victory and thus undermined the Democrats' effort to retake the House.[52]

Balanced Budgets, Impeachment Politics, and the Limits of the Third Way

Clinton staked his success as president on forging "a third way" between Republican conservatism and Democratic liberalism. In part, Clinton's remarkable popularity—his resilience in the face of scandal and a hostile Congress—followed from his ability to rise above the conventional left-right political spectrum. This gift for forging compromise was displayed in May 1997, as the White House and Republican leadership reached a tentative plan to balance the budget by 2002. Arguably, this deal was struck on Republican terms. The most dramatic measures in the budget—the first net tax cut in sixteen years, the largest Medicare savings ever enacted into law, and constraints on discretionary spending below the expected rate of inflation over five years—decidedly shifted priorities in a Republican direction.[53] Just as many liberal Democrats felt betrayed by the president's negotiated settlement, so a number of Republicans acknowledged that Clinton had played a principal part in enacting a conservative policy, one that would have been far more difficult to achieve were one of their own in the White House.[54]

Nonetheless, Clinton exacted some important concessions from the Republicans, enough so that he prevailed on a majority of his partisan brethren in Congress to support the plan. Most significant, the balanced budget act ameliorated, if it did not "fix," the tough remedies of the welfare reform bill. It provided substantial additional funding for immigrant benefits and a bit more for food stamps. It also included $16 billion in spending to cover a new children's health program for low-income working families who were not eligible for Medicaid. Clinton thus accepted certain Republican budgetary priorities but stood his ground on partial fulfillment of his promise to renegotiate a fair new social contract with the poor.[55]

To be sure, this uneasy agreement between the White House and the Republican-controlled Congress was made possible by a revenue windfall caused by the robust economy, thus enabling Clinton and GOP leaders to avoid the sort of hard choices over program cuts and taxes that had animated the bitter struggles of the 104th Congress.[56] Those hard choices would still have to be made if long-term entitlement reform was to be achieved. Even so, this rapprochement, which brought about the first balanced budget in three decades, testifies to the potential of modern presidents to advance principles and pursue policies that defy the sharp cleavages characteristic of the nationalized party system. As Levin and Landy note in chapter 1 of this volume, the partial emancipation of presidential elections and governance from partisan squabbles represents potentially an important ingredient of a moderate policy regime.

Yet, as the House impeachment and Senate trial of Clinton dramatically revealed, the "extraordinary isolation" of the modern presidency has its limits.[57] Just as the Reagan and Bush presidencies were plagued by independent counsels who investigated abuses in those administrations, so Clinton's troubles started with the Ethics in Government Act. Republicans had long opposed reauthorization of the independent prosecutor statue, considering it an unconstitutional infringement on the executive's prosecutorial authority, but their resistance to Democratic efforts to reauthorize the statute came to an end in 1993, when the Whitewater scandal emerged.[58]

In early January 1998, Independent Counsel Kenneth Starr was authorized to expand the scope of the Whitewater inquiry to pursue allegations that the president had an affair with a White House intern, Monica Lewinsky, and that his intimate Vernon Jordan had encouraged her to lie under oath about it. Remarkably, as the Lewinsky scandal unfolded in 1998, the public continued to express overwhelming approval of Clinton's performance in office. This expression of support reflected not only approbation for the president's third-way policy positions and his management of the economy but also general disapproval of Starr's tenacious investigation into Clinton's peccadilloes as well as the eagerness with which the Republican-controlled Congress exploited the results. Nonetheless, few Democrats came to the president's defense, underscoring that while Clinton may have had allies in Congress, he had few close friends there. Most Democrats did oppose an impeachment inquiry, but this stance represented their disdain for the Republican majority rather than support for a president who appeared indifferent to their programmatic commitments and election prospects. In fact, as the *New York Times* reported, "it is the people who know [Clinton] best—from his own former aides to his wary fellow Democrats in Congress—who have been most disappointed and angry about his handling of the Monica Lewinsky matter, and who have held it against him more harshly than a detached and distant public."[59]

With the decline of Clinton's personal stature, nearly every political expert predicted that the Republicans would emerge from the 1998 elections with a tighter grip on Congress and, by implication, on the president's political fate.[60] But having been preoccupied by the Lewinsky scandal for the entire year, the Republicans were left without an appealing campaign issue. They were unable to increase their 55–45 margin in the Senate and lost five seats in the House, leaving them a slim 223–211 margin. Just as Clinton was the first Democrat since FDR to be reelected, so he now became the first president since Roosevelt to see his party gain seats in a midterm election. Bitterly disappointed by the results, the Republicans fell into soul-searching and recriminations; ironically, it was the hero of their 1994 ascent to power, Speaker Newt Gingrich, and not Clinton, who was forced from office: after the elections, Gingrich announced that he was giving up not only his leadership position but also his seat in Congress.

The 1998 elections and their aftermath appeared to take the steam out of the House's impeachment inquiry. But as the president gathered with friends and aides to celebrate what seemed to be another remarkable political resurrection, the Republicans prepared to move forward with the impeachment inquiry. A centrist, poll-driven politician, Clinton, as well as most pundits, underestimated the willingness of Republicans in Congress to defy they survey-tested will of the people.[61] In December, after a year of dramatic and tawdry politics on both sides, Clinton was impeached on charges of perjury and obstruction of justice by a bitterly divided House of Representatives, which recommended virtually along party lines that the Senate remove the nation's forty-second president. Hoping to become a great president in the tradition of Franklin Roosevelt, Clinton now became the first elected president to be impeached by the House of Representatives.

Even impeachment, however, did not undermine the president's popular support. Soon after the House's historic action, large majorities of Americans expressed approval of Clinton's handling of his job, opposed a Senate trial, and proclaimed Republican members of Congress as "out of touch with most Americans."[62] The public's support of the president and the small Republican majority in the Senate encouraged discussion among senators about the possibility of substituting a motion of censure for a protracted, agonizing impeachment trial. But Republican leaders were determined not to abort the constitutional process, even though acquittal of the president on the articles of impeachment seemed foreordained. After a five-week-long Senate trial, the president's accusers failed to gain even a majority vote on either of the charges against Clinton: on February 12, 1999, the Senate rejected the charge of perjury, 55–45, with ten Republicans voting against conviction; then, with five Republicans breaking ranks, the Senate split 50–50 on a second article accusing the president of obstruction of justice. Clinton's job was safe. Moreover, the trial and tribulations of the impeachment process encouraged bipartisan opposition to the Ethics in Government Act, which Congress failed to reauthorize when its authority lapsed in the summer of 1999.

Still, whatever moral authority Clinton may have had at the beginning of his administration to establish a new covenant of rights and responsibilities between citizens and their government was shattered by the public disrespect for his morality. Indeed, the virulent partisanship that characterized the impeachment process forced Clinton to seek refuge once again among his fellow Democrats in Congress, thus short-circuiting plans to pursue entitlement reform as the capstone of his presidency.[63] In the wake of the impeachment debacle, Clinton positioned himself as the champion of Social Security and Medicare, urging Congress to invest a significant share of the mounting budget surplus in the salvation of these traditional liberal programs.[64] Clinton's extraordinary resiliency, it seemed, was achieved at the cost of failure to fulfill his promise to correct and renew the progressive tradition.

Conclusion: Clinton and the Politics of the Welfare State

Clinton's dramatic ups and downs are attributable both to his qualities as a leader and to the political circumstances he faced. The wayward path of new democracy reveals how the third way can all too easily degenerate into a plebiscitary form of democracy, in which citizens directly invest their support in an individual leader and then, all too often withdraw it. Just as surely, Clinton's tainted success sheds light on his political time, on the love-hate relationship that Americans have formed with the welfare state. Even as liberalism became a discredited doctrine, the Reagan revolution failed to roll back many of its programmatic achievements. Republicans won dramatic electoral victories, most notably in 1980 and 1994, by promising to get government off the backs of the people; yet, the public's persistent commitment to middle-class entitlements, such as Social Security and Medicare, environmental and consumer protection, and health and safety measures raises doubts about Clinton's claim that "the era of big government is over."

Most Americans are hopeful that the late New Deal era can provide them with all the good things, with programs they support, without the centralized administration they have long been taught to shun and fear, and with benefits that secure the general welfare, without destroying individual responsibility. These are not necessarily incompatible goals, but they are unlikely be reconciled without the renewal of principles and institutions that foster a sense of collective obligation. In calling for reciprocal responsibility, and in slouching toward the reform of entitlements, Clinton "ingeniously addressed the political liabilities of the Democratic party," one of his close advisers has noted. "But," he continues, "'new' Democratic politics were crafted to serve Clinton's own political ambition; the Third Way did little to help the party's strength in Congress and the States."[65] Indeed, it has been coopted not only by the new Republican president, George W. Bush, but also by leaders in Great Britain, Holland, Germany, and even Italy. For better or worse, today there is a real sense in which we are all "New Democrats."

One does not have to be a devotee of the present party system— or one of the shrinking core of partisan loyalists—to find some aspects of the third way deeply troubling. In relying on personal charm and organization to advance new Democratic principles, and in subordinating the collective mission of his party to his personal political fortunes, Clinton may have further weakened, rather than invigorated, civic life in the United States. In the final analysis, a meaningful "reinvention" of government can be conceived only from a great contest of opinion, by a painful but necessary struggle over the relative merits of the Democratic and Republican understandings of constitutional government. Clinton's view that the debate between these two understandings was forlorn did not excuse him from partisan engagement; rather, such a position demanded the building of a third party, of a collective organization with a past and a future. All previous realignments have required extraordinary partisan leadership, in which reform presidents have played a principal part in forming a new party or remaking an existing one.[66] But developments since the Progressive era—the direct primary, campaign finance laws, the expansion of national administrative power, and the rise of the mass media—have encouraged presidents to seek office and govern as the heads of organizations they have created in their own image. Although this "extraordinary isolation" has enabled modern presidents to become the common center of American democracy, it has deprived them of an opportunity to make a lasting mark on the nation. In the end, the successes and failures of third-way politics shed light on the imposing power yet fragile authority of the modern presidency—as well as the unsteady ground on which the "moderate policy regime" described in this volume sits.

Notes

1. Cited in William Leuchtenburg, *In the Shadow of FDR: From Harry Truman to Ronald Reagan*, rev. ed. (Ithaca, N.Y.: Cornell University Press, 1985), 49.

2. Oscar Handlin, "A Self Portrait," *Atlantic Monthly* (November 1963): 68.

3. Richard Neustadt, *Presidential Power and the Modern Presidents: The Politics of Leadership Roosevelt to Reagan*, 4th ed. (New York: Free Press, 1990), 139.

4. Robert Blake, *Disraeli* (New York: St. Martin's, 1967), 477.

5. On the concept of "political time," see Stephen Skowronek, *The Politics Presidents Make: From John Adams to Bill Clinton* (Cambridge, Mass.: Harvard University Press, 1997).

6. Theodore White, *America in Search of Itself: The Making of the President, 1956–1980* (New York: Harper & Row, 1982), 124.

7. I make this argument more fully in Sidney M. Milkis, *The President and the Party: The Transformation of the Party System since the New Deal* (New York: Oxford University Press, 1993).

8. Benjamin Ginsberg and Marin Shefter, *Politics by Other Means: Politicians, Prosecutors, and the Press form Watergate to Whitewater*, revised and updated edition (New York: Norton, 1999), 41.

9. Linda Greenhouse, "Ethics in Government: The Price of Good Intentions," *New York Times*, February 1, 1998; and Cass R. Sunnstein, "Unchecked and Unbalanced: Why the Independent Counsel Act Must Go," *The America Prospect* (May–June 1998): 20–27.

10. For a more complete treatment of the "new" party system, see Sidney M. Milkis, *Political Parties and Constitutional Government: Remaking American Democracy* (Baltimore: Johns Hopkins University Press, 1999), chapter 6.

11. Alan Brinkley, "Roots," *New Republic*, July 27, 1992, p. 45.

12. William Clinton, "The New Covenant: Responsibility and Rebuilding the American Community," Washington, D.C., October 23, 1991. This speech marked the first pronouncement of these "sacred principles." From then on, Clinton repeated them at every defining moment of his journey to the White House: the announcement of Senator Albert Gore, who shared his ideas, as his running mate; the party platform; his acceptance speech at the Democratic convention in New York; and his victory remarks in Little Rock on election night.

13. Similar ideas and attendant policy proposals are spelled out in detail in Will Marshall and Martin Schramm, eds., *Mandate for Change* (New York: Berkeley, 1993).

14. William Schneider, "A Loud Vote for Change," *National Journal*, November 7, 1992, p. 2544.

15. "Champions of the People," *Esquire* (December 1984): 447.

16. Interviews with Will Marshall, president, Progressive Policy Institute, and Al From, president, Democratic Leadership Council, May 20, 1997.

17. Dan Balz, "Democrats' Perennial Rising Star Wants to Put a New Face on the Party," *Washington Post*, June 25, 1991, p. A4; E. J. Dionne, "Democratic Hopefuls Play for Solidarity, *Washington Post*, March 15, 1992, p. A21; Helen Dewar and Kenneth Cooper, "Clinton Seeks Partnership for Change on Hill," *Washington Post*, April 30, 1992, p. A16; and David Von Drehle, "Clinton's Movers and Shakers," *Washington Post*, March 23, 1992, p. A1.

18. Richard Nathan, *The Administrative Presidency* (New York: Wiley, 1983).

19. Sidney Blumenthal, "Bob Dole's First Strike," *New Yorker*, May 3, 1993, pp. 40–46; Douglas Jehl, "Rejoicing Is Muted for the President in Budget Victory," *New York Times*, August 8, 1993, pp. 1, 23; David Shribman, "Budget Battle a Hollow One for President," *Boston Globe*, August 8, 1993, pp. 1, 24.

20. David Osborne and Ted Gabler, *Reinventing Government: How the Entrepreneurial Spirit Is Transforming the Public Sector* (Reading, Mass.: Addison-Wesley, 1992).

21. Al Gore, *Creating a Government That Works Better and Costs Less: Report of the National Performance Review, September 7, 1993* (Washington, D.C.: Government Printing Office, 1993).

22. Donald F. Kettl, *Reinventing Government: Appraising the National Performance Review* (Washington, D.C.: Brookings Institution, 1994), ix.

23. "Democratic Chiefs Apply Brake to Spending-Cut Juggernaut," *Congressional Quarterly Weekly Report,* November 23, 1993, p. 3186. For a discussion of the political damage Clinton suffered in the budget battles of 1993, see Paul Pierson, "The Deficit and the Politics of Domestic Reform," in *The Social Divide: Political Parties and the Future of Activist Government,* ed. Margaret Weir (Washington, D.C.: Brookings Institution, 1998), 148–152.

24. Penny cited in Fred Barnes, "Gored," *New Republic*, September 20 and 27, 1993, p. 12.

25. William Clinton, "Address before a Joint Session of Congress on Administration Goals," *Weekly Compilation of Presidential Documents,* February 17, 1993, pp. 215–224; Jill Zuckerman, "Pared Funding Speeds Passage of National Service," *Congressional Quarterly Weekly Report,* August 7, 1993, pp. 2160–2161. The story of Americorps's creation is told in Steven Waldman, *The Bill: How the Adventures of Clinton's National Service Bill Reveal What Is Corrupt, Comic, Cynical—and Noble—about Washington* (New York: Viking, 1995).

26. Steven Waldman, "Nationalize National Service," *Blueprint* (Spring 1999): 20.

27. Indeed, during the early days of his presidency, Clinton sought to identify with his party's leadership in Congress and the national committee—partly, one suspects, to avoid the political isolation from which Carter suffered. Whereas Carter kept party leaders in Congress and the national committee at arms length, Clinton sought both to embrace and to empower the national organization. The White House lobbying efforts on Capitol Hill focused almost exclusively on the Democratic caucus, and the administration relied heavily

on the Democratic National Committee to marshal public support for its domestic programs. Interviews with White House staffer, November 3, 1994, not for attribution; David Wilhelm, chairman, Democratic National Committee, October 18, 1993; and Craig Smith, political director, Democratic National Committee, October 19, 1993. Also see Rhodes Cook, "DNC under Wilhelm Seeking a New Role," *Congressional Quarterly Weekly Report*, March 13, 1993, p. 634.

28. On the 1938 "purge" campaign, see Milkis, *The President and the Parties,* chapter 4.

29. Al From and Will Marshall, *The Road to Realignment: Democrats and the Perot Voters* (Washington, D.C.: Democratic Leadership Council, July 1, 1993), 1-3–1-5.

30. David Shribman, "A New Brand of D.C. Politics," *Boston Globe*, November 18, 1993, p. 15; Gwen Ifill, "56 Long Days of Coordinated Persuasion," *New York Times,* November 19, 1993, p. A27.

31. Address to Congress on Health Care Plan, printed in *Congressional Quarterly Weekly Report,* September 25, 1993, pp. 2582–2586; Robin Toner, "Alliance to Buy Health Care: Bureaucrat or Public Servant," *New York Times,* December 5, 1993, pp. 1, 38.

32. For a fuller account of the health care reform battle, see Haynes Johnson and David S. Broder, *The System: The American Way of Politics at the Breaking Point* (Boston: Little, Brown, 1996); and Theda Skocpol, *Boomerang: Clinton's Health Security Effort and the Turn against Government* (New York: Norton, 1996).

33. Adam Clymer, "National Health Program, President's Greatest Goal, Declared Dead in Congress," *New York Times,* September 27, 1994, pp. A1, B10. For a sound and interesting case study of the Clinton health care program, see Cathie Jo Martin, "Mandating Social Change Within Corporate America," paper presented at the Annual Meeting of the American Political Science Association, September 1–4, 1994, New York City. Martin's study shows that health care reform became the victim of a battle between "radically different worldviews about the state and corporation in modern society."

34. William Schneider, "Clinton: The Reason Why," *National Journal,* November 12, 1994, pp. 2630–2632. Schneider cites a nationwide poll by Voter News Service revealing that voters who approved of the job Clinton was doing as president (44 percent of all those who voted) cast their ballots for Democrats in House elections by 82 percent Democrat, 18 percent Republican. Those who disapproved of his performance (51 percent of all who voted) chose Republicans by 83 percent Republican, 17 percent Democrat.

35. Dan Balz and Ronald Brownstein, *Storming the Gates: Protest Politics and the Republican Revival* (Boston: Little Brown, 1996), 205–206.

36. Ibid., 207.

37. Remarks of William Galston, lecture at Harvard University, December 2, 1994.

38. Steven Gettinger, "'94 Elections: Real Revolution or Blip on Political Radar?" *Congressional Quarterly Weekly Report,* November 5, 1994, pp. 3127–3132; Richard L.

Berke, "Epic Political Realignments Often Aren't," *New York Times*, January 1, 1995, section 4, p. 3.

39. Michael Wines, "Republicans Seek Sweeping Changes in the House's Rules," *New York Times*, December 8, 1994, pp. A1, B21; Wines, "Moderate Republicans Seek an Identity for Gingrich Era," *New York Times*, December 26, 1994, pp. 1, 22.

40. Republicans disagree about whether the appropriate path to a conservative revolution is federalism or national conservative policy. With respect to re-forming the Aid to Families with Dependent Children program, for example, the Republican Contract with America proposed to expand the flexibility of the states, allowing them to design their own work programs and determine who participates in work programs. In fact, states would have the option to opt out of the AFDC program and convert their share of AFDC payments into fixed annual block grants, thus removing federal control over the program. For those states that would stay in the program, however, the contract called for national standards to determine eligibility, to attack illegitimacy and teen pregnancy, and to establish work requirements. As John J. Dilulio and Donald Kettl argue in their analysis of the contract, "every relevant study indicates that nationally initiated contract-style welfare reforms can be achieved only where significant resource increases are made in the government bureaucracies." Similarly, with respect to regulatory policy, the Contract envisioned strengthening federalism by ending the practice of imposing unfunded federal mandates on state and local governments; at the same time, it called for the protection of property rights against "takings" in a form that would greatly reduce the discretion of states and localities to control land use. See Richard A. Harris and Sidney M. Milkis, *The Politics of Regulatory Change: A Tale of Two Agencies*, 2d ed. (New York: Oxford University Press, 1996), chapter 7.

41. Although many pundits were quick to view the 1994 election results as the end of the New Deal, neither Democrats nor Republicans sought to make changes in the largest entitlement program, Social Security, or to end the enti-tlement status of Medicare. See Robert Pear, "Welfare Debate Will Re-Examine Core Assumptions," *New York Times*, January 2, 1995, pp. 1, 9.

42. Peter Baker and John F. Harris, "Clinton Seeks to Shift Focus by Using Executive Powers," *Washington Post*, April 11, 1997, p. A1; John H. Cushman, "Clinton Sharply Tightens Air Pollution Regulations Despite Concerns over Costs," *New York Times*, June 26, 1997, p. A1; Allan Freedman, "Oversight: Lack of Focus Leaves GOP Stuck in the Learning Curve," *Congressional Quarterly Weekly Report*, November 1, 1997, pp. 2649–2655; Robert Pear, "The Presidential Pen Is Still Mightier Than the Sword," *New York Times*, June 28, 1998.

43. William Clinton, "Address Before a Joint Session of Congress on the State of the Union," January 23, 1996, printed in *Congressional Quarterly Weekly Report*, January 27, 1996, pp. 258–262.

44. Al Gore, *Commonsense Government* (New York; Random House, 1995), 7.

45. Many public officials and journalists claimed that the new law put an end to "a sixty-one-year-old entitlement to welfare." In truth, the AFDC program never existed as an entitlement in the sense that Social Security and Medicare

did. The program only guaranteed federal matching funds to states that established AFDC programs. See R. Shep Melnick, "The Unexplained Resilience of Means-Tested Programs," paper delivered at the Annual Meeting of the American Political Science Association, Boston, September 3–6, 1998.

46. William Clinton, "Remarks on Signing the Personal Responsibility and Opportunity Reconciliation Act," August 22, 1996, *Weekly Compilation of Presidential Documents,* no. 1484.

47. R. Kent Weaver, "Ending Welfare as We Know It," in Weir, *The Social Divide,* 396.

48. Clinton, State of the Union Address, January 23, 1996.

49. Bob Woodward, *The Choice* (New York: Simon & Schuster, 1996), 344.

50. Not surprisingly, Clinton's speech received praise from the Democratic Leadership Council's president, Al From, who celebrated it as an attempt "to speak to the main concerns of the millions of disaffected voters in the political center" who were estranged from the ideological and institutional combat between liberal and conservatives and "were likely to be the margin of difference in the 1996 election." From "More Than a Good Speech: The State of the Union Address Could Have Marked a Turning Point in History," *New Democrat* (March–April 1996): 35–36.

51. Anthony Corrado, "Financing the 1996 Elections," in *The Elections of 1996,* ed. Gerald Pomper (Chatham, N.J.: Chatham House, 1997). "Soft money" was provided for in the 1979 amendments to the campaign finance legislation of 1974, as part of the broader effort to strengthen national party organizations. By 1992, both Democrats and Republicans had come to depend on it to finance the expensive media campaigns that dominated national elections. As such, the parties violated the spirit of the 1979 amendments, which were dedicated to increasing party spending on traditional grassroots boosterism and get-out-the-vote drives rather than mass media campaigns. More to the point, the institutional separation between the president and parties allowed—indeed, encouraged—the exploitation of these funds by presidential candidates. See Beth Donovan, "Much-Maligned 'Soft Money' Is Precious to Both Parties," *National Journal,* May 15, 1993, pp. 1195–1200.

52. Michael Nelson, "The Election: Turbulence and Tranquility in Contemporary American Politics," in *The Elections of 1996,* ed. Michael Nelson (Washington, D.C.: Congressional Quarterly Press, 1997), 52; and Gary Jacobson, "The 105th Congress: Unprecedented and Unsurprising," in Nelson, *The Elections of 1996,* 161.

53. Daniel J. Palazzolo, *Done Deal? The Politics of the 1997 Budget Agreement* (Chatham, N.J.: Chatham House, 1999), 189.

54. "Can you imagine what they would be doing to us if this was a Republican-only plan?" admitted one GOP Budget Committee member. "They would be killing us," he continued. "Clinton gave us the cover to do some things. I think this is better than if Dole were president." Cited in Palazzollo, *Done Deal,* 100. For the Democratic reaction to the budget package, see Alison Mitchell, "Despite Angry Colleagues, Clinton United His Party," *New York Times,* May 6, 1997, p. A12.

55. Weaver, "Ending Welfare as We Know It," 397.

56. Richard Stevenson, "After Year of Wrangling, Accord Is Reached on Plan to Balance the Budget by 2002," *New York Times,* May 3, 1997, p. 1.

57. The term "extraordinary isolation" is Woodrow Wilson's. See his *Constitutional Government in the United States* (New York: Columbia University Press, 1908), 69.

58. Kathy Hariger, "Independent Justice: The Office of the Independent Counsel," in *Government Lawyers: The Federal Bureaucracy and Presidential Politics* (Lawrence: University Press of Kansas, 1995), 86.

59. Adam Clymer, "Under Attack, Clinton Gets No Cover from His Party," *New York Times,* March 16, 1997, p. 1; Todd S. Purdum, "Clinton Most Charming at a Distance," *New York Times,* September 17, 1998, p. 18. One Clinton official who knew the president well acknowledged that even as he went into the administration eagerly, his enthusiasm was tempered by "Clinton's lack of firm attachment to any principles and his undisciplined nature. . . . Clinton is a talented leader, but his major influence is one of effect—there is no moral compass or sense of direction." Interview with Clinton official, not for attribution, May 28, 1998.

60. Janny Scott, "Talking Heads Post-Mortem: All Wrong, All the Time," *New York Times,* November 8, 1998, p. A22.

61. Richard L. Berke, John M. Broder, and Don Van Natta Jr., "How Republican Determination Upset Clinton's Backing at the Polls," *New York Times,* December 28, 1998.

62. "Early Views after Impeachment: The Public Supports Clinton," *New York Times,* December 21, 1998.

63. Interview with Will Marshall, president, Progressive Policy Institute, June 14, 1999.

64. David E. Rosenbaum, "Surplus a Salve for Clinton and Congress, *New York Times,* June 29, 1999.

65. Interview with Democratic official, not for attribution, July 12, 1999.

66. On this point, see Marc Landy and Sidney M. Milkis, *Presidential Greatness* (Lawrence: Kansas University Press, 2000).

16

Two-Tier Politics Revisited

Wilson Carey McWilliams, *Rutgers University*

Two-tier politics framed discussion of the presidential crisis of 1998–99, with almost all analysis referring to the distinction in attitude between political insiders and the general public. Interestingly, the ordinary stereotypes were reversed: it was people in the governing circles who moralized about the presidency, deploring conduct unworthy of the office, while mass opinion seemed to reflect a subtle pragmatism.[1]

In August 1998, Thomas Mann of the Brookings Institution reported that Washington conversation dominantly held that Clinton should leave office, one way or another; Democrats were only a little less likely to share in the general indignation, even though, for partisan reasons, they eventually rallied behind the president.[2] From the beginning, by contrast, polls indicated the broader public's belief that Bill Clinton's "improprieties"—his affair and even his deceptions under oath—were less damaging to American institutions than his opponents' insistence on *exposing* them.[3] Mass opinion, Alan Wolfe wrote, was "in tune with Realpolitik," while "official Washington," insistently didactic, could not let go.[4]

Social conservatives such as William Bennett, like Beckett characters waiting for Godot, expected a popular outrage that never materialized.[5] Most Americans, while believing that Clinton had lied and lacking respect for him as a person, considered the scandal irrelevant to his presidency. Like the Kansan George Pyle described, they apparently considered Clinton a "successful example in a line of work—perhaps in a nation—where success requires doing things we all used to see as slightly crooked."[6]

In that view, Clinton's capers only confirmed the more depressing perception that, like the king in the old story, democratic government itself has no clothes.

In part, the problem of two-tier politics inhered in the American founding, with its creation of a large republic defined by forms—legal distinctions, relatively complicated institutions, and an artifactual politics in which we are equal "before the law." Necessarily, the government established by the Constitution lacked the affective qualities and organic relationships of smaller communities, so that even the states, themselves relatively large republics, seemed more or less homelike.[7] The national government, Alexander Hamilton conceded, would be "less apt to come home to the feelings of the people, and in proportion, less likely to inspire a habitual sense of obligation and an active sentiment of attachment." The Framers were content to hope for the moderate allegiance likely to be won by a "much better administration" and by a relatively thin and expert representation. The virtues of the federal government, Hamilton predicted, would "chiefly be perceived and attended to by speculative men."[8]

This aspect of the American regime, however, has been grotesquely exaggerated in our time: the increasing scale and complexity of public and economic life, the escalating pace of change, the fragmenting of local community, the ascendancy of the mass media, and the decline of party organizations and loyalties—all the familiar lyrics of political lament—have strained or snapped the linkages between most citizens and policymaking elites. (For the sake of clarity, I should add that when I refer to policy "elites," as I do when the synonyms seem exhausted or inappropriate, I am not speaking of a social stratum—"the elite"—with a coherent view or interest. Rather, following a grand tradition in political science, I am thinking of individuals with skills, offices, or other resources that afford them disproportionate influence in shaping public policy alternatives.)[9]

Inside the beltways, the society that surrounds the centers of government is thick with organized interests, policy advocates, and officials and characterized by a high level of knowledge about the intricacies of policy and the networks of power. Outside, at varying degrees of distance, the mass electorate is weakly articulated, mostly baffled, and certainly removed from policy deliberations.[10] In policymaking, the members of the first tier speak, broadly, in their own voices and are allowed to develop their positions with considerable nuance and complexity. The second tier, by contrast, speaks largely through aggregate data assembled from comparatively simple responses to questions posed by others.[11] In deliberation, Harvey Mansfield observes, even passionate or biased speakers are constrained to give reasons; in mass politics, "individuals do not even have to state their opinions, much less defend them."[12] What passes for public opinion, increasingly, is solicited in private places and defined in private terms, while the inner circles address the electorate almost exclusively in sound bites and slogans.

American political life offers most citizens only a voicelessness that—especially in a country so inclined to discount loyalty and to cherish the individual's liberty to exit—leads not only to a lessened interest in politics but to *deauthorization,* the qualification of allegiance.[13] This retreat leaves first-tier experts relatively unencumbered but limited in the support they can expect and, consequently, in what they can hope to achieve. In public, policy has to be defended largely in terms of a "no-pain" politics that asks for no significant sacrifices. In 1997, for example, Congress and the White House could draw on the electorate's traditional support for the principle of balancing the budget and, as Eric Patashnik indicates in chapter 2 of this volume, there was no longer any strong basis for disagreement among policymaking elites. But while it favored the idea abstractly, the public also was in no mood for austerity; consequently, Congress and the president agreed to cut taxes in a time of considerable prosperity, avoided addressing the problems of the entitlements, and postponed major spending cuts until the later years of the project. That prosperity, increased revenue, and the vision of a surplus seem to have taken governing elites off the hook—at least, for the moment—does not change the quality of the decision at the time or its implications for democratic politics.[14]

Since important policies do involve costs and hurts, policy elites face a growing temptation to rely on covert (or "low-visibility") politics—on deliberations and policies that, if not literally secret are so defined as to be arcane, impenetrably technical, and shrouded by a rhetoric of deception (as in such ugly neologisms as revenue enhancement, downsizing, and outsourcing) or by acrobatic accounting. (The fact that so much more information is screened or printed paradoxically amounts to another sort of disguise, only increasing the public's confusion. Even where the facts are tolerably clear, the majority of citizens are apt to be muddled. In 1996, for example, most voters believed that the deficit had increased rather than decreased during Clinton's years in office, probably because, while the *annual* deficit had fallen, the *total* deficit continued to rise.) Policymaking moves off the political stage, away from elections, public forums and clearly defined statutes, and public principles lose importance relative to the application of those principles by administrations and courts.[15] (At the same time, the public is intruding, via cameras, in areas such as criminal investigations and trials where, although administration *should* be insulated, the issues are personal and more or less comprehensible.)

Moving away from elections and statutes, policymaking seems to be mirroring postmodernism's distrust of structures and categories, just as the turn to administration and to courts parallels the postmodern emphasis on particular contexts and singular events.[16] It might even be said, with only a dash of mischievousness, that postmodernism is an ideology of the administrative state.

Be that as it may, both "no-pain" and covert politics are asking for trouble, the first because it ignores problems or treats them superficially, and the second because—found out or suspected—it increases the public's distrust and resentment of government, sentiments the media are all too ready to reflect and amplify.[17]

And at best, government's legitimacy is under siege: increasing numbers of Americans doubt government's ability to deal with the forces at work in their lives, and any serious effort to confront those dark and shadowy powers—rapidly changing, high-level technologies in the context of globalization—requires government to make itself over in their image, accentuating two-tier politics. For too many of us, government is simply another incomprehensible and overwhelming presence, prudently regarded as malign. The national mood skirts the borders of paranoia: One poll in 1995 found that some eleven million Americans regarded government as an enemy; almost half the public, *Newsweek* told us, believes in UFOs and is convinced the government is covering up the story, while close to a third (29 percent) believe the government is in contact with aliens.[18] Conspiracy theories are a staple of the entertainment industry, to say nothing of ostensibly serious public figures.[19] A great many, if not most, of us would rather believe that government is malevolent than that it is incompetent or powerless, and there are plenty of indications of a widely felt desire for someone who can "take charge."[20]

It is easy to understand why policy experts, feeling the need for informed action, are not eager to rouse a public that seems short-sighted and recalcitrant when it is not simply goofy. But both tiers are inclined to agree that American democracy faces great problems and a shadowed future, and the *strong* democratic policy that seems to call for, like strong democracy generally, presumes public support proportioned to its measures and to the powers of the time.[21]

My primary aim is to discuss resistance to policymaking elites, but I want to begin by acknowledging the force of Martin Shapiro's argument (see chapter 18 of this volume): consensus among elites is powerful and often decisive in shaping policy, not the least because it has a powerful claim to our respect. Of course, policy elites do not always or even often agree; ordinarily, they appear on the public stage in conflict or competition. Partly for that reason, however, a high degree of commonality among elites, where it exists, is likely to seem unarguable, setting the terms and limits of intelligent debate.[22]

Consensus among elites is almost certain to be decisive under two conditions: (1) where ordinary citizens see no clear *prescriptive* basis for judging policy and (2) where *experience* and the working principles of everyday life do not testify against what elites say. The 1996 presidential campaign offered a dramatic instance in the rapid decline of Steve Forbes's "flat tax" proposal. Attractive in its simplicity, initially well received and not greatly damaged, among Republican primary voters, by "populist" critiques, Forbes's scheme was badly hurt by a consensus among economists, who agreed it would add to the deficit and work to the disadvantage of the middle class. (By contrast, economists had not spoken with similar authority against Reagan's "supply-side" notions, a fact many economists had come to regret.) But where moral convictions or experience intervene, elites may find the going more difficult.

For example, if the American Psychological Association (APA) announced that a fetus does (or doesn't) have a soul (or a psyche, the soul's more secular equivalent), its opinion would make a difference, just as it did when the APA removed homosexuality from the list of "mental diseases," but no one would expect such an intervention to be *decisive*. Where issues seem morally comprehensible, voters show a kind of tenacity, which is just what the tradition of political theory would lead us to expect: when theorists have praised ordinary citizens, it is chiefly for their ability to prescribe, to weigh policy in the scales of decency.

However, for contemporary voters, issues do not often present themselves as clear moral alternatives. Parties and political groups, after all, adapt to the prescriptions registered by polls and elections: those on the wrong side of majority moral judgment move, at least rhetorically, toward the center, hoping to blur the moral lines of division.

But precisely because they are more confident of their ability to prescribe, voters are insistent about keeping issues that pose moral alternatives high on the political agenda. Political insiders often find this irksome or surprising. In the early going in 1996, Senator Robert Dole's position on abortion was astonishingly confused, probably reflecting a desire to preserve his freedom to maneuver or compromise; he should have known, however, that any such strategy would be difficult or impossible, especially in Republican primaries.[23]

The fact that the broad public is attracted to issues that pose morally comprehensible alternatives suggests that any major change in policy should be cast in prescriptive terms capable of mobilizing popular support. By contrast, in developing its health care plan, the Clinton administration sought a broad elite consensus through a covert politics that avoided public debate and sought to enlist the widest possible range of interested groups, particularly in the insurance industry. The resulting proposal epitomized "first-tier" politics: it was a Dungeons and Dragons of policy, so maddeningly complicated that it lent itself to distortions by opponents who played on the public's fears and its knowledge that it can easily be deceived. In effect, the Clinton plan obscured prescriptive choice, a crucial factor in its ultimate defeat.

By contrast, to overcome entitlement "rights talk," buttressed by the claims of compassion, welfare reform depended on a moral case: the argument that justice links benefits to obligations and that the very dignity of those who receive requires that they be expected to contribute. The plan Congress enacted is full of defects—somewhat masked by the comparative prosperity of the times—but the lack of a moral basis for public assistance is not one of them, which accounts for its continuing popularity.

Opposition to elites, if only of a sullen sort, is also likely where their arguments seem disconnected from day-to-day existence. In most nonprofessional circles, the claim that America faces a "labor shortage" (and hence, among other things, that we need immigration) is at least suspect. Even at the recent strikingly low levels of unemployment, experience seems to teach a different lesson. Relatively few Americans can define the Phillips Curve, much less account for its new unreliability. Millions know firsthand, however, that fear that jobs may disappear works to moderate wage demands; they may even intuit that the dread of inflation set off by labor scarcity—so common at the Fed and among economic elites generally—reflects a perception that we may be entering a market favorable to labor as opposed to capital, one in which enterprises will be compelled to pay higher wages even at the cost of borrowing. For great numbers of American wage earners, that seller's market seems overdue, a position that may be interested and parochial, but not one that policymakers can afford to discount.

The disparity between elite consensus and mass experience, in fact, points toward a familiar political dialectic. In the first instance, the gap is apt to result in two-tier thinking, as it did in the mid-1980s, when it was common for surveys to report that a plurality of respondents regarded the economy as doing well, while feeling that they themselves were doing badly. Given an adequate army, Bertrand Russell wrote, he would undertake

> to make the majority of the population believe that two and two are three, that water freezes when it gets hot and boils when it gets cold. . . . Of course, even when these beliefs had been generated, people would not put the kettle in the refrigerator when they wanted it to boil. That cold makes water boil would be a Sunday truth, sacred and mystical, to be professed in awed tones, but not to be acted on in daily life.

Dissenters, Russell concluded, would be "frozen" at the stake.[24]

Russell came too close for comfort, but—even discounting for hyperbole—he exaggerated the power of elites, even in totalitarian states. In a liberal democracy, if two-tier discontinuity is radical and persistent, it is almost inevitable that antielites will emerge to challenge the dominant consensus.

In the late nineteenth century, to cite a familiar example, American farmers were told, plausibly enough, that declining prices were the result of "overproduction."[25] But the facts of American life offered an opportunity for populist orators such as Mary Ellen Lease, who questioned whether it was possible to speak of overproduction "when 10,000 little children, so statistics tell us, starve to death every year in the United States." Lease suggested, in other words, that the problem lay not with production but with distribution, buttressing her case with that elite-rivaling appeal to "statistics."[26]

Yet while antielites may offer counterexplanations better suited to experience, except in very unusual cases and situations, these counterdoctrines will be *synthetic*, adopting some—possibly crucial—elements of elite theorizing. Even Lease, after all, suggested that the farmers of Kansas "raise less corn" along with "more Hell," and populism's strategy of inflation remained tied to the belief—"magical," Russell called it—that money must be based on precious metals.[27] Whatever its defects, that deliberative process is democracy's way of reaching for political community.

Epitomizing the bases of public resistance to elites, the crisis of 1998–99 also signaled the need for that sort of democratic deliberation. To most citizens, experience seemed to testify on Clinton's behalf, in the most immediate of ways: on the whole, Americans associated his administration with prosperity and suspected anything that might rock the ship of state. It was even more important that Clinton's critics were unable to dent the popular *moral* judgment that lying about sexual matters is nearly universal and largely appropriate and that the president's "personal weakness" did not amount to a "willful abuse of public trust."[28]

Yet this implicit popular analysis is open to very serious objection. It turns on a *privatized* view of the presidency, holding that the office, attorney-like, exists to serve our interests, and that personal character is irrelevant, so long as the president "gets the job done." This is Machiavellianism in its bourgeois, Anglo-American form, a disposition that, looking askance at sacrifice, is all too prone to exchange democratic citizenship for personal comfort.

By contrast, elites were more likely to think about Clinton's conduct in terms of *public* principles, especially the government's ability to challenge our habits and interests in the name of self-government. In the impeachment debate, conservatives—scandalizing Republican pragmatists—were evidently willing to pay a significant price to do what they took to be their constitutional duty. And liberals, though they came down on the president's side, saw his lapses as more than private failings. Effectively, Richard Cohen wrote, the president made Lewinsky "a gift of his power," betraying his own vocation, risking and almost certainly losing great public things for tawdry and private ones.[29] And in the House and Senate, perhaps the strongest argument against removing the president was the contention that the charges against him were not grave enough to warrant overturning the verdict of that constitutional sacrament, a democratic election—a defense, in other words, not of a person or an interest but of a *form*.

Democrats still have faint hopes of profiting from the lingering irritation with the impeachment process and the congressional Republicans who spearheaded it, but in general, both tiers have seemed eager to move on to less painful things. The health of American democracy, however, requires serious effort to bridge the rift between the tiers, and soon.[30]

In our time, too many discontents smolder in the dark corners of two-tier politics. It is hardly surprising, for example, that elites—"out of touch" almost by definition—underestimate the public's ambivalence about technological change. Popular doubt is evident in the almost unchallenged support for environmentalism, a vague persuasion but one certainly committed to "preservation" or "conservation"—that is, to setting *limits* to change, even though most stop well short of outright Green hostility. Gingrich's futurism, now back in the closet, put the GOP too visibly on one side; the Clinton administration, and especially Vice President Gore, tried to play a safer hand, combining an airy devotion to nature with a passionate embrace of the "information revolution." But the first tier has been put on notice that it still tends to underrate its opposition.

In December 1999, a coalition of labor, environmental, and human rights groups successfully derailed meetings of the World Trade Organization (WTO) in Seattle, also throwing the city into disorder. For elites, the result was unexpected, an evident "miscalculation" of the strength and intensity of the distrust of and opposition to globalization. Characteristically—and shrewdly—Clinton bent with the wind, the president making himself into something of a spokesman for the protesters' concerns, and at this writing, subsequent protests have only been shadows of Seattle's. But the demonstrations are an indication of our discontents: fascinated with the new gadgetry and eager for its advantages, Americans are also—and increasingly—aware of their own vulnerabilities.[31]

Rapid technological change (and here, Gingrich conspicuously got it wrong) never democratizes. It undermines old elites, but it creates new ones, the princes of technique; most of us will, with effort, master a piece of the new technology only to discover that it has become obsolete. Most of us suspect, as Kurt Vonnegut predicted in *Player Piano*, that the new order threatens to displace even mental labor.[32] At the same time, the new technologies seem on the way to completing the fragmentation of local communities and social control. They make it possible to overcome pluralistic ignorance, enabling our better angels to find and sustain each other, but as we are learning, they allow at least as many very nasty imps to discover that they, too, are not alone. Perhaps most important, the new technologies do not remove, and may accentuate, the inequality of power: as recent elections continue to demonstrate, the massive resources it takes to make a difference in national politics are still a matter for elites.[33]

At the lighter level of nuisance, ordinary citizens have similarly mixed feelings about deregulation. Policymakers, and especially consumer advocates, speak with near unanimity about the benefits of competition, a theory that the public by and large accepts. In practice, however, matters are not so clear.[34]

Telephone service is an illustrative case, and probably not an extreme one. Competing for customers, companies avoid any simple standard of price comparison, confronting us with an array of plans, each with its nuances and special costs. And this says nothing about added complexities such as "slamming" or phone booths operated by obscure and very expensive companies. The advantages, in this sort of competition, go to elites who can afford the "information costs" of sorting through plans and who can negotiate from strength. Deregulation, Robert Reno writes, "bewilders us with life-complicating incomprehensibility and revenue-enhancing nonsense," turning "what used to be a public service into a lactating cash cow."[35] Whatever the truth of Reno's criticism, the evidence testifies pretty clearly that ordinary citizens, exasperated, are inclined to tune the competitors out, so that price competition becomes ineffective and almost beside the point. In 1996, NYNEX, sensing the mood, found it useful to run ads on television appealing to the desire for "peace" as opposed to competitive "war." And so far, the deregulation of electricity—on the experience of California—only underlines such impressions.[36]

Irritations like these, however, are symptoms of a more fundamental problem. The "mantra" of contemporary economic policy elites, Louis Uchitelle observes, has been the doctrine that long-term prosperity, in the "competitive intensity" of the new marketplace, requires a freedom to innovate of which downsizing and wage inequality are inescapable elements.[37] In this conventional wisdom, "unrelenting pressure" on the labor force is crucial to the economy's well-being, and business, Stephen Roach argues, has become "fixated" on cutting labor costs.[38] And not only business: those who aim to "protect anyone from losing," Vice President Gore said in 1997, are in effect willing to "pull the nation down."[39]

This prescription for a two-tier society, and the two-tier politics necessary to sustain it, is at least a "recipe for mounting tensions" in the short term and, as old experience tells us, is not likely to survive any sharp downturn in our economic fortunes.[40]

It is a straw in the wind that the 1997 UPS strike—to the surprise of economic elites—evoked a broad sympathy for labor.[41] More and more Americans are part of—or feel an uneasy sympathy for—the economy's second tier, with its low or stagnating wages and its growing reliance on part-time labor, less rewarded with benefits and easier to discharge.[42] Especially if the economy falters, there is reason to expect stronger support for the view that social stability, work, and home are goods at least as important as an increasing gross national product (GNP) and probably more important to civic dignity and self-government.[43]

The best example of this mood is also the most obvious— Clinton's 1997 retreat from his doomed request for extended "fast-track" authority in international trade. When the North American Free Trade Agreement (NAFTA) and fast-track policies first appeared on the public's horizon, their consequences were theoretical and speculative, and while there were forebodings and bleak forecasts, most Americans accepted the assurances of that vast majority of policy experts who championed freer trade. So far, however, practice—in personal encounters or through the media—tells a different story: imports are outpacing exports, with a net loss of high-paying jobs, accompanied by a continuing series of horrendous accounts of working conditions and human rights violations.[44]

Policy elites again supported the president's 1997 request with remarkable unanimity, but their very confidence may have been a problem. The "sin of certitude," Representative Sander Levin (D-MI) called it, one that discounted present troubles in favor of futuristic abstractions: Vice President Gore, Representative Bill Pascrell

(D-NJ) remarked, "is caught up in 21st century macroeconomics." And John Broder and Lizette Alvarez, reporting in the *New York Times*, could not resist making the ironic comment that the White House and its allies were shocked that members of Congress would listen to "the petty parochial concerns of their constituents, mere voters."[45] Even so, the president's defeat should not be interpreted as a victory for protection: dozens of members of Congress who opposed the president's request went out of their way to declare themselves, in principle, to be supporters of free trade, even as they insisted that such trade be "fair." An optimistic reading might even treat the result as a signal victory for democratic deliberation.[46] And in fact, that the administration won congressional approval, in 2000, for "normalized" trade with China testifies to its intense attention *to* members of Congress and their local problems. Warned in 1997, Clinton and his allies fought a better campaign in the political trenches.

The half-empty aspect of that glass, however, is that the setback for fast-track—like the defeat of impeachment—was merely a negation, another instance of deauthorization, and that, for policy and for the polity, is not good enough. (Nor is it adequate, for that matter, that the president persuaded Congress on trade with China: judging by the polls, popular sentiment inclined to the other side, not yet persuaded that the prospect of economic gain trumps the risk of losing jobs and the tacit acceptance of China's abysmal record on human rights.)

Among American citizens, the level of disenchantment is already dangerously high. No one, I think, has said it better than Howard Baker did in trying to understand the electorate in 1994: "I don't know where they are going," he remarked, "and I don't think they know where either. But . . . if we do not address their feelings, they may develop a tendency to savage our institutions."[47] As the aftermath of that election ought to suggest, the majority were not voting to dismantle government so much as seeking a government that speaks for them as well as to them. A politics of reauthorization is not simply mobilizing citizens to support government; it includes limiting policy initiatives to those that have made their case in and through the democratic process.[48]

Taken literally, bringing government closer to the people suggests devolving its functions, wherever possible, to localities and states, a program with a distinguished history as well as contemporary support. Tocqueville, admired these days around almost all political campfires, taught that, in America, decentralization was the foundation of public authority: "In no country in the world does the law hold so absolute a language as in America, and in no country is the right of applying it vested in so many hands."[49] And on the whole, voters seem to favor the "new federalism," their suspicions of the federal government warming their feelings for governments nearer home.

This tendency is worth supporting, but its possibilities are severely limited. In the first place, state governments are only comparatively close to us; especially in the large states, they are large-scale, complicated bureaucracies, only marginally more accessible to citizens. In fact, during the crisis of 1998–99, *local* elites were often almost as much out of touch with mass opinion as their national counterparts.[50] It is probably even more important that, in at least two respects, constitutional and fiscal, states and localities lack the resources to address our problems and concerns effectively, which radically limits their claims on our allegiance. In relation to the Constitution, this is part of an old story: John Smilie, a Pennsylvania Antifederalist, warned that a centralization of loyalties was only a matter of time, since the Constitution made state governments "weak and useless to every beneficial purpose" and the people would not forever "idolize a shadow."[51] For us, it's easy to see Smilie's wisdom: the regulation of commerce, especially in an age of global economics, is beyond the constitutional reach of states; even Vermont, with statewide zoning, is apparently unable to resist the intrusion of Wal-Mart, protected as that locally destructive retailer is by the federal commerce power.

And financially, states depend on the federal government's power to tax and spend. "Block grants," favored by conservatives and partisans of state authority generally, offer the states *discretion* in spending but do not change the fact of dependence. This is especially true since the motives of the supporters of this sort of federalism are mixed, partly decentralizing but partly economizing, and in their new form, federal grants are not cast as entitlements. It seems likely that governors and state officials will find it even more necessary to make an annual, hat-in-hand pilgrimage to Washington. Too much of the "new federalism," in other words, seems to offer a decentralized *government* on the basis of a centralized *politics*.[52]

Another strategy for bridging the two tiers aims at improving the quality of representation, giving citizens a more adequate voice in federal councils, and campaign reform is at least one logical place to begin. In our version of democracy, elections are the crucial link between the public and its government, the one institution in which citizens act as sovereigns.

Today's electoral campaigns, however, do not greatly increase our confidence in or strengthen our authorization of public life and policy, and they may even make matters worse. Around the country, prevailing opinion is increasingly apt to hold that money and organized interests call the political tune. Before Clinton's more intimate improprieties forced them off-stage, the Democrats' 1996 fund-raising was the Republicans' scandal of choice, but in 1997, congressional inquiries were met with little more than indifference. Week after week, the press reported new instances of Democratic sleaziness, and it was made abundantly clear that there wasn't much that the president and vice president wouldn't do for a campaign buck.

In and around the District of Columbia, these revelations caused a considerable stir. In the broader public, the hearings did begrime Vice President Gore's hitherto clean image, and they convinced most voters that Democrats had raised more money than Republicans in 1996, an idea several parsecs wide of the truth. They did surprisingly little damage to the Democrats, however, because citizens in the second tier took it more or less for granted that the GOP had been just as bad, just as they discounted as a trivial technicality the question—had President Clinton broken the law by engaging in fund-raising from the Oval Office?—that had engrossed members of the first tier.[53] In the election of 2000, the electorate seemed at least as indifferent to renewed Republican attacks on fund-raising improprieties by Gore and his party, a fact that only underlines the extent of deauthorization.

Some campaign reform legislation is certainly desirable, and while Republican zeal has waned as Democratic sympathies have waxed, enough Republicans remain committed to make at least cosmetic changes a possibility. But serious campaign reform faces a formidable obstacle in the Supreme Court's finding, two decades ago, that campaign contributions are speech, broadly protected by the First Amendment.[54] Scott Turow is kind when he calls that decision "puzzling." As Turow points out, the "act of spending money is not in and of itself an expression of political opinion," and on the Court's reasoning, vote buying would seem equally entitled to be enshrined by the Bill of Rights.[55] Still, even within the limits set by *Buckley v. Valeo,* it would help if Congress, while permitting continued "soft-money" contributions for "party-building activities," enumerated such activities so as to include support for local party staffs, organizations, meetings, and conventions but excluding advertising on television. Legislation of that sort would at least have the effect of extending face-to-face politics and reweaving, if only marginally, the personal connections between citizens and policy.

More generally, strengthening the relationship between citizens and their representatives—ideally to the point of political acquaintance and friendship—calls for civic trust, which demands political judgment and courage more than mere promise keeping. Christine Whitman based her 1997 New Jersey gubernatorial campaign around the slogan "Promises Made, Promises Kept," and she almost lost, partly because voters who admired her for trustworthiness often decided, in retrospect, that they did not like what she had done or, even more, what she had failed to do. And it is hard to tell whether Republican efforts to fulfill the Contract with America did the party more good than harm.

The representative relation, moreover, is two sided: voters need to feel responsible *toward* those they elect. Strong representation presumes mutual accountability and hence, to sound the most familiar and ignored theme of political science, the reciprocal loyalties of party.

Clearly, something is wrong with the American party system. It may be that we are—as interest in third or fourth parties suggests—on the edge of a major partisan realignment, even though the Reform Party's catastrophe in 2000 suggests otherwise. But the major parties also have a very mixed record when it comes to translating voter resentments into responsible policy alternatives. The Republicans get better marks; I have devoted most of my attention in this essay to economic concerns because popular discontent with the cultural elites *has* found a voice, if not always a coherent or constructive one, on their side of the aisle. The Democrats, by contrast, have been lucky to do as well as they have. Led by the president, the party has softened its stance on the old social "wedge" issues, but the president's disinclination to conflict reinforced the Democrats' tendency to be the "party of things as they are." They need, I think, to be much more articulate in speaking for the economic grievances of working Americans.

In general, both parties have become overcentralized bureaucracies, overdependent on money and those who donate it, armed with polls and slogans and sound bites but fearful of real public debate. Our politics, in fact, has lost the capacity to amuse, which once was, H. L. Mencken said, its saving grace.[56] Unlike our government, there is no constitutional barrier to rebuilding local parties and politics, although it would surely require some friendly legislation and the repeal of at least some of the antiparty measures enacted in the name of reform. In the end, a decentralized *politics* may be the best and safest means of reauthorizing the central *government* that seems a political necessity in these times.

Notes

1. John R. Zaller, "Monica Lewinsky's Contribution to Political Science," *PS* 31 (1998): 182–189.

2. Richard L. Berke, "Split between Commentators and the People May Help Clinton," *New York Times*, August 20, 1998, p. A20.

3. In January 1998, respondents were already blaming the president's "political enemies" by a margin of 51 to 39 percent; almost two-thirds said, in a February poll, that the public did not need to know about the scandal (*New York Times*, January 27, 1998, p. A13, and February 24, 1998, p. A16). By August, 68 percent were saying the country would have been better off without the investigation (Carey Goldberg, "The People, Just Wanting It All to Be Over," *New York Times*, August 15, 1998, p. A8). The numbers dropped slightly, and briefly, after Clinton's first confession, but then reasserted themselves (*New York Times*, August 22, 1998, p. A10).

4. Alan Wolfe, "Oh, Those Beltway Innocents," *New York Times*, August 30, 1998, Week in Review section, p. WK13; E. J. Dionne referred to Washington as "obsessed" with the scandal in his Pi Sigma Alpha lecture, "1948–1998: Harry Truman Meets Monica Lewinsky," delivered to the New England Political Science Association, Worcester, Massachusetts, May 1, 1998.

5. William J. Bennett, *The Death of Outrage: Bill Clinton and the Assault on American Ideals* (New York: Free Press, 1998).

6. George Pyle, "In Kansas, We Call It Politics as Usual," *New York Times*, March 8, 1997, p. 23.

7. Cato, Letter to the *New York Journal* (undated) in *The Complete Anti-Federalist*, ed. Herbert Storing (Chicago: University of Chicago Press, 1981), 2: 111.

8. *The Federalist*, ed. Jacob Cooke (Middletown, Conn.: Wesleyan University Press, 1961), number 17; see also number 27, 63.

9. Paul Goldstene, *Revolution American Style* (Novato, Calif.: Chandler & Sharp, 1997), 110; for the tradition of elite analysis, see Harold Lasswell, *Politics, Who*

Gets What, When, How (New York: McGraw-Hill, 1936), or Gabriel Almond, *The American People and Foreign Policy* (New York: Praeger, 1960), 136–157.

10. Douglas Arnold makes similar observations in *The Logic of Congressional Action* (New Haven, Conn.: Yale University Press, 1990).

11. In the Lewinsky scandal, as in similar Washington imbroglios, it mattered that members of the elite had been lied to *personally,* an offense more deeply resented than being lied to *en masse,* especially if one feels, as so many citizens do, that in the latter setting, lying is the rule. See Wolfe, "Oh, Those Beltway Innocents."

12. Harvey C. Mansfield Jr., *America's Constitutional Soul* (Baltimore: Johns Hopkins University Press, 1991), 170.

13. I am drawing here on the terms developed by Albert Hirschman, *Exit, Voice and Loyalty* (Cambridge, Mass.: Harvard University Press, 1970).

14. Robert McIntyre and Michael Ettinger, "Will the President Sign Tax Bills That Don't Add Up?" *Washington Post National Weekly,* July 28, 1997, p. 23. The current policy consensus, of course, excludes any serious attention to the strong case against making budget balancing a fetish. See, for example, Robert Levine, "The Economic Consequences of Mr. Clinton," *Atlantic Monthly* (July 1996): 60–65. For a broader, more theoretical discussion, see Paul Pierson, "The New Politics of the Welfare State," *World Politics* 48 (1996): 143–179. Paul Krugman indicates that the fundamental issues remain largely unresolved: "The Pig in the Python," *New York Times,* June 21, 2000, p. A23.

15. Theodore J. Lowi, *The End of Liberalism* (New York: Norton, 1969); Benjamin Ginsberg and Martin Shefter, *Politics by Other Means* (New York: Basic Books, 1990); John Kenneth Galbraith, "Coolidge, Carter, Bush, Reagan," *New York Times,* December 12, 1988, p. A16.

16. On postmodernism, see Leslie Paul Thiele, *Thinking Politics* (Chatham: Chatham House, 1997), 81, 83.

17. Reporting that eight out of ten professors of education regarded the public's views of education (including those of students) as "outmoded and mistaken," Richard Marin was inclined to agree with Deborah Wadsworth of Public Agenda that such "rarified blindness" is so detached from education's sources of support as to be "counterproductive." "Lessons from the Education Professors," *Washington Post National Weekly,* November 17, 1997, p. 31.

18. *Washington Post National Weekly,* May 22–28, 1995, p. 37; *Newsweek,* July 8, 1996, p. 50.

19. Frank Rich, "The New World Order," *New York Times,* April 27, 1997, p. E15.

20. Richard Rorty, *Achieving Our Country* (Cambridge, Mass.: Harvard University Press, 1998), 90–91. Consider only movies like *Independence Day* or *Air Force One.*

21. Benjamin R. Barber, *Strong Democracy* (Berkeley: University of California Press, 1984; Theda Skocpol, *States and Revolutions* (New York: Cambridge University Press, 1989), 4, 33. Jack L. Walker observed that stronger policy goals create an imperative for a stronger organization of the public, at least in interest groups ("The Origins and Maintenance of Interest Groups in

America," *American Political Science Review* 77 [1983]: 403). Also, as Cathie Jo Martin notes, the importance of organized interests has risen with the declining effectiveness of Congress and the parties as links with the public ("Business and the New Economic Activism," *Polity* 27 [1994]: 57). But interest groups, structured by private concerns, are no adequate defenders of civic values. On the problem of self-government and the future of democracy, see Theodore J. Lowi, "Think Globally, Lose Locally," *Boston Review* (April/May 1998): 4–10.

22. Bryan D. Jones, *Reconceiving Decision-Making in Democratic Politics: Attention, Choice and Public Policy* (Chicago: University of Chicago Press, 1994).

23. In the politics of the abortion issue, pro-life advocates have focused on the attempt to ban late-term abortions as a "wedge," a first acknowledgment that there are some limits to "choice," and the moral terms of debate—virtual infanticide versus the health of the mother—tilt in their favor. Many Democrats, from conviction or convenience, now support the ban, but—fearing the very slippery slope their opponents hope for—the president's prochoice allies, if not his own principles, kept him from accommodating himself to opinion.

24. Bertrand Russell, *Unpopular Essays* (New York: Simon & Schuster, 1950), 95.

25. Of course, this reference to problems caused by overproductivity is startling to contemporary ears.

26. Cited in John D. Hicks, *The Populist Revolt* (Minneapolis: University of Minnesota Press, 1931), 160.

27. Russell, *Unpopular Essays,* 91–92; Willard Fischer, "'Coin' and His Critics," *Quarterly Journal of Economics* 10 (1896): 187–208.

28. Sean Wilentz, "Pleading for Their Political Lives," *New York Times,* August 24, 1998, p. A17; Janny Scott, "Bright, Shining or Dark: The American Way of Lying," *New York Times,* August 16, 1998, Week in Review section, p. WK3. Moral distaste for the president's enemies—widely felt in relation to Kenneth Starr, virtually universal in the case of Linda Tripp—was also a major weapon in Clinton's arsenal.

29. Richard Cohen, "For Clinton, Truth Is Optional," *Washington Post National Weekly,* August 10, 1998, p. 27; see also Robert Kuttner, "Collateral Damage of the Clinton Mess," *Berkshire Eagle,* September 13, 1998, p. A9.

30. David Broder, "Time for National Soul-Searching," *Washington Post National Weekly,* November 30, 1998, p. 4; Michael Sandel, *Democracy's Discontent* (Cambridge, Mass.: Harvard University Press, 1996).

31. David Sanger, "The Shipwreck in Seattle," *New York Times,* December 5, 1999, p. 26, and "President Chides World Trade Body in Stormy Seattle," *New York Times,* December 2, 1999, p. A1; see also Joseph Kahn, "Clinton Shift on Trade: 'Wake-Up Call,'" *New York Times,* January 31, 2000, p. A6.

32. Kurt Vonnegut, *Player Piano* (New York: Dell, 1952).

33. Jacques Ellul, *The Technological Society* (New York: Vintage, 1964), 208–218.

34. Robert Kanigel, "Too Much of a Good Thing," *Washington Post National Weekly,* January 12, 1998, p. 25.

35. Robert Reno, "Phone Companies Give No Quarter," *Newsday,* October 12, 1997, p. F9. See also Seth Schiesel, "The No.1 Customer: Sorry, It Isn't You," *New York Times,* November 23, 1997, Business section, p. BU1.

36. Agis Salpukas, "Power Deregulated, Customers Yawn," *New York Times,* February 26, 1998, p. D1. By 2000, a great many California customers were actively complaining about brown-outs in the Bay Area and radically rising electric bills in San Diego, leading the state to a measure of reregulation. James Sterngold, "In Reverse, California Acts to Cap Some Electric Bills," *New York Times,* August 22, 2000, p. A14.

37. Louis Uchitelle, "Puffed Up by Prosperity, the U.S. Struts Its Stuff," *New York Times,* April 27, 1997, p. E1.

38. Stephen Roach, "The Worker Backlash," *New York Times,* August 24, 1997, p. E3.

39. Dan Balz, "The Battle to Seize the Heart and Soul of the Democrats," *Washington Post National Weekly,* June 9, 1997, p. 11.

40. Roach, "Worker Backlash"; Thomas Palley, "The Forces Making for an Economic Collapse," *Atlantic Monthly* (July 1996): 44–58.

41. Steven Greenhouse, "In Shift to Labor, Public Supports UPS Strikers," *New York Times,* August 17, 1997, p. 1.

42. Louis Uchitelle, "Strike Points to Inequality in Two-Tier Job Market," *New York Times,* August 8, 1997, p. A22; Jeff Madrick, "The UPS Strike Delivers a Message," *Washington Post National Weekly,* August 18, 1997, p. 21; academics, in their increasingly adjunct-ridden profession, know the problem only too well.

43. Alan Greenspan has indicated some support for this view, though as a warning rather than a prescription. Richard W. Stevenson, "Trade Support Is Dwindling, Fed Chief Says," *New York Times,* August 26, 2000, p. C1. For a more sympathetic perspective, see Roach, "Worker Backlash"; it is worth remarking that the classics of political theory associate Republican government with austerity.

44. Before NAFTA, in 1992, the United States recorded a $5.4 billion surplus in its trade with Mexico; in 1995, it ran a deficit of $15.4 billion (Palley, "The Forces Making for an Economic Collapse," 58). See also Kenneth Lynn, "Second Thoughts on Free Trade," *New York Times,* July 13, 1997, p. F12.

45. Katharine Q. Seelye, "Gephardt, Long on Sideline, Scores a Touchdown at Last," *New York Times,* November 12, 1997, p. A28; John M. Broder and Lizette Alvarez, "Democrats Sound Like a Couple in Need of Therapy," *New York Times,* November 15, 1997, p. A11. The Pew Research Center found that 82 percent of policy experts and officials supported "fast-track" authorization, as against 47 percent of the general public. John F. Harris and Peter Baker, "The Public Wasn't Sold on Fast Track," *Washington Post National Weekly,* November 11, 1997, p. 11.

46. Similarly, when Democratic House leaders wrote the president opposing an amendment to the International Monetary Fund (IMF) Charter that would promote the unrestricted movement of capital across national boundaries—without corresponding provisions allowing restrictions to protect workers or human rights—they did so, party strategists said, to keep Democrats united in support

of the administration's request for $18 billion in new IMF funding. Eric Schmitt, "Top Democrats May Not Back IMF Outlay," *New York Times*, May 2, 1998, p. A1.

47. *New York Times*, November 10, 1994, p. B4.

48. An argument anticipated, in every way that matters, by Dwight Waldo, *The Administrative State* (New York: Ronald, 1946).

49. Alexis de Tocqueville, *Democracy in America* (New York: Knopf, 1980), volume 1: chapter 5.

50. For example, the *Canton Repository*, which had endorsed Clinton in both 1992 and 1996, called for his resignation after the release of the Starr Report, arguing that Clinton had "destroyed" his presidency, only to discover that ordinary people in its relatively conservative area supported the president. Michael Winerip, "Bellwether's Rank and File Strongly Support Clinton," *New York Times*, September 30, 1998, p. A1.

51. John Bach McMaster and Frederick D. Stone, eds., *Pennsylvania and the Federal Constitution, 1787–1788* (Philadelphia: Historical Society of Pennsylvania, 1888), 270–271. Hamilton pretty much agreed: arguing that the federal government would not usurp state authority, he offered the less than reassuring comment that to any person of ambition, state powers would seem only "troublesome" and "nugatory." *The Federalist*, number 17.

52. Paul Peterson, *The Price of Federalism* (Washington, D.C.: Brookings Institution, 1995). On the recent politics of decentralization see Adam Clymer, "Switching Sides on States' Rights," *New York Times*, June 1, 1997, p. E1.

53. Carey Goldberg, "Response to a Furor: Ho-Hums," *New York Times*, February 28, 1997, p. A26; Garry Wills, "Politics by the Old Rules," *New York Times*, March 4, 1997, p. A23.

54. *Buckley v. Valeo*, 424 U.S. 1 (1976).

55. Scott Turow, "The High Court's Twenty Year Old Mistake," *New York Times*, October 12, 1997, Week in Review section, p. WK 15.

56. H. L. Mencken, *Prejudices: A Selection*, ed. James T. Farrell (New York: Vintage, 1955), 123–124.

17

Exit "Equality,"
Enter "Fairness"

Eugene Bardach, *University of California, Berkeley*

Unlike the rest of the chapters in this book, this one is not mainly about policy outcomes or political institutions but about policy ideas. More precisely, it is about the conceptual frameworks in which ideas and policies are debated at both the elite and the mass-public levels. Such frameworks are significant because they reflect the ways in which politicians and the public define problems and evaluate solutions. They also affect the political fortunes of the parties to the debate.

I describe here a seeming shift in the relative prominence of two partially overlapping but partially competing frameworks that organize America's dialogue about "social justice." These are the traditional "equalitarian-individualist" framework and the newer "social reciprocity" framework organized around arguments over the "fairness" of terms in an evolving social contract. My principal intention in this chapter is to explicate the newer, and hence the less apparent, of these two. Although I offer some conjectures about the reasons for the seeming shift in frameworks and about the speed of the shift, I do not mean to assert them with much force, as much more research on these matters is clearly needed.

The Traditional Framework

Since the New Deal, the ideological dialogue about social justice has been organized around two questions: How much should the government do to promote greater equality of opportunity?[1] How much should it do to help those in distress? This dialogue has taken place within a conceptual framework built on differing evaluations of equalitarianism and individualism. Liberals traditionally have believed in government action to promote equality of opportunity (and, for some, equality of condition) and to aid unfortunates. Conservatives, valuing individualism and property rights and rejecting governmental efforts to abridge greatly either of these through taxation or regulation, have regarded both inequality and a certain amount of distress as more or less inevitable. Because most people do not hold extreme or particularly well-organized liberal or conservative ideologies, popular attitudes toward social policy have been distributed on a rough equalitarian-individualist (EI) continuum with clustering toward the center.

This framework for dialogue has endured in part because it has in some sense been "useful." That is, it has pointed to real problems, real solutions, real shortcomings in proffered solutions, and real trade-offs. But the EI framework is much less useful today in organizing the dialogue about social justice than it has been. Though it continues to be a useful source of partisan rhetoric, particularly for the conservatives, it is declining in "realism" or "relevance." This decline, in turn, can be traced to the declining relevance of one end of the EI continuum, equality. As Ronald Dworkin writes, "Equality is the endangered species of political ideals."[2] Why should this be so?

First, if the ideal of equality is defined as what most Americans seem to care about, equality of opportunity for the population somewhere below the median, this seems increasingly far-fetched. "Opportunity" is accessed not only by means of tangible assets such as education and training but by many sorts of intangible family, community, and cultural assets as well.[3] Both types of assets, but particularly the latter, are acquired by growing up in stable, safe families and communities that successfully inculcate habits of discipline and self-restraint in many or most of their members. Almost by definition, the millions of people who live in that loosely defined stratum "the underclass" are undersupplied with such assets.

In some cases, no amount of compensatory effort by government subsidies, professional "interventions," or other such external agents will compensate for failures in basic socialization processes. More generally, when compensatory efforts are possible at all, they are not cheap. For instance, the noted economist James Heckman estimated in 1994 that simply to restore the *lesser degree of inequality*

between the college educated and those with a high school education or less that had prevailed in 1979 would require an investment
of \$1.66 trillion.[4] Clearly, little would be left over for all the other
things that "justice" and other pro–social values also prescribe, such
as extending access to medical care, cleaning up the environment,
and supporting the arts. Furthermore, as the economic returns to
better education are now increasing, the social groups that are relatively less able to take advantage of education are going to fall farther behind. From almost any point of view, "social justice" now is
not so much a question of furnishing the disadvantaged with
"equality" of opportunity but with sheer *adequacy* of opportunity.[5]

Second, trust in governmental institutions as reliable instruments for achieving any goals at all, including equalitarian goals,
has declined. In 1958, 72 percent of a national sample said they
could "trust the government in Washington to do what is right" either "always" or "most of the time," whereas the comparable response in 1996 was 32 percent.[6] This skepticism has washed almost
equally across all income classes and ages. Whites and blacks,
women and men, liberals and conservatives, Republicans and
Democrats—all have been affected to about the same degree.[7]
Furthermore, with the exception of providing education and nutritional assistance, the sorts of tasks that would be involved in rebuilding the needed base of human and social capital—intervening
in family life and altering the content of popular culture—are exactly those for which "big government" seems least suited and that
would attract the greatest skepticism.[8]

Third, to the extent that economic equality has been pursued as
a consequence of full citizenship status in a community of demo-
cratically equal citizens—the rationale advanced in T. H. Marshall's
famous Cambridge University lectures in 1949 and by many who
have followed in his footsteps—this rationale has faded in the West
as national communities have grown more heterogeneous.[9]
Marshall's England is now home to substantial numbers of East
Asians and West Indians along with lesser numbers of Arabs and
Africans. America is even more diverse with respect to ethnicity
and native-born and immigrant subpopulations. The presence of
large numbers of individuals with "dysfunctional life-styles" in
American cities adds another important divisive element.[10] The
bonds of fellow feeling and the presumptions of common identity
are weakening. "Community" is not necessarily fading, but it is

now built on foundations of enlightened interdependence. In this new formulation, citizens are connected by bonds of reciprocal self-interest and empathy that vary considerably within and between different social groups.

Finally, though the traditional bonds of community may be loosening—and to a certain degree *because* they are—people hunger to preserve what remains and to create new bases for community.[11] As idea and as object of affection, "community," wherever we find it, seems fragile. One of the central challenges for any community is to adopt and enforce norms that discourage free-rider behavior. Increasing consciousness of this problem leads people to ask how equalitarianism and individualism, respectively, might contribute to or detract from the desired bundle of norms. They might plausibly conclude that a moderate degree of both values would contribute to community while an excess of either would not. They might further conclude that responsibility-enhancing norms such as reciprocity and fairness must be included in any bundle of anti-free-riding norms. Such conclusions would depress the salience of the EI framework in political debate and would enhance the salience of a framework that engaged citizens in a dialogue over what exactly the "fair" terms of exchange were for any relationship allegedly based on reciprocity.

In an ideal democracy, intellectuals—and, indeed, people at large—would somehow manage to invent such a framework. A successful framework would permit the dialogue to go on and would help policymakers focus on key policy problems and think up a menu of creative solutions. Moreover, this framework would also suit the needs of political party elites seeking to position themselves strategically for the purpose of contesting elections. Might this have been happening in America in the recent past? If so, what exactly is the evolving framework? And what are the odds that it will be able to displace the very powerful historical attachment of the American people to the traditional EI framework? In what follows, I consider these questions in order.

Signs of Creativity

First, has it been happening? Consider first ordinary citizens. Sociologist Alan Wolfe conducted intensive interviews with two hundred middle-class Americans in eight communities about a wide range of contemporary social, cultural, and political concerns. For our present purposes, the views he elicited concerning welfare are most germane. They are a textured weave of ideas about tolerance for human frailty, an insistence on individual responsibility, an ideal of individual autonomy, and a commitment to the idea of contract and the principle of reciprocity. Wolfe's summary is worth quoting at length:

> [M]iddle-class Americans believe that everyone is deserving until proven otherwise; the benefit of the doubt works to the advantage of those in need. That is how people reconcile their support for welfare with their generally favorable disposition to individualism. Given the importance middle-class people attach to responsibility, they believe that everyone ought to be capable of supporting themselves. But they know that not everyone can—at least not all the time. The way you protect the dignity of those who cannot is to help them in return for their promise to support themselves when they can. . . .
>
> [Doris Casey, an unmarried mother of five, receiving welfare, who was included in Wolfe's sample,] does not advocate abolishing welfare. But she also knows that her support is contingent on the generosity of the taxpayer, which bothers her. Help me, she reasons, and I will do what I can in return: go to school, give my children the attention they need. In this way, she reflects the fact that "mainstream" attitudes toward welfare are often found most strongly among those who have had experiences with the system. Reciprocity is the contract that undergirds welfare, a contract implicitly recognized by most Americans no matter on which end of the welfare bureaucracy they find themselves.[12]

Consider next political elites, particularly partisan elites. Even more particularly, consider partisan elites who are seeking to regain lost power or who fear they might lose power to threatening competitors and who might regard a new and improved ideology as a competitive weapon. Perhaps the leading instance of such an elite faction is the New Democrats in the years after 1984, when President Ronald Reagan, as the standard-bearer of traditional EI conservatism trounced his liberal Democrat counterpart, Walter Mondale, in the presidential election. As Democrats, they needed a counter to the Republicans. As centrists, they needed to have an alternative to the liberals within their own party.[13]

Not surprisingly, the New Democrats have created a sort of think tank, in the form of the Progressive Policy Institute, as well as a political forum, the Democratic Leadership Council. But we should not necessarily expect even this highly motivated collection of self-consciously innovating individuals to succeed. Many obstacles stand in the way. The problem is itself very difficult. In a sense, they face a challenge of normative political theory very like those facing political philosophers of centuries past. After all, the erosion of equality as the touchstone of social justice is rather a major challenge for inheritors of the Enlightenment and Liberal traditions.[14]

Somehow, though, out of all this effort successes have emerged. They have even been copied by New Labour in Great Britain.[15] A prime example is the proposition that Bill Clinton, in the late 1980s an intellectual and political leader among the New Democrats, put forth in many contexts and in many forms since his 1992 campaign for the presidency that "no one who works hard and plays by the rules" should be poor or miss out on the American dream. There may be many more, to be sure, but in the space available here I propose to concentrate mainly on this one. I believe it is a highly suggestive sign.

Like any sign, this one needs interpretation. One can ask, What does it point to? The Clinton proposition was applied to justify, directly or indirectly, many concrete policy proposals, from increasing the minimum wage to easing the terms of federally supported student loans to extending the reach of the Earned Income Tax Credit (EITC) to lifting the ban on gays in the military.[16] Of all these the EITC is the most interesting for our purposes, since it has nothing to do with the old liberal agenda of promoting equality of opportunity, as does the idea of education loans, or with a populist agenda (but not only that) of forcing business to pay a nonexploitative minimum wage. It is intended pretty much as a transfer of wealth pure and simple from those who have "enough" in some sense to those who haven't, and it is justified, in Clinton's rhetoric, by reference to an implied social contract.

The EITC had been part of the federal tax code since 1975. At its inception it had not been accompanied by any grand ideological justification. It had been just another (relatively small) tax expenditure to a political constituency, poor working folk, of particular interest to a powerful elected official, Senator Russell Long, chair of the Senate Finance Committee. It was a constituency important to Long's political base in his home state of Louisiana and for which he felt, in addition, a personal empathy.

The EITC became more visible in the early 1980s. Following President Reagan's large tax cut in 1981, which disproportionately benefited high-bracket taxpayers, Democrats in the 1982 congressional elections charged Republicans with unfairness to the little guy and used their control of the House Ways and Means committee to publicize their case.[17] But Republicans refused to concede "the fairness issue" entirely. Reagan announced his intention to seek—or at least study—comprehensive tax reform in his 1984 State of the Union message. Tax relief for low-income workers thus became absorbed into the continuing dialogue in American politics over the appropriate efforts of government intervention to reduce inequality and achieved a certain level of consensual legitimacy within that dialogue.

In the mid- to late 1980s, the EITC acquired three additional ideological dimensions. The Democratic Leadership Council made "strengthening the family" into one of its core issues, and the EITC held a high place on this agenda. Second, the DLC and its intellectual allies depicted the EITC as a way to "make work pay." Third, the idea was not just that a sympathetic constituency would benefit. So would the idea and the institution, one might say, of work itself. As Isaac Shapiro and Robert Greenstein wrote in 1989 in *Making Work Pay: A New Agenda for Poverty Policies*:

> "Making work pay" could lift many of the working poor—especially many working poor families with children—out of poverty or much closer to the poverty line. It could also have a strong work incentive effect, bringing more people into the labor market and making work relatively more attractive as compared either to public assistance or to various illicit endeavors in the underground economy. . . .
>
> In the inner cities . . . a key policy goal . . . should be to transform the working poor more into role models who *do* escape poverty, through their effort, and to make them seem less like "chumps" who work all day at jobs that pay little more than what can be obtained through public assistance or minor hustling. A strategy to make work pay might in the long run prove to do as much (or more) to affect attitudes and norms in such communities as the exhortations for changes in values now so widely sounded.[18]

It was only left for candidate Bill Clinton to pick up the "make work pay" idea in the 1992 presidential election campaign and enrich it with the implication that work was part of a larger constellation of "playing by the rules."

At this point, as interpreters of signs buried in political rhetoric, we might wonder, "The rules" of what, exactly? A social contract seems implied, and a novel one at that. Traditional EI conservatives could well ask whence comes the warrant for taking taxpayer money and giving it over to the hard-working but, let us say, naturally untalented or unskilled. The market is hard but just, they might say, and there is no obvious reason to take money from those it rewarded justly in order to subsidize those whom in its justice it chose not to reward. By what reason has society a duty to support the able-bodied but untalented? Yet the implied contract does not resonate with traditional liberalism either. After all, the rhetoric seems to imply that if you *don't* work hard and play by the rules, then maybe you *do* deserve to be poor and cut off from the American dream. The traditional liberal could ask, Is there no duty at all to treat even the undeserving poor with "compassion" or, better yet, "empathy"? These and other such questions can be posed quite constructively as questions about what would count as "fair" terms within our social contract—call it the Social Reciprocity (SR) contract—and the desirability of maintaining or adjusting the terms.[19]

The Contract Design Space

One of the great virtues of social contract metaphors is the centrality—and the legitimation—of self-interest as a theoretical building block. In a large-scale industrial and postindustrial society, the essence of the SR contract has broadly to do with the sort of insurance contract people would want for themselves and their families. Thus, citizens create a collective insurance contract because it serves their individual interests to do so. This means that they are willing both to pay "premiums" in the form of taxes and to allow their fellow citizens, as well as themselves, to accept benefits under certain conditions. They are also prepared to adopt and enforce rules to prevent abuse, whether on the part of claimants or of the agents of the payer, typically agencies of "the government," though in principle other such agents could be invented.

For some people, especially those who have had no personal experience of misfortune and/or who expect none (perhaps unrealistically), extending assistance may seem like an expression of empathy, not the fulfillment of a merely utilitarian insurance contract, which they never personally signed in any case. While I do not quarrel with the existence of empathy—indeed, I think contemporary academic moral philosophy is profoundly mistaken to ignore empathy, as it has generally done[20]—empathy cannot alone guide society in its collective efforts to extend help to strangers. Short of embracing Christian self-effacing universalism, invoking empathy cannot lead to useful answers to questions about how much, for what, and to whom. Indeed, it cannot even lead to raising the questions. The mutual insurance contract, founded on self-interest, is a much richer medium for reasoning about such issues because it permits us to use the touchstone of "fairness."

Now, "fairness" is a complex, multidimensional, concept. At a minimum, it has to do with (1) the absence of deceit and coercion, (2) the use of rational methods to resolve disputes, (3) the like treatment of people and situations that are alike in relevant ways, and (4) the appropriately differential treatment of relevant differences. But these are all abstract ideas, and they need to be filled in by considering the concrete issues that arise in the course of working out the terms of an insurance-based SR contract. The terms of the SR contract are dictated by a generic "design space" that pertains to virtually any insurance contract. I therefore turn now to exploring this design space. By way of providing an overview, the discussion here touches on which perils should be covered, how to guard against moral hazard, the size and character of the deductible, the benefit level, and the nature of loss prevention measures.

Some Process Matters

Before turning to the substance of insurance contracts, however, let us briefly stipulate certain features of the collective choice process. First, all members of the society—call them "voters"—involved in choosing a collective insurance contract are both potential beneficiaries and actual premium payers. Hence, they all face incentives to find efficiency-maximizing arrangements.

Second, I assume that the individual premiums are scaled to ability to pay. Hence, there are no incentives for one class of persons to load the contract with extra benefits, say, while counting on others to pick up a disproportionate share of the burdens. Correspondingly, no one is less motivated than anyone else to hold down costs.

Third, for many perils, such as fire and theft, private insurance products are available on fair terms. For some insurance products, however, there are private-market imperfections; and in those cases voters will attempt to create provisions in the SR contract that suit their risk preferences.

Finally, though voters prefer to decide on contract terms by consensus, if consensus proves too elusive or time-consuming, they rely on majority rule. In doing so, they at least potentially risk coercing minorities and also making the outcomes vulnerable to strategic manipulation; and both of these effects, by violating fairness norms, are presumptively unjust.

What Perils Should the Collective Contract Cover?

Insurance companies in private competitive markets typically worry about adverse selection—that is, attracting subscribers with above-average exposure to the perils insured against and whose condition is known to the subscribers but not to the company. A health insurer that offers especially generous mental health benefits, for instance, is in danger of attracting subscribers with a taste for therapy. The equivalent problem with regard to government programs is special-interest lobbying by parties who expect to be beneficiaries. Low-wage workers, for instance, or more precisely those who competed to represent them, did in fact lobby for an EITC. Special-interest organizing strategies familiar to public choice theorizing and adverse-selection incentives familiar to theorizing about insurance markets tend, therefore, to merge with one another. "Fair" contract terms would give no special benefits to such self-seeking parties.

The mirror image of adverse selection is skimming: insurers, using their own knowledge of who is an above- or below-average risk, take measures to skim the low-risk subpopulation into the subscriber pool and turn away the rest.[21] HMOs and other health insurers are notoriously prone to this practice. Since the political process shapes the terms of our collective insurance contract, small and weak minorities are the most likely to have their particular perils excluded. Hence, "fair" SR contract terms would not involve any sort of skimming strategy on the part of the dominant majority.

John Rawls's famous theory of justice can be construed as having been erected on insurance contract imagery, with its central design objective to prevent unjust skimming.[22] This objective explains Rawls's device of individual and collective choice of fair principles of social distribution behind a hypothetical "veil of ignorance," in which ignorance of their situations prevents the currently fortunate from discriminating against the currently unfortunate. Although the particular details of Rawls's choice process are of doubtful value, the basic intuition about the need for some sort of imagination is sound. The imagination required, in my view, involves empathy, putting oneself in the other guy's shoes, bolstered by thoughts such as "There but for the grace of God go I." This corresponds to what social scientists are discovering to be a natural sense of justice.[23] Arguments about the proper kind and degree of such imaginative efforts clearly are part of the current debate over the justice of various social programs.

How to Deal with Moral Hazard?

Private insurers use various strategies to counter moral hazard—that is, the disincentive to guard against perils that insurance itself creates. With regard to public sector insurance, such as our hypothetical SR contract, benefit claims attributable to moral hazard are not only inefficient but unfair, in that they exploit one's fellow citizens and taxpayers.

For our present purposes, the important strategies are keeping benefit levels relatively low, imposing deductibles (front-end losses the insured must absorb before claiming the first dollar of benefits), and requiring coinsurance payments (proportionate reductions of every benefit dollar paid out) or their functional equivalent. The EITC presents only a slight problem of moral hazard, since receiving the benefit is conditioned on job-related earnings and work on the job itself is the functional equivalent of a coinsurance payment. The EITC's "welfare" counterpart, Temporary Assistance to Needy Families (TANF)—formerly, Aid to Families with Dependent Children (AFDC)—pays low benefit levels in most states, although it is hard to say how much this reflects a desire to protect against moral hazard as opposed to other values. The workfare requirements imposed on TANF recipients by the 1996 federal welfare reform legislation[24] are also supposed to work as a kind of nonmonetary coinsurance payment forced on aid recipients. That is, they make TANF benefits less valuable than their simple cash value to the recipients and so decrease the moral hazard that would be associated with the cash payments alone. In regard to TANF-type welfare programs, one might also think of community stigma, and of administrative hassle in establishing and maintaining eligibility, as forms of coinsurance. Fairness also requires that society not impose excessively high coinsurance costs, of whatever kind.

What Sort of Deductible?

Deductibles discourage moral hazard, but they also save on administrative costs by screening out relatively small claims for relatively small losses and inconveniences. As in the case of coinsurance, deductibles in a collective insurance policy take different forms. Medicaid coverage for long-term nursing home care requires "spending down" one's assets. In unemployment and disability insurance, a waiting period until benefits kick in is common. In theory, the higher the deductible, whatever form it takes, the greater the incentive for individuals and their families to act providently. In practice, when providence has been inadequate or misfortune especially harsh, a "high deductible" means improvising solutions to problems of varying desperation with the help of family, friends, and local charities.[25]

Setting the deductible "too high" implies that some, perhaps many, people end up homeless and hungry or imposing on family and friends who very badly want no part of them. Setting it too low means that those needy individuals who value providence, self-reliance, and informal mutual aid and who have chosen to rely on these supports rather than on the collective insurance policy feel unjustly treated. More precisely, they feel that their neighbors who had chosen to rely on the collective insurance, and hence indirectly on their own premium/tax payments, had received unfair advantages.[26]

What Is the Right Benefit Level?

One might think it "fair" that the benefit level should somehow be proportional to the loss incurred. However, this conclusion is too simple. Much depends on the purposes for which benefits are supplied. In cases in which the insurance is intended by the voters only as a safety net or lifeline, proportionality would not necessarily be thought fair. Furthermore, the benefit level, like the choice among perils to be covered, indirectly affects adverse selection, skimming, and the similarity or dissimilarity between one's personal attitudes toward self-reliance and those of the hypothetical median voter, which all have an impact on perceived justice or injustice. For instance, those who think they are likely to be beneficiaries desire high benefit levels, while those who do not think so will prefer low benefit levels. Low benefit levels also discourage moral hazard and alleviate the sense of unfairness on the part of individuals who believe they are denied benefits rightfully theirs.

Fairness is an issue in another way as well. Benefit levels must be kept low enough so that nonrecipients who think themselves substantially like recipients do not feel that recipients are being treated better than they are. In the run-up to the 1996 welfare reform bill, the complaint was strongly registered that working people didn't receive wage or salary increases when they had more children, though welfare recipients did.[27]

Under real-world conditions, some unfairness of this last sort is inevitable; the only questions concern its scale and the degree of countervailing justification. The inevitability arises from the fact that the individuals who are awarded some benefit[28] often look very similar, even identical, to those who are not. They may be distinguished only by small and seemingly arbitrary characteristics, or by a slightly higher level of effort in pursuing the benefit, or simply by appearing to have good luck.[29] In the case of affirmative action, for instance, beneficiary groups defined in categorical terms always contain individuals who lack the characteristics supposedly associated with the group as a whole that would justify their receiving the benefit. And many who are not in the categorically defined group have characteristics that, in appropriate ways, match the within-group characteristics thought to warrant the benefit.

How Much Intrusiveness Is Acceptable?

Private insurers sometimes take pains to help—or force—their insureds to prevent losses (e.g., by requiring the installation of sprinkler systems and smoke detectors or by sponsoring research on the flammability of building materials). Customer turnover, competitive rate pressures, and other market forces probably discourage optimal investment in loss prevention by private insurers. A society-wide insurance scheme from which subscribers (by assumption) cannot exit, on the other hand, is well positioned to design and implement loss prevention strategies. As long as the members of the collective who have been the objects of investments in prevention do not exit, which by assumption they cannot, all members benefit from cost-justified investments in prevention. Loss prevention measures represent unusual opportunities for voters because they can in principle benefit both premium payers and individuals and families who are at high risk of certain perils. I have in mind such measures as drug treatment and counseling, preventive medical care, parenting instruction, and community-provided night basketball—all of which measures might prevent losses down the road both for the society and for the individuals who are the focus of such measures.[30]

But such measures, however efficient overall, raise issues of fairness. On the one hand, the focal individuals might not, for any number of reasons, want to cooperate. They might resent intrusions in their lives. They might be willing in principle but object to the precise terms available. They might accept the terms but believe that the implementers do not behave competently. On the other hand, advocates of such loss prevention measures can argue, in paternalistic fashion, that cooperation benefits the focal individuals whether they know it or not and that, anyway, dysfunctional behavior, while perhaps legal, has negative spillovers that society, in fairness to the great majority, has a right to try to prevent.[31]

Collective Security and Equality-Individualism as Frameworks for Dialogue

Assume for the sake of argument that fairness is to some extent displacing equality as the core idea in debating issues of social justice and that the SR contract framework is displacing the EI framework.[32] Why might this be so? I suggested four reasons earlier: (1) as an ideal, equality of opportunity is becoming increasingly unattainable, perhaps even unthinkable; (2) the sense of membership in a shared national community is declining; (3) governmental capacity looks smaller than it once did; and (4) the fragility of community in the face of extremes of both egalitarianism and individualism is now better recognized. But the weakening of the EI framework is only half the explanation. The second half is that the SR contract framework and its core moral ideal of reciprocity have many intellectual and cultural strengths. Its method is inductive and incremental, it ducks divisive attributions of blame, it defines a constructive middle ground, and it does not disallow compensation for social groups as well as for individuals. I discuss these intellectual and cultural assets in this section and in the next section turn to how partisan political considerations might also bear on the displacement process.

Inductive and Incremental

Like the common law, the SR framework can approach the dauntingly large and complex question of "social justice" empirically and a step at a time. It owes this to the centrality of "fairness" and the inductive method inherently prescribed by trying to figure out whether group X,[33] whose just treatment is in question, is similar, or dissimilar, to some other set of groups about whose treatment we are more sure. This comparative procedure has led to the slow expansion of "victim"-like groups in the society entitled to some sort of special consideration.

Given the variety of terms in the SR insurance contract, this comparative exercise must be completed several times for a given case. For instance, compared to other victimlike groups, how high a "deductible" is group X being asked to pay, and have they done so? In the case of the working poor, for instance, liberals might say, "These people are struggling valiantly [paid a high deductible]. It is unfair not to give them rewards that are at least a little more like the rewards of other people who don't even work as hard." Choosing a different comparison group, conservatives might respond, "No, in my time [or my parents' time] the struggle was even harder, so it would be unfair to support them." Similar comparative questions can be asked with respect to the level of benefit to be accorded and about the type of coinsurance to be paid.

The comparative method is especially helpful in thinking about the question of adequacy of opportunity.[34] Falling below some "adequate" threshold of some resource (e.g., money income or educational opportunity) is a condition to be insured against. But what is "adequacy"? Clearly, beyond some threshold of survival, "adequacy" is a socially constructed, not an objective, norm. Ideas of adequacy differ among individuals, across societies, and, in any given society, across time periods. Today many people think it egregiously unfair and unjust, for instance, that many children are not given adequate—that is, grade-level—reading skills by the time they are in the higher elementary grades, though fifty years ago proportionately fewer people might have thought so.

Sidestepping Blameworthiness

Suppose that liberals can get conservatives to agree that the working poor have a very hard life and, at a human level, deserve sympathy, perhaps even some hard cash. The deductible, it is agreed, has been paid. Liberals would still need to meet conservative questions about the worthiness of the recipients. Is their low condition somehow "their own fault?" it will be asked. No, reply the liberals, it is the fault of forces over which they have no control: "globalization" or "downsizing" or "the recession" or "the new information economy" or "the stress getting by on little money and both parents working full-time and overtime" or "the absence of traditional community supports" and so on. In reality, attributing blameworthiness is often (though not always) a sterile enterprise. The causes of any condition are often multiple, and they often interact. In the social realm, they typically include a host of preventive actions *not* taken and benign conditions *not* present. It is hard to know which of these nonactions and nonconditions really deserve to have causality, and hence blameworthiness, attributed to them. Worse still, since many of the nonactions refer to *compensatory,* or second-best, strategies that individuals or society might have taken in response to various troubles or insufficiencies, one must always wonder how well such strategies would have worked.

The insurance contract framework, which by definition deals with chance and contingency, can rhetorically handle the ambiguities of blameworthiness by blaming "bad luck," without trying to parse too carefully exactly what this bad luck consists of or how it came to pass.[35] Debaters who agree to attribute a present condition to bad luck may be in effect agreeing to disagree about the past. They can then get on to the typically more interesting question of whether extending some benefit will create unacceptable moral hazard with regard to future conduct.

Defining Common Ground and Joint Tasks

Historically, the EI framework more or less segregated the liberal partisans of empathy and equality from the conservative partisans of self-reliance and fiscal restraint. The liberals were not interested in talking about the problems of moral hazard, dependency, and abuse. Conservatives were not to be bothered with news of human hardship, especially if the humans in question were very different from themselves. The insurance contract framework, however, presumes self-reliance and is matter-of-fact about the existence of moral hazard. This should please conservatives. But it need not for that reason trouble liberals, since an honest discussion of contract terms can force conservatives to acknowledge the existence of hardships, and hence perils, not hitherto covered and to confront the adequacy or inadequacy of compensation packages.

Once traditional liberal and conservative opponents have been drawn into recognizing each others' most cherished facts (or allegations of fact), it is a short journey to the common ground that they can occupy together. Both camps, for instance, can agree on many investments in paternalistic prevention of the sort described earlier, though they might do so for different reasons and might therefore disagree about the proper expenditure level and type. To oversimplify somewhat, because many such interventions can be characterized as variants on "tough love," conservatives could emphasize the "tough" and liberals the "love."

The insurance contract framework also provides abundant raw materials for liberals and conservatives, working together, to fashion interventions that meet their respective requirements. Because the SR insurance contract presumes a complex social system with many dimensions and many contract-relevant interdependencies, there are many opportunities for subtle trade-offs and adjustments. The 1996 federal Welfare Reform bill, for instance, limited total benefits (with time limits) and imposed tougher coinsurance (workfare) but increased the states' fiscal incentives and capacities to invest in prevention (more work-related education and training).[36] I suspect that the EI framework is not nearly so rich, although I acknowledge that this could be a case in which my biases, and the possibility of having created an EI straw man, are distorting my view of the matter.

Justice for Groups

Historically, American conceptions about justice revolve around individuals, not groups. The traditional EI conception has no room for minority group set-asides in the admission of students into public universities, the promotion of employees within firms or agencies, or the awarding of public contracts. More precisely, it does have conceptual room but pronounces such group-oriented benefits flatly unjust.

Such pronouncements, however, do not adequately acknowledge many minority individuals' feelings of exclusion and the moral intuition of many observers that set-asides, by whatever euphemism they are called or however fuzzily they are calibrated, are not categorically "unjust." The challenge is a technical one (albeit an extremely difficult one) of designing and administering set-asides that count as "fair" given the multidimensionality and the administrative limitations of our real-world SR insurance contract. Or consider another collective concern, environmental risks and uncertainties imposed on poor communities. Like the peril of "working hard, playing by the rules, and nevertheless being poor," the cumulative impact of happening to lose out in a large number of life's arenas—albeit fairly and squarely—is a new peril to be insured against.[37] This, I believe, is what has prompted current demands in minority communities for "environmental justice." These are demands to be exempted from having to accept incinerators, dumps, and the like, just because low land costs in their low-income communities make it otherwise logical to site such facilities there. Like the experience of caste-based discrimination, being "forced" to be a dump site by the better off is a collectively experienced pain and, some would say, a matter for concerned debate before an action is taken.

An adequate debating framework would acknowledge the legitimacy in principle of compensation for collectivities. The insurance contract framework is able to do so. It says, in effect, "If it's a collectivity that can be thought of as having (1) borne some contribution to the society and (2) experienced bad luck—or something even worse, such as slavery—then it's the collectivity that can be thought of as the appropriate recipient of compensation." Of course, this leaves open the question of what it means to be a collectivity of this sort. This question does not have simple or uncontroversial answers. Nevertheless, it is a question that cannot even be asked under the traditional EI framework. It is the legitimacy accorded by the contractarian framework to *create* justice-related norms using will and imagination, and not merely to deduce them, that gives the SR framework this advantage.

Partisanship and the Coexistence of EI and SR Frameworks

It would be astonishing if a shift in the framework for our dialogue over social justice were to occur rapidly and decisively. Such a rapid and decisive shift is not occurring. A very long transition involving both generational replacement and within-generation change is the more realistic picture. Although it is hard to define the benchmarks to characterize an amorphous thing like a "shift in ideological framework," perhaps twenty to twenty-five years would be a plausible conjecture. We are probably less than halfway through the transition. During the ongoing transition, two of the most venerated ideological symbols that evolved during the ascendancy of the EI framework, "equality" and "big government," are continuing to affect the quality of the dialogue, though in different ways.

The liberal attachment to "equality" seems to be getting recycled without much logical difficulty into meaningful equivalents in the SR framework, such as attributing much of people's misfortune to "bad luck," insisting on greater empathy with others by "putting yourself in their shoes," and claiming that compensatory benefits for "playing by the rules" ought simply to be more generous. Some liberals, at least, have been acknowledging the problem of moral hazard and the unfairness to the more effortful poor that is associated with it. To generate as much support as possible for investing in human and cultural capital for the disadvantaged, they have been trying to make hard-headed arguments about the payoffs in eventual tax savings and in improving the capacity for self-reliance. One can easily find such themes in the house organ of the New Democrats (titled *The New Democrat*), who are admittedly only one variant of "liberals."

Of course, the real-world debate between liberals and conservatives is not about the terms of the SR contract alone. Our real-world SR contract uses government as the administrator of the collective insurance contract and will likely do so for the foreseeable future. There is some evidence that association of the "big government" symbol with the debate over justice strengthens the conservative side of the EI debate independently of citizens' attitudes on all the SR justice-related design issues discussed earlier.[38] This has given EI conservatives, particularly Republicans, a powerful reason not to let go of the EI framework in favor of the SR framework. The New Democrats have been countering with their own prescriptions for trimming government and for devolving many of its historical functions via contract to for-profit and nonprofit entities.

Conclusion

I have conjectured that equality is slowly losing its relevance, and therefore its potency, as the touchstone of what "social justice" is to mean in America. I have also conjectured that it is being displaced by the idea of "fairness." "Fairness" is a multidimensional and abstract idea, the meaning of which gets worked out in an open-ended political dialogue over the terms to be found in a certain kind of social contract. This is a collective insurance contract among all citizens to provide compensation for a variety of perils. The contractual terms at issue are the perils to be covered, how to guard against moral hazard, the size and character of the deductible, the benefit level, and the nature of loss prevention measures.

If this displacement is in fact occurring, it is probably being driven in part by politics and in part by the good fit of the social contract framework to the real issues of current controversy. These are, for example, fairness-based demands that the working poor be treated at least as well as welfare recipients, that racial and ethnic minority communities not be treated as environmental dumping grounds, and that people who "work hard and play by the rules," in Bill Clinton's rhetoric, not be left solely to the untender mercies of the market. Political incentives exist on the Republican and conservative side, however, to keep the equalitarian idea alive as a subject for debate, since it permits them to bash "big government" as the unpopular—but in truth not at all inevitable—instrument of equalitarian policies. Liberal Democrats have to some degree played into Republican hands, though the New Democrat element of the party has been trying, with some success, both to promote reciprocity-based themes and to invent more popular (and more effective) instruments than "big government."

As I stated—forcefully, I hope—at the beginning of this essay, all of this is largely conjectural. Much research, and perhaps the passage of some years, would be needed before these conjectures could be accepted as more or less realistic. My object has been to illuminate a number of pertinent questions.

Notes

1. In the legal, political, and moral (or "social") spheres, Americans care greatly about equality of condition and treatment. However, with respect to material or economic goods, where the debate over social justice is focused, they care about equality of opportunity rather than condition. See Jennifer Hochschild, *What's Fair? American Beliefs about Distributive Justice* (Cambridge, Mass.: Harvard University Press, 1981); James R. Kluegel and Eliot R. Smith, *Beliefs about Inequality: American Views of What Is and What Ought to Be* (New York: Aldine de Gruyter, 1986).

2. Ronald Dworkin, *Sovereign Virtue: The Theory and Practice of Equality* (Cambridge, Mass.: Harvard University Press, 2000), 1.

3. See Jens Ludwig, "Information and Inner City Educational Attainment," *Economics of Educational Review* 18 (1999): 17–30; Katherine Newman and Chauncy Lennon, *Finding Work in the Inner City: How Hard Is It Now? How Hard Will It Be for AFDC Recipients?* (New York: Russell Sage Foundation, 1995); Meredith Phillips, Jeanne Brooks-Gunn, Greg J. Duncan, Pamela Klebanov, and Jonathan Crane. "Family Background, Parenting Practices, and the Black-White Test Score Gap," in *The Black-White Test Score Gap*, ed. C. Jencks and M. Phillips (Washington, D.C.: Brookings Institution Press, 1998); Robert D. Putnam, *Making Democracy Work: Civic Traditions in Modern Italy* (Princeton, N.J.: Princeton University Press, 1993); Steven Raphael, "Inter- and Intra-Ethnic Comparisons of the Central City-Suburban Youth Employment Differential: Evidence from the Oakland Metropolitan Area," *Industrial and Labor Relations* 51, no. 3 (1998): 505–524; William Julius Wilson, *When Work Disappears: The World of the New Urban Poor* (New York: Knopf, 1996).

4. James J. Heckman, "Is Job Training Oversold?" *The Public Interest* (Spring 1994): 94.

5. Adequacy can be expensive, too, of course. Moreover, when "adequacy" implies "compensatory," as it might in regard to educating some students from disadvantaged families, it can also imply spending above-average resources. See William H. Clune, "The Shift from Equity to Adequacy in School Finance," *Educational Policy* 8, no. 4 (1994): 376–394.

6. I read these figures off the graph supplied in Gary Orren, "Fall from Grace: The Public's Loss of Faith in Government," in *Why People Don't Trust Government*, ed. J. S. Nye Jr., P. D. Zelikow, and D. C. King (Cambridge, Mass.: Harvard University Press, 1997), 81. A similar decline is evident with regard to state and local government; see Joseph Nye Jr., "Introduction: The Decline of Confidence in Government," in Nye et al., *Why People Don't Trust Government*, 1.

7. Orren, "Fall from Grace," 86–87.

8. This is not to say that publicly financed programs, carried out by a mix of public and nonprofit agencies, could not have some success. On the scale that would be required to achieve real equality of opportunity throughout the population, however, it is unrealistic to think that government could do the job.

9. T. H. Marshall, *Class, Citizenship, and Social Development: Essays by T. H. Marshall* (New York: Doubleday, 1965).

10. Lawrence M. Mead, "Citizenship and Social Policy: T. H. Marshall and Poverty," *Social Philosophy & Policy* 14, no. 2 (1997): 197–230.

11. See Amitai Etzioni, ed., *Rights and the Common Good: The Communitarian Perspective* (New York: St. Martin's, 1995), and Ronald Inglehart, *Culture Shift in Advanced Industrial Society* (Princeton, N.J.: Princeton University Press, 1990).

12. Alan Wolfe, *One Nation, after All* (New York: Viking, 1998), 207–209.

13. The other instance of an elite partisan faction with a return to power on its mind is the Gingrich Republican conservatives, interested in restoring Reaganite populist conservatism within their own party during the Bush years

and in using the party as the political arm of something like a social movement. Gingrich Republicanism, however, has not been particularly creative ideologically. It has simply offered a harder-edged version of traditional EI individualism and opposition to "big government."

14. Apart from mobilizing mass movements of the nationalist or totalitarian variety, political science does not have any theory about how an elite-driven process of ideological creativity might work itself out successfully. But we can be sure that it could fail in many ways—for example, with simple-minded but accessible ideas crowding out more sophisticated ideas of greater complexity, or with personal and clique rivalries overwhelming audiences' interest in any kind of ideas at all. It is not enough that policy intellectuals or philosophers recognize a new framework for dialogue about justice as being analytically more useful or in other ways more meaningful than some older framework. It must make sense to a broad spectrum of political professionals and ultimately to the much broader spectrum of ordinary citizens. If understanding is limited or distorted—perhaps willfully so—in such quarters, failure is likely.

15. Anthony Giddens, *The Third Way: The Renewal of Social Democracy* (Cambridge: Polity, 1998); Desmond King and Mark Wickham-Jones, "From Clinton to Blair: The Democratic (Party) Origins of Welfare to Work," *Political Quarterly* 70, (1999): 62–74.

16. CNN interview with President-Elect Clinton, November 11, 1992, Transcript 208, on gays in the military; Presidential Announcement of March 9, 1994, on the EITC; Presidential Statement of September 22, 1998, on the minimum wage.

17. I rely heavily throughout on Christopher Howard's history of the politics of the EITC, and on his chapter in this volume (see chapter 10).

18. Isaac Shapiro and Robert Greenstein, *Making Work Pay: A New Agenda for Poverty Policies* (Washington, D.C.: Center on Budget and Policy Priorities, 1989), 7–8. Shapiro and Greenstein also credited David Ellwood, of the Harvard Kennedy School of Government. His 1988 book *Poor Support: Poverty in the American Family* was an accessible and influential contribution to the intellectual case for the EITC and "making work pay."

19. It should be apparent that in my formulation "the social contract" is not merely a metaphor. Although it is intangible, evolving, and subject to interpretation, it is nevertheless real. As a suitable analogy, think of Britain's unwritten but very real constitution.

20. Three important exceptions are Allan Gibbard, *Wise Choices, Apt Feelings: A Theory of Normative Judgment* (Cambridge, Mass.: Harvard University Press, 1990); Elliott Sober and David Sloan Wilson, *Unto Others: The Evolution and Psychology of Unselfish Behavior* (Cambridge, Mass.: Harvard University Press, 1998); Ken Binmore, *Game Theory and the Social Contract II: Just Playing* (Cambridge, Mass., MIT Press, 1998)

21. This is a common practice in the private health insurance industry, for instance.

22. John Rawls, *A Theory of Justice* (Cambridge, Mass.: Harvard University Press, 1971).

23. Matt Ridley, *The Origins of Virtue: Human Instincts and the Evolution of Cooperation* (New York: Viking, 1997).

24. Formally, the Personal Responsibility and Work Opportunity Reconciliation Act (PRWORA).

25. Ironically, having family and friends act as a second line of defense (after the individual him- or herself) can sometimes create as much dependency in the focal individual as reliance on government and can diminish the capacity for self-reliance of those relied on. For an insightful discussion, see Robert J. Goodin, *Reasons for Welfare: The Political Theory of the Welfare State* (Princeton, N.J.: Princeton University Press, 1988), chapter 12.

26. The one sure way to avoid such a trade-off is to make the collectivity into less of an insurer and into more of a routine supplier of subsidized goods and services to the needy and the less needy alike—in the manner of the Scandinavian welfare states.

27. Of course, much depends on how one frames this fact. It would have been very reasonable to say that welfare grants were reduced for families with fewer children on the ground that need was less and therefore tax dollars were being saved. This framing does not, to be sure, take into account the fact that children born while the mother was on welfare were generally illegitimate as well as simply additional.

28. Or suffer the imposition of some burden, as I explain in the next paragraph.

29. Bo Rothstein implies that this sort of unfairness is a problem of imperfect administrative discretion alone; see his *Just Institutions Matter: The Moral and Political Logic of the Universal Welfare State* (Cambridge: Cambridge University Press, 1998), 160–162. However, it arises even when eligibility rules are clear and legislated. The problem lies not so much in our institutions or implementers but in the complexity of the world.

30. Unfortunately, "in principle" is only that, and many seemingly attractive programs of this sort do not work out in practice.

31. On "the new paternalism," see Lawrence Mead, ed., *The New Paternalism: Supervisory Approaches to Poverty* (Washington, D.C.: Brookings Institution, 1997).

32. Actually, the SR framework, if properly understood, subsumes the EI framework; therefore, equality is a particular expression of fairness, and the only appropriate one in some contexts, such as voting for elected representatives.

33. In this context I use the term *group* to refer to a category of people who have in common the exposure to some situation or condition.

34. As I said earlier, the debate over adequacy of opportunity is that over equality of opportunity.

35. On the political virtues of "ambiguity" in the EITC case, see Howard, *The Hidden Welfare State*, p. 141. More generally, on the virtues in law and politics of analogical reasoning and "incompletely theorized agreements," see Cass R. Sunstein, *Legal Reasoning and Political Conflict*, New York: Oxford University Press, 1996.

36. The incentive of allowing states to keep some portion of the savings also motivates states to dump cases from the rolls relatively indiscriminately.

37. I borrow the cumulative impact notion from Jon Elster, *Local Justice: How Institutions Allocate Scarce Goods and Necessary Burdens* (New York: Russell Sage Foundation, 1992), 132–134.

38. The (liberal Democrat) pollster Stanley Greenberg and his associates presented what I construe as Empathy and Self-Reliance "stories" of four to five sentences apiece to respondents, though Greenberg does not use these labels. They found very high—74 percent—support for the Empathy story. Paradoxically, 63 percent of respondents also supported the Self-Reliance story. How to account for this? I believe that respondents were reacting against negative characterizations of "government" that appeared in the Self-Reliance story. It appeared three times, accompanied by words and phrases such as *big, inflexible, centralized,* and "imposing burdensome taxes and regulations." The Empathy story had no mention of *government* at all but instead used the phrase "we should ensure" three times. See Stanley B. Greenberg, "Popularizing Progressive Politics," in *The New Majority: Toward a Popular Progressive Politics,* ed. S. B. Greenberg and T. Skocpol (New Haven, Conn.: Yale University Press, 1998). It is not clear from Greenberg's account of the polling procedure whether the same individuals responded to both stories. If they did, the apparent reversal of opinions when presented with the big-government cues is all the more striking. Of course, something other than an aversive response to the big government cue may account for this pattern in any case.

18

The Politics and Policy of the Regulated Market, Efficiency-Constrained Welfare State

Martin Shapiro, *University of California, Berkeley*

A series of themes recur in story after story in this book. Low-visibility interest group, old-style policymaking persists. There is, however, a significant high-visibility overlay characterized by electoral competition between the parties and a politics of credit claiming and blame avoidance. Neither party wishes to appear unfair or mean-spirited. Both push their claims to possess new ideas and/or higher competence to govern. Skrentny's chapter particularly emphasizes the blame avoidance theme (chapter 6). There is also a low-visibility politics of experts in which technical consensus on relatively narrow, programmatic policy ideas dominates. Entrenched vested interests, dissensus among experts, or more or less deliberate political manipulation reinforced by the media may move particular policy issues from low to high visibility. Skerry tells one such story in the census chapter of this volume (chapter 12). Beam and Conlan make this dynamic the central theme of their analysis of tax policy (chapter 4). In an era of sometimes divided government and powerful appeals to "rights," both policy persistence and policy change occur. Divided government can act. Even the rights ratchet can sometimes slip a cog. A politics of ideas coexists and interacts with a politics of interests as Schuck shows in his immigration chapter (chapter 5).

Two aspects of the politics of ideas are explicitly and repeatedly dealt with by the contributors to this volume. One involves policy ideas that are the currency of the politics of experts. In chapter 14, Mayhew notes the political efficacy of such ideas. Howard's chapter on the earned income tax credit (EITC) shows a subtle interaction of politics, policy ideas, and party politics (chapter 10). The other involves more or less symbolic ideas such as balanced budgets and welfare reform that sometimes become the currency of party electoral competition. At this point I want to press upon the reader a broader politics of ideas in which all of the themes of this volume are deeply embedded and that contributes heavily to the policy dynamics described here. This politics of ideas is more or less global, but for our purposes it makes little difference whether the United States is responding to internal or external ideological forces.

This politics of ideas may be briefly and bluntly stated. First and foremost, socialism is deserted. It is deserted not because we passionately love its rival, the free market, but because socialism just does not work. Its failure to solve the incentive problem results in failure to produce the levels of goods and services that capitalism produces. In the United States the failure of socialist aspirations is translated into the language of small government versus big government highlighted by my coeditors. As Mayhew says, "the 1990s was a very poor decade for the national public sector." On the other hand, some form or other of the idea of equality remains very much with us. It remains with us, however, accompanied by an acute awareness of the same incentives or efficiency problems that haunted socialism. What level of equality can we afford if we are to successfully maintain a market system that is the only key we currently hold to the gates of material prosperity? Markets and equality—or, as Bardach argues in chapter 17, equality transmuted into fairness—are the ideas behind the public opinion that Mayhew sees as winning in the 1990s.

Those concerned with the politics of policymaking or, indeed, any kind of politics in the developed world would be foolish indeed to neglect this fundamental decline in confidence in government direction of the economy and the fundamental devotion to some sort of human and humane equality that are the yin and yang of contemporary political thought, both elite and popular. One vector of that yin and yang appears in Vogel's "The Postwar Liberal Trade Regime: Resilience under Pressure" (chapter 13). The "resilience" flows from faith in an international market system; the "pressure" from concern that left to itself such a system may make the rich richer and the poor poorer.

The failure of socialism as a political ideology in the United States is well known and often explained. The proclivity of the early

New Deal to sample international isms of every variety is slightly less well known, given the leftist caste of American historical writing since World War II. Of course, the fascism of the National Industrial Recovery Administration (NIRA) complete with flag and jack-booted General Johnson has been noted, although seldom called by its right name. The New Deal's great experiment with socialism, however, the Tennessee Valley Authority (TVA), is never called by name. It is presented instead as a success or failure of democracy not of socialism. Yet socialism it was and a socialism that survived longer than the fascism of the NIRA thanks to the durability of concrete and the hunger of the nuclear weapons program for electric power. For all the early enthusiasm and serendipitous survival, however, the TVA was not much repeated. Power remained largely publicly regulated rather than publicly owned. Socialisms proceeded so little in the United States that our participation in the global—that is, European—disillusion with socialism took the mild form of deregulation rather than privatization because in America there was not much to privatize. Indeed, about all we could privatize were those things that even antisocialist Americans had once believed were naturally public, like prisons and schools.

In the immediate pre– and post–World War II periods, Americans much praised and feared Sweden, a nation that fascinated the college students of the late 1940s as the guru and dope-laden Indian subcontinent did the Beatles' generation. There, even aside from the glories of free love, was thought to flourish a democratic, as opposed to a Stalinist, socialism. In reality, of course, Sweden was not a socialist but a highly developed welfare state with a left syndicalist economy—that is, a partially cartelized economy in which basic investment, fiscal, and wage decisions were made by a small circle of labor, management, and government executives. The syndicalism was almost invisible to Americans. What they saw and labeled socialism was the welfare state.

Here again the New Deal had done its sampling, most notably, of course, with Social Security and the Federal Housing Administration (FHA). Other bits and pieces had long existed at state and local levels. After the war, some further expansion could be camouflaged as veterans' benefits. By persistently incremental strategies, we adopted Scandinavian modern styles, although with lingering nostalgia for the Americana of Cedar Rapids and Sears Roebuck.

As we all know, the Scandinavian style began to lose fashion when the cheap teak disappeared. The welfare state either actually generated or was said to generate the government budget deficits that loomed larger and larger in political perception. Even the jovial Swedes, prepared to accept the most enthusiastic tax rates, began to ask whether they could entirely embrace their ever-growing welfare sweetheart. The Dutch decided that a country could not operate if everyone in it were allowed to suffer on pension from disabling lower-back pains. Americans began to tote up the incrementally attained costs of welfare and, worse yet, project them far into the future. During the great perceived budget crunch described by Patashnik and Pierson in chapters 2 and 3, respectively, "nondiscretionary spending" and "entitlements" became key bugaboos in the war on the deficit. During the succeeding perceived budgetary surplus, the debate has been about putting existing entitlements on a sound financial basis and what increments to entitlements would not cost too much.

Biology was the king of the politics of the 1960s and 1970s; economics wore the crown of the 1980s and 1990s. At least until the Asia debacle, anyone who has dared to question the glories of free markets has branded him- or herself a fool. And suddenly the costs of welfare have come center stage. In absolute terms, can we afford all this welfare? In terms of global competitiveness, can we afford all this welfare? And, particularly for Europeans, is all this welfare contributing to our persistent unemployment problem? Free benefits and free markets—can we afford the one if we are to engage in the other?

A sustained phenomenon across the Western world is a continued commitment to the welfare state along with nagging concerns about its costs, both its projected costs as a share of gross national product and government spending and its costs in terms of the international competitiveness of national economies. In Europe these concerns were encapsulated in the run-up to the euro. In the United States they have brought welfare reform, repair of the Social Security system, medical care, and the deficit center stage. Even as miraculous prosperity has led to seeming triumph over the deficit, the general tension between universal support for the welfare state and nagging concerns over its costs remains at the center of both American and European politics—the love-hate relationship with the welfare state to which Milkis refers in chapter 15.

It is precisely this tension that leads to the stability *and* change dialectic, or layering, that is so prominent in this volume. The United States has incremented welfare entitlements, refusing to elaborate an overall ideology of the welfare state beyond the rudimentary notion of the "safety net." Federalism allows us an even more piecemeal approach. Such a bits and pieces welfare state generates a fragmented politics of entitlements, a distributional, nonzero-sum, interest group, pluralist, "normal" politics of incremental change. At the same time the unavoidable, cumulative and rising costs of the welfare state, which press upon all the political actors continuously but do not seem to require or to be amenable to immediate, wholly successful rationalization, lead to periodic outbreaks of perceived crisis and bold, entrepreneurial proposals for their resolution. Central to politics become the who, where, what, when, how, and why of declaring a crisis and its proposed resolutions. What is in reality a constant macropressure is translated into a series of episodic microcrises.

If the pressure is macro—that is, about the massive impact of the whole welfare system on the performance of the whole economy—then the solution might lie in a critical or realigning election or set of elections that generated a new consensus. The current situation is exactly the opposite. The fall of international socialism has left a currently unchallengeable intellectual consensus that government ownership of the means of production and central economic planning fail and fail precisely because they cannot solve the incentives problem. At the same time, there is really no inclination to abandon the welfare state along with socialism. Quite the contrary, there is almost total agreement in both Europe and America in persons of every political persuasion and economic circumstance that the rigors of free markets must be tempered by the welfare state. Of course, work is best, but no one is going to be allowed to starve to death in the street. Thus, in both the United States and Europe left and right political parties move to the "center" not only because of the standard American dynamic of two parties and an essentially bell-shaped electorate but for other reasons as well. Both (formerly real and now nominal) socialists and conservatives in Europe and Democrats and Republicans in the United States fully accept the welfare state. Both are concerned about its costs. Both favor private ownership of the means of production. Both, at least short of a true international economic breakdown, incline toward not only domestic but international free markets. Both, therefore, can only offer the electorate a claim that they can manage the current, private enterprise, welfare state, international markets regime better than can the other party. Thus, Milkis's chapter 15 in this volume describes President Clinton's attempt at a "third way" between Republican conservatism and Democratic liberalism, notes European parallels, and emphasizes the growth and persistence of the administrative state even in the face of popular distrust of the competence of the administrators. That distrust is, of course, the theme of McWilliams's chapter 16, which he presents largely in terms of a public concern that governing elites have not struck quite the right balance between markets and regulation.

Because the problems are constant, there is a constant low-visibility incremental politics of policy adjustment and implementation. Because nominal left and right must still confront one another electorally, there is also a politics of crisis-policy innovation. Because the two sides fundamentally are in agreement about private ownership and welfare, they vie with each other either simply in terms of better management, entitlement "reform," "time for a change," personality politics or, when possible, with announcements of welfare crises that they have better solutions to than their opponents. Thus, a politics of droning choruses punctuated by arias is what can be expected unless and until an economic crisis of fundamental proportions disrupts the current free markets welfare state consensus.

The contributions of Pierson and Patashnik to this volume announcing the fiscalizing or budgetizing of the politics of the 1990s, together with the contributions of Teles and Prinz (chapter 9), Martin (chapter 11), and Derthick (chapter 8), reveal a fairly clear pattern. The various currents sketched by Pierson led after 1975 to an increased visibility of welfare costs at the same time a politics of rights reinforced the familiar pattern of interest group politics in which groups plant and nourish government spending programs and the programs in turn nourish vested interest groups. The fall of Keynsianism noted by Patashnik as a major cause of the new politics of budgeting is, of course, the American version of the fall of socialism—that is, the fall in confidence in government to manage the economy. Given the consensus I have noted, the result is not a wholesale dismantling of welfare but instead, as Pierson proclaims it, a politics of austerity in which the costs of welfare are a continuous worry and constraint. Within this austerity the whole volume then notes a layering of politics that fits neatly within the markets-welfare consensus. Many welfare programs remain low-visibility, interest group, incremental policy as usual. Experts and other idea merchants and policy entrepreneurs offer up new policies designed to harmonize markets and welfare. Party electoral competition, credit claiming, blame avoidance politics chooses some of these to bring to high visibility. In this process, some now high-visibility policy initiatives succeed, and some fail because they encounter too high a barrier of entrenched interest groups or too much dissensus among experts. Various factors peculiar to the policy area or the particular set of political circumstances of the moment contribute to success and failure. But overall a new configuration of government financial decision-making institutions evolves that tends to stabilize a greater concern for costs in relation to revenues.

The most outstanding policy successes noted in this volume, at least in terms of survival and growth, are workfare and EITC. Bardach emphasizes the potential conversion of "equality" to "fairness." All of these phenomena are fueled by the desire to address the incentives and competition challenges to markets posed by welfare costs, rendering welfare and markets as compatible as possible while refusing to abandon humanitarian reserves against market forces. Both workfare and EITC seek to reconcile our ideas about welfare and market efficiency by turning welfare recipients into workers and workers into welfare recipients. Conversely, when Teles and Prinz, Burke (chapter 7), and Levin (chapter 1) take up rights and rights' retraction, they tell an AFDC (Aid to Families with Dependent Children) kind of story in which a complicated political dynamic of judicial declaration of rights, party competition, divided government, and federalism is ultimately directed to produce a workfare solution by the consensus on market constrained welfare.

None of this means that American politics does or should necessarily enjoy an era of good feeling. Indeed, certain dimensions of partisan controversy between the political parties have been maintained or sharpened, as Mayhew and others in this volume note. As President Clinton repeated his mantra of growing the economy, to which he contributed almost entirely by leaving the market economy alone, Republicans became increasingly frustrated by his easy *ex officio* credit claiming. As already noted, with a basic economic policy consensus between the parties, partisanship is expressed increasingly by mutual attacks on the administrative competence of the other side. The impeachment controversy was a pinnacle of such attacks, with the Republicans again frustrated by the economic credit mileage the president got out of just being there in an extended period of miraculous prosperity. Both sides agree on the preservation of a sound Social Security system in the face of demographic pressures. The two parties disagree about the details of fiscal strategies to achieve this goal. Again much shouting at the margins but a durable central policy.

This shouting at the margins is well illustrated by the 2000 presidential campaign. Following the Clinton seizure of the middle described by Milkis, the Democrats and Republicans argued about how big a tax cut and to whom, how much the national debt should be reduced, and how fast and how best to put Social Security on a sound financial footing. The two parties offered slightly different increments to Medicare. McWilliams's elites want to respond to McWilliams's people's concerns about education, so both candidates proclaimed largely symbolic education plans, both of which are in the Levin and Landy small government mode (chapter 1). Pushed by the third-party developments to which McWilliams calls our attention, both candidates experienced hesitation about moving toward their own party's or the national voter median. The Democratic candidate did not propose major new federal government programs. The Republican candidate did not propose any radical surgery. Of course, given the probabilistic quality of all economic analysis, even a consensus on markets plus welfare yields the traditional marginal policy differences between Democrats and Republicans on precisely how much regulation and how much welfare are desirable, with the Democrats inclining toward a little more and the Republicans toward a little less.

Even the great environmental awakening has been largely reduced to marginal controversies over economic efficiencies. It is the economic costs of global warming, not its aesthetic consequences, that come center stage along with the international trade consequences of doing more or less, sooner or later, about cooling things off. Some old-growth redwoods are saved but with less regulatory expropriation and more tit for tat. Negotiated rule making is in vogue alongside regulatory impact analysis, "soft law" modes of regulation, and the new magic word, *deliberation,* as the stairway to the promised land of regulatory answers that are both right and consensual. We shall now deliberate the polluters rather than smiting them.

To put the matter slightly differently, the consensus on the free market is actually a consensus on the regulated market, on the substitution of government regulation for government ownership of the means of production. Much of this regulation can be rationalized by laissez-faire true believers in terms of market failures, the proper assignment of externalized costs, correction of information deficiencies, and so on. But in reality few are interested in preserving their ideological purity. Regulation is accepted to achieve health, safety, environmental, and other values whenever the market is not thought to be sufficiently achieving them. And while no one would contend that we should pay more than is necessary to achieve our goals, only a few contend that our goals themselves need be efficient. We may choose, if we wish, to protect worker safety or research the causes of cancer far beyond the point where benefits outweigh costs because we do not accept the proposition that we should allow a man to lose his arm if it is cheaper to compensate him for the loss than to install the safety devices that would have prevented the loss. We should, however, install the safety devices that will save the arm at least cost.

As Bardach tells us, the "fair" or humane distribution of risk, or distribution of protection against risk, is now a durable feature of our policy thinking and is not the same as the efficient or rational response to risk. Risk regulation takes place in conditions of considerable uncertainty and often of probabilities that cannot be estimated accurately. More generally, much regulation involves intangible values such as the glory of knowing that a wilderness that you are forbidden to see is still there or a guppy still lives in some mud hole. Thus, regulation provides a fertile ground for partisan conflict at the margins. The general regulatory agenda of the Democratic and Republican parties would look much alike, no matter how much one loved and the other hated corporate capitalism. But the devil in the regulatory details can and does inspire plenty of both interest group and party-electoral controversy.

Indeed, it has been widely noted that at both U.S. and global levels, more market means more regulation. Everyone knows of the great health, safety, and environmental regulatory outburst of the 1970s and 1980s. But everything that Burke says about the persistence of rights, and the comments throughout this volume directed to the persistence or layering of various styles of politics, applies to regulation. The rights to clean air and so forth are not going to go away. It is true that a lot of "deregulation" has occurred where pure market entry or rate regulation was at issue, but much of the enthusiasm for that kind of deregulation was fueled by the unparalleled U.S. economic prosperity of recent years and an alliance between true free marketeers and pragmatists who found that in some regulatory arenas regulatory abuses cost the citizenry even more than free market abuses would. At this very moment we are pressing regulation of financial institutions on the third world and flirting with import quotas ourselves. The consensus on markets is also a consensus on regulation.

The general consensus on regulation, both economic and other kinds, brings to the fore a cleavage that cuts across those between Democrats and Republicans and is treated extensively by Beam and Conlan, Skerry, Patashnik, and Martin. In modern high-tech economies, regulation necessarily implies a tension between technocratic and democratic government. Cincinnatus cannot come from the plow to regulate the nuclear power industry. On the other hand, we have learned that experts have their own interests and preferences that will be privileged if experts are allowed too large a voice in policymaking. Every act of regulatory policymaking is also an act of determining the relative strength of expert and nonexpert in policymaking.

The 1990s experienced a peak in the charisma of one brand of expert—the economist. Not only did economists tell us that free trade and a globalized economy was our only option, but, far, far more important, economists told us the proper moment-to-moment interest rate to grow the economy. The economy may have been President Clinton's cloak, but it is Alan Greenspan's baby. Should the national economy stumble, as has the international one, the Federal Reserve Board may lose charisma, as the International Monetary Fund has. Particularly where there is perceived regulatory policy failure, rival expertises are likely to become prominent and expertise as a whole is likely to lose some of its leverage over the policymaking process.

This volume places a good deal of emphasis on experts as providers of ideas for which they act as entrepreneurs themselves or turn over to politicians. We must also remember the continuing power of experts in providing the millions of implementing details required to make regulatory programs run. It may be even more important that experts are in at the landings than that they are in at the takeoffs.

The consensus on markets and welfare tends to channel partisan energies into policy areas in which less consensus exists, the so-called social issues: crime, education, abortion, gender, and ethnicity. Crime produces its own consensus. Neither side can really be for it. Liberals long clung to the pro-crook science of criminology, but for the most part they eventually joined the anticrime crusade. Here again the dispute becomes a marginal one over management competence and fairness issues such as police brutality and the inflexibility of sentencing guidelines and three-strikes laws. But the conflict is muted by the consensus. It is a Republican administration that stages a double jeopardy, political trial of police officers accused of brutality, with Democrat civil libertarians remaining absolutely silent about the politically correct lynching because for once it is the brutalizers who are being brutalized by the justice apparatus. Both parties want more cops, the death penalty, and more jail time, but Democrats are more interested and Republicans less in drug rehabilitation programs. The Democratic voices for drug programs sing the song, however, that rehab is cheaper than prison.

Race, gender, ethnicity, and "family values" remain as the major sticking points outside the dominance of the free market–welfare combination. In such areas both policymaking processes and policy outputs of unusual sorts may be anticipated but may not always materialize. Thus, we find the tortured and somewhat inexplicable story of the persistence of affirmative action policies in the face of majority negative sentiment, but a more or less normal story of the ethnic politics of immigration. In education both parties pretend to bold education strategies, but even the Democrats are careful not to propose major shifts of responsibility to the central government.

The most partisan of all matters currently is the gender-abortion cluster. In their introduction, Levin and Landy note the long-standing, "old politics" phenomenon of each of the two great parties seeking its own center and thus moving away from the general voter center in the periods between general elections and then either scrambling back or paying dearly when the general elections occur. The Democrats have stubbed a toe on gay issues. The Republicans have contracted a life-threatening disease on the abortion issue.

Abortion and gender discrimination issues, more than almost any other major policy issues of Western societies, have become a special domain of courts. The judicialization of policymaking in these areas has not, however, necessarily removed them from the arena of party politics. Generally speaking, the judicialization of gender employment discrimination has been moderately successful. The idea of gender employment equality is unchallengeable. The actual costs of implementation are largely borne piecemeal and relatively gradually by the private sector, and general economic gains from opening the vast female employment pool exceed losses. Only where judicial intervention creates very large, concentrated costs to governments, as in some of the pension decisions of the European Court of Justice, is the judiciary likely to encounter serious opposition. Abortion, of course, is quite a different story. Where courts have intervened, they have stimulated rather than sublimated partisan political controversy.

The debate is still open about the degree of success of courts when they took the lead in race policy. Clearly the politics of race is a central phenomenon of American politics, legislative and executive as well as judicial, and the comparable problem of ethnicity is becoming central in Europe. These problems are partially defined and exacerbated by the perceived need for constrained welfare in a market regime, but the basic tensions lie along quite a different dimension. It is no coincidence that race has had a deeply negative effect on the electoral viability of the Democratic party and abortion on the Republican party while both move merrily to the center on regulated markets and constrained welfare. It remains to be seen whether race and gender issues can be subordinated to some combination of the stability of the old interest group politics and the market-welfare consensus of the new politics of public policy.

When we turn our attention to the ideas component of American politics and the impact of the regulated market constrained welfare consensus on American policymaking, it is difficult to keep our eyes from drifting eastward across the Atlantic. There we see constrained welfare as central to the political economy of the euro, socialist parties deserting socialism but claiming to be more efficient at managing market-embedded governments than the rival parties, pushes for free markets and more regulation deeply intertwined in the policymaking of the European Union, debate over technocratic versus democratic governance, and a cross-cutting and potentially explosive race-ethnicity-citizenship issue. What may be different is employment, full in the United States and far from full in Europe. But even here the market-welfare connection may be crucial to both. Europeans tend to see the difference in terms of the United States' falsely solving the problem of market utilization of the most inefficient by employing them at wages below the poverty line, while Europe places them on welfare above the poverty line. It is often said in Europe that for many people it is better to be unemployed in Germany than employed in the United States. Ultimately the problem of not letting the least efficient starve is a problem on both sides of the pond.

At the more purely political level, on both sides of the Atlantic we can note elections keyed to the claims of party leaders to competence, the closely connected themes of corruption and campaign finance reform, and above all the push toward the center by the major competing parties. All of the inattention to ideology, particularly at election time, for which Europeans used to chide Americans, is now a determining quality of European electoral politics as well. And so is a judicialization of politics and a political discourse of "rights."

Without speaking the dreaded name of globalization, it does appear that the market-welfare consensus and tension is shared by Europe and the United States, as are very roughly similar democratic political institutions and processes and the tensions between democratic and technocratic regulatory governance. Perhaps the general ideas hovering behind concrete policies are the most trans-Atlantic in character and the particular policies adopted the least, but it is increasingly hard to offer purely American analyses of American regulatory and welfare policies or even social policies.

Contributors

Eugene Bardach is professor of public policy in the Richard and Rhoda Goldman School of Public Policy at the University of California at Berkeley. He is the author of *The Eight-Step Path of Policy Analysis: A Handbook for Practice,* for which he received the 1998 Donald T. Campbell award of the Policy Studies Organization for creative contributions to the methodology of policy analysis; and *Getting Agencies to Work Together: The Practice and Theory of Managerial Craftsmanship.*

David R. Beam is professor of political science and director of the Master of Public Administration program at the Illinois Institute of Technology. A former senior analyst with the U.S. Advisory Commission on Intergovernmental Relations, his published works examine contemporary American federalism, and his current writings address the political challenges facing public policy analysts and ethical issues in privatization. Beam is the author of *Taxing Choices: The Politics of Tax Reform.*

Thomas F. Burke is an assistant professor of American politics at Wellesley College. He is author of *Litigation and Its Discontents: The Struggle over Lawyers, Lawsuits, and Legal Rights in America.*

Timothy J. Conlan is professor of government and politics at George Mason University, where he directs the university's Federalism and Public Policy Research Center. Previously he served as assistant staff director of the Senate Subcommittee on Intergovernmental Relations and as a senior analyst with the Advisory Commission on Intergovernmental Relations. Conlan is the coauthor of *Federal Regulation of State and Local Governments: The Mixed Record of the 1980s; Taxing Choices: The Politics of Tax Reform;* and *New Federalism: Intergovernmental Reform from Nixon to Reagan.*

Martha Derthick is Julia Allen Cooper Professor of Government and Foreign Affairs at the University of Virginia. She is the coauthor of *The Politics of Deregulation,* which won the Louis Brownlow Award from the National Academy of Public Administration; and is the author of *Policymaking for Social Security,* awarded by NAPA and the American Political Science Association; and *Agency Under Stress.*

Christopher Howard is the David D. and Carolyn B. Wakefield Associate Professor of Government at the College of William and Mary and author of *The Hidden Welfare State.*

Marc K. Landy is professor of political science at Boston College. He is an author (with Marc Roberts and Stephen Thomas) of *The Environmental Protection Agency from Nixon to Clinton;* the coauthor of *Presidential Greatness;* and coeditor of *The New Politics of Public Policy.*

Martin A. Levin is professor of political science at Brandeis University. He is the author of *The Political Hand: Policy Implementation and Youth Employment Programs; Urban Politics and the Criminal Courts; After the Cure: Managing Aids Other Public Health Crises; Making Government Work;* and coeditor of *The New Politics of Public Policy.*

Cathie Jo Martin is a professor of political science at Boston University. She is author of *Stuck in Neutral.*

David R. Mayhew, Sterling Professor of Political Science at Yale University, is the author of *Congress: The Electoral Connection; Divided We Govern;* and *America's Congress.*

Wilson Carey McWilliams is professor of political science at Rutgers University. He is the author of *The Idea of Fraternity in American Politics* and of numerous essays about American political thought and American politics. He is a frequent contributor to *Commonweal.*

Sidney M. Milkis is professor of government and senior scholar at the Miller Center of Public Affairs, University of Virginia. He is the author of *The President and the Parties* and *Political Parties and Constitutional Government,* as well as the coauthor of *Presidential Greatness.*

Eric M. Patashnik is an assistant professor of political science at Yale University. He is author of *Putting Trust in the U.S Budget: Federal Trust Funds and the Politics of Commitment.*

Paul Pierson is a professor of government at Harvard University. He is the author **of** *Dismantling the Welfare State?: Reagan, Thatcher, and the Politics of Retrenchment;* coeditor of *European Social Policy: Between Fragmentation and Integration;* and editor of *The New Politics of the Welfare State.*

Timothy S. Prinz is Senior Health Policy Analyst at the United Hospital Fund of New York City. He is coauthor of *Ten Virginia Papers 1990–1995.*

Peter H. Schuck is Simeon E. Baldwin Professor of Law at Yale and author of *Suing Government: Citizen Remedies for Official Wrongs; Citizenship without Consent: Illegal Aliens in the American Policy;* and *Agent Orange on Trial: Mass Toxic Disasters in the Courts.* He has also been principal deputy assistant secretary for planning and evaluation in the U.S. Department of Health, Education, and Welfare (1977–79); director of the Washington Office of Consumers Union (1972–77); and consultant to the Center for Study of Responsive Law (1971–72).

Martin Shapiro is Coffroth Professor of Law at Berkeley's Boalt Hall School of Law. He is one of the founders of Berkeley's program on Jurisprudence and Social Policy. His books include *Who Guards the Guardians; Judicial Control of Administration; Courts: A Comparative and Political Analysis;* and *Law and Politics in the Supreme Court.*

Peter Skerry is an associate professor of government at Claremont McKenna College. He is the author of *Counting on the Census: Race, Group Identity, and the Evasion of Politics* and *Mexican Americans: The Ambivalent Minority;* and coauthor of *What, Then, Is the American; This New Man?;* and *Christian Schools, Racial Quotas, and the IRS.*

John David Skrentny is a professor in the Law and Society program at the University of California, San Diego. He is author of *The Ironies of Affirmative Action: Politics, Culture, and Justice in America.*

Steven M. Teles is a professor of political science at Brandeis University. He is the author of *Whose Welfare? AFDC and Elite Politics.*

David Vogel is professor at the Haas School of Business, University of California, Berkeley, and author of *Benefits or Barriers? Regulation in the Trans-Atlantic Trade; Kindred Strangers: The Uneasy Relationship between Business and Politics in America;* and *Trading Up: Consumer and Environmental Regulation in a Global Economy.*

Index

Aaron, Henry, 207
Abortion issue, and Republicans, 365, 435–436
Abraham, Spencer, 130
Act for Better Child Care (ABC), 250
Adarand Constructors v. Pena, 152, 159
Affirmative action
  antipreference policy, control of, 154–156
  beneficiaries of, 132–133
  business sector view of, 142–144
  durability of, 22, 133–134, 141–151
  educational setting, 138–139
  initiation of, 136
  interest groups for, 147–148
  low-visibility amendments/riders, 151–153
  minority-owned business assistance, 137–138
  Philadelphia Plan, 136–137
  policy context and agenda, 153–154
  public opinion of, 133, 141–142
  regulations related to, 136–139
  Republican Party, 132–159, 143–151
  retrenchment, areas for, 139–141
  support for preferences, divide and conquer strategy, 156–158
  Supreme Court interventions, 152, 158–159
Aid to Dependent Children of 1935, 219
Aid to Families with Dependent Children (AFDC)
  creation of, 219
  end of, 215–227
  history of, 217–226
  low participation rate, 219
Aid to Families with Dependent Children (AFDC). *See also* Welfare reform
Aleinikoff, Alex, 124
Alvarez, Lizette, 392
America Leads on Trade, 330
American Association of Retired Persons (AARP), 60, 68
American Enterprise Institute, 244
Americans with Disabilities Act (ADA), 18, 175
Americorps, 352, 360
Anti-Terrorism and Effective Death Penalty Act (AEDPA), 120–121, 180
Apportionment
  effects of census adjustment, 296–299
  redistricting, 298–299
Archey, Bill, 280, 281
Armey, Richard, 120, 145
Austerity, fiscal policy, 58, 60–74
  of 1970s–1980, 61–64, 66–67
  policy trends related to, 61–65
  political trends related to, 65–74

Baker, Howard, 392
Baker, James, 196, 245
Balanced budget. *See* Federal budget
Balanced Budget Act of 1997, 24, 30–31, 48
Ball, Robert M., 196, 205, 207
Banking reform, 4, 25
Bardach, Eugene, 401

Baumgartner, Frank, 178
Beam, David R., 81
Beer, Samuel H., 92
Bell, Daniel, 56
Bennett, William, 120, 381
Bentsen, Lloyd, 252
Binder, Sarah, 38
Bipartisan support, areas of, 8, 26–27, 50
Blendon, Robert, 264
Block grants, 234, 393
Boehner, John, 281
Bolick, Clint, on affirmative action,
    139, 143, 148, 154, 156, 157
Bond, Christopher, 152
Borjas, George, 126, 128
Bosso, Christopher, 102
Bradley, Bill, 88
Brady, David W., 36
Breaux, John, 206
Brimelow, Peter, 127
Brinkley, Alan, 355
Broder, John, 392
Brown, Jerry, political agenda of, 6
Brown, Robert, 59
Brownlee, W. Elliot, 57
Brunell, Thomas, 295
Bryant, Barbara, 303
Buchanan, Pat, 31
    on immigration policy, 118, 124
    on trade policy, 330, 331
Buckley v. Valeo, 395
Budget. *See* Federal budget; Federal
    budget deficit; Federal budget
    deficit reduction
Budget Act of 1974, 38, 40
Budget Enforcement Act (BEA) of
    1990, 40, 48, 68
Bunning, Jim, 281
Bureaucratic approach, health care
    reform, 277–278
Burke-Hartke bill, 319
Burke, Thomas F., 172
Bush George, H.W.
    and health care reform, 269
    on taxation, 36–37, 90, 98
    and welfare system, 225–226
Bush, George W.
    on immigration, 129–130
    slogan of, 6, 11, 20
    on Social Security, 208
    tax cut, 49
Business Opportunity Development
    Reform Act 1988, 138

Business sector
    on affirmative action, 142–144
    and health care reform, 271–273,
        282–285
    on trade policy, 330
Butler, David, 298
Butler, Stuart, 224

Cain, Bruce, 298
California Civil Rights Initiative
    (CCRI) (Proposition 209),
    140–141, 151
Campaign finance, interest group con-
    tributions, 105
Canada
    health care system, 268
    immigration policy, 114
Canady, Charles, 139–140, 155
Capital gains, tax cut, 69, 87
Carson, Rachel, 102
Carter, Jimmy, 60, 89, 355–356, 361
Cato Institute, 202, 205
Census adjustment, 292–306
    apportionment effects, 296–299
    and ethnic minorities, 294, 299–301
    fiscal effects, 296
    impact on states, 295–296
    process of, 294–295
    right to be counted issue, 303–306
    sampling issue, 294–295
    scientific approach to, 301–303
    undercount, 293–294
Center on Budget and Policy Priorities
    (CBPP), 243, 245, 251
Center for Equal Opportunity, 143
Center for Immigration Studies, 130
Chafee, John, 363
Chamber of Congress, and health care
    reform, 280–281, 282
Chandler, Alfred D., Jr., 348
Charter school program, 6
China, most favored nation status, 5, 322
China Permanent Normal Trade
    Relations (PNTR), 5, 10
Christian Coalition, 141
Citizens for a Sound Economy, 274
City of Richmond v. J.A. Croson Co.,
    158–159
Civil Rights Act of 1964, Title VII and
    affirmative action, 136–137
Civil Rights Act of 1991, 181
Civil Rights Act of 1997, 141, 145,
    153–154

Clegg, Roger, 143, 149
Clinton, Bill
    and 1992 presidential election,
        20–21
    and 1996 presidential election, 9,
        12, 367–369
    on affirmative action, 148
    balanced budget bill, 367
    on entitlement programs, 6
    fund-raising issue, 394
    health care reform efforts, 264–286,
        362–363
    on homosexuals in military, 358,
        364, 366
    impeachment, 14, 28, 351–352,
        370–373, 388–389
    limitations of, 351–352, 358–360,
        364
    politics as president. See Clinton-
        era politics
    public approval ratings, 15, 286,
        352, 369–370, 372
    reinventing government (REGO),
        359
    Republican treatment of, 354–355
    and taxation, 67
    and trade policy, 321, 324–325,
        329–333, 361–362
    welfare reform, 6, 7, 226–235,
        251–256, 367–368
Clinton-era politics
    Democratic Leadership Council
        (DLC), 248, 356, 361
    and divided government, 353–354,
        360–366
    new covenant, scope of action,
        355–360
    New Democrats, 11–12, 353–360,
        406–408
    and partisanship, 355–356, 359–366,
        370
    Republican congress, 358–372
    and Republican policies, 351, 354
    third-way politics, 352–353, 355,
        369
    two-tier politics, 382–396
    and welfare state, 373–374
Clinton, Hillary Rodham, and health
        care reform, 264, 277, 362
Coalition on Jobs and Health Care, 285
Cohen, Richard, 389
Communitarianism, 20
Community, bonds of, 403–404

Community Development Block
        Grants, and census adjustment,
        292, 296
Congress
    apportionment and census adjust-
        ment, 297–300
    Republican, and Clinton, 358–372
Congressional Budget Office (CBO),
        38–40
    creation of, 38
Conlan, Timothy J., 81
Connerly, Ward, 140
Contract with America, 88, 90, 105,
        119, 231, 363, 365
Cooper, Horace, 145, 149
Cost-of-living adjustment (COLA),
        Social Security, 195, 196, 197
Crime, by illegal aliens, 125–126

Danforth, John C., 199
Defense spending, reduction in, 58, 61
Deficit reduction. See Federal budget
        deficit reduction
Democratic Leadership Council
        (DLC), 248, 356, 361, 407
Democratic Party
    competition with Republicans
        (1990s), 8–10
    and economy, 20–21
    as "moon" party, 8, 21–22, 27
    New Democrats, 11–12, 353–360,
        406–408
    and small government, 19–20
    on spending surplus of budget, 8
    on trade policy, 10, 314–316, 330–331
Democratic Party. See also Clinton, Bill
Department of Health, Education, and
        Welfare, 219
Deregulation
    banking reform, 4
    Freedom to Farm Act, 4, 25
    impetus for, 434
    telecommunications reform, 4
    telephone service, 390
Derthick, Martha, 55, 193
Destler, I.M., 317
Devolution alternative, welfare
        reform, 228–231
Dickerson v. United States, 22–23, 185
Dingell, John, 284
Divided We Govern (Mayhew), 10
Dole, Bob
    on abortion, 386

Dole, Bob *(continued)*
  on affirmative action, 90, 145, 151
  and Equal Opportunity Act of
    1995, 139–140
  on taxation, 90
  on welfare reform, 232–234
Dole-Candady bill, 139–140
Domenici, Pete, 35, 197
Dukakis, Michael, 12
Dworkin, Ronald, 176, 402
Dymally, Mervyn, 305–306

Earned Income Tax Credit (EITC), 30, 72
  cutbacks, 253–256
  Democrats on, 252–253
  entrepreneurial advocacy for, 242–243
  expansion of, 239, 241–243, 255–256
  future view, 256–257
  largest increase in, 244, 252
  as means-tested program, 241
  and moral hazard, 411
  operation of, 6, 240
  politics of, 406–407
  values upheld by, 240–241
Economic Recovery and Tax Act of
  1981, 246
Economy
  and Democratic Party, 20–21
  and market efficiency, 25–26
  and Republican Party, 21
  stagflation, 26, 43
Ed/Flex, 8, 19
Education legislation, 102. *See also*
  School-related issues
Eisenhower, Dwight D., 350–351
Elementary and Secondary Education
  Act for 1965 (ESEA), 102
Elites
  consensus with, 385
  local elites, 393
  opposition to, 387–389
Ellwood, David, 227
Employment, immigrants versus citi-
  zens, 128–129
Employment discrimination, legal
  restrictions, 137–138
Employment discrimination. *See also*
  Affirmation action
Engler, John, 339
Enthoven, Alain, 269
Entitlement programs
  and austere fiscal policy, 62–63
  and budget process, 45–47

Entitlement programs. *See also specific*
  programs
Environmental issues, 432–433
Environmental Protection Agency
  (EPA), 179
Equal Employment Opportunity
  Commission (EEOC), functions
  of, 137
Equal Opportunity Act of 1995, 139
Equal Protection Clause, 175. *See also*
  Rights
Equality, decline in relevance of, 402–404
Esping-Anderson, Gosta, 57
Estate tax, 12
Ethics in Government Act of 1978, 354,
  373
Ethnic minorities
  and census adjustment, 294, 299–301
  equal opportunity regulations,
    136–137
  federal assistance for businesses,
    137–138
  origin of groups, 138
Ethnic minorities. *See also* Affirmative
  action
European Union (EU), 321, 328–329
Evans, Donald, 293
Expansionism
  fiscal policy, 26, 30, 57–60
  immigration, 113–117

Fairness
  elements of, 409
  and policymaking, 24
Family Economic Security Act of 1988,
  247
Family Educational Rights and Privacy
  Act of 1974 (FERPA), 102
Family Research Council, 141
Family Support Act (FSA) of 1988, 227
Federal Acquisition Act amendments,
  138
Federal agencies, increase in, 45
Federal budget
  Balanced Budget Act of 1997, 24,
    30–31, 48
  balanced budget concept, 30–31, 43
  Budget Enforcement Act (BEA), 40,
    48
  classical period of, 45
  and entitlement programs, 46–48
  fiscalization of policy concept, 6,
    12, 17, 23, 26–27, 36–40

future view, 48–50
Gramm-Rudman Act, 27, 40, 47–48
Keynesian economics, 41–44
long-term budget items, 44–47
and policymaking, 23–24, 35–36
Federal budget deficit, 47–48
and moderate policy, 6, 17
and 1960s, 41–43
and 1970s, 43
and 1980s, 43–44
as theme of 1990s, 26–27
Federal budget deficit reduction
and Clinton 1996 victory, 12
effects on fiscal policy, 74–77
mechanisms of, 7–8
and policymaking, 23–24
post-deficit skepticism, 74–76
surplus, uses of, 8, 50
surplus amount, 74
and tax reductions, 69–70
Federal government
public opinion of, 384, 392–393, 403
small government programs, 19
Federal Insecticide, Fungicide, and
Rodenticide Act (FIFRA) of
1947, 102
Federal Insurance Contributions Act
(FICA), 194
Federal Reserve Board, influence of,
43, 434
Federation for American Immigration
Reform (FAIR), 114, 128
Feldstein, Martin, 206
Finney, Leon, 299
Fiscal policy
austerity, 58, 60–74
deficit reduction, effects of, 74–77
expansionism, 26, 30, 57–60
fiscal activism, 41
fiscal regime concept, 56–57, 77
sociological perspective, 56–57
Fiscalization of policy concept, 6, 12,
17, 23, 26–27, 36–40, 243
Flat tax proposal, 93, 98–99, 385
Flynn, Ray, 295
Food stamps, 43, 121
Forbes, Steve, 385
Ford, Gerald, 60, 132
Fordney-McCumber Act of 1922, 315
Freedom to Farm Act of 1996, 4, 25
Freeman, Richard, 128
Friedman, Lawrence, 177
Friedman, Milton, 201

Full-employment budget, 42
Fuller, Ida May, 60
Fund-raising scandal, Democratic, 394

Gender discrimination, Civil Rights
Act of 1964, 136–137
Gender discrimination. *See*
Affirmative action
General Agreement on Tariffs and
Trade (GATT), 314, 325, 329,
331–332
Gephardt, Richard, 88, 330
Gingrich, Newt, 21
on affirmative action, 145, 153,
154–155
on census adjustment, 292–293
Contract with America, 88, 90, 105,
119, 231, 363, 365
on health care reform, 280
on immigration, 120
negative attitudes toward, 27, 28
Republican Revolution, 27, 88
resignation of, 21, 372
Giuliani, Rudolph, 339
Glendon, Mary Ann, 107, 173
Goldberg v. Kelly, 220
Goldwater, Barry, 201–202
Gore, Al
fund-raising scandal, 394
on immigration, 130
and National Performance Review
(NPR), 359, 367
and 2000 presidential election, 12,
76, 130
Graham, Hugh Davis, 158
Gramm, Phil, 140, 206, 233
Gramm-Rudman Act 1985, 27, 40, 47–48
Great Society, 26, 30
Greenberg, Stan, influence of, 278–279
Greenspan, Alan, 348
influence of, 43, 434
Greenspan Commission, 196, 210
Greenstein, Robert, 242–243, 245, 407
Gregg, Judd, 206
Greider, William, 97
Guinier, Lani, 306

Hall, Peter, 116
Hall, Robert E., 99
Hamilton, Alexander, 382
Handlin, Oscar, 351
Harkin, Tom, 330
Hart, Peter, 203

Haskins, Ron, 225
Hastert, Denny, 285
Hatch, Orrin, 250
Health Care Equity Action League, 281
Health care reform, 73, 264–286,
    362–363
  bureaucratic approach, 277–278
  business sector support, 271–273
  and Clinton public approval rating,
    286
  goal of, 279
  Heritage Foundation plan, 268, 269
  ideas and interests in formation of,
    270–275
  interest groups, 274, 278, 281–285
  Kennedy-Kassenbaum proposal,
    19, 276
  managed care developments dur-
    ing era of, 276
  managed competition, 269–270,
    273–275
  and National Association of
    Manufacturers (NAM), 271, 279,
    282–284
  opponents of, 274–275, 279–286
  play-or-pay system, 268–269
  political salience of, 275–286
  political significance of, 265–267
  and Republicans, 279–282
  single-payer approach, 268
  task force for, 277
  voucher system, 269
  weaknesses of plan, 277–278
Health and Human Services (HHS),
    and welfare program, 223
Health Insurance Association of
    America (HIAA), anti-health
    care reform, 274
Heckman, James, 402
Heritage Foundation
  health care reform plan, 268, 269
  on Social Security, 205
Higgins, Foster, 273, 276, 278, 283
Hobbs, Chuck, 223
Hochschild, Jennifer, 144
Hohfeld, Wesley, 174–175
Homosexuals in military, 358, 364, 366
Hopwood v. Texas, 159
Howard, Christopher, 64, 239

Illegal Immigration Reform and
    Immigrant Responsibility Act of
    1996 (IIRIRA), 121

Immigration Act of 1990
    (IMMACT90), 113–117
  conditions leading to, 114–117
  provisions of, 113–114
Immigration issues
  citizen workers, damage to,
    128–129
  criminal aliens, 125–126
  economic recession and restriction,
    114
  expansionist policy, 113–117
  future view, 129–130
  good immigrant/bad immigrant
    concept, 124–125, 127
  and idea politics, 115–116, 123–124
  intergovernmental aspects, 127–128
  nonassimilating immigrants,
    126–127
  and presidential election of 1996,
    120–121
  Proposition 187, 118–120, 127–128
  and Republican Party, 119–121,
    129–130
  restrictionist interest groups, 114,
    128
  welfare reform and immigrants,
    117–118, 121, 126, 130
Immigration laws
  Illegal Immigration Reform and
    Immigrant Responsibility Act of
    1996 (IIRIRA), 121
  Immigration Act of 1990, 113–117
  Immigration and Nationality Act
    (INA), 117
  Immigration Reform and Control
    Act of 1986, 118–119
Immigration and Naturalization
    Service (INS), 115, 118, 121–122
Impeachment, Clinton, 14, 28, 351–352,
    370–373, 388–389
Indexing, of Social Security, 195–196
Individual Retirement Accounts
    (IRAs), Roth IRAs, 69
Inter-Modal Surface Transportation
    Efficiency Act of 1982 (ISTEA),
    138, 152, 153, 156
Interest groups
  affirmative action, 147–148
  contributions of, 105
  health care reform, 274, 278,
    281–285
  immigration restriction, 114, 128
  and policymaking, 60, 68, 85

predominant types of, 105
trade policy, 330–331
Interest rates, rise in 1980s, 63
International Monetary Fund, 332, 434
International Trade Commission, 320
Iron triangle, pesticide industry, 102
IRS Restructuring and Reform Act of
    1998, 69

Jasinowski, Jerry, 279, 283
Johnson, Lyndon B., 18, 87, 92
    on gender discrimination, 136
    Great Society, 26, 30
Jones, Bryan, 178
Jordan Commission, 122
Jordan, Vernon, 371
Justice, Rawls theory of, 410–411

Kagan, Robert, 177
Kasich, John, 206, 360
Katz, Lawrence, 128
Kemp, Jack, 120
Kennedy, Anthony, 158
Kennedy, Edward, 252
    on health care reform, 19, 276
Kennedy, John F., 41
Kerrey, J. Robert, 199, 205, 206
Kettle, Donald, 359
Keynesian economics, 41–44
    effectiveness 1960s–1980s, 41–44,
        48–49
    public opinion of, 42
King v. Smith, 220
Kitzhaber, John, 339
Kosovo crisis, 31
Kristol, William, 120, 279

Laffer, Arthur, 244
Landy, Marc, 183
Lash, William III, 317
Leadership Conference on Civil
    Rights, 147
Lease, Mary Ellen, 388
Lesher, Richard, 281
Levin, Sander, 391
Lieberman, Joseph I., 140
Lindberg, Tod, 275
Lipsky, Michael, 219
Long, Huey, 15
Long, Russell, 406
Lott, Trent, 145
Low Income Opportunity Advisory
    Board (LIOAB), 223–224

McCain, John, 152
McConnell, Mitch, on affirmative
    action, 152–156
McDermott, Jim, 228
McInturff, Bill, 279
McLaughlin v. Boston School Committee, 24
McWilliams, Wilson Carey, 151, 381
Magaziner, Ira, 277, 362
Managed care, forms of, 273
Managed competition, health care
    reform, 269–270, 273–275
Managed Health Care Association, 274
Mann, Thomas, 381
Mansfield, Harvey, 383
Market efficiency, and policymaking,
    25–26
Marshall, T.H., 403
Martin, Cathie Jo, 264
Martin v. Wilks, 158
Matsui, Robert, 228
Mayhew, David R., 43, 339
Media, and policymaking, 90–91
Medicare
    federal expenditures in 1980s, 63
    prescription drug benefit proposal,
        76
    strengthening of, 8
Megan's Law, 181
Melnick, Shep, 178
Mencken, H.L., 396
Middle East crises, 31
Milkis, Sidney M., 350
Miller, Dr. Herman, 299
Minimum wage, increase in, 247–248
Minimum Wage Restoration Act,
    247–248
Minority Small Business and Capital
    Ownership Development,
    137–138
Miranda rule, 184–185
    durability of, 22
Mitchell, George, 363
Moderate policy
    and budget deficit, 6
    deficit reduction, 7–8
    deregulation, 4
    dualism related to, 18–19
    enduring and non-enduring poli-
        cies, 21–23
    policies, types of, 4–5
    and Republicans, 21
    trade initiatives, 5
    welfare reform, 4, 7

Moderation
  meaning of, 6–7
  resistance to change, 14–15
Mondale, Walter, 12, 197, 405
Morone, James, 266
Morris, Dick, 231, 352
Most favored nation status, China, 5
Moynihan, Daniel P., 92, 206, 230, 303
Murray, Charles, 230

National Association for the
  Advancement of Colored
  People (NAACP), 143, 147
National Association of Manufacturers
  (NAM), and health care reform,
  271, 279, 282–284
National Coalition of Minority
  Businesses, 145
National Environmental Policy Act of
  1969, 346
National Governor's Association, on
  welfare reform, 233–234
National Organization for Women
  (NOW), 147
National Performance Review (NPR),
  359, 367
Negative Income Tax (NIT), 220–221
New Covenant, 355–360
New Deal, 25–26, 41, 179, 194
  anticompetitive devices of, 25–26
New Democrats, 11–12, 353–360,
  406–408
New Frontier, 26
Nivola, Pietro, 316
Nixon, Richard, 60
  and affirmative action, 132
Noah, Timothy, 297–298
North American Free Trade
  Agreement (NAFTA), 5, 10, 25,
  314, 324–325, 330–333, 361–362,
  392
Nunn, Sam, 358

O'Connell, Jim, 272
O'Connor, Sandra Day, 158
Office of Federal Contract Compliance
  (OFCC), 136
Offner, Paul, 230
Oklahoma City bombing, legislation
  related to, 120–121
Old-Age, Survivors, and Disability
  Insurance (OASDI), 199

Omnibus Budget Reconciliation Act
  (OBRA) of 1990, 81, 89, 94
  child care provisions, 250–251
Omnibus Budget Reconciliation Act
  (OBRA) of 1993, and Earned
  Income Tax Credit (EITC), 251
O'Neill, Thomas P., 197
Opportunity, access to, 402
Organized labor, decline of, 67–68
Ornstein, Norman, 35

Packwood, Bob, 88, 230–231
Panetta, Leon, 252
Partisanship
  and Clinton politics, 355–356
  and policymaking, 87–90
  and Social Reciprocity (SR) con-
    tract, 417–418
Patashnik, Eric M., 35, 383
Patient's bill of rights, 19–20, 73
Patterson, Orlando, 141, 144
Pay-as-you-go systems, 68, 216, 217
  operation of, 59
Payne-Aldrich Act of 1909, 315
Payne v. Tennessee, 182
Payroll tax, 194
Pechman, Joseph A., 93
Perot, Ross, 12, 15, 124, 252, 330,
  355
Perry, Tim, 360
Personal Responsibility and Work
  Opportunity Act (PRWORA),
  218–219
Pesticide control, 102
Peterson, Mark, 268
Petri, Thomas, 248
Pickle, Jake, 196
Pierson, Paul, 54, 135, 182, 197
Pitts, Billy, 281
Planned Parenthood v. Casey, 23, 181,
  182
Play-or-pay system, health care
  reform, 268–269
Pluralist perspective, policymaking,
  86–87
Policy
  elimination of, 134–135
  elite-directed policy, 135–136
  meaning of, 4
  policy image, 183–184
  policy lock-in, 182
Policy. *See also* Moderate policy

Policymaking
  bipartisan support, areas of, 8,
    26–27
  competing for the middle concept,
    13–14
  and concept of work, 24–25
  and Congressional procedures, 91
  and fairness, 24
  and federal budget, 23–24, 35–36
  fiscalization of, 6, 12, 17, 23, 26–27,
    36–40, 243
  general concepts related to,
    340–348
  ideas, importance of, 91–94
  innovative, 15–17
  and interest groups, 60, 68, 85
  and market efficiency, 25–26
  and media, 90–91
  opportunistic elements of, 11
  and partisanship, 87–90
  pluralist perspective, 86–87
  policymaking process, meaning of, 4
  and political parties, 85
  president versus Congress, 11–13
  and public opinion, 29–30
  symbolic aspects, 94–100
Political organizations, and policy-
    making, 85
Political parties
  competition of, 8–10
  and policymaking, 85
Political parties. *See also* Democratic
    Party; Republican Party
Politics
  deregulation example, 390
  elites, consensus with, 385
  elites, opposition to, 387–389
  moral judgment aspects, 386
  new federalism, 393
  and political party system, 395–396
  and public view of government,
    384, 392–393
  symbolic politics, 104–107
  two-tier politics, 382–396
Politics. *See also* Clinton-era politics
Pollack, Sheldon, 87
Powell, Colin, 358
  on affirmative action, 140
Powell, Lewis, 158
Primus, Weldell, 243, 245
Prinz, Timothy S., 215
Prison Litigation Reform Act, 180

Prisons, foreign-born inmates, 125–126
Progressive Policy Institute, 11, 406
Proposition 187, 118–120, 127–128
Proposition 209, 140–141, 151
Pryor, Pam, 145
Public Citizens' Global Trade Watch,
    331
Public opinion
  of affirmative action, 133, 141–142
  of federal government, 384,
    392–393, 403
  of Keynesian economics, 42
  and policymaking, 29–30
  of Social Security, 201
  of welfare state, 405
Pyle, George, 381

Rabushka, Alvin, 99
Rawls, John, 410–411
Reagan, Ronald, 18, 132, 405
  on affirmative action, 132
  on Social Security, 196–197, 199, 202
  and tax reform, 88, 96–97, 407
  and welfare state, 27, 223, 224
Recession, and immigration restric-
    tion, 114
Reciprocal Trade Agreements (RTAA)
    Act of 1934, 313, 324–325
Reform Party, 395
Regan, Donald, 93
Regulation, 433–434
  expansion of, 73
  risk regulation, 433–434
Reich, Robert, 43–44
Reinventing government (REGO), 359,
    367
Reischauer, Robert, 39, 207
Rendell, Edward, 339
Republican Party
  and abortion issue, 365, 435–436
  on affirmative action, 132–159,
    143–151
  and budgetary politics, 66
  Clintonizing of, 11
  competition with Democrats
    (1990s), 8–10
  Congress, and Clinton, 358–372
  and economy, 21
  family values position, 249
  and health care reform, 279–282
  and immigration issues, 119–121,
    129–130

and moderation, 21
on race issues, 148–151
and small government, 19–20
on spending surplus of budget, 8
as "sun" party, 8, 21–22, 27
on taxation, 88–90
on trade policy, 314–316, 330–331
and 2000 presidential election, 27
and welfare reform, 73–74, 223–225,
    228–234
and welfare system, 73–74, 223–225
Republican Revolution, 27, 88
Ricardo, David, 323
Rights
    and census adjustment, 303–306
    cost shifting and policy, 178
    defining features of, 174, 221
    as entrenchments of duty, 174–179,
        184–185
    and nationalization of policymak-
        ing, 177–178
    negatives attributed to, 173–174
    opposite of rights, 179
    policy feedback to, 182–184
    politics of rights, 173
    proliferation, reasons for, 176–177
    reduction of rights efforts, 180–181
    resilience of, 181–182
    right to know, 1781
    rights revolution, 172, 174, 176–177
    sources of rights, 172
    venue shifting and policy, 178
Rights retraction
    Aid to Families with Dependent
        Children (AFDC), 215–227
    welfare reform, 218–235
Riordan, Richard, 339
Roach, Stephen, 391
Roman, Nancy, 155
Roosevelt, Franklin D., 87, 195, 324,
    356, 361, 369
    New Deal, 25–26, 41, 179, 194
Rostenkowski, Dan, 88
Roth IRAs, 69
Rubin, Robert, 348
Russell, Bertrand, 387, 388

Samuelson, Robert, 105
Sanford, Mark, 205–206
Savage, John, 41
Schier, Steven E., 38
Schlesinger, Arthur M., Jr., 127

Schneider, William, 363
School-related issues
    and affirmative action, 138–139
    Ed/Flex, 8, 19
    education legislation, 102
    school uniform proposal, 19
    school vouchers, 153
Schuck, Peter, 113
Schumer, Charles, 303
Shapiro, Isaac, 407
Shapiro, Martin, 425
Shapiro v. Thompson, 220
Shribman, David, 296
Simpson, Alan K., 205
Single-payer approach, health care
    reform, 268
Skerry, Peter, 292
Skocpol, Theda, 40, 56
Skrentny, John David, 132
Slattery, Jim, 284
Small Business Administration (SBA),
    assistance to minority business-
    es, 138
Small government
    and Democrats, 19
    and Republicans, 19–20
Smilie, John, 393
Smith, Lamar, 119
Smith, Nick, 205–206, 278
Smoot-Hawley Tariff of 1930, 315, 326
Social Reciprocity (SR) contract,
    408–419
    benefit level, 412–413
    coverage, areas of, 410–411
    deductible, 412, 415
    and fairness, 409, 414
    and justice, 417–418
    moral hazard peril, 411–412
    and partisanship, 416–419
Social Security
    and budget surplus, 8, 50, 75, 76, 208
    cost-of-living adjustment (COLA),
        195, 196, 197
    declining rates of return, 200–201
    durability of program, 22, 182
    financial problems of, 45, 200
    first recipient, 60
    growth pattern, 46
    and immigrants, 127–128
    indexing of, 195–196
    personal security accounts (PSAs),
        204

privatization of, 76, 193, 203–204,
    207, 222
public opinion of, 198–201
strengthening of, 8
Social Security Act of 1935, 194, 219
amendments to, 194–195
Socialism, failure of, 426–427
Socialist ideology
    failure in U.S., 427
    and New Deal, 427
Soft money, 105
Stagflation, 26, 43
Starr, Kenneth, 371
Stein, Herbert, 42
Steuerle, C. Eugene, 58, 89, 93, 243, 256
Stockman, David, 196
Supplemental Security Income (SSI), 121
    and immigrants, 126
Supreme Court
    and affirmative action preferences,
        152, 158–159
    welfare-related cases, 220
Symbolic pathway
    characteristics of, 96
    policymaking, 94–100
Symbolic politics, rise of, 104–107

Tax cuts
    Bush era (2001), 49, 50
    capital gains tax, 69, 87
    estate tax, 12
    as federal activism, 76
    Kennedy-Johnson era, 42
    Reagan era, 88, 97, 407
Tax Equity and Fiscal Responsibility
    Act (TEFRA) of 1982, 81
Tax expenditures
    financing of, 65
    IRS Restructuring and Reform Act,
        69
    losses, sources of, 64
    rise from 1970s–1990s, 64–67
Tax Reform Act of 1986, 105, 106
    effects of, 82, 93–94, 244
Taxation
    bracket creep, 61–62
    Earned Income Tax Credit (EITC),
        239–257
    flat tax proposal, 93, 98–99, 385
    increases, 66–67
    policymaking, pathways of power
        model, 84–100

relationship to spending, 56–58
Tax Equity and Fiscal
    Responsibility Act (TEFRA), 81
tax expenditure politics, 64
Tax Reform Act of 1986, 82
tax reform and working poor,
    244–247
Taxpayer Relief Act of 1997, 70,
    81–82, 87, 89, 94
Taylor, Charles, 173
Telecommunications reform, 4, 25
Telephone service, deregulation, 390
Teles, Steven M., 143–144, 178, 215
Temporary Assistance for Needy
    Families (TANF), 72, 411–412
Terrorism, legislation related to,
    120–121
Thatcher, Margaret, 203
Third Millennium, 201–203
Thompson, Tommy, 339
Tobacco legislation, 69, 73
Total Justice (Friedman), 177
Trade agreements
    China, most favored nation status,
        5, 322
    China Permanent Normal Trade
        Relations (PNTR), 5
    Fordney-McCumber Act of 1922,
        315
    General Agreement on Tariffs and
        Trade (GATT), 314, 325, 329,
        331–332
    North American Free Trade
        Agreement (NAFTA), 5, 314,
        324–325, 330–333, 391–392
    Payne-Aldrich Act of 1909, 315
    Reciprocal Trade Agreements
        (RTAA) Act of 1934, 313,
        324–325
    Smoot-Hawley Tariff of 1930, 315,
        326
    Trade Act of 1974, 325–326
    Underwood Act of 1913, 315
    Uruguay Round Agreement, 314,
        320, 321, 325, 333
    World Trade Organization (WTO),
        5, 314, 317, 321, 329, 333
Trade policy
    and Clinton, 321, 324–325, 329–333,
        361–362
    and declining economy, 318–322
    Democrats on, 314–316, 330–331

Trade policy *(continued)*
  and European Union (EU), 321,
    328–329
  historical view, 313–329
  interest groups, 330–331
  liberal trade, resilience of, 322–330
  opposition to liberalization,
    329–333
  protectionist efforts, 319–320
  Republicans on, 314–316, 330–331
Turow, Scott, 394
Two-tier politics, 14–17, 382–396
  covert politics, 383–384
  first/second tiers in, 382–383
Two-tier politics. *See also* Politics
Tyson, Laura, 317

Uchitelle, Louis, 391
Underwood Act of 1913, 315
Unemployment insurance, 43
Unfunded mandates, 178
Up from Dependency, 222
Uruguay Round Agreement, 314, 320,
    321, 325, 333

Ventura, Jesse, 15
Vogel, David, 313
Volden, Craig, 36
Voucher system, health care reform, 269

Waivers, welfare system, 222–226, 235
Waldman, Steven, 360
Walker, Jack, 60
Wallace, George, 15
Wallach, Lori, 331
War on Poverty, 92
Wards Cove Packing Co., Inc. v. Antonio,
    158
Watergate, 354
Watts, J.C., 145
Weaver, Carolyn, 205
Welfare reform, 4, 218–235
  and Clinton, 6, 7, 226–235, 251–256,
    367–368, 373–374

devolution alternative, 228–231
and Earned Income Tax Credit
  (EITC), 6, 239–257
history of, 222–235
as moderate change, 6, 233
moral aspects, 221
Personal Responsibility and Work
  Opportunity Act (PRWORA),
  218–219
and Republicans, 73–74, 223–225,
  228–234
success of, 431–432
as theme of 1990s, 27–28
waivers, 222–226, 235
welfare rights advocates, 220
Welfare system
  and Bush,, 225–226
  and noncitizens, 117–118, 121, 126,
    130
  public opinion of, 405
  and Reagan, 27, 223–224
Wharton, Joseph, 323
Whitewater scandal, 371
Whitman, Christine, 395
Wildavsky, Aaron, 37
Wilson, James Q., 42, 91, 106, 134
Wilson, Pete
  on affirmative action, 140–141, 150
  election loss, 129
  and Proposition 187, 118, 129,
    150–151
Wolfe, Alan, 381, 404–405
Women
  equal opportunity regulations, 137
  federal assistance for businesses, 138
Work, and policymaking, 24–25
Workfare. *See* Welfare reform
World Trade Organization (WHO)
    Agreement, 314, 317, 321, 329,
    333
World Trade Organization (WTO), 5
  Seattle riots, 389

Zimroth, Peter, 304